CHEF AL
RAW AND UNCUT

CHEF AL

ALAN MICHALS

CONTENTS

After twenty-five years as a private chef to some of the
most powerful families across the country, Chef Al tells true stories about
the rich and famous and what they're like—and holds nothing back.

Chapter 1
GROWING UP

FOR THE MOST PART, I had a good childhood growing up in a small farm town in Ohio. It wasn't bad fishing in the summer, going to the swimming hole every day, smoking a little weed, and banging the girl next door. Mom worked in a factory, so she was gone most of the time, and Dad just stayed drunk and was never around much. He was a good dad, just not around. I guess you could say we were a middle-class family. We had clothes and food on the table but no money for college, cars, and extras. But it was not all bad, better than some kids I grew up with. My brother finished high school and joined the Navy for thirty years. These days, he's is still a prick. So much for him.

I didn't make it through school and got into some trouble, so I joined the Marines. This turned out to be the best thing I ever did—besides putting some other woman's panties in Andy Anson's wife's drawer on his yacht.

Back then, I never dreamed of becoming a chef. I just thought I would go into the Marines and figure out what to do later. I guess I was already a jar head in the making. The Marines were good to me. I learned some discipline and how to drink, and I scored the best weed ever in Thailand. Oh, and the girls! A piece of ass was three dollars in the Philippines. I would go through three or four a day when on liberty. I was seventeen, a kid from a farm in Ohio, getting laid and a blow job for a couple of bucks. I wanted to live there for the rest of my life.

I don't want to get off track here. I want these books to be about some of the pricks I worked for, not about me. That will come later. I've got some great shit you will not believe. FYI, not everybody I worked for was a prick; I worked for a few nice guys as well. We'll cover that later: names, pictures, the whole truth about me and some of these families. I mean, who do they think they are? So what if they have some cash? That does not make them better than me, but they sure as hell thought so.

We never had that issue in Ohio. Growing up, everyone was pretty equal. Folks worked in a factory or owned a farm or local hardware. Most of my hometown was a cool place to grow up. I still have friends there today, and they will love this book. Smart-ass kid makes good in the Marines and then becomes top chef to the rich. What a great life I have had. I've been around the world and back and had lots of good times, and I will share some of them with you in this book.

Some of my friends never left the farm. They knocked up some farmer's daughter, married her, and never left town. Poor bastards. I've always had big plans, though. I knew I did not want to spend the rest of my days in a small town with nowhere to go, plus the cold Ohio winters suck, and the girls are a little thick, if you no what I mean.

After my brother joined the Navy, my folks got divorced. That year, everything went to shit quick. I started doing more drugs, ditching school, and hanging out with the wrong crowd, and it wasn't long before I dug myself a hole that I could not get out of. Finally, I got caught with a pound of weed and was expelled from school and sent to juvie for thirty days.

When I got out, a local cop, Miles Standish, visited me. He'd always liked me, even though I was a smart-ass and thought I was a tough kid. Turns out Miles was a former jar head and said I needed to join the Marines if I wanted to get my life straightened out. Otherwise, I'd end up in jail for the rest of my life—or dead. He said he could get my record cleared and, if one of my parents would sign for me, he was sure he could get me in, as he knew the recruiter.

Well, Dad was living with a new woman in the next town over. One thing about my dad was that he was a good-looking man. He was also a ladies' man and always had women on the side. The apple didn't fall far from the tree, as I've had more than my share of ass, and I am still getting my fair share, even though I'm turning sixty-four next year. He also gave me my tough side. He was a big, tough guy, too.

I planned to go see him when he was drunk, which was every day, and get him to sign for me because Mom would not. When I asked her, she said, "No way. Get your dad to do it. He don't care about you." She always busted his balls. Once, she hit him in the head with a frying pan and opened it right up. Then she called the cops and said he was picking on her. They almost laughed. They knew my dad was a drunk but no wife-beater. It was her; she was tough on him, and me as well.

I went to see my dad on a Friday because I knew he would be in the sauce pretty good, but I also made sure it was early evening, before he got too hammered. We had a few beers together, and then I dropped the boom: "Dad, Standish said he could get my record cleaned and get me in the Marines. I could finish my school and get my diploma." Then I lied, saying, "Mom is cool with it, but you have to sign since you're my dad."

He fell for it. I had the enlistment papers with me, so I got them out and had him sign them, and the next Monday, I was at the recruitment office, getting sworn in. Then, a week later, I was off to Paris Island, crazy shit for a seventeen-year-old.

The night I signed up, my dad and I got drunk at the local bar, and he told all his pals his son was going to be a Marine. By the next week, the whole town knew I had joined. Most thought I would not make it and would be home in a few weeks. They were all wrong.

Mom found out from the neighbor and was mad as hell, so I moved out and stayed with dad and his girlfriend until I went off to boot camp. She got over it once she knew I was shipping out in a few days, and we made up. All was good on my way to a fresh start in the Marines. I had no idea what was in store for me, but I must say I needed to get my ass kicked. When it was time to ship out, I said goodbye to everyone, and the old cop Standish told me to make him proud and not come home unless I graduated.

Well, I did graduate. Mom and dad both came down, and it was one of the best days of my life. If you are a Marine, you know what I am talking about. I even made PFC top 10 percent, not bad for a dropout. I was meant to be a Marine, and I never felt so proud in my life. I had finally done something besides getting stoned and in trouble. I had a new view of life, and my whole outlook had changed. You could see it in my swagger, the way I stood tall and straight and said, "Yes, sir," and, "No, ma'am." My folks were proud. Even my dad said that, and for him, that was tough. He'd served in the Navy during the Korean war.

For me, the Marines were the best, and everyone knew it. Their dress blues are the best uniforms in the service. All the other branches know who rules: the few, the proud, the Marines. Enough said; we all know the Marines' history.

Well, I went home on leave for fifteen days, and when I got there, the first thing on the list was to see the old rat bastard Miles, the cop, to show off my first stripe. He was proud of me, and we had a few beers together and talked about boot camp and how I had turned my life around. I had quit smoking weed, and hard drugs were for sure out the window. None of that shit for me now. I was in the best shape of my life, able to do a hundred push-ups at a time.

I went out west to grunt school and got to see California for the first time. It was great back in the '70s. I did my twelve-week training there and got sent to the Rock, aka Okinawa. When I got there, I was told I had been selected to be a Recon Marine, but I had to pass their school and twelve weeks of training before I could join the unit. What a rush, the top one percent in the corps.

I couldn't wait to get home and brag to the guys and Miles that I had been selected to be a Recon Marine. I had thirty days of leave before starting, and then I would be on the Rock for thirteen months.

When I got back to Ohio and told my mom, she was proud, and my dad was as well. I had bought a set of dress blues in California, and man, did I look good in them. I felt like I could walk through a brick wall. Confidence was not an issue. No one in town could believe how much I had changed and what a fine young man I'd turned out to be.

I hung out with all the guys, got drunk, smoked some weed, nothing hard. It was a great time, and I got some tail from a few of the old girls from school. Out of everyone, Miles was the most impressed. He told me he knew I had it in me. All the teachers at school were proud of me, too. My friends were just graduating, and here I was, off to Okinawa. What a great adventure for a young kid, now a young Marine.

The thirty days flew by, and before I knew it, I was on my way to the Rock. When I got there, I was met by a bad-ass Marine, my platoon sergeant during training. If I made it, I would be sent to a unit. It was like boot camp, only worse, but I kicked ass and soon was with a unit and off to the Philippines to train. It was heaven, except for the training. Beers were twenty-five cents, and the Thai sticks were out of this world, laced with opium. Talk about a high. I still remember it thirty years later, and I will never forget the girls.

So, I did my thirteen months, and I had a great time. Hong Kong, Korea, Bangkok, Japan. Lots of good weed and plenty of chicks, what more do you need? And I was getting paid—if you can call $36 a month getting paid—but I did get my ass kicked every day. I was seeing the world. What a great experience for a kid from Ohio.

Finally, it was time to go back to the States, to Camp Lejeune, and do my last few months until I got out. I did my time, got my honorable discharge, all my benefits, and then it was back to Ohio to go to college and get on with my life. I had saved a few bucks, and I had the GI Bill for school: thirty-six months paid for, what a great deal. Plus, I had all these great stories and had finished as a Recon Marine after taking all the schools: Scuba, Airborne, Pathfinder, Mountain Warfare, Jungle School.

I was one cocky young man with a swagger, but I could back it up. I had gone into the Marines as a 112-pound, skinny little prick and come out 145 pounds with no body fat, a lean, mean killing machine, but that is history now and one for the books. Now I was in college and back to being a slimy civilian, as the Marines called them. Before joining the Marines, I had done nothing to be proud of. Now my mom and dad were proud, and Miles, too. Plus, I had a clean record and was off to a fresh start. I mean, I did bang the preacher's daughter, the newspaper girl, which was where my nickname "Dispatcheo" came from (the local paper was the *Columbus Dispatch*). Leave it to Dale Collins. We still talk about that. She was a little hottie, not as hot as the three Phelps sisters, whom I'd also had.

On to school, and thank God for the GI Bill. Mom and Dad could never afford school for us; it was never discussed. Anyway, in my mind, I was already working on being a legend. As some of my close friends say, "The legend is still alive and kicking, and what great stories he tells,"

I promise to tell them to you, and I am sure you will get a few laughs, unless you are one of the pricks I worked for. In that case, the joke is on you, asshole. Now the whole world will know what pricks you were and what bitches your wives were.

I know it sounds bad, but I know for a fact that they do not live in the same world as we do, and they truly think their shit doesn't stink.

Recon Team

Jungle School Philippines

San Miguel Beer

Young Jar Head

Recon Team

Mom and Dad

chapter 2

CHEFS SCHOOL

MOM GOT ME A JOB at the General Motors factory, where she had worked for twenty-five years. I hated that factory job. What a bunch of losers, I thought, breathing all these chemicals. This could not be healthy and was not what I had planned.

In college, I was already having a tough time. I thought I knew it all. I was nineteen, had one of the best jobs in that part of the country, had already bought my first house, been in the Marines, and on top of all that, I was a dropout with a diploma from Kubasaki High School in Okinawa, Japan, which no one believed until I showed it to them. I was doing ok, plus I was getting laid and smoking weed all the time. Back then, chicks liked good weed, but they like Quaalude's even more—liquid panty removers, we called them. I was already reading *Money* magazine, had a rental unit, and was well on my way.

One day in the middle of winter, I was sitting around my house, freezing my dick off and doing a bunch of bong hits while reading *Money* magazine. There was an article about jobs for the '80s and beyond in the hotel and restaurant service industry. I was already a pretty good cook; at least, the thick chicks at home thought so, but I'd get them so stoned they would eat dog shit and think it was filet mignon. I thought, why not? That is a career I could get into: work the ski resorts in the winter and the beached in the summer, travel the world, play the best golf courses, and screw all the hot-ass chicks who worked in the hotels. What a job. I knew the factory job was not for me. Who could live after twenty-five years of breathing that shit and in a dark factory, plus there were all those drunk old fucks trying to get their thirty years in. So, I said, "What the hell?"

I looked into the best chef schools. NY was too cold and full of New Yorkers, so that was out. I found a great school in Clearwater, Florida, called them up, and talked to the French chef there, Chanton. He said I was making a great decision. There was good money in it, travel, and I would never have to look for a job once I got in the business, and yes, there were plenty of chicks. Later, I found out he had four wives around the world and was still going strong at sixty-five. Chanton was a true legend, and I wanted to be like him—except for the four wives.

The next day, I dropped out of college and went to the VA to make sure they would pay for two years of culinary school. Then I quit my job, rented my house out, and was on my way to sunny Florida: hot chicks, sunshine, good weed, and a real career I could wrap my arms around. When I told mom, she said, "I cannot believe you are quitting GM. It's the best job in town. What will the neighbors think?"

I said, "I don't give a shit. It's my life, and I am not going to work in some shithole factory for twenty-five years and not live long enough to get my pension. I am going to go to chef school, work in the hotel industry, and travel the world."

After that, she was still not on my side, but I did not care. I had already learned to be my own man from the Marines. Dad liked the idea and was very happy for me. We got shitfaced before I took off to Florida, and he wished me good luck. He just said, "Finish school," and I did.

So, I packed up and moved south. When I got there, I rented a room from two girls in Indian Rocks Beach. The place was close to school and on the beach, and I was already off to a good start. I met the chef a few days later and signed up for classes. Then I got a part-time job the next week at a steakhouse, and my plan was in motion.

This was the first time I had lived on the beach, and I knew that this was what I wanted for the rest of my life: sunshine and all the tourist chicks from up north—all they wanted was to meet a guy on the beach and hook up while they were on vacation, easy pickings for me.

Class started in a few weeks, and I could not wait to get started. This was a real culinary school, with a restaurant open to the public. It was where you learned to make hotel and chain-restaurant-style food, including cost, portion control, and all the basics of the business. This all happened in the first year. After that, you took advanced classes, learning classic French and international cuisine. At the restaurant, you also learned to wait on tables, bus, all that. It was a first-class operation, and Chanton was a real pro. He knew everything and had worked all over the world. He'd had a few restaurants, a few wives, worked for presidents, celebrities; he had done it all and was even working on his book at the time. Yes, he was the man.

At first, we did not get along. He was always riding my ass, giving me shit. I was on pots and pans for one whole quarter. Then one day, all that changed. Dominica was in the kitchen before lunch was served. She came in almost every day. She saw him giving me shit, as he did every day, and man, did she let him have it. I don't know what she said, as it was in French, but Chanton was no match for her. I had never seen his face get red like that. Then came a big smile and a kiss, and that was it; my fate had changed. He called me over, told me no more pots and pans the rest of the year, and said I would be the new maître d'hotel until I graduated. That was the best job in school, reserved for the best students and the ones ready to graduate.

I knew I was one of the best. I had left the steakhouse and was working for Chanton's friend Michele Dennison, who had a great French restaurant on the beach, La Pomeno. He was a great chef and taught me a lot. I was on my way to becoming a great chef someday and was having a great time as well.

Back at school, a few students were pissed at me. I guess they were envious that Chef and I were very close now and I had become his favorite student, thanks to Dominica. A few days later, during our Friday weekly critique, someone said, "Why does Alan get to be maître d' every week?"

Chanton, never one to mince words, said in his loud voice, "Alan is a leader and the best in the class, and Dominica said that is how it has to be, so there will be no more talk about it, or that person will be on pots and pans forever." That was that, and the subject was never brought up again.

My main job as maître d' was to greet and serve Dominica's and Chanton's guests and the other high-end clients and school staff. It was a very demanding role, but with it came a lot of clout.

I was in the spotlight every day. One of the perks was I got to meet all the hot chicks at school, teachers, and Chanton's close friends, and I became one hell of a waiter. I was already building a reputation around the Tampa area and at school as someone with style who was on his way to becoming the next top chef. Whenever Chanton needed a person in his home or a private event, I was at the top of the list. He would just call Michele and say he needed me and I had to have the day off, no questions. I even cooked for the owners at the Super Bowl that year in Tampa in the owners' suite; that was the shit. Chanton made it happen for me, and Dominica as well. I was her favorite. I could do no wrong. I was the only one allowed to have a glass of wine with Chef in the morning. It was his daily ritual. We would talk about my work, my future, and he said he would help me get to the top. Plus, he liked hearing about all the chicks at school and the beach, not to mention the waitresses at work I was banging. Like I said, he was French, and I had good stories and pictures— he liked that even more. It was a great time in my life.

Finally, graduation drew near. Two years had gone by so fast, and I had learned so much and worked in a few of the top restaurants in Tampa and Clearwater Beach. I'd had a great time living on the beach with the two girls and nailing all the tourists, but it was time to start my career and get to work. I had no idea what Chef had planned for me, but I knew it would be good. He said I needed to get on the road to learn the business.

Near the big day, Chef and I were having our daily glass of wine in his office when he asked me what I wanted to do and where I wanted to go. I looked at him and said, "Chef, wherever you think I should go." I was single and had a few bucks, as I had sold the house in Ohio, so I was way ahead of the rest of the students, who did not have a pot to piss in. I was in good shape, no bills and cash in the bank—I have lived my whole life like that. The Marines taught me that, and my mom as well. She was a good saver, and she taught me the value of money.

Chef looked at me and said, "What do you think of Montreal?"

"Where is that?" I asked.

He looked at me and said, "You little whore, in Canada."

"Oh, sorry, I did not know."

"My friend is the chef at a famous hotel there, and if I can get you into their apprentice program, would you be interested in going there to work and study? It would be one year, with room and board and a small salary."

I looked at him and said, "Whatever you think is best for me. I just want to travel, build my reputation as a chef, make some money, and yes, have plenty of fun as well."

That was it; it was done. He made the call, and in a few weeks, I was heading off to a new adventure in a different country, even if it was just next door.

This was about the same time Chef's book was about to come out, *Recipes for Success*, so I got a signed copy of the book along with my diploma and a big hug and kiss from Dominica. In my two years at school, I had worked with three world-class chefs and had a good base to draw from. I was great at soups and sauces and still am to this day; it's my favorite, next to a nice glass of wine and cheese.

Chef was to mold my career for the next five years until he died in Florida. That was a sad day. He was truly a legend in the culinary world. Dominica passed a few years later—what a great woman. I still think of her and Chef today, as they both changed my life and were so good to me. I don't know what he saw in me, but he prepared me for what was to come.

Just like that, I had graduated top of my class and was off to Montreal. I had left all my stuff at Mom's house back in Ohio, so, with just the clothes on my back, I headed north.

Marines

Dress Greens Ohio

Olongapo City Philippines

Chapter 3
THE BUSINESS

SOON I WAS IN MONTREAL, working at the famous Hotel Queen Elizabeth.

I lived down in the basement storage room, but it was clean and warm, which was great, as it was now winter.

I spent a year there, mastering French cuisine. I worked all stations. The days were long, and the pay low, but I ate and drank whatever I wanted—part of the deal. I was a novelty, the only American working in the hotel. The other cooks did not care for me too much, but the girls did. The chef looked out for me just like Chanton did. I was serious about my work, and he knew it. This was not just a job for me, but a career. My plan wasn't to be the best chef around, but to be well known in certain circles, and if I did get to that level, that was the icing on the cake.

Even today, if you were to talk to someone who employed me, they would tell you I am a hard worker, clean, organized, an all-around chef with style. I have not changed my practice. I never waste food, and to this day, after three decades in the business, I have never missed a day of work in my life. That, my friend, is one hell of a track record. People always ask me, "Al, what makes a good chef?" Some of the high-profile chefs today will give you a line of shit that it's about knowing the business. These young chefs—they call themselves chefs, though they've never gone to culinary school or formal training—if they had to get on the line and pump out some food or do more than one task at a time, they would be lost. I have seen it. What a joke.

The truth is, if you can put out six courses, all hot, different entrees, fish, chicken, say a piece of meat or pasta, get it all out at the same time, hot but not overcooked, that is a good start. Having a touch of flair or a degree of temperature tis a big part. The rest is just years of learning the business, doing all the prep, soups, and sauces, ordering all the paperwork.

That is a good base to draw from. The rest is just paying your dues, and hopefully, you get lucky like I did and work for some great chefs. If you do, listen to them and win their respect, and they will teach you their secrets and help you build your career. Great chefs are like that. They want to say they trained you. It's like you are their children and they are proud of how they raised you and how you have become a fine young chef. I know it sounds crazy, but it's true. I know. I've been there, and it's a great feeling.

I was on a great roll and having lots of fun. I worked for some top chefs at the time and was learning a lot and well on my way to becoming a great chef.

I spent the next eight years or so traveling and working at resorts, restaurants, and country clubs around the country. Life was grand, and I was making good cash for the first time in a while. Lots of nice girls and some great stories along the way, and I met a lot of great folks, and some crazy ones as well. Like in life, you learn to take the good with the bad.

I will share a few stories of the business and some of the crazy cast along the way, like Habbs in Vermont, Billy Joel on his boat in the Hampton's, and the party animals in Florida and Hilton Head. I just did one season there. It was great; the Southern girls sure do give it up, along with all the hotel interns. That was a great summer. I played lots of golf there; Hilton Head is great golf country, Harbor Town, Palmetto Dunes, Oyster Reef, too many to name, but what a great place. I had my way there. I worked at the big plantations for the summer, as Vermont was just the winter gig.

Hilton Head was the bomb, with tons of tourist chicks. I think I got more ass there than any place I have ever been. Well, except for Colombia, that's a different story. But I had great fun. I picked up a new skill, Low country cooking: BBQ, shrimp, red beans and rice, all that great food. It will stop your heart if you eat it all your life, but it's good cuisine. It was a real party town. I think, at the hotel, I was banging four girls at the same time, and none of them knew. I will share a few pics of the girls and the hotels and golf courses. I have not been back there since—too many other places to go.

The highlight of my time there was cooking on August Busch Sr.'s yacht. We did a catering job there from the hotel, and I was picked to cook. He was a great guy, treated all the staff well and left a big fat tip to boot. It was a great day. The boat was at Harbor Town Marina, of course. I knew this was my style; I just had to figure out how to work my way into these circles. I ran into August years later at La Quinta in the desert, and he remembered me. Like I said, he was a great guy.

That is pretty much the highlight of Hilton Head. I knew then that this was my calling, to be a private chef to the rich and famous, hanging out with good-looking women, eating the best food, and drinking the best wine, all on their dime. Live like the rich and famous and get paid to do it. Doesn't sound bad, does it? That's what I thought. I just had to figure a way in, but that would come later by pure luck when the first lady appeared. More on her later.

Summer was over, and it was back to Vermont for foliage season and to get ready for ski season and the snow bunnies. I had some great times in Vermont and am still friends and keep in touch with a few of the guys there. If you are in Stowe, you must go to the Sunset Grill. Go see Haabs and Nancy and tell them Chef Al sent you. If you do, the first beer is on the house. He will tell you a few more stories about him and me. We smoked a lot of weed and drank too much but still managed not to kill ourselves. Haabs married Nancy, raised a few daughters, and built the Sunset Grill, a Stowe Landmark and still there today.

The best was Haas's bachelor party at the Matterhorn. Pat Burgen helped me put it together. Ask anyone who knows him, and they'll all agree: he's one great skier and one crazy son of a bitch. Pat was also one hell of a bartender. He worked at the Stoweflake Resort, but his main gig was the Matterhorn. He was a legend in town, and we had some great times together. For the bachelor party, we hired a stripper from Burlington, some college chick. The party was at the Horn, and all the normal criminals came: Pat Persico, Ernie, Will Spalding, Jim Malone, the whole gang. Then we took a cab to the Montreal red light district. We were on a tear; it's a wonder we did not get thrown in jail. We got kicked out of a few clubs, but man, what a good time, and Haabs had the time of his life. Nancy was cool about it. We smoked a ton of weed and drank ourselves sober.

The second great story involves a few of the same criminals: me, of course, Pat, and Kevin Venter. I had old man Baraw's Caddy. He was the owner of the Stoweflake, where I'd spent a few seasons. His two sons ran it, Stew and Chuck, not bad guys. They had their moments but liked me.

Their dad liked me, and whatever he said, that was it. So, when I started taking Mr. B to the airport, he told Chuck I had to have Mondays off to drive him. That was it, no questions. We would have lunch, and he would give me a few dollars. He wanted to know about all the girls I was sleeping with. He was a dirty old man; I think he was already in his late sixties.

I already had a rep as a lady's man, so I would share some stories and a few new pics of the latest chicks. His drinking buddy at the time was Walter Cronkite. Like I said, some great stories, and he liked me and gave me a lot of good advice. I could go on and on about Mr. B, like the trip to Montreal where he tried to pick up my girlfriend. He was a character, and I liked him. He took me to play golf, and later, when I went to work for Marriott in Atlantic City, he came to see me and told the GM they were lucky to have me. One great reference. He knew everyone in the business on the East Coast.

Back to the scene of the crime. After dropping him off at the airport, I picked up Pat and Kevin. We played golf, got stoned, and then went back to town to get some lunch. After that, we hung out in the parking lot, talking shit. I acted like I was going to drive off, but then I turned around like I was going to run over Pat. What does this guy do but jump right through the windshield. We all almost shit, that crazy bastard Burgon. We were all high, so no one got hurt, but the Caddy was in bad shape, and Mr. B would have my ass. Thank God Chuck was out of town.

So, we called a windshield place in Burlington and told them who I worked for, and they came right over and got her looking good. They did not believe the deer story, but it was not their job to tell Mr. B. I called Ernie at the Flake; he was the head maintenance guy. I did not tell him the whole story at first but said I needed the company credit card to pay for the windshield for the Caddy. He knew damn well that if he did not, Mr. B would have all our asses. That is where I got the name Teflon Kid—nothing ever stuck to me; shit just rolled off my back. Even today, I am one lucky guy. The shit I pulled off—bosses wives, daughters, housekeepers, you name it. I did them all. Never got caught. Lived to fight one more day.

Back to the Caddy. When we got back to Stowe, I was still not in the clear. Pat and Kevin said they would keep quiet, but it was so cool that we had to tell the rest of the guys.

The Caddy looked fine; you could not tell anything had happened. First thing I did was call Mr. B in Boston. He was cool and wanted to make sure I was fine, and that was it. I said I was fine, a little shaken up, but not injured, and the car was fine. That was it. Ernie, on the other hand, knew better. He could tell I was high, but we were always high, like every day, so what was the big deal? He knew better than to buy this deer story. I will never forget Ernie's face when I told him the truth. He said, "Are you fucking crazy? I don't want to hear one more word, and you had better never pull shit like this again, or I will not be there to save your ass again. I don't believe this shit story, either, but I don't want to know what happened, so stick to the deer story." But Ernie did save me again and again over the next four seasons; I was always in the shit. What's funny was that everyone knew, and they loved it. I was like Mr. B's little pall. I could do no wrong. But the Baraws never found out. Well, maybe not. We were always doing something stupid back then to see if we could get away with it.

Pat and Kevin are still laughing, along with Habs, Persico, and the chef. Even Ernie said, "Chef Al, you are one crazy bastard." They would have never thought I would be working for a president or the likes of Jerry Weintraub. But I cleaned up pretty good once I quit smoking pot.

I had many great years in Stowe, Vermont. We did some crazy shit. I will share a few more stories, and if you are in Stowe, pop in and see Habbs, and he will verify them. He was in on a few of them, but I was always the ringleader.

Back in the eighties, Stowe was a real ski-bum town—young kids just having fun, getting high, and all about the skiing and drinking, with lots of both every day. We used to call it the mountain crawl. When you were done skiing for the day, the first stop was the Horn, and you'd work your way down the mountain road, stopping at every bar and seeing all the gang. Hell, it would be 10:00 sometimes, and we would still be in our ski clothes. That is how you tell a true ski bum.

I don't know how, but I was in the kitchen every morning on time and ready for work. I had to be there at 5:00 every morning to prep, check in deliveries, the whole shit. It was not an easy job. I made all the soups and stocks and did breakfast every day off the menu—150 was an average day for breakfast. By myself, that was kicking some ass. I was done by noon and off to the mountain to go skiing.

I had room and board, a free ski pass, and use of the golf cart, Mr. B's private one. That's the next story, and you will love this one. It was just Habbs and me. Once again, I was the one with the idea, aka the ringleader. The BS were all out of town. I think it was the week before Christmas, because it was really slow. We were having one hell of a snowstorm. You could not drive, and Habbs was in my room at Elmer's staff housing. We were getting high and drinking, and I came up with the crazy idea of taking Mr. B'd golf cart to do the mountain crawl.

So, off we went to the first stop, Stoweaway, a Mexican place where our friend Tim was the bartender. We pulled in, and the guys shit. "Chef Al, what's up with Mr. B's cart?"

I said, "We're doing the crawl in the cart."

They said, "For sure, you guys are going to jail if you get caught."

But we did not. We hit all the bars, and we were almost home when we started fighting. Next thing you know, we were in front of the Flake, and I crashed into a snowbank. The staff was in Charlie B, the bar at the Flake, drinking: Pat, Will, and Ernie. They could not believe what they saw. We were stuck, so we went into the bar.

Ernie said, "What the hell are you two doing?"

I said, "We're stuck, and we need all of you to help us get it out of the bank."

They knew they had no choice but to help, or all of us would be in the shit, so, once again, Ernie saved the day. We got her out, no damage, and I got her all cleaned up the next morning, good as new. Pat and Ernie were mad as hell at first, but they could not stop laughing, so we had a few more beers and told them all we'd done the mountain crawl in the cart. That was a first.

Just let me tell you about Pat, a great chef and a cool guy. On top of that, he's an old-school pothead. To this day, we get high. Last time I saw him was in Stowe a few years back. I cannot say enough about Pat, the Snake, Persico.

I will never forget the old gang from the Stoweflake. A few have passed on. Habbs, Pat, Will, Ernie, Tim, too many to go on, are still in Stowe, and to this day, I consider them some of the best friends I have met in all my world travels. I cannot wait till the guys get a copy of the book. We did some crazy shit, and the BS never found out.

I went back to Stowe a few years back, and when I walked into the Stoweflake, there was Loretta. She could not stop crying, and then we both started laughing. The first thing she said was, "I still remember the night you and Habbs were in the golf cart. Everyone still tells that story. Man, were you two drunk."

That was a great time, and we had so many of them back then, from ski-bum races to road trips with a keg in the trunk and a bag of dope. You name it, we did it. I had it pretty good at the Flake, as you can tell. I went through the whole staff the first year. There were a few cuties, plus all the ski bunnies; that was my deal.

We helped Ernie get ready for winter in the off-season, raking leaves, putting all the summer shit away—whatever Ernie needed, we did. That is how I got all the keys. I had keys to the gym, the indoor pool, and most importantly, the hot tub. I would take all the chicks there late at night for a hot tub and a little rub-a-dub. Ernie soon found out, but he was not pissed. He said, "Just make sure you lock up at night, and don't leave no evidence."

By now, Ernie and I were good friends. I spent four or five seasons in Stowe. Then I stayed the whole year. It was great until Pat left to open his own place and Habbs bought the Sunset Grill. Then everything went to shit, and it was time for me to move on. Stowe still holds a place in my heart. When I was not in Stowe, I spent a few summers in the Hampton's. That was a blast as well, but I never did so well with the girls there. I mean, I had more than my fair share, but I never liked girls from New York or Boston

I worked a few places in the Hampton's and met some wonderful folks there as well. I got my first write-up here in the local paper: best new chef. I worked my first season at the Royal Atlantic Hotel, owned by two Greek brothers, nice guys. But I had my sights set on the Montauk Yacht Club, and I had the chef job set up for next season. I would be in charge of the off-site cooking on the guest yachts and private parties.

I had a room above the restaurant. While working there, I met Jimmy Dean, cooked on his yacht, and Billy Joel and Christie. They were cool and nice to me. I always liked him. Nice guy. Then there was the mob guy, Nick Monte. He owned Monte's steakhouse in Brooklyn, and I am not sure what else he did, but he loved to play golf. That is how we meet. His son was a Marine, so I was in already. We hit it off, and I cooked on his boat as well. He tipped me well and took me to play golf and into the city a few times. We had some good times, but I would not want to be on his bad side. You'd find yourself in the Hudson River, if you know what I mean. I would see guys come in the front door and never leave. What do you think happened to them? I don't want to know or care. He was good to me.

I was always running into guys like these. When you run in the Hampton's, Stowe, Hilton Head, Boston, Montreal, you are in the big league. Me, I was just a working stiff trying to get laid, make some money, have a great time, build my reputation, and go on to the next gig. I look back, and I had it pretty damn good: skiing all winter, golf all summer, getting laid, meeting all kinds of cool folks, and making good cash. As long as I had a new pair of boards and new sticks, that is all I needed, and of course, some good weed and some ass here and there. What else is there in life?

I did these for about five years, working the resorts, building my resume. There were a few good chefs, and I had my own deal one summer in Montauk. Chef at the golf course was a cool gig. I was humming in my skills and making a name for myself on the East Coast. That was a big deal. Back then, I never had to look for a job. I'd make a phone call, or someone would track me down.

I ended up with Marriott down the road. It was in New Jersey, where I'd started with them. I'd done a summer gig for them a few years back, so I had an in. This was the year Pat left the Stoweflake, and we all moved on, Habbs to Sunset Grill and me to Atlantic City. Trump was opening his new place, and I needed a change from Vermont. It was time to move on.

I took a job there as a saucier but quit as soon as I ran into an old chef from Montauk in town at the Seaview Country Club. Marriott had just bought it, and Mike was the sous chef. I was playing golf and ran into him. He was a great guy, Greek. He said, "Hey, we need a chef for our new gourmet seafood restaurant. It's only open four days a week, but we'll put you on salary, and you can help out on banquets when you are free. You write the menu and do your own thing. That would never happen today in Marriott, and we will make you a restaurant chef, big title, or room chef."

It was a good job, and I liked Mike, a real stand-up guy and a good young chef. We were about the same age. I banged one of his wife's sisters. She had three, and they all lived with Mike. What a fuck story, but she was fun.

Mike already had two kids and a mortgage and was well on his way to the poor house for the rest of his life. Some guys want that. Not me—I just wanted to build my career. I'd had a lot of good times at Seaview. I did all the girls at the hotel. I'm lucky I did not get shot by one of those psycho Jersey bitches. I got a lot of ass there—I mean a lot. I will put a few pics in.

Let's start with FB Tony, ex-chef Tony, and Frank, the purchasing agent. That was my new rat pack, and Mike, of course. I played a lot of golf there. At the time, it was the home of the Cadillac Open for the WPGA, as I say, dikes on spikes. Never went to a tournament. I mean, who cares?

FB Tony taught me a lot about the numbers and my future in the business with Marriott. He was a great friend and F&B director. We hung out a lot and had some great dinners. He was a little pissed when he found out I was banging his secretary, Phillis, this old broad, but what a set of tits and ass on her. She was in her late forties. That was old for me, but what a horny one. Frank caught us getting in on in the wine cellar one time, and he always gave me shit for that. They were all married and wanted to get ahold of that big set, but I beat them all to it.

Tony got over it in a few weeks, but Chef Tony was an asshole about it; he was a prick, anyway. His English ass could not cook for shit, but man, could he write a menu. Too bad he could not cook it. What a schmuck. That's all most executive chefs I meet do: push paper and write menus out of magazines. Plus, he was a shit golfer and probably still is today. Mike, on the other hand, was a great chef, golfer, and father. I am sure he is still out there and doing well. He had a great work attitude and was not mad, as I'd gotten rid of his wife's sister.

Seaview was a blast. At one time, I had several of them going: Phyllis, Mike's sister, a waitress, the manager of the gift shop, and the housekeeping manager, and I never got caught. What a summer. Almost all the managers were married, so I had the women all to myself.

Between shifts, I would sneak out and play the back nine. Frank and I would go to Atlantic City and gamble once in a while. He was good at blackjack and taught me a few things. On top of that, he was a great golfer. We used to win a few bucks from the Tony's. They were no match for us. I owe Frank a lot. If it weren't for him, I never would have made peace with my dad, and now that he has passed, I can look in the mirror and smile. We made up and had a few good years together. Thanks, Frank. I love you, man, from Hot Rod. That's the name Frank gave me.

I will never forget him.

After a year, it was time to move on. I had my sights set on California. I talked to Tony, the F&B, and said I wanted to head out west. Winter season was approaching, and we would shut the gourmet room down, and I would be on banquets.

There was an opening at the Palm Desert Marriott in Palm Desert, California. He knew the F&B and said he could get me in if I wanted. He also knew the chef and I did not get along and it was only a matter of time before I kicked his ass and got fired. It was a good move.

They wanted me to do two jobs: executive steward and banquet chef. It sounded great, plus it was out west. This was a new property and their flagship, with two golf courses on top of that. I drove cross-country, stopping in Ohio to see my dad on Frank's orders.

Dad was glad to see me, as were Mom and the rest of the old gang. I saw Peggy, too, and threw a shot in her for the road. Then it was on to Cally.

I had just bought a house in La Quinta, sight unseen. One of my pals had checked it out for me. With the new house and new hotel, things were going as planned. Now I just needed to break into the private chef scene and get out of the hotel business. I had been doing this for almost ten years now: resorts, fine dining, restaurants, country clubs, yacht clubs. I needed a change and had my sights on LA.

Don't get me wrong. I was still having fun. I just wanted more, and I did not see myself as some paper pusher taking shit from some GM or asshole F&B director. I wanted to be in charge and report only to the boss. Not a bad plan.

I got all moved in and went to work at the new hotel. Man, was I in for a pile of shit. They forgot to tell me the steward was in charge of the dishwashers, silver and glassware inventory and keeping it polished.

I had to supervise fifty dishwashers and cleaners over three shifts, and only a few spoke English. Man, did they fuck me. That's Marriott for you. Plus, I was doing banquets.

The only good news was my new friend Kevin, who'd just bought the house across the street. He did not get high, as he was a Secret Service agent working for the Fords, but we'd go out drinking, grab a few chicks. We had some good times, even if he was a New Yorker.

He was one crazy dude—Marine as well, if I remember right.

Things were bad at the hotel. I could never make payroll, and my overtime was out the window. Every day, I had a few no-shows, and the day after payday, forget it. I never had a full crew, so I had to keep guys overtime, or the dishes wouldn't get cleaned and the trash wouldn't get emptied. It was a nightmare. I never got help. Man, was I screwed.

I called Tony, and he said, "Just hang in there for a year. Then I'll move you."

"I will kill myself or someone else if I have to stay here a year," I replied.

There was no time for chicks; it was all work and no play from the time I got onto property till when I left. I was on a dead run and never looked up, just kept going, the Marine way. That was all I knew, but still, I was not making progress.

When the INS came in because half my staff was illegal, with fake Social Security numbers, man, that is a day I will never forget. I never saw my crew move so fast to get off the property, and a few were at a dead run. I lost half my staff in one day, but HR got more shit than I did, as they'd hired these guys. So, on that note, I was cool, but I still had no staff and had to get some dishwashers. Not an easy task. For the first time, I got a little help from the rest of the staff

They knew I was just about ready to walk and would kick someone's ass if they gave me more shit about overtime or the trash or back dock being a mess. I needed help and in a bad way.

I got some luck. We got some staff from the other Marriott down the street, and within a week, I had hired a new crew and was back on track, but I was still not happy. "Tony, one year, you are killing me, man," I said to myself. I knew I could not make it, and the new F&B was an asshole. I wish I could remember his name. What a real piece of work. He thought he was the shit. I would love to call him out; he always needed a good ass-kicking. As I remember, the chef was not too far behind, but man, could he carve some ice. That was all he did all week.

I knew my days were limited; I just had to line something up, as now I had a mortgage, but I did have two hot chicks living with me to help pay it. One was a striper and hot, so life was not all bad. My car was paid for, and I had no credit cards, so my mortgage was my only concern. If I quit, I could get by for a few months. I was always lucky back then. A good chef was hard to find, and I knew that if I had to, I could find work in any other hotel or fine dining restaurant, as my resume was getting there and I had a history of being a hard worker and a very good cook on the line or buffets. I could do it all. So, I was not worried if I quit. Then I got the break of my life.

Around Christmas, the annual Betty Ford party was held at the hotel. I was working banquets that night, helping plate up and making sauce for dinner. When the first lady walked through the kitchen with my pal Kevin, she did not stop to say hi to the chef or F&B, as she was with the GM. Luckily, Kevin saw me and waved me over to meet the first lady. He told her I was his new neighbor and a former Marine. She said that Kevin had told her all about me and it was nice to meet me.

The rest of the staff almost shit themselves: the lead dishwasher/ banquet chef was shaking hands with the first lady. It was a real feather in my cap, and I owe it all to Kevin. Semper fidelis, brother. Afterward, everyone asked, "Hey, Al, how do you know the first lady ?" I just smiled and said, "I cannot say." They were all so envious. What a great feeling.

A few days later, Kevin and I were drinking beers, and I thanked him. He said, "No big deal. Betty is like that once you get to know her." He never called her that in public, only when they were alone. I did the same, but mostly, I called her ma'am, and she called me Alan.

Needless to say, I was on my way to my first big break. I'd had it with all the bullshit at the Marriott, so I gave them my two weeks' notice. The GM even tried to get me to stay, but I'd had it. I could not make it a year; the job was shit, and I was killing myself, so I knew I had to move on. I thought getting a job in a different hotel or a nice restaurant would be easy. Palm Springs was full of hotels and nice restaurants. I just had to get out and talk to a few chefs.

I was at the house, having a few cold ones, when Kevin stopped by for a beer. He said, "Betty asked about you, and then she asked me if I thought you would be interested in working for them as a chef slash house manager. You know, help out around the house and just kind of be an all-around Johnnie on the spot."

I thought he was bullshitting me, but he said, "No, she's going to call you this week and talk to you."

I still did not believe him. Then the call came.

Disco Nights LA

The team

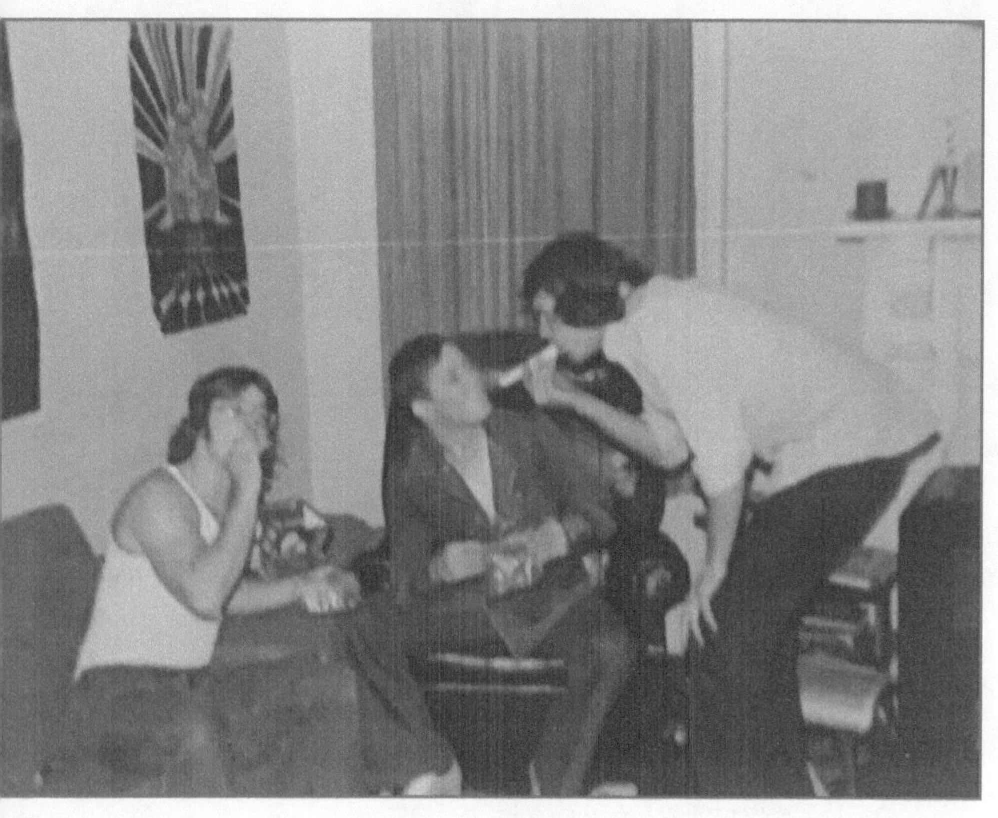

Home on leave getting stoned.

Chapter 4

FIRST LADY

KEV WAS RIGHT. THE CALL came that week. Thank God I was not drinking. I will never forget the conversation for the rest of my life, though it only lasted a few moments. There was a nice voice on the phone, like your grandma or your mom calling to check on you. "Is this Alan Michals, the Marine? Kevin's neighbor?"

I said, "Yes, ma'am," in a weak voice.

"This is Betty Ford. Are you ok?"

"Yes, I am, just a little in shock that you would be calling me. How can I help you."

"Kevin said you quite the Marriott. We called there and asked for you, and they said you had given notice and they were sorry to see you leave. Our chef has just left, and President Ford would like to hire you. When can you come by the house to talk and see if you are interested in the job? We know you are a Marine, and we have already checked you out. Could you come by tomorrow before lunch?

"Yes, ma'am. What time?"

"Eleven AM."

"I will be there, and thank you. I look forward to tomorrow."

"We do as well."

Wow, holy shit, a meeting with the first lady and former president. Man, was I in shock. My friends had laughed at me and said I was a dreamer for thinking I could work in LA for the rich and famous and travel the world, but who was laughing now?

When Kevin got home, I rushed over to see him with a couple of cold ones. I was about to say something, but then he said, "Yes, I know. Betty called and you are to come by in the morning. She asked me if I would bring you by." As we drank the beers, he gave me some solid advice on what and what not to say. They liked that I was a Marine and from Ohio, as President Ford was from Michigan.

I could hardly sleep that night. I knew I was up for it, but I was still nervous. I mean, it's not every day that you meet a first lady and president. Well, I said, just be yourself, and I know they will like you.

The next day, Kev came by for coffee and gave me some more solid advice. Then I was off to the Fords. I had on my best suit at the time and was a little nervous. This was the biggest interview of my life—or so I thought at the time. I had no idea there would be many more to follow over the next twenty years.

When I arrived, Mrs. Ford's assistant showed me into the dining room and said the first lady would be there in a few minutes. She asked if I would like something to drink, and I said water would be fine, thanks. I did not know it at the time, but Kevin was banging her. Her name was Ann.

A few minutes passed, and then in came the first lady. Beside her was a cocker spaniel, Happy Ford. He jumped all over me, and just like that, we were friends, and I landed the job. Betty said, "He likes you. That's a good sign."

We talked about money. I would get a ski pass to Beaver Creek, and she asked if I would mind traveling there to work. We talked about food, and she said they ate very simply and then asked if I could do dinner parties. Then she said, "You will have to help Mr. Ford get dressed sometimes, as he just hurt his hip. Help him pick out ties and shirts and pack for him when he goes on trips, kind of like a butler."

I said, "I've never done it before, but I would not mind, and I am a fast learner."

She said she would help me and show me his favorite ties, shirts, things like that. She was one great first lady. She respected President Ford so much and loved him. I was very impressed. She always referred to him as President Fort, and I liked that. I just called them sir and ma'am, but in private, after a few weeks, I was supposed to refer to her as Betty.

Wow, what a day. We talked for a few hours, and then she showed me my room if I needed to stay over for any reason. I told her I could start next Monday and that was it for the day. We covered all the bases: breakfast, lunch, Beaver Creek, travel, and all my duties, which ended up growing a lot every month, but I was cool with that.

I will never forget that she asked me about growing up in Ohio, my folks, and the Marines. Then she asked me if I wanted to get married and have kids. She was concerned about me and wanted to know a little about me; that was a great feeling. They truly were great folks; I can never say a bad word about them. They could have paid me more, but this was my first full-time private chef job, so I was cool with the money—and a ski pass, to boot. Not bad.

She called in Ann and told her, "Alan will work out just fine. If Happy likes him, that is all that counts. He will start Monday. Get him a credit card, tell him the codes for the house, and give him a set of car keys."

Ann had been on board for years, I think since the White House, and she was one sharp woman—and well connected. I did not pick up on that at the time. I think we never hit it off because Keven and I were friends, and later, Kev kicked her to the curb for a school teacher. She could have been a great ally for jobs later down the road, but I was not thinking ahead yet.

She called Kev, said we were done, and asked him to take me home. We said our goodbyes, and then I said, "I will see you Monday."

Just like that, my life had changed for good. Chef Al was now a full-on private chef.

Man, did I get drunk that night. Kev and I tore it up. He had this old Caddy. It was like a damn yacht, it was so long. Somehow, we got home alive, and the next morning, I started planning for the next week. I wanted to blow the Fords away. I wanted them to be unable to live without me.

So, I got busy planning menus and working on my game plan. I had notes that Betty and Ann had given me. I just had to be myself and work hard, and if all else failed, the dog loved me. That carried a lot of clout.

Well, the weekend flew past, and before I knew it, Monday arrived, my first day.

The first week was pretty easy, and a few weeks after that, I had it down. They were very simple people; even the dinner parties were pretty casual. After having all the staff in the White House, you just want things to be simple and easy. There were a few dinners where we put out the good china and I hired a staff member to help, but that was it. Holidays were spent with family and pretty standard.

One friend regularly took me golfing at Thunderbird and a few other private courses, which was cool. I think he was the son of the paper company up north, the big one. He had an old place on the course, but it was bad-ass. Ford's place was nothing special, but at the time, I was impressed—then I started working in LA. One thing about the Fords' friends: they were all pretty nice. They were a few pains in the ass, like Nancy. She was a ball-buster, must have been a mean first lady like Hillary.

After a few months, the job got boring. I had a fixed menu. Breakfast was usually fruit, homemade muffins or banana bread, eggs, and bacon—very simple. I fed Ann sometimes and the housekeeper but never the agents. Betty treated all the staff and agents like family. I never heard her say a cross word to a single person. The Fords went out a few times a week, which meant I got off early those evenings. They never worked me too hard, unlike some of the assholes I worked for later.

Here is a great lunch story, and you will love the guest—pretty cool shit. It was a deli lunch for all the women, cold cuts, potato salad, mac salad, hoagies, clubs, chips—I mean, it was a full-blown deli spread. I made it all from scratch. It was easy for me, and they loved it all. The guests were Firestone, Annenberg, Nancy, the paper guy's wife, Duich's wife, and—believe it or not—Whoopi

Goldberg. Don't ask me how she fit into the picture, and man, was she a real bitch. I am sure she has gotten worse over the years. I never ran into her in LA, thank God. I would have killed myself.

It was a buffet lunch, and I poured glasses of iced tea, water, and soda. They all talked about their husbands, the White House, traveling around the world, not at all what you would think. That was my first big lunch. I know, boring—I will get to some juicy stuff later. That was how many lunches went: easy lunches and dinners, fried chicken, meatloaf, all that Midwest stuff. I was cool with that; I still love to cook some of those dishes, like a good meatloaf with a real brown sauce, not some shit jar or packet garbage.

They always talked politics and business; that's when I started listening for tips. They all liked me. I was young and fit, a former Marine, and a hard worker. I got used to helping Mr. Ford with his packing, and I sometimes helped him with his shirt and things like that. They treated me well and were sorry to see me leave.

They say no one quits, but it happens after the first year. It's usually the money; they don't pay. I was making almost the same at Marriott, around thirty thousand dollars a year, with two weeks' vacation. Weintraub paid me fifty thousand to start the next year, and I still went skiing every year. Plus, I had a car at my disposal at all times, not some piece-of-shit Suburban, but a Rolls and the 57 T-Bird from *American Graffiti*, and I was living in Malibu, not the desert. But still, I had it pretty good, and I was just not ready to quit. I wanted to make it one more year, but I just couldn't. I lasted around a year and a half.

It was one of the great jobs of my life. I mean, cooking for a president? Where do you go from there? The answer for me was nowhere but up.

I did two holidays dinners in Beaver Creek, Thanksgiving and Christmas, with family and a few friends, but nothing exciting. I skied and met a few locals, whom I would run into later in my travels. I hung around for a while doing lunch parties, helping Mr. Ford pack and unpack, polish silver, polish the marble floor. And as for my best new pal, Happy Ford, I would take him to the vet and the groomer and feed him. I was his pal. He was a cool little guy.

I did not want to give notice until I had a better gig, but it was time to make a move. If I had to do one more boring dinner party, I would die. A few days later, I was at the supermarket, and I ran into a chef working for a family in Palm Desert. We started hanging out, and I told him the Ford gig was boring and ok money, but I wanted to work in LA, so he turned me on to an agent there named Dori. She owned the International Agency, the best in town, only A-list clients.

The next week, I called her and drove to Beverly Hills to meet her, and we hit it off. She said, "Stay by the phone and don't give notice yet, but I will have something in a few days."

Well, the offer came in a few days, just like she said, some hotshot attorney. I would be a driver, chef, and house manager, but the pay was around forty thousand dollars, and I would be living in Malibu. I drove up for the interview, and they hired me on the spot. I said I had to give the Fords two weeks' notice, and they were ok with that.

Now I had to break Betty's heart. This was not going to be easy, as I liked them. I just needed more money, and I was dying there. The Fords were truly great folks, and their friends were as well: Jack Nicklaus, David Frey, Hooker, some business guy in Beaver Creek, Pepi Granshamme—I mean, shit, he was Mr. Vail, Colorado. Betty tried to talk me into staying, but I said I wanted to live in Malibu. I stayed two more weeks, and we all left on good terms. I thought I would be there for years, but the low pay and same routine every day had worn me down, and there was no ass to be had.

Just like that, I was on my way to Malibu. I had a few good stories, met some great people, played a few private golf courses, and skied Beaver Creek, so I was off to a good start. That was one hell of a first private chef job.

After the new gig, I took a few days off, just hung out in the desert, drinking and playing golf, some of my favorite things to do.

US Open Shinnecock. Chef, Steve, Mac O'Grady

Chef, Payne Stewart

Chef, and the Shark

Chapter 5

THE ATTORNEY, THE HODGES, AND LAKE TAHOE BEACH AND SKI RESORT

WORKING AS THE PERSONAL CHEF of an attorney was not my dream job, but Dora made it sound great. Later, I found out it was just a test for me. It was more cash, though, and I would live in Malibu, so I thought, what the hell. Go for it.

The Hodges, Richard and Terri, seemed nice in the interview. I had a great little guest house and a Benz to drive. I should have known it was too good to be true. I was supposed to start Monday morning, so I left the desert around 5.00 PM on Sunday to get there in plenty of time, but I hit PCH about four miles from the house, and they had closed the road: a bad wreck, someone had gotten killed, and there was no way to turn around for hours. When I finally arrived at my destination around midnight, the old bastard was pissed. He didn't believe me. The next day, he apologized after hearing they had shut down the road. But still, I already had a bad feeling about the fuck.

It turned out he was a full-blown alcoholic. His drink of choice was scotch, Johnnie Walker, and he downed at least a bottle a day, all while in court and running a huge law firm. He was a tough old man and mean as hell. I thought maybe I should have stayed in the desert and worked for the boring Fords. But things got better after I started fucking Terri, his wife. He had to have been in his sixties, but Terri was probably in her late thirties, maybe forty, blond, not bad looking, skinny. She worked in the office as a kind of office manager. She used to be a secretary till she started banging old man Hodge. Then they got married, and now she was running the firm. She was one bossy bitch, but with me, she was cool. I mean, shit, I gave it to her almost every morning. I would drive old man Hodge to the office in Santa Monica, and if I did not have to drive him to court or a meeting, I was to return home to do the house and personal stuff for Terri—errands, food shopping, and laying some pipe.

She was a horny old broad, and she'd be down in the guest house as soon as I got back with nothing on but a "come get me" smile. I knew the old man was not taking care of business. He was drunk all the time, and I was sure he could not get it up even with a crane

I did not do a lot of cooking for the Hodges. I'd make breakfast, maybe a few eggs and some toast, but they ate out for lunch every day, and a lot of dinners as well. When I did cook dinner, it was usually something very simple, like pasta, fish, chicken. I never cooked for dinner parties, but I was not there for the holidays.

This was also one of my shortest jobs; I think I was there for six months. Dora said I had to make it till spring. I did not know it at the time, but if I quit in less than six months, she had to replace me free of charge.

The main job was to keep the old man happy and in scotch, so I bought it by the case. I was also the driver and did errands for the firm as well. I had weekends off, which was great. I met some cool folks in Malibu and Santa Monica and learned the lay of the land in LA, who all the players were.

Terri did not eat much. She drank like a fish, though, which was why she had that skinny little ass. I would make her a light salad for dinner, and that was it. I don't think Richard could taste the food. The more he drank, the meaner he got. At first, I felt sorry for Terri, but it was her choice to marry some mean old bastard for his money. She'd made her bed, so now she had to sleep in it.

Besides the law firm, Richard owned the Lake Tahoe Beach and Ski Resort. His son ran it. Terri did not like him; he was from a former marriage. He was an ok guy, far nicer than the old man. We got along fine.

The coolest thing about the job was that I was out doing something every day. I had a credit card, and I could buy my lunch with it when I drove in the city or worked at the office, so that was cool. The partners at the firm all liked me. I am sure they were thinking, how long will this kid last before he quits or kills the son of a bitch?

Just when I thought it could not get any crazier, Richard's new assistant, Susan, asked me to lunch to go over the next week's schedule. Richard had a very busy week and some court appearances downtown. She was hot, about thirty-five, and lived in Huntington Beach. I think she knew I was doing Terri and wanted to fuck me just to get at her, because a few weeks later, Terri knew I was fucking both of them. But what could she do, fire me? The old man was happy with me.

She asked me, "Are you fucking Susan, because she was bragging to the girls in the office about what a great lover you are." I told her that I'd run into her one weekend in Huntington Beach and then we'd gotten drunk and it had just happened. At first, she was jealous, but then it blew over, and I cooled it with Susan. We got back together after I quit, but she blew me off after a few weekends. I knew she just wanted to fuck me to piss Terri off, and she did.

Man, what fun I was having. Even with the old man being a dick, I was still having fun and saving a few dollars. Some weekends, I'd go back to the desert. The two strippers were still living there, and Kev was still in town, so life was pretty damn good. I never met people while working for the Hodges. They never had parties and knew no one. Their world consisted of the firm, the resort, and his son.

I don't even think the partners liked them; everyone was always on edge, except me. I was used to him—just keep him in scotch, and he was fine. I'll say one thing—he was a sharp old guy, and from what I heard, one hell of an attorney, drunk all the time but a true functioning drunk. The firm was in the Waterford Plaza in Santa Monica. I heard he owned the building, but I don't know for sure. He was also a sharp dresser and kept his beard nice and trimmed.

I'd made some new friends in Santa Monica. There was a great little cafe where we met to eat a few times a week, and they would pick up my tab once in a while. Before I knew it, six months was getting close. I had to make a trip to Beverly Hills and see Dora. She knew I had it rough, and later, she told me, "If you can work for the Hodges for six months, you can work for anyone," and she was right. I did not tell her I was sleeping with the wife; she would have died.

On the weekends, I was off. My only job was to make four dinners, two salmon and two chicken, and leave them in the fridge halfway cooked so they just had to reheat them. Most importantly, he wanted to make sure he had at least four bottles of Johnnie in the cabinet. I had never seen someone drink that much scotch—and neat, too, just ice. Terri was a vodka and white wine queen, and she could drink as well; no lightweights here.

I look back at the job now, and it's pretty damn funny what a circus it was. I knew it was only a matter of time before the old man caught me or Terri got tired of me and fired me. I mean, he would get drunk and just argue with me. He'd yell at me for driving too fast or too slow, and if he spilled his scotch, there would be hell to pay. It was time to move on, and I had a meeting lined up with Dora at the International. But before I get into that, I want to share one last story.

We were driving through downtown LA to the main courthouse. Keep in mind that this was the same day the Rodney King verdict was coming out, and the city seemed ready to explode. The night before, Richard had called me into his office. This was a weekly routine, but he did it every time we traveled downtown.

"Alan," he would say, "come to my office." I would leave my guest house and meet him in his office, and from his desk, he would very calmly say, "Alan, in the bottom drawer, you will find a Louis Vuitton flask. Make sure we take that tomorrow and that it is full, and bring one highball glass and put it in the glove box of the Benz. I will be out of court at eleven, and I will call you when I am heading out. Make sure you have some ice for my drink."

After the second time, I put a cooler in the trunk and kept ice in it. I would pick him up in front of the curb and hand him his glass of ice, and he would pour his own drink. What a trip. I mean, he had it down to a science. He would have that thing killed by the time we got back to the office, and I had to refill it for the ride home, or he would make a big one for the road. I think we kept a case of scotch at the office as well. Hell, I should have bought stock in Jonnie.

Back to the courthouse story. So, I got the call to pick him up, and when I arrived, I pulled in front, got out, opened the door, and handed him the glass full of ice. He opened the glove box and poured himself a fat one as I pulled away. As I worked my way over a few lanes to get on the expressway, he spilled his drink in his lap and just went ape-shit on me.

"You should stop," he said.

"Sir," I replied, "I am in the middle of traffic in downtown LA. I cannot just pull over and let you make a refill in traffic."

He went off on me, saying, "Don't argue with me. Y should drive better and never question what I say."

Well, a few minutes later, all hell broke loose. We were on our way to Beverly Hills for a meeting when the riot started.

I could see the march starting a few blocks behind me in the rear-view mirror. It was not a pretty sight. I told Richard we should cancel the meeting and get back to Malibu as soon as we could, because LA was going to be nasty. He looked around and made a few phone calls, and then it started to happen—he could see them marching behind us a few blocks away. So, I beat hell back to the office, he closed it early, and then I drove him back to Malibu.

And as we all know, shit hit the fan that night and for the next couple of days. I thought for sure we were going to get stuck downtown and be in deep shit—nice Benz, rich old white guy, and his driver. It would not have had a good ending. But we got out of there and back to the beach.

He was still giving me shit about him spilling his drink hours after we got home, saying that I had to pay more attention. I almost hit the old bastard and walked out, but I knew I had a meeting coming up with Dora and I had to keep my cool if I wanted to move up the food chain with her. So, I just kept quiet and swallowed my pride.

I had to work that weekend in case the riot came to Malibu. I stayed on guard all weekend with a shotgun in my guest house. It was a crazy two days.

I had a meeting with Dora at the end of the week. She called me and said she had something for me and needed me to come to her office. I could hardly wait. Dora had the keys to LA. She knew everyone, and if she liked you, you were in and would never have to look for a job again. People would find you or steal you from someone else once. I was on my way there; I just did not know it yet. I had proved I could work for anyone.

Later that week, I told Terri, "I need a half-day off. I have some personal stuff I have to do."

She checked the schedule and said, "Thursday will be ok. I'll drive Richard home. Just take the rest of the afternoon off since you worked last weekend."

She did not have a clue I was going to an interview. I called Dora, who told me to be at her office at 1:30 and put on my best suit and look proper. Then she asked, "Could you go to the Valley to meet someone?"

"Yes," I replied, "I'm on my way."

I got to Dora's office, and she told me I looked nice. "Are you ready to step up?"

I said I was, and then she told me about a family that wanted to hire me. They had interviewed a few chefs, but they wanted someone like me who could do it all, cook, drive, run the house, and who did not mind working weekends. Live-in was a must, which was also up my alley. She said the husband was in the movie business. At that time, I did not know who the players were in town, but that was about to change in a matter of hours.

She said, "Call this number and tell them who you are. Say that I sent you and you have a meeting with Mr. Annericho at three." She told me it was around fifty thousand to start, plus a car, and I would be living in Santa Monica, Pacific Palisades—on the cliff, the Necklace, I think it was called, because you saw the whole coast from the cliffs. The houses there were off the chart.

I had no clue where I was going or what to expect. I'd never been on a studio lot. When I got to the Warner Brothers gate and said who I was, before I could get the words out, the guard said, "Mr. Michals, park here. Mr. Annericho is excepting you."

We got in a golf cart, and he droves me to the building and said, "Go inside and ask for Susan." Inside was a huge lobby, and as I wandered around, looking lost, a hot young brunette greeted me. "Are you Alan Michals?" I told her I was, and she said, "Art wants to meet you."

"Who?" I asked.

"Art. We all call Mr. Annericho Art. That's what he prefers. Art is short for Arthur. He's the owner of the company."

I still did not know who he was. Google was not around back then to help you—I mean, shit, I still had a pager. Even back then, I had a few Armani suits, all black and dark blue, white shirt, and spit-shined shoes, Johnston Murphy, still a great shoe today. I still have a few pairs. So, I felt I was looking my best and up to the job.

Susan was real cool. She said, "Art is running a few minutes behind, but I am supposed to take you to his office and get you whatever you need till he arrives."

As I waited, I watched the clock. I'd have to get across town soon and out to Malibu. Finally, Arthur walked in and said, "I'm sorry about being late. Grab a chair over here, and let's talk."

He saw me look at my watch. I did not know it back then, but that is not good to do in an interview. He said, "Do you have to be somewhere?"

"I am very sorry," I said, "but I am on a job now, and I have to be back in Malibu in a few hours, or I might get fired. Dora only said you wanted to meet me and gave me a few details."

He asked who I was working for, and when I told him, he said he'd heard of the firm but did not know the Hodges. He asked why I was leaving, and I said, "I don't want to get into it. I am new to LA. I don't want to say bad things about my current employer and start on the wrong foot with you."

He asked again, and I said, "Mr. Anaracho, you want to know, and you will not hold it against me?"

"It's Art," he replied, "and tell me what's going on."

I looked him square in the eye and said, "The old man is a drunk, and a mean drunk at that. He curses at me and says rude things to me, and his wife is mean and a drunk, too. Once I give notice, they will kick me out of the house and maybe not pay me. Dora told me not to tell you this."

He sat back for a minute. He could see I was a little uneasy about telling him these things. He looked at my shoes and said, "Marine spitshine."

"Yes, sir," I replied.

"Can you get my shoes looking like that?"

"Yes, I would."

We talked about food, the Marines, and his wife, Betty. I said something about pasta, and that was it.

"You have to meet Betty tomorrow," he said. "Come over and cook dinner for us. I know she will love you. I have to go to a meeting now, so I will have Susan give you some money for coming over here today and to buy food for dinner Saturday. If you cook half as good as you say you can and my shoes look that good, you have a job. We will work on the details. If the Hodges fire you, let me know, and I will send a car to get you, or get to the studio, and I will get you a car till we sort things out."

He called Susan in and said, "Give Alan a thousand dollars to buy food for Saturday and money for today. In case something comes up, I want to make sure he is ok." Then he said to me, "Alan, I have to run. It was a pleasure, and I will see you on Saturday. If you need anything, call Susan. She will give you my address, phone number, and all the info you need."

I was blown away. After he left, Susan said, "He never does this. He must like you. He is the best guy to work for, and Betty is a sweetheart. You will love working for them."

I was blown away. I had no idea who Art was. I had been told he was a producer and had a few shows on TV, and that was it. The building was huge, with the company logo on the building, and I had never seen an office like his, full of awards, autographs, a pool table, a wet bar, and some sick artwork. I did not know who the artists were, but they looked damn expensive. These would be the first of many trips to the office and the studio. I had no idea what I was in for.

Susan and I talked for a while, and then I said I had to get back to Malibu. She gave me Art's home address, phone number, and some cash and said, "We will talk next week." Then I hauled ass back to Malibu. I did not know what to tell the Hodges; I wanted to quit that day, but first, I wanted to make sure I had the job with Art. That night, I prepared and served dinner, got everything on the to-do list done for the weekend, and made sure Richard had plenty of Johnnie. Then I retired to my guesthouse for the weekend.

It was nice having weekends off. I could hang out at Malibu beaches, catch some rays, and down a few cold ones. It was not bad, just the mean old drunk, but that was about to end. I was tired of the old lady as well. Things hadn't been the same since she'd found out I was banging the girl in the office. Even though I'd told her it was over, she was still a little pissed.

The big day came, my first trial dinner. Art loved pasta, so I thought, what better way to win them over than his favorite food. I would hit him with one of the classics—how could I go wrong with that? The menu was simple but made with love. I got that from Shari, who will come into the picture later.

The salad was tomato mozzarella on a bed of arugula with fresh basil. Very clean.

Dinner was a hit. I made pasta primavera with a light sauce of white wine, garlic, basil, and tomato. I know this dish is old, but it was very popular back then, and it tastes great when done right, with lots of fresh diced vegetables.

Dessert was my flan, and Art and Betty loved everything. Art was a wine collector and had a great cellar as well, and he had picked out a Borella, a super Tuscany red. After dinner, he said, "Please sit and have a glass of wine, and let's talk about you moving in and working for us." They both enjoyed food and liked the dinner.

As I enjoyed a great bottle of wine and got to know a nice couple, Art laid out what the job entailed: five-day workweek, holidays and most weekends off, though, for some busy weeks, I may need to work six days. I told them this was not an issue. They wanted someone to watch the house when they were gone, oversee the gardeners and housekeeper, do all the shopping for dinner parties, help Betty around the house and with whatever she needed to be done, maybe drive them to events, help Art at the studio—cater lunch, drive him places, whatever he needed, and help out with Art's shoes and clothes. He was one sharp dresser, as was Betty.

I said, "I can do all of these things, and I would be very happy to come on board and work for you."

I was to have a company car, pager, and petty cash. Back then, that was a thousand dollars. My starting salary was fifty-eight thousand dollars plus bonus and tips. This was more money than I had ever made. Plus, I was living in Pacific Palisades, just outside Santa Monica, in a Mediterranean villa on a cliff overlooking the ocean. As we talked, they asked about the Marines, the Fords, my folks in Ohio, and how I had come to California. They also wanted to know more about my hobbies, and all this gave me a great feeling, just like I'd had with the Fords.

I said goodnight and headed back to Malibu. It was a twenty-minute drive to the Hodges' place. Then I took the day off and hung out at Zuma Beach, drinking a few beers and just letting it all sink in. This was the big league in LA. I could not wait to tell the Hodges I was quitting. He was a mean old fuck, and I was tired of the abuse. When I look back at how he treated me, I realize I should have kicked the old drunk's ass, taken some nude pics of his wife, and told him what great head she gave; that would have been cool. But I was moving on to bigger and better things.

So, Monday came, and I was ready to drop the hammer. I talked to Art, and he said, "If they fire you on the spot, just come to the house. We will work it out. Don't worry about their reference. They probably won't give you one, anyone."

After taking Hodge to his office, I headed back to the house to pack my stuff and move it over to Art and Betty's house. It was only ten minutes from Hodge's office. I had to do a few things for Terri, and I threw one last shot in her just for good measure. Then I headed back to the office to pick up Hodge. As we drove back to Malibu, I told him I was moving on and going back to work for Marriott, that private service was not for me. I politely said, "Thank you for the opportunity to work for you. I would like to give two weeks' notice." He agreed and said, "Just finish the week. Terri and I will be fine. Just get the house stocked up on a few things." By this, he meant a few cases of Johnnie. And that was it. He was nice to me for the rest of the week, but Terri turned back into a complete bitch.

I could not wait for the week to end. Art was cool. He said, "Move in Saturday and start Monday, or take a week off." What a great new boss. I said, "I just need the weekend off to go home to the desert and check on my house, and I will start Monday."

I headed to the desert for the weekend hook-up with Kev. We caught up and drank a few beers, and I told him about the Hodges and what I had been up to in LA. It was a great weekend, but now I was ready to embark on the next path. One door opens as another door closes had been the story of my life.

Playboy Club bound CA.

The Stowe Gang

Chef, Haabs. The Snake

Haabs Bachelor Party

Heather, Great Ass

Heather, Sam and Sherie

Chef, Sherie and Sam

chapter 6

THE ARTHUR COMPANY.

I COULD WRITE A WHOLE book about the time I worked for Art and Betty, possibly the two best years of my life. I was young, living in the Palisades and working for one of LA's hottest new TV producers. My boss was great, and his wife was nice as well.

Let me give you a little background on Art. He was Italian and proud of it. Betty was his second wife. He'd started in the business as a sound guy and worked his way to the top. When I came on board, he was living large, with several hit shows.

I will say one thing about Art: he knew how to live. He had a couple of custom Harleys, a restored bi-plane, and a few hot cars, and man, did he dress sharply, nothing but the best. Art was a nice guy but full of himself. Betty was nice, just a little weird. It took a while to learn all their quirks, but they were not that bad, just a little different, as Shari used to say. She did not like to hang out with them, as they always had to name-drop and impress everyone around them. I did not know this at the time, but that's Hollywood—the same shit goes on today, just with different players. Some folks don't live in the real world, and they don't have a clue how the rest of us live. Art and Betty treated me very well, far better than Hodge, the old drunk.

Some of Art's shows were *Airwolf, The New Monsters, FBI: The Untold Stories, Adam-12,* and *Rocky Road,* just to name a few, and he won three Emmy's, so he was prime time. I just did not know it then; this was my first big gig in LA.

I was supposed to meet Susan at the studio to fill out paperwork and meet all the office staff. If you've never been on a studio lot, you don't know what you are missing. It's cool, way cool. I was to meet Art to go over all my new duties. I was given a pager—they were big back then—and a cell as well. My house car was a big black suburban; that was the in-thing in LA at the time.

When Art finally made his way into the office, he greeted me with a big smile and said, "Welcome home." He asked me how things had gone with the Hodges, and I told him, "They were not too happy, but everything was ok." People in LA hate it when you quit. They think they are so special. They don't have a clue. I soon learned why they called LA "La-La Land."

I filled out all the paperwork, and Art did not even check my references; he just went with his gut. He said, "I like you, Marine, and if the first lady says you are ok, that's good enough for Betty and me." Then we talked about food, wine, dinner parties, ad helping out at the studio

There was no budget for food and wine at the house. Art had a dinner party every Friday night. He had a screening room at the house to show movies, new releases or stuff in the works. So, we went over that; they would be casual dinners for the most part. Then there would be formal dinners a few times a month, and I was told that I could hire staff—bartender, server, whatever I needed.

Money was not an issue, first class all the way. I would cook dinner for Art and Betty a few times a week, or I might drive them to a dinner party or restaurant. I would also help around the house, oversee the housekeeper and gardeners, take care of the cars and bikes, and help Betty with errands. That was a tall list, and it would keep me busy.

After our conversation, I was ready to go. Art said he had a meeting so I should head to the house and get settled in. That night, I would cook for just him and Betty, and he told me he felt like having fish.

I headed back to the Palisades to meet with Betty and unpack. I met her at the house, and then I went out to get some fish for dinner. This was a great place to live, down the street from the beach and a short walk from town.

At dinner that night, we talked about food, parties, house duties, time off, all that stuff. Betty said that a lot of the time, I could just prepare dinner and then retire, as Art might be late or she might have a late meeting. They were very easy. They just wanted nice food—and I also had to take care of Lacy, the house dog.

I had a full plate, but this was a cool gig. I don't want to bore you with two years of anecdotes about cooking for the A-list in LA, so I will stick to a few stories that I think you might enjoy.

So, where to start? Let's do the first big dinner party and my first true test for Art. I have never lacked confidence, and I knew I was a great cook. The rest was just being charming, looking the part, and taking care of business. Art was having a screening party and had invited a few guests: the mayor, Richard Riordan, Shari and Sam, Warren and his wife—she was on her way out; Warren was trading up—and Pernell, who was solo.

Warren Trepp was Michael Milkin's partner and a top bond trader. Milken went to jail, but Warren never did. Warren lived around the corner, and we became friends. He was a great guy, and man, did he know how to live. I did not know it at the time, but he was a big-time guy, wealthy enough to buy Art a few times over and still have cash to piss away. He was a monthly dinner guest, along with a few others. Later, I did a few gigs for him at his home.

Dinner was a buffet on the patio, weather permitting, right next to the screening room. Betty liked doing these dinner parties, and we decided on Mexican. That was easy for me, and I liked cooking it as well. I gave Betty a few ideas, and we nailed down the menu: chicken enchiladas; fish tacos; beans and rice; guac, salsa, and chips; my kick-ass margaritas; and my special homemade flan.

Dinner was a hit, and all the guests were raving, so Art was in heaven. He told the guests that he'd stolen me from President Ford, and they ate it up. Art was a showman, and I loved it, too; it was good for my ego.

Part of my job was to answer the door for guests, offer them a drink, and make them feel at home. Then Art would come down, and I would prepare dinner.

Art would usually take them to the bar to talk shop, and sometimes he invited me back and introduced me to new guests. If Sam, Don, or Warren were there, I would chat with them for a few minutes, maybe make a tee time at the Riviera for later in the week. Warren knew I liked good wine and always brought me a nice bottle, and I mean the best great reds.

I would eavesdrop on their conversations on stocks, new movie deals, and local politics—Richard was the mayor of LA at the time. Warren was a smoker, so he would smoke outside my kitchen door, and I would join him once in a while and bullshit. He was a great guy, and we came to be good friends. At the time, I did not know he was a big-league guy.

I also became close friends with Sam and Sheri, but there will be more about that later. The mayor was a nice guy. We did not get too close, but we were friends. Pernell was another great guy. He was the voice for *FBI: The Untold Stories*. He was winding down his career and living in Malibu, enjoying life. He liked good food and wine, so we hit it off. Later on, I did a few dinner parties for him, and he was a first-class guy.

On movie night, once dinner was over, I would make popcorn in the movie theater and tell the guests it was show time. Art had a guy come from the studio to show the movies in the production room. I got to watch them, too, once I cleaned the kitchen. After the movie, I would offer the guests a coffee or a nightcap, get their coats, and say goodnight, and then I was done. It was a cool deal.

On weekdays, I would take care of the cars and Art's Harley stuff or do errands for Betty. If she had nothing, I would head to the studio and take care of Art: cater lunch, pick up and drop off scripts, get petty cash from Susan, shop, you name it; I did it all. I was having the time of my life, meeting all the celebs playing the best golf course in LA, and making good cash, and I was getting my share of tail as well

From the chicks at the studios to the cashier at Gelson's, I was loving life. Art knew it and asked me all the time, "Are you fucking Susan or one of the other girls from the office?" He loved that sort of shit. He never cheated on Betty—not his style. He just lived vicariously through my stories, and he always asked who I was doing, and I showed him the pics. We became very close. Art was cool with me and liked my style and work ethic and that I was a Marine. Plus, he loved my food. We often played golf together. He thought he was a golfer, but he sucked. I still played with him, though. I mean, shit, free golf? Come on. Plus, he was the boss.

I worked for Art for almost two years. It was a blast. He tipped me a lot for Christmas, gave me a G for bonus cash. As time went on, though, my relationship with Betty grew strained. She thought I should not hang out with their guests and friends, particularly Sam Behrens and Shari Belafonte. Sam and Sheri were good golfers, and we had fun and hit it off.

My first Hollywood experience was with Sam and Shari, and I will never forget that night. I'd just finished dinner with Art and Betty when the house phone rang. Betty answered, but it turned out to be Shari calling for me. Betty was not real happy about that. Art did not care, so I picked up the phone, and they asked me if I was off tomorrow night. It just so happened that I was, so they asked if I would like to go to the screening of Stallone's new movie *Cliffhanger*. They had an extra pass, and they told me to meet them at Man's Chinese Theatre. Wow, this was a first. Art said, "You will have a blast. Go have a good time." So, I finished cleaning the kitchen and called it a night.

The next day, I was off, but I still had coffee ready for Art and Betty. I mean, I lived at the house, in the back. I asked Art what to wear, and he said just nice jeans and a cool jacket. I could hardly wait for the evening to come. I had no idea what I was in store for. I met Sam and Shari at a restaurant an hour before the screening to have a drink and a bite to eat. When we got to the event, I was in shock—it was the real deal, red carpet, the whole shit.

We walked in just as Sly was finishing his interview. He said hi to Sam and Shari, and they introduced me. Turned out we were setting right behind him. We watched the flick, and then, to my surprise, Sam told me we were going to the after-party, which was across the street in a tent in the parking lot. He had style, and man, he was one good-looking dude. Shari was hot, too—look at the old *Playboy* pictures—and was she ever nice and down to earth, not like these new celebrities, who are so full of themselves.

We headed to the after-party, and the area inside the tent had been made to look like the *Cliffhanger* movie set, with cliff climbing and fake snow. There was also an open bar and free food. We hung out for a few minutes with Sly, and he asked me if I liked the movie. I said, "Yes, it was great."

I hung with Sam while Shari talked to her agent. Sam said, "What do you think?"

"I am in awe," I replied.

"You get used to it. I come to these things all the time."

We had a few beers, talked about golf, and met Sharon Stone's sister, Kelly. Sam tried to hook me up with her. Shari came back, and we met a few friends and talked a bit. Sam and Sheri had to leave early, so we said our goodbyes, and I was on my own.

I walked around, had a few more beers, and ran back into Kelly. We had a drink and started chatting. I told her I was a chef, and she asked if I did dinner parties and small events. I said I did, and it turned out that she ran the charity Planet Hope. We talked about food, and I said I had to be getting on my way.

"What's the hurry?" She asked.

"I have to drive out to the Palisades."

"Why not come by my place and have a drink? It's close."

I said ok, and we were on our way. When we got to her place, we had a glass of wine, and next thing you know, we were going at it. What a great night. We had some great sex. I spent the night, got up early, and threw one more shot into her. Then we exchanged phone numbers, drank some coffee, and I was on my way.

I had to get back to Art's. I had a busy week ahead of me. Art was always on the move, and he kept me busy. I did not mind. I liked the fast-paced lifestyle back then.

The next day, Art asked how the premier went. I told him about the party and going back to Sharon Stone's sister's home and banging her. He went crazy and said, "That is great!"

"I had the time of my life," I said.

"I knew you would enjoy it," he said. Then he added, "If Betty has nothing for you, I need you to do lunch at the office for a couple of studio heads at one today. I also need you to do a few things at the office. I feel like pasta today, so let's do that for lunch."

Man, did Art love food, which was why he had a gut, not too big, but he could have stood to lose a few pounds. One thing I loved about Art was that he knew how to live. Sometimes, first thing in the morning, we'd be having a cup of coffee together, talking about the day's schedule, and he would say, "Alan, I feel like lobster tonight, with those garlic mashed potatoes and a nice Pouille-Fuissé." It would be eight in the morning, and he would already be thinking about what he wanted for dinner. I liked that. On the other hand, Betty was simple: salad, iced tea, easy.

By the time I got to the office, Art had told all the office girls I'd gone to the screening of *Cliffhanger* with Sam and Shari, and they said they knew: they'd seen me on TV with them and talking to Sly. They were like, "Chef Al is the shit." Man, Art ate this up. He would love to get them going about his chef hanging out with all these folks. It was a great time in my life. I had no idea who the studio executives were at the time, but after lunch, I did.

There was a kitchen at the studio, not great but ok for small stuff. I was preparing salmon with a pink vodka sauce on linguine with Asparagus tips—a great dish that I still like today. The two studio heads were Lew Wasserman and Sid Sheinberg.

Sid and Lew ran MCA Universal, and what a couple of pricks. They were not real friendly. I would do a few more lunches for these guys over the next year, and they came to Art's house a few times to watch a movie and called the house a lot, looking for Art. Lew had been the agent for Jimmy Stewart, Jack Benny, Henry Fonda, Fred Astaire, Gene Kelly, Gregory Peck, and the list goes on. Sid was the COO. They ran the show. All I know is that when they called Art, he was always on his good behavior; he knew who ran the show. They acted like I did not exist when they came for lunch or dinner, but who cares? Some folks are just assholes.

All I heard them talk about was that they would renew *FBI: The Untold Stories* for one more season. When lunch was over, Art was in a great mood. He told me that he and Betty were going out to dinner and that I could take the night off. He said, "Go bang Kelly."

"Thanks," I said, and then I cleaned up and headed back home. I did a few things around the house, and then I called Kelly to see if she was free for dinner. She said she was and that I should pick her up around eight.

We had dinner at Dan Tanners, the hot spot back then, and after a few drinks, we went back to her place for a little playtime. We did not go out again after that. I would see her around, but I think she thought she was better than me.

That's how it went for me the next few years. I worked for all the big players in LA, and I got a lot of hot pussy. At Art's, it was dinner parties and working at the studio, but he was good to me. I got to ride his Harleys, and he even took me flying in his by plane. The old wacko did a barrel roll and a few dives. He was a half-assed pilot, but he could fly the bi-plane. Art thought he was the best at everything, which is why Sahri and Sam did not hang out with him and Betty much. It took me some time to catch on. Art and Betty thought the world revolved around them.

Most celebrities are so full of themselves and have no friends. That's why they kill themselves or just lose it—drugs, booze, whatever, they self-destruct. I remember having Robert Downey Jr. over for the screening of his first big movie, *Chaplin*. He was a piece of shit. He had no money and was a coke-head. He'd been busted a few times and had broken into some folks' house in Malibu. I mean, if not for Hollywood, this guy would be dead or in prison, and now look at him, making like fifty million dollars a year. He was doing blow in the bathroom at Art's house. What a loser. I never liked him. I only met him a few times, but he was always wasted and thought he was the shit. Forget him.

The good thing about working for Art was that I was always meeting new people. It was never boring. I mean, at lunch could be Sid and Lou or some new writer or one of the folks next door, Walter or my favorite, Ali

MacGraw. She was nice. She came by for dinner and lunch a few times. Betty did not like her. Ali still looked hot, and Betty was just Betty, kind of dumpy. I don't know what Art saw in her. I mean, she was no trophy wife, but she let Art do what he wanted. Maybe that is why he kept her. She was a little thick. Her daughter was the same—you would not catch me fucking her. Better be a lot of tequila, if you know what I mean.

I prepared a cool dinner party for James Brolin, Sally Kirkland, Warren and his wife, and some new writer. We were showing a movie with Jimmy and Sally in it. I had met Jimmy a few times and his son, Josh. They lived around the corner. I dropped off a few scripts, Christmas gifts, and lunch a few times. Nice guy, first class, and he always drank tequila and soda. He was nice to me, and I liked him.

It was a normal dinner party until Sally came into the kitchen. I had the new *People* magazine where she was flashing her tits, and I was going to ask her to sign it for me. She was kind of an old broad but still hot, and what a set of tits. The other guests were heading into the screening room, and I had already made popcorn and had it all set up.

Out of nowhere, she said, "I cannot sign this unless you agree that these are a great set," and she opened her top and showed me her tits right in the kitchen. I think she had a thing for younger guys. I told her they were nice, and I gave them a little kiss and some tongue. Then Sally said that when I saw her go to the bathroom, I should give her a few minutes and follow her in. The bathroom was behind us, so knew one could see me go in except Frank, the guy from the studio, and we were friends.

The movie started, and about twenty minutes into the flick, Sally got up and made her way to the bathroom. I told Frank, "I am going to fuck Sally in the guest bathroom."

He said, "Yeah, right." Then, when I left, he almost shit himself.

I knocked on the door, and she opened it with a smile I will never forget. We did not say one word, just got right to business. I bent her over, and what followed was ten minutes of hard-core fucking. She was one horny chick. She could not get enough. Afterward, she gave me her phone number, and we got together a few times just for sex. She never was a guest at Art's again—I don't know why; it just never happened.

I did not tell Art I fucked her in the guest bathroom—he might have been pissed—but I did tell him she gave me her number and I hooked up with her and took care of business. Sally was one crazy broad. I am sure everyone who knows her would say the same, but what a set of tits, and she could give one hell of a blowjob. She loved sex—my kind of woman.

I told Sam when we were golfing, and he laughed and said, "What are you doing, fucking these old broads?"

I said, "It's just for fun, and shit, it's Sally Kirkland."

He agreed, and we both laughed about it the rest of the back nine.

Sam said, "I will hook you up with some young fresh stuff."

"Cool," I replied, and we laughed.

"I have to tell Shari about the bathroom."

"Sure," I said. Why not? We were becoming good friends. He said Sheri would get a laugh out of it.

That was a dinner party I will never forget. Look at the pics and tell me you don't agree: that is a great set of tits. We had a few more rolls in the sack, and then I never saw her again. If Betty had found out, she would have fired me so fast, but Art would have just laughed. I tell you, I've pulled some shit over the years and never got caught. What a lucky bastard, the Teflon Kid.

The next week, I had dinner with Sam and Shari. The first thing Shari said was, "Have you had any more bathroom blow jobs?" I mean, she was so cool. We all just laughed, and I said I was just having fun.

Back at Art's, it was just more of the same routine: help out wherever and with whatever Betty needed. I started building my client base around this time. I was already starting to be well known. Art's guests would ask me, "Do you hire yourself out?" At first, I said no. I did not want to mess my gig up with Art.

After the first year, Art and I were having a drink, and the subject came up, and he said, "I'm fine with it if you do it on your off days. Just don't let it interfere with our schedule."

"It would just be some small dinner parties and helping some folks get organized, go to the store, get their cars detailed, easy stuff," I said.

Art was cool with that. "Just don't tell Betty."

I was always on the go, shopping, cooking, running errands. I liked not doing the same thing every day, going to the studio, meeting all kinds of cool folks.

Here is a cool dinner party story.

The guests were Don Johnson, Melanie, and Pero from Valentino's restaurant, an LA landmark—Art loved this place, and Don did as well; that's why he was on the guest list—and Warren and his wife, soon to be divorced. I always thought she was a bitch, but she thought she was something special. Trophy wives are all like that; they look better on their backs. To hear them talk, you'd think they were born into money. Truth is, they're not much different than a whore and cost a whole lot more. Now, back to a great dinner party story.

Don was trying to get back with Melanie for the third time. He said she was a great piece of ass. I still find that hard to believe. She was dumber than a bag of rocks. This was before she married Antonio. I wondered what he saw in her like. He said the sex was great, so maybe that was it.

There was a nice cocktail party before dinner. Don wanted Art to look at a script called *Tin Cup*. That was the main reason for the dinner party— and to watch a movie.

We were in the formal dining room, with all the good china, and I'd pulled out all the stops: a four-course dinner of lobster bisque, house salad, veal chop Tuscany style, and tiramisu for dessert. Don loved a good veal chop and a super Tuscan red.

I had just cleared the salad plates and poured some more wine when Melanie lit up a cigarette. To my surprise, Betty asked her to step outside with it. Instead, she put the cigarette out on the B and B plate. These are hand-painted plates from Italy. You should have seen Don's face; he almost shit. He was so embarrassed. Melanie thought nothing of it—like I said, dumber than a bag of rocks and no class. I picked up the plate as quickly as possible, but it was too late; everyone saw it. Wow, what a stupid move.

After dinner, Don came in and said, "Try the super red." He poured me a glass, and he was right; it was a great wine. He said he was sorry for the cigarette incident. I said it was cool, and that was it. Pero came in and said, "Great dinner," and poured me some more wine. Art was cool with that; he always saved me a glass for my dinner after I took care of the guests. Pero said, "You need to come by the restaurant and have dinner and meet the chef." I said I would like that. Pero's place was a LA landmark. All the A-listers went there, and I was a regular there for a few years till I met Wolfgang.

Movie time came, and when the ladies returned from the restroom, it was show-time for the guests while I cleaned up the kitchen.

These dinner parties happened nearly every Friday or Saturday, and I loved doing them. I got to show off, and there were some great guests. One couple who came over was an attorney and his wife: Heather Thomas. She was one cool chick, and we had some fun. I know why she married this guy big-time celebrity attorney: he had some of the biggest and deepest pockets in town. I don't think he was a good-looking guy, but when you have that kind of money, chicks don't care.

When the movie was over, I gave the guests their coats and said goodnight. Don had a limo get him, and Warren always had a driver. Pero said good night and told me I was welcome at his restaurant anytime.

I visited Valentino's the next week, and my money was no good. He treated me like an A-lister. Pero was a showman; he knew all his guests' first names, and even their kids' names. In all my travels, he was by far the best restaurateur I have ever seen. That is no secret. I met the chef that night. He was from somewhere in Northern Italy. We talked about food and drank some wine, and he invited me to spend a day with him in the kitchen. At the end of the evening, I thanked Pero and went home.

The next morning, Art asked how it was, and I told him Pero would not let me pay and I met the chef and had a great dinner. Art was cool about things like this. After every dinner party, he would tell me thanks, and the next day, he would give me some tip money and let me use the credit card for lunch.

The following week, I went back and spent the day with Pero's chef. It was a real European ran kitchen. If you've never worked in one, then you don't have a clue. I picked up a few new dishes and got Pero's tiramisu recipe. The best part was the staff lunch. Waiters set the table and waited on the kitchen staff as they ate lunch, drank a glass of wine, and talked about the night's specials. It was a one-hour break, and then the chefs cleaned up, and it was back to work. I spent a few days in their kitchen, and I always had a great time. It was an honor for a chef to open his kitchen to a guy like me. They liked my stories of the stars I cooked for, and they all knew who Art was. I will never forget Pero's kindness.

This next story is a good one. It's about Skip, Art's partner, and Heather. Skip was an attorney for the stars, and I mean big time. He had houses in Bellaire and Montana. He and Art were into fly fishing. Nice guy, but he was not taking care of business at home. Heather is Heather Thomas, an up-and-coming star in the day. She never made it big, but man, was she hot.

I first met them at lunch at Art's. He had some legal stuff for Skip to look at. It was a casual lunch: chilled gazpacho soup, poached lobster on a bed of arugula, Chef Al's "you make me crazy" sauce, Champagne, and flan for dessert. After lunch, Heather told me they were looking for a person like me, that their chef had quit. I told her I could help her out on my off days if Art said it was ok. I knew he would not mind. She gave me her number and said to call in the next few days.

This was going to be fun. I called a few days later, and she gave me the address of the house and what time to come by. I showed up, and we had a cup of coffee and a great talk. She said she needed some shopping done, gas in the cars, and for me to cook some stuff and leave it in the fridge for that night or the next day. I agreed and said I could do that, and that was it. She knew I would not leave Art and I lived at his place, and she was cool with that. She asked me if I would help interview when they found someone, and I said I would.

This went on for a few weeks, no big dinner parties, just helping out one day a week. I needed at least one day off, and I was cool with that.

Art and Betty were leaving town for a long weekend. I told Heather I couldn't help that week, as I had to stay around the house. She was cool about that and said, "Maybe I will stop by and say hi." Turned out Skip was going out of town on business as well.

I never thought about it. I was so naïve; I did not have a clue. These chicks were pros. They knew what they wanted, money and a sugar daddy.

Not Shari, though. She was not like that; she had her own money. And Sam, what a stud and a nice guy. Heather had Skip, a boring attorney with lots of dough. She could not make it on her own, but she was nice—a little snobby, but I could put up with her. I am sure, as the years passed, she became a pain in the ass. I'm glad I was not around. I had my roll in the hay, or should I say, hot tub action.

Back to the story. I took Art and Betty to the airport on Friday. They were going to the Cayman Islands for a week. Art had a place there and did his offshore banking there. I met his attorney a few times, and Art had me take him out to play golf. He was a real nice guy. Art was sending a lot of cash down there—I am sure of that.

When I got back to the house, I lay by the pool to catch some rays and drink a few beers. Then I made some lunch and took a nap. Afterward, I thought I would head into Santa Monica and hang out, get home early, and just chill.

I was drinking a beer in the back when the doorbell rang. I thought it was Betty's daughter checking on me, though it wasn't the first time they had left me in charge of the house, so I put a shirt on and answered the door.

Holy shit, it was Heather and one of her friends, and they were buzzed and looking hot and horny. I said, "Come on in. Art and Betty are not home. They're in the Caymans."

Heather said, "I know, and Skip is out of town as well." Then she asked, "Are you going to offer us a drink?"

"Of course. How about my signature margarita?"

They said yes, and then they asked me what I had planned for the weekend. I told them I had to watch Lacy and keep an eye on the place. Then Heather saw the hot tub was on and said, "Is it hot?"

"Yes," I said, "I was just warming it up to jump in there."

Next thing I knew, they had busted out some blow, and Heather said, "Do you want to do a few lines with us?"

I said sure, so we did some rails. Next thing you know, we were all in the hot tub with nothing on but smiles. Heather was grabbing my dick, and the other chick was all over me as well. So, we had a wild-ass threesome, drinking more and doing more lines, and I mean to tell you, it was some of the best ass I ever had. This went on for an hour or so. I had them both every way you can, in and out of the hot tub. I always look back and think, what if Art and Betty had come back or Skip had stopped by. Man, would I have been fired. Betty would have shit, but Art would have loved it. I never told him—that was kind of going over the limit, don't you think?

We had some more sex, more drinks, a few more lines, and then they cleaned up in my room off the back of the house. Then I nailed them both one more time. I figured, this will never happen again, so I better take care of business and enjoy it while I can. I was right.

They got dressed and asked me to join them for a late dinner at Spago's. I said, "Sure, I will meet you there. I just have to let the dog out and clean up, and then I will head over."

After cleaning up, I headed over and met them at the bar. Wolfgang got us a table; this was my first time meeting him. Heather and Skip were A-listers, while I was just a working stiff who'd just had sex with two hot married broads. I was walking on cloud nine.

Heather told Wolfgang I was Art's private chef. He knew who Art was. We had drinks, and then they bought me dinner. They kept saying that they had not had sex like that in a long time and we must do it again. I knew it probably would not happen, but it was a great ego boost. They were both married to older guys with money, so you get what you pay for.

We finished dinner, and then I had to get back because of the dog. I told Heather I would call her when Art and Betty got back in town. She said, "Sure, just call. Good night," and that was it.

I went home, let the dog out, sobered up, and finally went to bed. What a night for a high school dropout from a one-horse town in Ohio, banging Heather Thomas and some billionaire's hot bitch. What a rush. I still think about it thirty years later.

The next morning, I got up to go for a run, let the dog out, cleaned the hot tub, washed the towels, and cleaned the kitchen so the house-keeper would not know. I had to cover my ass. Art did not have cameras at the house, just an alarm, so I knew I was cool. When I was done, I walked down to Santa Monica beach and hung out for the day, just loving the sun and all the hot chicks and drinking a few beers.

The weekend flew by, and then it was time for Art and Betty to return home—and for me to go back to work. No more fucking off, and the hot tub was no longer in play.

I picked them up at the airport, and of course, I brought Lacy. That made Betty's day and put me in her good graces. She and that dog—I wont get into that. It was just over the top. The damn dog lived better than I did. That's LA. La-La Land. Bunch of phonies.

I did not know what life had in store for me the next few weeks, but Art was not himself. Something was up. Out of nowhere, Betty started checking the receipts for food. She had no idea what things cost. The dinners parties slowed down. I lost the GMC and was now driving some piece-of-shit Ford station wagon. Oh, and the flowers. I had been spending about a hundred dollars every two weeks buying flowers for the whole house. She cut that down to just having some in the entryway

Turned out that I never went back to the MCA lot till I started working for JW.

Things went to shit in a matter of a few weeks for Art. Sid would call, and Art would not take it. I knew something was up.

Art's series, *FBI: The Untold Stories*, had just been canceled three shows before it could go into syndication. That was big money, and Art was having a shit fit. He told me, "It's in the millions if it gets renewed," but it did not. To this day, I still don't know what happened, but within a few weeks, Art was closed down and no longer allowed on the lot. Everyone was fired, except for a few writers and Art's secretary, but she would go later. I was the last to go.

Art started a new production company with some investors, mainly Warren Trepp. He had the real money, and all the Wall Street guys wanted to be in Hollywood, so it was a good fit.

Art had some new shows lined up and was working on a deal with King World, but I guess the shows belonged to Universal, and they closed Art down in less than a month. I am sure Warren took it in the ass for a few dollars. The next thing I knew, Art had the house for sale, and it was like a fire sale; he could not get out of town fast enough. He let me go a few weeks later, but he gave me a month's pay Art was cool like that. He said, "Just don't tell Betty." Plus, he gave me a great reference.

I never saw Art or Betty again. He was done in the business, black-balled. You don't fuck with Sid and Lew. I learned that when I was working for JW—that's Jerry Weintraub. I heard Art moved to Colorado. He wrote me a nice letter, and that was it.

Early that week, I said, "Hey, I had better line up a new gig," so I called Dora at the International, and she said to come on in and asked what happened. Then she called Art just to check up on me, and he gave me a clean bill of health.

She said, "I have a dream job in Malibu and Beverly Hills. You'll have to travel with the family, and they have multiple homes in different states. Would you mind that?"

"Of course not," I said.

"It's for one of the LA moguls."

"Who?" I asked, as if I would know.

"Jerry Weintraub. Do you know him?"

"No."

"They want to meet you tomorrow. Mrs. Weintraub will interview you at their Malibu estate. Can you be there at one?"

"I have to call Art to make sure I can get off," I replied.

I called Art got the green light. Then Dora lined the interview up. She said, "They just came back from Camp David with the Bushes, and I told Mrs. Weintraub you were a Marine. She wanted to meet you right away."

I guess the Marines at Camp David had made one hell of an impression on her.

I went back to Art's place to make dinner for them. This was my last week, and tomorrow would be a big day. I told Art about Weintraub, and he said, "He's a whole different league. Have them call me if they have questions about you."

I fixed Art and Betty one of their favorite dinners that night: lobster ravioli with a Gorgonzola cream sauce and a super Tuscany red Antora. I believe Art loved that stuff, and the pasta was to die for. After dinner,

Betty went upstairs, and Art and I finished the wine. He said, "Alan, you have a long and bright future ahead of you. They will hire you for sure; just be yourself. You are one of the best in town, so don't worry. If you need something, just ask me." Art was cool with shit like that. We talked for a while and then said goodnight. I went to bed early as I had to be in Malibu at one.

For the interview, I put on my best suit. I already had two nice Armani suits. Black suit, white shirt, black tie, all business.

I fixed Art and Betty breakfast, and they said that after I cleaned up from breakfast and took Lacy for a walk, I could take the rest of the day off for the interview. I thanked them, cleaned up, and was on my way to Malibu.

I had no idea who Jerry Weintraub was but I was about to find out, and my life would change forever.

When I got there, I rolled up to the gate and was met by a security guard. Before I could say one word, he said, "Are you Alan Michals?"

"Yes."

"Mrs. Weintraub is waiting for you in the kitchen. Park at the guest house and walk up."

I had never seen such an estate. It made Art's place look like a tract home, with stables, two guest houses, tennis courts, an Olympic-size pool, and a private road to the beach. I walked up to the main house and rang the bell, and to my surprise, this old broad answered the door.

"Alan," she said, "come on in. I've been wanting to meet you." Before I could thank her, she said, "I talked to Betty, and she said they love you and hate to see you go. Why are you leaving?"

I told her the truth: "The money, and I want to live in LA."

"What happened with the Hodges?" She asked.

I told the truth again: "He was a drunk and mean." She got a kick out of that. Then she asked about Art, and I said, "I love the job, but Art and Betty are moving and don't need me any longer. They're downsizing." That's what they say in LA when someone is out of money or having trouble.

She asked if she could call Art, and I said, "Yes. This is my last week, and if I don't get a job, I will stay at my house in the desert till something comes up."

"You have a house in the desert?"

"Yes, in La Quinta."

"That's nice. We have a house in Palm Springs. We spend Thanksgiving there every year".

We chatted for some time, and she asked about the Marines, my family in Ohio, why I became a chef, and if I liked what I did.

"Of course," I said, "and I love to travel."

She laid the job out for me. My main responsibility was the Malibu estate, keeping it ready for the weekend. Plus, I would travel with the family to Lake Tahoe for Christmas, where they skied every year. Thanksgiving would be in Palm Springs. In the summer, they might go to Kennebunkport, Maine, where they had a blueberry farm next to the Bushes. I would cook lunches at the house in Beverly Hills, and dinner parties as well. I might be required to drive her sometimes and do all the personal errands, and I would take care of the cars, including the Rolls-Royce's—he had three—and drive the kids to school when the nanny was off. It was my first estate job. Man, was I in over my head.

She asked, "What is Art paying you?"

"Fifty thousand dollars, plus petty cash, a car, dry cleaning, and room and board."

"We will start you off at sixty-five thousand, and after the first year, we will move you to seventy thousand. We will give you a car, and everything Art was doing for you, we will do as well. Just keep your receipts and do a budget for what you spend it on. Now I would like to show you the guest house and give you the tour."

Mr. JW was not there, and neither were the kids. She said I would report to her but whatever JW wanted was the top priority. First, we walked back to the guest house, a two-bedroom, two-bath beach bungalow. I thought, holy shit, dreams do come true. She asked, "Will this do?" As if I would not like it.

"Yes, ma'am," I said. "This is great."

We headed back to the main house, and she showed me the master bedroom, the china room, and the wine cellar. We talked some more, and then she asked me if I would like to work for them. I said, "Yes, ma'am," with a big smile. She called the security guard up and told him I would be the new estate manager and chef and to please see to whatever I needed.

She then told the story of Camp David with the Bushes and the Marines. That was why she liked me. "They were all so professional and polite," she said. Then she asked, "When can you start?"

"Next week," I said.

"Take a few days off, and then we'll meet at the house, and I will give you my list of the family's likes and dislikes. You can pick up the Suburban keys, and we will get started." She had already spoken to the Fords, and I guess that was enough. I am sure Dora gave me a great review as well; like I said, I was one of her favorites.

We talked a little bit, and she said, "I look forward to having you work for us. Now I must get back to Beverly Hills, as I have dinner plans."

We said our goodbyes, and I headed back to Santa Monica, but not before having lunch at Alice's Restaurant on the Malibu Pier. What a hip spot to be seen having lunch. Back at home, the first call was to Dori. Before I could say one word, she cut me off and said, "Mrs. Weintraub already called me. She liked you and offered you the job. She said she was very impressed with your honesty and posture." Then she added, "You got the best job in town. Don't screw it up. Other families will try to steal you, so be careful about what you say to guests and other people you meet. Keep who you work for very private."

"Yes, ma'am, I said. "I will stop by and bring you up to speed once I get the job down and I am in a routine."

"Great job. I knew they would like you."

Then I called Art and told him the great news. He said, "I told you so. Take the weekend off. We will see you Monday. Do whatever you need to do. Don't worry about us." Then he added, "Congratulations. You are in the major league now, so act like you belong there." I will never forget that. Art was cool like that.

I had no idea who this guy Weintraub was or how powerful he was, but like I said, my life was about to change. This was one of the biggest days of my life.

I had a great lunch at Alice's and drank a few beers while doing my favorite thing: girl watching. Believe me, this is one of the best spots in Malibu for that. Then I headed back to Art's, packed a bag, and went to my home in the desert for a few days to relax and work on my tan before starting the new job.

What a great feeling. I had just gotten one of the best jobs in LA as a private chef—maybe even the best job in the country. I had no idea what to expect, but man, this was going to be one hell of a ride.

Once I got home, I stopped by Kev's place to tell him about the new job. "Yes," I said, "Jerry Weintraub."

He knew him from the Bushes. He said, "He is one powerful man. Keep your shit together, and you can ride his coattails for a long time."

We had a few beers and caught up, and he told me that Betty Ford asked about me every once in a while. That was a great feeling.

Finally, I said goodnight, went across the street to my place to crash, and let it all sink in.

Julien Home, Del Rey Beach

Pacific Palisades Art house

Malibu Beach

chapter 7

THE WEINTRAUBS

I CALLED MRS. WEINTRAUB ON Monday, as planned, and she said, "Meet me at the house tomorrow at noon. There will be a car there for you to get back to Malibu, and we can go over all the details and what we expect of you." We chatted for a few minutes, and then she said, "I will see you tomorrow, and be sure to bring a few suits in case you have to drive on John's day off."

"Yes, ma'am," I said. "Goodbye. I will see you tomorrow."

Wow, one more day to hang in the desert and party before the new job started. I figured I would go to the Marriott in Palm Desert, play a round of golf, and have dinner at the Italian restaurant there. Then I'd see the asshole executive chef, Chris, and brag about the new job I'd just landed.

I put on my signature black Armani suit and a white shirt—I was wearing this way before George was. I had dinner at the bar, and then I asked if Chris was around. He came out a few minutes later. I had not seen him since I'd worked for the Fords, well on my way to the top.

He came over and said, "Hey, Chef Al. Good to see you." I knew he was full of shit. He said, "I heard you left the Fords and were living in LA." He'd probably heard that from the Asian pastry chef I was still fucking when I was in town.

I said, "Yes, I just got a new gig working for Jerry Weintraub, running his Malibu estate and the family chef as well." I wish you could have seen his jaw drop.

I mentioned a few names and places I had been hanging out at. He was speechless, and he ended up comping my dinner and a super Italian red on top of that. He had a glass of wine with me and said, "Man, am I impressed with you. I know you are cocky, but man, you can back it up."

"Thanks," I replied. "All the best to you." Like I said, he was a real asshole. I finished my dinner—and I did ring up the tab a little more. I never felt so on top of the world. I am sure word of my new job sailed around the Marriott.

The next morning, I packed all my things. I still had a few clothes at Art's, but I could pick them up in a few days. Kevin and I had coffee together, and I said, "I will see you in a few weeks." Then I was on my way to Beverly Hills and a new adventure.

First Day.

When I got to the house in Beverly Hills, I saw Wolfgang playing tennis as I passed the tennis courts. I gave him a quick wave as I headed into the house to meet Mrs. Weintraub. She said, "You know Wolfgang?"

"Yes, ma'am," I replied. "I met him when I worked for Art."

"That's nice, because his restaurant is one of Jerry's favorite lunch places, and they're quite good friends. If you ever need something from him, feel free to ask him. Just say it's for Jerry."

The housekeeper gave me a cup of coffee and a few folders as Mrs. Weintraub told me what would be expected of me. One folder was a phone book, and I mean a phone book from hell, with numbers for George Bush, Arnie, you name it. If they were powerful, they were in there.

Another folder had a list of the things each family member liked: beer, food, candy bars. It was all in there, and my job description as well. The Malibu beach house was my main priority; that is where they did most of their entertaining. I would travel with the family and oversee the security staff, stables, housekeepers, cooking, and cars. I had to have the house ready twenty-four-seven in case JW showed up with guest—or as I learned later, a few young chicks out the back door.

The hot tub and Olympic-size pool would stay heated all year. That, I thought, must have cost an arm and a leg, but with the Weintraubs, money was never a question—it was always the best of everything. This was not like Art, who could be cheap sometimes. Like with bottled water. Art hated that guests would not finish them. He saw me throwing them out once and told me to fill them back up and use them a few more times. I almost shit. I laughed, but Art was serious. So, I would fill them up a few times with tap water. Then, after a few uses, I would toss them. I could not believe Art asked me that.

Mrs. Weintraub and I talked for an hour or so about the family. Then the three girls came in, all adopted. They seemed nice, but later I would find out that they were little spoiled bitches. JW had a son from a previous marriage, and I met him later. He had a great wife, but he was a real pussy. When his dad said shit, he squirmed like a little kid.

There was a nanny as well. She had to have been in her sixties, way too old to be taking care of the two young girls, and she was sick all the time. Part of my job was to shuttle the kids if she was not around.

If you don't know who Jerry Weintraub was, let me bring you up to speed. He was from New York, moved to LA to make it big. He married Jane Morgan, a singer and old Hollywood starlet and quite a bit older, but from what I heard, she opened all the doors in LA for him. He managed the likes of Sinatra, Elvis, Led Zeppelin, and Neil Diamond and produced several hit movies: *The Karate Kid*, *Oceans 11*, *Diner*, and the list just keeps going. He was a real mogul. I had no idea the guy was that huge.

A loyal staff was already in place at the house: housekeepers; security; John, the butler, the nanny—all great folks. I was to keep the show running: cooking, making sure the house was always ready, and traveling with them. I had the normal stuff: credit card, petty cash, all that was taken care of. You name it, I did it—Johnny on the spot, as I've been called over the years. I won't get in to the boring daily routine. They normally came on the weekends, so I made sure it was ready, and I might have to go to Beverly Hills once a week for a business lunch or dinner, or to the studio, depending on John's schedule, so as you can see, I was very busy and had to be ready for anything. That was cool.

I want to tell you some of the cool stories, the people I met and the shit I pulled there. I could write a whole book on the Weintraubs: the kids, the girlfriends, the fights, all the drama, the trips, the Bushes. But I want to give a little insight into every family I worked for, the good and the bad. How some of them don't think their shit stinks.

At the Weintraubs, I met them all, good and bad, so let's start right in.

The old lady, Mrs. W., aka Jane Morgan, was a cool old broad. I liked her. She was hot shit in the day, but she was past her prime when I came along. For the most part, we were great friends, and she liked me. I am told I was the only one to drive the old T-Bird besides her. It was the pink '57 from *American Graffiti*, the one Suzanne Somers drove. We had some good times in that ride.

For the most part, the three girls were ok, just spoiled little shits. Julie was already in some art school in Valencia, so I did not have to deal with her shit every day, just Jamie and Jody and their friends, but that was enough.

The son, Michael, only came around on weekends and holidays. He was a little twit. Yeah, that's a good word for him. You know the sort—can't wipe his own ass, but he will sure let you know who his dad is. We got along, though. I just put up with his attitude and let it roll off my back. JW was a true man's man, a big guy, and he took care of himself.

JW just had this presence about him; he was almost regal. I have met a lot of famous people, but none like him. He was larger than life. He would run three or four miles and then play eighteen holes. He was always on the go, reading scripts and making deals. He hardly ever slept, just go. I picked that up from him. He would not have just one beer but pound down two or three. Not one Advil, but a dozen. He used to guzzle orange energy drink like it was water. I guess you would say he was compulsive.

The first time I talked with JW, he gave me a business card and told me to keep it with me at all times and not to be afraid to use it. It was for the head of the California Highway Patrol, a real-life get-out-of-jail card.

He also gave me a letter on official letterhead from President George Bush, saying to please give the bearer of the letter all due respect and show him the same courtesy you would give the president, signed George Bush, and it had a number to call, too. I never used it, but I did use the Highway Patrol card a lot. Never had an issue. That was our first conversation.

Mrs. Weintraub gave me a list of everything I had to have on hand. I could not believe that list. In his private fridge off the master and his little closet by the wet bar, I had to have four kinds of beer, three imported and one domestic, all kinds of snacks, such as M&Ms, salted peanuts, Moon Pies, Almond Joy bars, Oreo's, and that was just a start. I also had to maintain a supply of cigars and cut them for him if John was not around. I mean, I've smoked my share of cigars, and I cannot believe he would not even cut them himself. I sometimes wonder if John had to wipe his ass, because he could not do shit on his own.

But that is what I was paid to do. The alternative was to quit and move on. That's the worst part of some of these jobs: the shit you have to put up with, and I do mean shit. The fax machine was by the wet bar, and JW would call me from my guest house on the other side of the property to bring it to him. The fucker could not get out of bed and walk ten feet. That's pretty sad. I almost said something one time, like, "JW, you can't walk ten feet?" But then I said to myself, "Fuck it. I want to keep the job a little longer. I like the perks."

There were some cool times, like Mrs. Weintraub wrecking the Rolls for the tenth time and slipping chicks out the back door, driving them back to LA, and giving them a few hundred bucks.

After a few weeks, I began to settle into the job. On one of my days off, I was in the main kitchen, having a cup of coffee, making my rounds. On my off days, I would do a walk-through of the property to make sure everything was cool. I mean, I had the place to myself, aside from the security guards. I would fix them lunch sometimes if I wasn't busy—it was good to keep them on my side.

I was enjoying the peace and quiet, no kids, sipping my coffee when I heard the back door open. I turned around, and it was Bruce Dern. He said, "Good morning," and asked who I was.

I said, "I am Alan, the new chef and house manager."

"Bruce. It's nice to meet you. How long have you been here?"

"About a month now."

He chuckled. "Oh, a long time."

I did not get the joke at that time. I guess they had a hard time keeping a chef and house manager.

As we talked, I fixed him a cup of coffee and gave him a muffin. He asked if Jerry was around, and I said, "No, he is at the studio today." Bruce lived down the street and had just popped in to say hi. He had seen me running and wanted to meet the new chef. He was pretty cool, and I looked forward to him stopping by for coffee once in a while. His career was kind of winding down, and I guess he and JW went way back. He would stop by once in a while, and we became good friends. We even had lunch one day at Alice's and dinner at Wolfgang's wife's restaurant in Malibu, Granita. We had a few laughs, but I never met his daughter. I wanted to; it just never came up.

A few days later, I was talking to the security guys as they were changing shifts. I said, "What's up with Bruce Dern?"

One said, "He just stops by from time to time and says hi to the chef and us." A

"He made a statement after he asked how long I'd been here, that a month was a long time. What's up with that?"

They laughed and said that he'd made a bet with them that I would not make it the first month. I got it now—other chefs hadn't been able to put up with the demands.

I said, "Thanks for letting me know the score." Dern lost the bet. I made it past the first month.

The estate had a guest house called the Bush Guest House. It was for George and Barbara to stay when they came. The tennis court was named after Jimmy Connors, who played there every few weeks. Wolfgang did, too, but he mostly played at the house in Beverly Hills.

Jimmy had a hot-ass wife, playmate of the month, Patti McGuire. What a set of tits. I saw them first-hand a few times. She used to lie on the beach while Jimmy played tennis with some of his friends, and I would fix them lunch. She was cool with me, but Jimmy, what a prick, and everyone knew it. I only saw them a few times over the two years I worked for JW, but I thought I should share the story. I mean, don't get me wrong—great player, hot-ass chick for a wife, but he could have been a little nicer. What a first-class prick. I am sure everyone who knows him will agree. Maybe they're just afraid to say it. Me, I don't give a shit.

On to golf legend Raymond Floyd. Man, what a nice guy. He stayed at the guest house when they used to have the Sharkskin Shootout at Sherwood Country Club. JW was a member there, and Mrs. Weintraub used to get me tee times there. JW didn't know this for the first year. She was cool with shit like that. Raymond stayed a week at the house. I cooked for him, and he took me out a few times. This was the year that he won the tournament. I had a VIP pass to the clubhouse; everything was pretty bad-ass. I met all the pros, like Norman and Freddie. It was a once-in-a-lifetime experience. Mrs. Weintraub gave me the weekend off—that hardly never happened. She knew I was a golfer, and JW was out of town, so the family stayed in Beverly Hills for the weekend.

Raymond treated me great, and the rest of the pros did as well. They all knew who JW was, and I was his private chef. Everyone at the club knew me, too, from playing there with Don Johnson and Shari and Sam on a regular basis. Plus, I was a ten handicap back then, not bad for a chef. Well, that's it for the Sharkskin Shootout. Raymond, thanks for the kindness. You are a true stud and a great guy. Thanks for dinner and the great conversations and tips. My game is still ok.

I used to see Johnny Carson every few days as well. He and JW were friends. I mean, shit, who did he not know? Johnny lived the next bluff down. I did a few lunches for him on my off days—funny, nice guy. He had a little coke issue, but everyone knows that; it's not news. But he was nice to me and tipped me well. I cannot say a bad word about him. Plus, he's a legend. I enjoyed his company. He was easy to talk to and not real demanding like JW, just an all-around nice guy.

The Bushes only came once while I worked there, but they came to the house in Kennebunkport once as well. That was a pretty cool weekend. Prince Bandar was there as well. I had two royal families. This was a pretty cool deal, I thought.

I won't bore you with all the day-to-day shit, but I will tell you about both parties and one good dinner story that I know you will appreciate.

The Bushes stayed in the guest house, and Bandar stayed in the main house, as he was by himself this time. I would bring breakfast out to the Bushes, and Bandar would join them or dine on the patio by himself. That is a pretty impressive guest list by any means.

Back to the dinner story. It was the last night, and all parties were leaving the next morning. The kids were in Beverly Hills that weekend, so I only had adults, thank God.

I made a nice dinner: grilled rosemary chicken breast with all the nice sides and my famous bread pudding for dessert. They all enjoyed it and were thanking me when, from out of nowhere, JW and Bandar fired up a couple of Montecristo No. 2s right at the dinner table.

I will never forget This. Right after the first big puff of smoke, Barbara looked at JW and Bandar and said to the both of them, "You two know better than to smoke them at the table. Now, either put them out or go outside, but you're not going to smoke them at the table."

I had never sent JW speechless before. He and Bandar looked at each other like a couple of little boys who'd gotten their hands caught in the cookie jar and gotten a tongue lashing. They both headed for the patio without a word, and George joined them out there as well. They enjoyed their cigars as I served them some Remy VSOP brandy.

The Bushes were first class, and Barbara must have been one hell of a first lady. The next morning, I fixed them breakfast, and then the Secret Service picked up the Bushes, and I drove Bandar to his jet in Van Nuys. It was a pretty cool weekend.

A few weeks later, a package was delivered to the house by private courier. Like all packages, I was to open it and put whatever was in it on JW's desk. I opened it to find a box of Dominican ropes cigars and a letter addressed to JW. It said, "Thanks for the great weekend and enjoy the ropes. They're not as good as Bandar's Cubans, but the king says they're pretty damn good. Enjoy them." I still have the letter today. Needless to say, I kept the ropes as well—great smokes, too. I did shit like this all the time.

Other guests who stopped by on a regular basis were Neil Diamond and the Fonz. They would go horseback riding. We had a pretty hot stable chick, Dawn, who groomed them and saddled them up when guests wanted to ride on the beach. I threw a few shots in her. She was pretty hot, kind of horsey but in a good way. There was no shower in the stables, so she would clean up at my guest house. Then we would have a little fun, if you know what I mean.

I was a pretty good rider, and once a week, I would ride on the beach, depending on my schedule. I was taking a ride one day down by Carson's place, and I saw a group of people shooting a commercial or something. I rode past at a nice gallop with my shirt off and then turned back in a full loop a few minutes later. A guy came running over. "Hey, what's up?" He said. "Nice horse. Would you mind if we used it in the commercial?"

I said, "Sure, why not?"

"Cool, I will be right back."

He came back ten minutes later with a couple of dicks. They said they wanted to use the horse but not me on it. I said, "Find someone else with a horse." They wanted to put some chick on it. I was thinking, what if something bad happened and JW found out? I would be fucked. I told them, "Me and the horse or nothing, and four hundred dollars cash."

They had a little meeting, and then the guy came back and said, "Ok, we just have to figure out a few things and change the shoot. Just hang out a few minutes till we figure these out." Meanwhile, all the chicks were coming over and petting the horse, and I was getting phone numbers.

Then they all came back over. And the guy said, "We want to use you in a background shot. You ride up and hang out a few seconds and then ride off with the girl."

"Cool," I said.

Then he said I would have to put my shirt back on and sign a non-compete or something like that.

"Cool," I said.

My deal was to ride up on the horse, and then the chick was going to leave this guy and then hop on the back of the horse with me and ride off into the sunset like some love story or bullshit romance novel. I got my four hundred dollars and a few numbers.

Never found out about the commercial. I heard it was for some lifestyle info, but I never verified that. I made good with a few of the numbers as well.

One more good beach horse story involves one of the hottest chicks I ever banged: Emilia Crow. Man, was she a great piece of ass. She was married to an oil guy and real estate baron out of Texas, Trammell Crow. I heard he was a piece of shit, but I never met him. I did, however, put the wood to his ex-old lady many a time. He was on *60 Minutes* one time, I heard for pissing millions away. He was a real piece of work, drugs, booze, you name it. I never knew what happened to him; they'd just gotten divorced when I met her, and she'd gotten the Malibu beach house and a shitload of cash. Chicks always take us to the cleaners and get the house and all the cash. Like I always say, what do hurricanes and chicks have in common? They both come in warm and wet, and when they leave, they take everything. I like that it's true. Guys, you know it's not bullshit.

I was going for my morning ride on the beach. There were a few small cliff houses down the beach, where I used to see the big-titted blond with her top off. I saw her many times in the past on the top-floor balcony with her top off, sunning those big tits and that long blond hair. I would look up, and she always waved at me. It made my day.

I looked forward to that ride, and on this day, after I rode past her place and was heading back to the house, she came down to the beach and waved me over. She said, "I've seen you riding lately, and I am a new owner in Malibu. My name is Emilia."

"I am Alan," I said, "and I am the new estate manager for the Weintraubs and JW's private chef."

"I know Jerry. Why don't you stop by some time and have a glass of wine and talk about food? I would love to have you cook for me."

We exchanged phone numbers and said our goodbyes, and I was on my way. Man, was she smoking hot. I loved those big tits. I will get back to when I came over and cooked dinner for her. Man, what a great time, one of the best pieces of ass I've ever had.

Back at the Malibu estate, everything was crazy as shit every day. The guests were amazing, a who's who of big names. For instance, when JW produced the movie *Pure Country*, George Strait stayed at the guest house.

He's a true legend and a stand-up guy. I won't bore you about that story—just one more dinner and a movie—but thanks, George, for the good times and conversation. You are a stud and first class in my book. He was great to all the staff. Great flick as well, *Pure Country*.

One lunch, in particular, was interesting. JW was making a movie with Sylvester Stallone, Sharon Stone, and James Woods called *The Specialist*. They were all coming over for Sunday brunch at the estate. They had already received the script, and JW wanted to have a sit-down. That was how he did deals—none of the bullshit "I'll have my agent call you." Instead, it was "You pick the script up and get back to me." I had met Sharon through her sister, whom I banged when I worked for Art, and I'd been introduced to Sly at the premier of *Cliffhanger*, but I'd never met Woods.

It was a Friday afternoon, and all the guests showed up on time. I made a simple lunch: club sandwiches and a nice salad. That was all JW wanted. He did not care what guests wanted; it was always about him. Lunch was on the terrace overlooking the coast. Sharon said hi to me and that it was nice to see me, and she asked if I liked the new job. I said yes, and we made small talk, and that was it. Sly and Woods and I exchanged greetings, and they all sat down to eat. I missed most of the conversation, but I caught the ending when they were all walking out. JW always had the last word.

"So, all parties are agreed," he said in his large voice. They all said yes and shook hands, and then JW said, "Let's get to it and start shooting. We will talk next week, get everything signed and wrapped up. We are all done here." Sharon left, and the guys returned to the terrace for a cigar and a drink.

They all left, and as I was cleaning up, JW said, "Take the night off." He was meeting some chick—I saw her come through the gate. I am sure she was some new actress, trying to break into the business. I knew he was a pig, like his buddy Weinstein. What a piece of shit he was, but everyone knows that, so we won't beat that dead horse. Plus, JW has passed on, so let the dead lie in peace. He died with his sins.

I don't know how, but I made it through the first year. Finally, it was Christmas, the whole family, including John and me, was going to Lake

Tahoe for the holidays and skiing. John and I drove up to rent a few SUVs and get everything ready. The family would fly up in the corporate jet the following week.

John and I had a little break before the family came. I mean, we still had a lot of work to do, but it wasn't bad. I got a few days of skiing in, and we went out to dinner every night. It was a great little vacation. This was my first vacation with the family. Sure, I'd done Thanksgiving in Palm Springs, but this was ten days of skiing and cooking—not bad.

The high point for me was that they all had private ski instructors, and to my surprise, Peter and Beth from Stowe were spending the winter out there and working with the kids and Mrs. Weintraub. When they came to the house for dinner the first night and saw me, they could not believe it. "Chef Al, we heard you were in LA, working for some big movie guy, but we did not know who." They did not know how big JW was, but they knew he was a VIP, and they told the family they'd known me when I was a ski bum back in Vermont and worked for the Baraw family at the Stowe-flake Resort. What a small world.

Mrs. Weintraub liked that, but the kids did not give a shit. For me, though, it was a big feather in my cap. I knew they would tell all the gang back in Stowe that they had seen me in Lake Tahoe, working for some movie mogul. Later on, I got calls from Haabs and a few others, and they all said, "Chef Al, you are the man. The legend is still alive and working in LA for the rich and famous. We are all proud of you. Keep in touch."

The rest of the trip was spent taking the kids to the slopes every day. I could ski a little, and then I had to get back to the house to cook dinner. At the end of the day, John and I would drive back together to pick up the family. Peter and Beth were invited to the house one more time, and we all got caught up. The trip went well; I did not miss a beat, and everyone was happy.

JW went back a few days early. He always did shit like that. I had the task of driving him to the airport, as John was doing something for Mrs. Weintraub.

On the way, we had our first real conversation. Before this, all our interactions consisted of him telling me to do things or asking how I was or how the kids were treating me—small talk and just bullshit. I was staff to him.

I will never forget this for the rest of my life: on the way to the airport, JW asked me what my name was again and said he was sorry that he'd forgotten it.

"Alan," I said.

"Oh, yeah, now I remember."

I mean, I had been taking care of his house, his personal shit, driving his kids to school, slipping chicks out the back door, basically lying for him, and he couldn't even remember my fucking name? Pretty fucking weak. I lost all respect for him after that.

He asked where I was from, and I told him Ohio for the tenth time. He said, "Oh, yeah, my pal owns the Indians." That was where he got his hot dogs from; he had to have them in the fridge in case he wanted one. What a primadonna.

I dropped him off at the airport and said, "Goodbye, boss. I will see you in Malibu, and thanks for the ski pass and Christmas bonus." Then I headed back to the house. I still think about this conversation. What a piece of shit.

Back in Tahoe, I cooked for the rest of the family for the next few days and drove them to the slopes. When it was time for them to leave, John and I took them to the airport, returned the rental cars, cleaned the house, and then spent an extra day in town just doing nothing.

I was upset because the kids left half their shit unpacked. I'd put some of it in garbage bags, and the rest, I'd tossed. John knew I was pissed and said, "Please don't quit. I need you to help me, and we can get through this together." Dora was his agent, too, so he knew I was trying to make two years.

We had a nice drive back home, and when we got back, Mrs. Weintraub was very happy. She thanked me and said she would make a tee time for me at Sherwood and then one in the desert at the Vintage. Meanwhile, JW didn't say shit, but that was normal; he never said thanks or made you feel appreciated.

The next day, I headed out to the desert. Kevin was still with the

Fords, but he was getting ready to leave in a few months. We hung out, played some golf, banged a few broads, and chilled—not a bad vacation place. The desert is nice in the winter. Shari and Sam came down and hung out for a few days. When they left, I chilled with Kevin and some friends, got some rays, and just took a break. I needed one after the ski trip. The week went by too fast, and then it was back to work in Malibu.

I had to go to the house in Beverly Hills first to do a lunch for JW and some guests, and Wolfgang was playing tennis. I stopped and said hi, and he said, "You're still here? Where have you been?" I told him that I mostly took care of the Malibu estate and had just returned from vacation.

"Well," he said, "stop in for dinner sometime."

"I will do that," I said. "Take care, and good to see you."

The guests for that lunch were Wasserman and Sheinberg. They came by often, and they were no prizes, let me tell you. They thought their shit did not stink. Real pieces of work.

I finished up and headed back to Malibu and my guest house by the sea. That was the best part of the job, living right on the beach. I miss that place—lots of good stories. I banged a lot of women in that place: half the staff, the Gelson's checkout girl, the florist next door, Emilia Crow, the housekeeper's daughter, a hot little Mexican, and whoever else I could find.

But the kids were busting my balls. I knew I had a tough year to get through, but I would make it. Then I would be golden with Dora at the International. I got a ten percent raise that second year, so it was not all bad. The kids spent most of the summer in Kennebunkport. I was there for the July Fourth weekend and a few other holidays. I was never crazy about Maine or the East Coast in general—lots of assholes, and New Yorkers are the worst. The Bushes came by a few times for dinner when JW was in town, but for most of the summer, I stayed in Malibu. Keeping that place up and running was a full-time job. JW still entertained, and I was driving back and forth to the Beverly Hills house as well. That was cool, as time passed quickly.

Before I knew it, Thanksgiving had arrived. They always spent the holiday at the Palm Springs retreat, a great old house. I got a few extra days to spend at my place in La Quinta as well. Afterward, when I got back to Malibu, Dern stopped by for a beer. He could not believe that I was coming up on my second year. He was a cool guy. I miss him—and all the regulars. Neil Diamond stopped by often as well. JW used to promote him, and they were still pals. He was a real nice guy, and humble as well. They don't make guys like him nowadays.

After Dern left, I took one of the horsed and down the beach. As I was coming back, while riding past Emileia's place, she came out. I stopped to talk to her, and she asked me why I hadn't called her.

"I've been in Maine, and I just now got back."

"When are you going to come over and cook me dinner?"

"How about next Tuesday?"

"Great! It's a date."

I asked her if she liked fish, and she replied, "I love fish, and I like all veggies—and everything else as well."

I told her I would call on Monday to confirm, and then I rode off, thinking, wow, holy shit. This could be great.

When I got back to the house, I cleaned up and started my day. First, I checked in with the security guards to see if anyone had stopped or any packages had been delivered while I was gone. We would shoot the shit for a few minutes. I always brought them something to eat.

Next, I'd check the stables, say hi to my girl, maybe bend her over in the barn. I did that quite often. Then it was on to the tennis courts to make sure they were clean, that the bathrooms were all in good order, and that the fridge had beer, water, and sodas. Next stop was the Bush guest house, where I'd do a quick walk-through if we had no guests, and then I'd check the pool, make sure it was clean and seventy-eight degrees all year-round. Then it was on to the main house to check the bathrooms, fridges, and hot tub on JW's private patio. It was always kept at 103 degrees in case he had some chick showed up. Finally, I'd check the fax machine and put all the faxes on his desk.

One day, as I was doing that, there was one fax that said, "Jerry, great to see you. I've got a little tip for you: buy all you want of Halliburton. Good things are coming. Your pal, Dick."

I called my mentor, Mike, a hedge fund guy in Newport. He told me about Halliburton and said, "Great tip. They're at an all-time low, like nine dollars a share. How did you get it?"

I told him about the fax and said, "It was from Dick." I didn't have a clue who Dick was, but Mike knew right off the bat that it was the VP. He knew my boss and the Bushes.

He said, "Buy all you can afford." I had some extra money around, so what the hell—I was all in. One of my better tips, next to QVC with that asshole Barry Diller.

I put the fax on his desk with the reports from his stockbroker, newspapers, and a few new scripts for him to read. Then I checked the humidor to make sure it was full of Montecristos and a few Cohibas. That was my typical day, along with fueling the cars, running a few errands, shopping for groceries, picking up wine and flowers—whatever had to be done, I did it.

The days went by fast, and I was constantly on the go. I liked that. The challenges were different every day. I'd take a little break in the afternoon if I could lie on the beach, get a little sun on my face and keep my tan up.

Next week arrived before I knew it. I called Emilia on Monday to make sure we were on. She said, "I look forward to trying your cooking. I think I am looking forward to fucking you as well."

Back then, all these broads in LA were down for whatever, and when they found out who you were working for, that was a slam dunk. Emilia was a little different. She had money from the divorce and she was a little older than me by seven or eight years. She wanted a little young action, and I was happy to give it to her.

I showed up two bottles of wine, fresh out of Weintraub's cellar—a Ramonet Montrachet Grand Cru and a Chateau d'Yquem—and food as well. Perks of the job. I made some martinis, and we chatted as we sipped them. She said, "You're a good rider. You don't see many guys riding a horse down the beach with their shirt off at full gallop every day."

"Is that a good thing?" I asked.

"Oh, yes, a very good thing."

She got awful close to me, and we had a little toast, and I gave her a little wet peck on her cheek.

She said, "I like that."

"I do, too, but I need to start cooking, or we are going to starve tonight, and I need some energy."

I whipped up dinner, just some fresh halibut, veggies, roast potatoes, and Caesar salad. We uncorked the Ramonet Montrachet Grand Cru. She was already wet, and I have not opened the Chateau d'Yquem yet; that was for after dinner.

We had a great dinner conversation, and her place was right on the sand, next to Albert Gurestan's place. I knew his kids from the Weintraubs. I took them home a few times when they needed a ride.

We finished our dinner, and she said, "Let me give you the tour."

Her bedroom was on the top floor, and it had a great ocean view. She said she wanted to take a hot shower, and she asked me to join her. I said, "Are you sure you want to do this?"

"Most definitely."

We got undressed and into the hot shower. I soaped her down, and we had some of the steamiest sex I have ever had. I love big tits, and man, did she have a rack from hell, bought and paid for. Glad it was not me. This was no cheap titjob. And it was out of my league. We fucked like a couple of teenagers. She could not get enough, and I was in heaven. She was one of the hottest chicks I ever banged, right up there with Heather.

I passed out after we finished the d'Yquem. I was off the next morning, so there was no rush to get back to the house. I made her breakfast in bed and threw one more shot into her, and she said, "Wow, what a great lover you are. You are a small guy, but you have a nice package." She seemed quite surprised by that.

I said, "Is that a good thing?"

"Oh, yes," she replied.

"Does that mean I will see you naked again?"

"Only if you cook and promise to fuck me in the morning again."

"I can do that."

We finished breakfast, and I said goodbye. Then I kissed her one last time and was out the door. I didn't even make it to the car before being busted. The two Gursten kids with their dad, Albert, watching me back the car up.

I had to stop and say hi, or they would know something was up. "Chef Al, were you supposed to take us to school today?"

"No," I said, "I was just having breakfast with Miss Crow and dropping a script off for her to read." The kids bought it, but Albert looked at me and smiled. I am sure he would have liked to bang her as well, but he liked them young and dumb. I said, "Have a great day, and Albert, if you need something, let me know."

Wow, what a close call. I got back home, and man, I was thinking, can it get any better than this? Marine from Hick town, Ohio, getting all this good ass, meeting all these famous people, and getting paid as well—what a great life.

Then my pager went off; it was Mrs. Weintraub. She'd backed into someone, and she asked if I could get her. "Of course," I said. "Where are you?" She was at the Ivy, and it was a mess, as always. I got there, and no cops were around, thank God. As usual, the valet guys had it handled. I just had to take her to the Beverly Hills house and call the dealer to get the car. If JW asked, it was getting serviced, and that was it. Just another crazy day.

This was the fourth time or so in the last year in a half where she'd thought she was the only one on the road, crazy old broad, but I loved her. We got inside the house, and she said, "Thank you. I'm sorry to ruin your day off."

"That's ok," I said. "It's no big deal. You come first."

"All right, then, I guess I have to make a tee time for you at Sherwood next week."

"That would be nice."

"And take the T-Bird for a spin as well. You have not taken it out for a while. Oh, Alan, I will make it for four. Call Sheri and Sam and ask if they want to join you."

"I would like to take Don instead, as I took them last time."

"Don who?"

"Johnson."

"Oh, how do you know him?"

"I met him when I worked for Art, and I've cooked for his attorney a few times."

"Ok, get back to Malibu in case JW needs you, and not a word about the Rolls. And say nothing to John as well."

"Yes, ma'am," I said, and I was on my way.

When I got back home, the day was almost over. Traffic in the afternoon going back to Malibu is hell. The stable girl was sitting on my patio. Weeknights, security left at six unless I was on the property; then they might leave a little early unless we had a VIP guest or something. I said, "I thought you would be gone by now."

"Yeah," she said, "but I hoped you might be up for a drink and a hot tub. I am horny."

I always had a bottle of vodka and beers in the guest house. I fixed us a couple of drinks, and then we went up to JW's private hot tub and did the wild thing. I was fucked out and tired from banging Emilia the night before, and now more pussy. I guess I could never get enough. We hung out a few hours, and then she rushed off to take a shower at my guest house. Then we did the wild thing one more time. Damn, she liked to fuck as well. I did say LA was great back in the day.

I was hungry as hell, as I had not eaten all day, so after getting cleaned up, I drove into Malibu for dinner. I loved Alice's Restaurant; what a great place. I had a nice dinner, said hi to Pete, and we caught up. I tell him about Emilia.

"Yeah, I know who she is," he said, "the blond with the big tits. Wow, what a great score."

I had dinner at the bar, and he bought me a drink. We talked some trash, and I told him the Rolls story and the stable girl and the night with Emilia. We laughed and had a shot of tequila.

Pete said, "Damn, must be nice to be Chef Al."

We had one more shot and then called it a night. Just another day in the life of Chef Al in Malibu. Man, I was tearing it up.

I knew I had to keep my nose clean till the end of the year. Then I would quit, get my bonus check, and go on one more free ski trip with the family. This year, we were going to Aspen. It would be a nice trip, and I had never been there.

I got through the summer—there were no house guests, and it was kind of slow for the first time. I mean, I was still busy with the estate duties, but JW was filming, so on weekends, it was just the kids and their friends. They were just kids but spoiled rotten and real pains in the ass.

But I made it work. That's the worst part of some of the jobs: the kids are assholes, the wife is a total bitch, the old man is a fuck, or sometimes they're all fucked up. I had a few families like that. I will talk about them later.

Mrs. Weintraub got me a tee time at Sherwood. I got ahold of Don, and he said he would love to play. I said, "I think it's just us two, but they might pair us up."

"That's cool with me," he said. "I will see you there."

I met Don at the range, and he ran into Jack Nicholson and said, "Let's play together."

"I didn't know you were a member here," said Jack.

"I'm not. I am a guest of Alan Weintraub's private chef." He laughed. "Yeah, Mrs. Weintraub likes him a lot. He's her favorite chef of all time, and he plays here a lot. I know; I've seen him around.

Don waved me over to meet Jack, and we shook hands.

"So, you're the chef," said Jack. "You are the only one I've ever seen drive the T-Bird and play here."

"I know," I said. "Mrs. Weintraub likes me, Jack."

I got a Bloody Mary, and we headed to the tee box. To play there, you had to have a caddy and be playing with a member. I was the exception. Once in a while, they would just let me go off by myself. This place was bad-ass. You didn't pay for anything. You just signed in as a guest and got a locker. At the range, you could get drinks, fruit, yogurt, whatever you wanted. The clubhouse was awesome, and the course was in mint shape. I had some great rounds there. On this day, I shot seventy-nine, and the guys were impressed.

Jack said, "We have to play again, and you have to cook for me sometime."

"Sure," I said. "Just let me know when. Weekends are tough because I run the Malibu estate, but weekdays are cool. Just give me a few days' heads up."

"Cool," Jack said. He is one cool cat. I always liked him; real nice guy, and what a hotshot. Don, too. I was cool with both of them, plus we are all golfers and liked pussy. I told them about Emilia Crow and the stable girl, and they both got a kick out of it. This was a great day—the first time I golfed with Don, and I got to meet Jack and play golf with him. I also had his private number, and Don's, too. We all talked some trash on the course and then had a nice lunch in the clubhouse, on Mrs. Weintraub, of course. Like I said, she liked me.

The next day, I called her in Beverly Hills to check in, and she said she was coming to the house for lunch today and asked if I would make her something.

I said, "Yes, ma'am."

"Fine. See you at noon."

There was a little Asian nail salon in Malibu she liked, and I knew she would be going there after lunch. She liked to check on me every once in a while and talk. I fixed her an egg white omelet—she liked those—and then we talked for a while. She asked me if I was happy, and she said, "I know the kids are testy sometimes, but we all like you."

"Yes, ma'am," I said. "I am happy and plan to stick around."

She smiled and said, "Good. I am going upstairs to change. Would you put my things in the Rolls?" I always did that for her; she always had around five bags of shit. I didn't know what was in them, and I did not want to know.

She called me on the intercom and asked me to bring up her juice. I headed up to the master, and when I turned the corner, she acted surprised and dropped her towel, and it was all hanging out—not a pretty sight, I can tell you. "Alan, please turn your head," she said, but I already had, as I did not want to see this old bag of bones in her birthday suit. Once she had the towel back on, I gave her, her juice and went back downstairs and loaded up the car.

When she came down, I walked her to the car and opened the door for her. She was getting up in age and always losing something or wrecking the car. I said goodbye, and then she headed to the nail salon.

I didn't even get to sit down and finish my coffee before she called me.

"Alan?"

"Yes, ma'am."

"I left my pantyhose on the dresser. Could you please bring them to the nail salon?"

"Yes, ma'am, on my way."

I went up to the master, and the pantyhose were on the dresser. The safe was wide open in the closet, and there was a lot of cash in plain sight: jewelry, watches, diamonds, a small fortune for the taking, but this might have been a test, so I locked it back up, grabbed the pantyhose, and was off to the nail salon. I think she liked showing me off sometimes, that I did all these small errands for her. The girls saw I was her friend, was always dressed sharp, and acted professionally. I liked helping her out; she always got me free tee times at Sherwood or the Riviera for doing some small task, and she always said thank you.

Before I left, I asked if there was something else she needed me to do, and she said, "No, go back to the house and let me know where you want to play next."

I said, "Thanks, and by the way, ma'am, you left the safe open."

"Oh, my God, did you lock it back up?"

"Yes, ma'am. I only took a few thousand and a diamond necklace. I did not think you would mind." She laughed and told me to be on my way. She was something.

Back at the house, my day was just about done. I made one last round, prepared dinner, and relaxed in the boss's private hot tub. That was a great deal.

Great thing about these jobs: I ate the best food, drank the best wine, smoked Cubans, played the best courses in the country, and didn't spend a dime. Not a bad job, and making nice cash as well. If I wanted a bottle of wine, I would just walk down to the main house and into the cellar and take what I wanted. I'd grab a Cuban for after dinner and take a bottle of Knob Creek back to my guest house and just buy a new one next week, all on the boss's dime. All perks of the job, just like banging the staff. I just learned to take what I wanted, and that's the way it was.

But I knew there had to be a better gig out there. For the time being, though, I would just do a good job and wait till something better came up. Dora told me I needed to make it two years; other clients would like that. We had talked, and I'd told her about the kids, how bad they were, and how demanding JW could be.

One Sunday, around like nine, Mrs. Weintraub called me. "We want brunch today. We'll have twenty guests in three hours."

I felt like saying, "Are you fucking crazy? Do I look like David Copperfield?" I had no staff, aside from a couple of Mexican house cleaners. They were not worth a shit, but I was fucking their daughter. Instead, I said, "Yes, ma'am."

I had to run to Gelson's in Malibu, get all the shit, and throw it together with not even a thank you from JW. It was not the old lady's fault; I am sure it was JW. They have no idea what the real world is like

Same with the shit-ass kids—just "give me money," and they have no values or work ethic. Look at all these celebrities' kids. They're all fucked up, drugs, lazy, just real pieces of shit. I knew it was time to get out of this job, plus the girls would go cry to mom, "Chef Al is being mean to me," because they did not get their way.

The last few months were the same. The nanny went on vacation, and I had to drive the little bitches to school. They were just so spoiled. It's nice to be adopted by some movie mogul and never have to work the rest of your life. I would have loved to see them in a different life. I am sure they would not be so arrogant. I had to drive the kids to their private school in Santa Monica. I felt like Mr. French. One good thing about it was meeting other folks, like the Gersten kids, Brandon and Brody Jenner, Mel's kids. That was kind of cool, and Mrs. Weintraub took care of me with tee times and a few nice tips.

Speaking of tips, I was cleaning the garage and the guest house, and there must have been at least eight cases of wine from a party. The place was a mess, but I got it all organized. When I made lunch for Mrs. Weintraub, she asked me why I was so dirty.

I told her I'd been cleaning the guest house and the garage and cleaning out the storage room. She said, "What did you find"

"A lot of old wine from a party," I said. "It's probably gone south. There were also a few pieces of artwork."

"I'll take a look after lunch."

We chatted as I served her an egg white omelet and a juice. Then we went to the garage and the guest house. I had everything clean as a whistle and organized. She loved that about me, as all my employers did. I was good at that stuff.

She said, "Take the wine home, Alan, and throw the rest away."

I saw this one painting by Erté, but I'd never heard of him. It was black and white, and I was not crazy about it, but it was signed by the artist, along with a few actors, and it had a little note on the back to JW. Mrs. Weintraub said, "JW hates the artist. Why don't You take it home?" It was of some chick walking a dog. I thought, what the hell. Someday it might be worth a few dollars, and was I right.

I said thanks, drove her back to Beverly Hills, and called it a day. That weekend, I took home the wine and my first real work of art. I mean, the wine was over the top. My cellar was already full. I haven't even mentioned the nice jackets and ski clothes for guests, tennis rackets, golf balls. I cleaned up. It was a great departing gift.

Like the rest of Hollywood, the Weintraubs didn't live in the real world. To this day, I do not understand why some people care about these assholes and read these magazines and watch these stupid-ass shows. I think most folks just don't have a life.

A few years back, my cousin in Ohio said at dinner that it was Tom Cruz's birthday, that he was turning forty. I said, "It's my birthday next month. I wonder if Tom knows? Who gives a fuck how old Tom is. He is one weird fuck, and on top of that, he goes both ways. I mean, you don't even know him, Lisa, and he is an asshole." There you go. Some people don't have a life, like my cousin in Ohio.

The family was going to Aspen for Christmas that year, and thankfully, they didn't know it would be my last family trip. I planned to quit after the holidays, get my bonus, and have something lined up so I could walk right into a new job.

Just like the year before, John and I drove up a week early to rent an extra SUV, get the houses all set up, pick up the ski passes and food, all that sort of stuff. It had become routine for me. I got a few days of skiing in before they got there, and John and I went out for a few great dinners. This was the best part of the job, next to the golf.

If you have not been to Aspen, let me tell you, it's full of all the stars, some good, some bad. Like I said, they don't live in the real world. I ran into Kurt and Goldie in town one afternoon. They had a place there, along with Kevin and lots of other stars. I told Kurt I was working for the Weintraubs, which was why I was in Aspen. We said goodbye and "hope to see you around," and I wished them a happy holiday.

The family arrived, and John and I picked up everyone at the airport. They went right to the slopes. JW was missing in action, par for the course. I was told he would follow in a few days. It was the same drill as usual: cook for the family, take them to the slopes, shop for them, wipe their asses—whatever they needed, that was what I did. Whenever I was having a bad day, I just put on my happy face and said, "Only a few more weeks, and I will be out of here." That kept me going, along with lots of vodka. JW showed up after four days and left a few days early. It was like he just made an appearance at these family outings, that he had bought their affection. I mean, come on. All of them were adopted. Whatever works for some people. I wish he'd adopted me and given me a trust fund with a few million dollars. I mean, who the fuck wouldn't?

Nothing interesting happened this Christmas, just family time and a few ski instructors over for dinner. They ate out a few nights, and they took John and me, too. JW liked to give you the bonus check in person— that was his thing after the big Christmas dinner.

Then he went back to LA, and we finished up. The family had a great time; even the old broad was still skiing at her age. She was something in her Bogner suit at her age, trying to look good, well past her prime decades ago. We wrapped up the vacation with a nice lobster and steak dinner for everyone. It was nice; even the kids were happy.

I'd gotten through the trip, and I was almost home free. The next morning, John and I drove the family to the airport, dropped off the rentals, and then headed back to the house to get packed and clean up everything. We spent an extra day just getting organized, and I went skiing one last day; that made the whole trip worthwhile.

John and I smoked a couple of the boss's nice Cubans and drank a good bottle of wine on top of that. Then we left for the long drive back to Malibu. As we headed back, I knew this would be my last Christmas with these fucks.

The first thing I would do would be to see Dora and get a new job before I killed myself. I'd made it two years. I'd thought old man Hodge was tough; at least I'd been fucking his old lady, so the job hadn't been too bad.

When we returned, I unpacked and then called Mrs. Weintraub to let her know. She told me to take a few days off. As for John, he only answered to JW. I was sure he was back to work wiping the old man's ass. Me, I was cool. I took the day and just lay on the beach and tanned my back. Then I called Emilia, lined that shit up, went over to her place, cooked her dinner, and took care of that business. Damn, I miss those big tits. She was one hot piece of ass.

The next day, I had to throw a shot into the stable chick. She was getting old but was still a good roll in the hay. After two days of fucking, I was good to go and on my way to Beverly Hills to see Dora. I called her, and she said, "I have something for you. Get in here today."

When Dora wanted to see you, you better got there that day, or you were on her shit list. I put on my best suit and went to see her. She was a tough old broad, but we got along, unlike her daughter. What a bitch. She was just starting to get in the picture.

I showed up on time with a fresh haircut and manicure, looking my best. She liked that I was a sharp dresser. We had a cup of coffee, and she asked me why I wanted to leave. I told her about the kids' schedule, JW's crazy shit with the girlfriends, and me having to lie all the time. It was just too crazy and too much drama. At least I'd made it two years.

She understood. She had placed a lot of chefs in that house, but none had lasted even a year. She said, "You will have to give them notice."

"Yes," I said, "of course."

"All right, I have something for you. Do you know Albert Gersten?"

"Yes, I met him a few times when I dropped his kids off at the house in Malibu. They go to the same school as the Weintraubs'."

"It seems like you made a big impression on him, and the two kids like you. He asked me if you were happy at the Weintraubs. I told him no and that you might be looking if it was a right fit, but not till after the holidays. He said he will pay you ten thousand more than JW and with the same set-up, car travel with the family, everything, only nice kids."

"Great," I said.

"He wants to meet you this afternoon at the beach house in Malibu. Here is the address and telephone number. You have the job. Just be yourself and make sure you give them notice, and let Mr. Gersten know. They might let you go on the spot. They hate it when the staff leaves. So, you might start in a week or so."

I knew the house, as I had dropped the kids off a few times and Emilia lived a few houses down the beach. I drove up to the house and met Albert, and he let me in and offered me a beverage. He had some hot-ass chick with him; I guess he'd just picked her up and she had moved in. I did not know much about Albert, but he drove a Ferrari, had a lot of money, and lived in a bad-ass house on the sand in Malibu. He asked about JW—they knew each other—and why I was leaving.

I just said, "It's not a good fit, and I've been there two years."

We made small talk, and then his girlfriend said, "When Albert has the kids, you will need to drive them to school and around."

"I am good with that," I said.

"I would like you to drive me to my club a few nights of the week," said Albert, "and we need to hire a new housekeeper. The last girl just quit."

"Cooking, travel with the family, vacations, taking care of the cars, yes, I can do it all."

"Great. Let me know what happens when you give notice."

"Ok. I still have a few days off, so I would like to drop a few things off at the guest house in case they fire me on the spot."

"No worries. Here are the keys to the Rover and house and all the security codes. Come and go as you please. I look forward to you joining the family. I agree with your salary. I told Dora I was good with that."

He gave me his number, and we shook hands, and that was it. I said goodbye to the girlfriend as well. As I pulled away, I saw Emilia leaving as well. She waved, pulled alongside me, and said hi.

"Dropping the kids off?" She asked.

"No," I said, "I just left the Weintraubs and will be working for Albert in a week or so. I just got the job."

"Watch it. He has a wild lifestyle."

"Thanks for the heads up. I will see you soon."

She drove off, and I headed back home. I called Dora on the way, and she said, "I told you so. Congratulations. Let me know what happens when you give notice."

"Will do," I said. "Thanks, and I will keep in touch."

I was feeling pretty good about myself. When I got home, the first thing I did was grab a big fat Cohiba out of the boss's stash, a nice Bordeaux from the cellar, and a steak from the fridge and head to my guest house. As I enjoyed a great dinner and bottle of wine, I thought about how I would give notice. They were not going to be happy. I knew I had to move on, though. Albert was paying me top dollar. No doubt, I was leaving. I figured I would wait till Monday morning when the kids were gone to tell Mrs. Weintraub.

The rest of the weekend was crazy, as usual. I had to fix ten different lunches for everybody. They thought I was just a short-order cook: "Alan, I want a BLT Wolfgang pizza," Mrs. Gerstend would say, and then Mr. Weintraub would want something crazy as well. They hardly ever ate together.

This was one fucked-up family. Monday morning came around, and I got a chance to be alone with Mrs. Weintraub. I said, "Ma'am, I have to talk to you. It's very important, and it cannot wait."

I think she saw it coming. She knew the kids were getting to me.

"I am sorry," I said, "but I must move on. I will give you two weeks' notice, but then I must go. The girls are just too much for me to handle, and they don't respect me. I got a job offer, which I took, and they want me to start as soon as I am done here."

"Who?" She asked.

"Ma'am, I cannot say."

"Ok, if you need a reference, have them call me, not JW."

I thanked her, and then she gave me a big hug and said, "Finish the week, and we will be fine. I will miss you, Alan. You are a good worker, the best we ever had. I am sorry about the girls. They're just kids."

"I know," I said, "but I cannot work like this."

We had a cup of coffee together and talked about the family vacations I'd spent with them and how she would miss me.

"Me as well," I said.

She told me to keep in touch and wished me good luck. She was a real nice old broad, and I'll never forget her. JW treated her like shit after all she did for him. I never saw JW again, but I would see the kids at school and the mall in Santa Monica. I had to drive them home from school a few times later on. They were nicer then, as I did not work for them and didn't have to put up with their shit. I'd stop and say hi to Mrs. Weintraub time and time again. She liked me. It's too bad things did not work out, but I was all about building my reputation and moving up the food chain.

I called Dora and said I would be starting next week for Albert and that Mrs. Weintraub offered to give me a reference if I needed it and was sorry to see me leave. She said, "Great. Be sure to call Mr. Gersten, and stop by the office in a few weeks and let me know how the new job is, and we will have lunch."

"Great," I said, "and thanks for the job."

"She must have liked you. People who quit never get a reference. You are the first."

"Must be the Marine and good looks."

She laughed and said, "Don't flatter yourself, and now you can buy lunch next time."

I called Albert next and told him I could start next week and would like to move into the guest house this week and pick up the Rover.

He said, "No problem. You have all the keys. We will talk next week, and we look forward to having you. If you don't mind me asking, what happened when you gave them notice?"

"She said to just finish the week and, if I needed a reference, she would give me one, but I did not tell her who I was going to work for."

"Great. See you next week."

Wow, just like that, I was making more cash than I'd hoped for and still living in Malibu. What a great life.

T Bird American Graffiti

"

Arthur Co. flies solo after 7-year MCA stint

BY BRIAN LOWRY

The Arthur Co. has ended a seven-year exclusive relationship with MCA TV and formed a limited partnership, the Arthur Company Entertainment Group L.P. The group is backed by a private investor group with $20 million for TV programming and another $30 million to move into feature film production.

Headed by Arthur L. An-

Stories" as well as such syndie series as "The Munsters Today," "What a Dummy" and first-run episodes of "Airwolf."

The company has moved off the Universal lot to offices in West L.A. and signed with ICM to represent it for both movies and TV. Financing, committed initially for a five-year period, is coming from a group of private investors that includes Leon Wagner.

After his seven years at U, Annecharico said the opportunity to

Arthur Annecharico

said there have already been talks with other syndicators.

The company is working on an

Dallas, TX

LA Riots. That's when I got mugged in Venice

CHAPTER 8
ALBERT GERSTEN
PLAYBOY AND POTHEAD

I DID KNOW MUCH ABOUT Albert before I took the job. I just knew he had two kids and a shitload of money. It was not like now, where you can just Google and find out everything about someone.

As it turns out, he made it the old-fashioned way: he inherited it. His father was one of the largest landowners in LA back in the day, and Albert was an only child, so he got a windfall. I have heard he owned two hundred fast-food franchises, a ridiculous amount of land, and apartment buildings, but he also had a few hundred Century 21 franchises as well. I don't think Albert worked a day in his life, just smoked weed and partied, living the dream.

At this time, Albert had the Malibu beach house and places in Beverly Hills, Cabo San Lucas, and Miami. Life was not bad for Albert. Too bad he was a drunk and a druggie. But I will say one thing: he knew how to live. Hot chicks, the best club in LA, a Ferrari—he had it all. He was not a good-looking guy, but chicks don't care when you have that kind of money. I'd learned that in just the short time I'd been in LA. Albert was a nice guy; I give him that much credit. He treated me well, and money was no issue. He was the only guy I knew who bought tequila by the case.

I met with Albert and his girlfriend after I moved in, and we went over the job, what he expected, days off, that sort of stuff. It would be pretty much like my last few jobs but with more driving and watching the kids when he had them. I was cool with all of that.

His girlfriend was a new one—she had just moved in, I think. Albert had known her a few months. When she moved in, he bought her a new Porsche, gave her a credit card, the whole nine yards. That's how he rolled. She was hot as balls but one money-hungry bitch from Tennessee. She was a pothead as well, smoking weed all day and lying on the beach. I mean, she was cool to me because I took care of the kids' duties—driving them to school, taking them places, that kind of shit. She could not stay straight for a day, so she could not drive the kids around. I cannot remember her name; she only lasted a few months and then she was gone. I will get to that later. I only lasted eight months—between the drugs and whores, I soon had enough. I will get back to that as well.

The kids were great. He had a daughter and a son who went to the private school in Santa Monica where all the rich kids went. That's where I met them in the first place. He had the kids every other weekend or whenever they wanted to hang out at the beach in Malibu. I would do Mexican buffets; they loved my fish tacos, beans, and rice.

I really liked the two kids. They were very good; their mom raised them well. I would take them to the arcade in Santa Monica, to the mall, over to Brand and Brody's, to lunch, to school, wherever they needed. It was kind of cool; I got to play dad. These were the first kids who really respected me, and I liked that and went out of my way to help them. They always said "thank you" and "please"—God forbid the Weintraub girls say anything polite.

For the most part, Albert was easy as long as he had weed, tequila, and blow. He had one hell of a life. The first time I drove him and his girlfriend to the Gate, we had dinner at Dan Tana's. I sat at the bar and drank an espresso while they ate. I had plenty of petty cash—I walked around with a grand just for tipping and myself.

That was the one thing I miss: sitting in a great restaurant, with everyone checking the boss and me out and asking, "Who are these guys?" It was not bad.

When they finished their dinner, we drove to the Gate. Albert told me to pull around back. The valets knew the car, and all the doors were open before I knew it. Albert said to me, "Wait here." He took the chick inside and returned a few minutes later. Then he told all the valets that I was his new driver and chef. We went to the front door, and he called a few bouncers over, and it was the same deal. It was also the same with the manager and the bartenders. He told them all, "Whatever he needs, take care of it." That was it—I was dialed in. Not bad.

We talked a few minutes in private, and he asked what I thought of the club. It was the balls, the hottest club in LA. I said it's great. He told me that if I wanted a bite to eat or coffee, to just order it, but to head back home when I finished, as he would take a limo home. That was the schedule from Wednesday to Saturday. Man, could he party. I went to the bar and ordered a snack and a club soda and cran.

I was sitting at the bar when Julian Lennon sets beside me. He said, "Hey, I know you." I'd met him at the Viper Room one night, doing some blow in the head. Man, what a loser, just a real piece of shit. He was a drunk and druggie all in one, living off his dad's name. He had been eighty-sixed from the Gate for starting a fight and being drunk out of his mind, but Albert had given him one last chance. We talked a few minutes, and I told him I was working for Mr. Gersten and had to get back to Malibu. Then I finished my food, said my goodbyes, and left for Malibu.

The next day, Albert heard I had spoken with Julian and asked how I knew him. I said I'd met him at the Viper Room some time ago, and he said, "Don't ever bring him out here."

"Why would I?" I said. I would never bring a guest to the house."

"Ok."

That night, after I'd left, Julian had started a fight and been eighty-sixed for the final time. When Albert told me, I said, "Wow. I only met him a few times. I know he is trouble."

That was the last I ever heard about Julian, and I never saw him again.

This was about the time I really grew up. I had quit smoking pot a while ago and was done with blow. I could see how it had destroyed people I'd worked for. I was finally getting my shit together, saving money and building my reputation in LA as a first-class guy and great chef. I was also still meeting A-listers and playing golf with Sam and Shari. Life was good. Plus, I was still fucking Emilia. On top of all that, the kids liked me, as did the ex-wife. I was the only straight one in the house.

Weekends at the Gate were always interesting. Depp, Cage, Downey, the list was endless at the Gate—all the A-listers in LA. One weekend, Janet Jackson was there, and she had a table next to Albert's in the VIP section. This was a roped-off area with a few big bouncers. Albert always had the back corner table and kept one next door in case a VIP showed up. On this night, Janet Jackson came in with her posse, a few gay guys and a bodyguard. She said hi, and we hung for a few minutes. I was not impressed.

Many guys think she is hot, but I tell you, that is one big ass for a tiny chick, and her ego is huge. She was nice to Albert, as he let her use the club in a video or something like that. Albert liked being around the assholes—I guess because he was one. He could be real a prick if he did not know you, but if you ever got in his face, he would cry like a pussy. He could not stand up for himself; instead, he would just call the bouncers over.

The next few months were kind of the same. Albert was already getting tired of his girlfriend. He buzzed me up to his bedroom one morning, saying he would like some breakfast and wanted to talk to me. I fixed him some scrambled eggs with ham and cheese and sourdough toast. He told me that he and the girl were done and she would come over at six to get her clothes. He was sending someone from the office to supervise the move-out and give her a check. "Have all her clothes in the garage, and she cannot take anything from the house."

"Ok. Is there something else?"

"Have the locks changed."

I said, "Of course," and took care of it.

Before she got there, Albert had someone from the office come over to make sure there was no conversation. When she arrived, she got her clothes, did a quick walk-through of the master, and that was it. I never saw her again. All she took with her were the clothes on her back and a check. Later, I heard Albert on the phone to someone, and he said he had given her twenty-five thousand dollars to beat it. What kind of girl is that, if not just a step up from a whore?

I knew why he'd paid her off. I had met an old girlfriend of hers and her husband a few months back. They were in LA from Tennessee and came out to the beach house to have brunch. The husband was a smoker, and he stepped outside to have a cigarette. He seemed like a nice guy, and we started to talk, and he told me the whole story. I still laugh about it sometimes: the fucking you give is the fucking you get. Apparently, her mother was a gold digger as well, married three or four times, and she'd raised her daughter the same way: marry a rich guy and make your living on your back. She'd banged every rich kid back there and gotten nowhere, thought she would have her way in LA. What a fucked-up family

She thought she had it made, but Albert kicked her to the curb. Good for him. Like I said, he had some good qualities, but he made a bigger mistake a few years down the line and married that dumb bitch Janice Dickinson. The first supermodel, my ass. She is so full of shit and herself. What a joke; just ask Ryan Seacrest and Sly. I think she fucked everyone in LA. What a slut. She's been married four times and still counting. What was Albert thinking? She was old then and way past her prime. I saw her at the Gate once—what a hag, even back then, and he bought her a twenty-karat rock. It lasted six months. I am sure he had to write a fat check that time; he did not get off easy, like he had with the dumb bitch from Tennessee, a Porsche and twenty-five thousand dollars, pocket money for Albert.

I am glad I left LA. I thought Vermont was full of mental cases and weirdos, but LA beats it hands down. And the money-hungry whores, so-called actress? Give me a break. They are so full of shit. They take your money and then turn around and sue you for sexual harassment if they don't get their way. That's why I never married. I saw all these guys and my friends getting taken to the cleaners. I was way smarter than that. Trophy wives come with a big price tag. Rent the shit; it's cheaper. My mentor taught me that.

Back at Malibu, things took a turn for the worse. Albert was doing more drugs and drinking more, as he was single again. He was bringing whores home every night, sometimes two, and I had to drive them back to LA. I don't think I am better than anyone, but I am sure worth more than an LA whore, and I don't answer to them or drive them around and take them shopping—not my deal.

This went on for a few months. Finally, I went to see Dora at the international and told her the story. She said she had heard that and to hang on until she found me something else.

In the meantime, Albert was planning a trip to his place in Cabo San Lucas. He asked if I had a passport, and I said yes. He said, "We are leaving in two weeks. I want you there a week before we get there to make sure the house is set up with food and drinks. I have a couple on site to help, and there is a car there, so they will pick me up at the airport. Take five thousand dollars in cash; the office will give it to you before you leave. There is a guest house for you, and buy whatever you need before you leave. Just put it on the house card."

I told Albert that was fine. Then we talked about the old girlfriend, and he told me thanks.

He gave me a checklist of what to get: a case of Chinocka tequila, plenty of beer, Champagne for the girls and guests. He also wanted me to plan a menu for seven days, all Mexican, fish and chicken. I said, "No problem."

This was my first trip to Cabo San Lucas.

A few days before I was set to leave, I asked Albert how many guests he would have so I knew how much food to buy and prepare. He said it would be Ralph and three women. I did not know who the girls were, but Ralph was a big-time hairdresser in Beverly Hills. He was cool; we hung out a few times. We had some common ground—we both liked chicks and golf—and I thought, this will be a cool trip.

A week passed, and then I packed and headed to Cabo. The housekeeper and her husband picked me up at the airport, and when we got to the house, I could not believe the size of the place—and the view of the coast was unbelievable.

I had three days until the guests showed up to get the house ready, plenty of time to go to town, get some sun, and check out the place. Marvin Davis had a house just down the way; he was a big oil guy. The place was an enclave called El Pedregal. All I can say is that it's only for people with big money. Over the next few days, I lay by the pool, went to town, got all the shopping done, and got everything ready for the guests.

Now that Albert was single, he was on a tear, more drinks, drugs, and chicks. I give old Albert credit—he enjoyed life. I am sure his health was never good. I never saw him work out, nothing physical. Getting out of bed was a workout for him. That is why he had a gut at a young age and no physical attributes at all, but when you have his kind of money, chicks don't care. The guests were going to be there four days; I guess a few of the girls did have real jobs, which surprised me. I knew Ralph had to be back at work.

The housekeeper and her husband picked them up at the airport while I stayed at the house to get the appetizers and drinks ready. I had no idea what to expect. This was my first trip with Albert, but I knew there would be a lot of drinking, drugs, and fucking. As it turned out, I was not far off—that was all they did for four days.

When they got to the house, I greeted them, helped carry all the bags in, said hi to Ralph, and, of course, got my marching orders from Albert. He was with this hot-ass blonde woman, tall—he seemed to like tall chicks, as the one he'd just kicked out was tall, and they were both dumb as a bag of rocks.

Ralph and the other two chicks had their own rooms. I got all their luggage in, and Albert said, "Be at the pool in thirty minutes and no tops for the girls."

I thought, ok, this will be crazy for the next couple of days, and believe me, it was. They all showed up at the pool with their tops off. As the music played, I made margaritas, fish tacos, chips and guac. They started doing lines, smoking weed, and just going wild—and this was just the first day. The chicks were demanding, saying, "Give me this," and, "I want that."

I get it, I thought. These chicks think they're A-listers, and they want to be big shots. I was going to say something to Albert, but he was too busy getting head from the tall blond, and Ralph was fucking the one redhead right in front of me at the pool. As for the other chick, I had seen her before at the Gate but did not know her. She was just lying there, exposed, getting her ass tan.

I made a few drinks and then waited until Albert was finished getting head. "Will there be anything else that you need?" I asked.

He said, "Take a break. We will not be going out tonight, so plan on us having dinner here and cook something local."

I headed to my guest house for a much-needed break and to cool off. What a first day.

Ralph stopped by to bullshit, and he asked if I wanted to do a few lines. I said, "No, I am working. Albert would have a shit-fit, and someone has to be straight if he decides to go into town. I also have to cook, but thanks for the offer.

"What a piece of ass," he said.

"Yeah, I saw it, you stupid fuck. I had to go jack off, between you fucking and Albert getting head. What a porn show."

Ralph was all jacked up, so I said, "Go take a break. I will see you at dinner. I need a break as well."

He headed back to his room, so I could finally take a deep breath and relax. What a day.

Some guys like these types of jobs, but not me. I hated being at the bottom of the food chain. Guys like Albert will always have money, but the chicks only last as long as their pussy is still good. Once they fuck all of Hollywood, that shit is worn out, and who wants it then? They cannot give that shit away.

At dinner, they were all still high. I made some coffee, and they started coming down one at a time for a snack. I tried to serve a nice dinner, tequila lime chicken, with all the sides, but it was not going to happen.

They all finally came down, but no one was hungry. They were all still doing shitloads of blow. I made a few pitchers of margaritas, and then Albert said, "Turn in and be ready for breakfast around ten." They were going out in the afternoon, into town. I said goodnight to all the girls and Ralph and went to bed. Man, what a long day.

My guest house was about a thousand square feet and a short walk from the beach. What a life.

The rest of the week was the same shit: they went into town to eat, shop, and drink. The girls would come back to the house and sunbathe in the nude. I made drinks, and Albert switched girls and then had them both, while Ralph stayed with the redhead. Then it was just more drinking and drugs for days on end

I could not wait to get back to Malibu. Like I said, I'd quit doing blow and pot around this time, and there's nothing worse than being straight around a bunch of bimbos doing blow and getting drunk out of their minds. Albert was the king of the party, just lying out their nude with his gut hanging out and the acne on his back looking like an ant farm. The chicks didn't care. Albert thought he was hot, but I don't think so. Look at the pitchers of him, and you will agree. I will say one thing: he knew how to live and got tons of ass. I am sure that is why he got into the nightclub business. It gave him a place to pick up chicks and drugs.

Finally, the end of the trip grew near.

They stayed high the entire trip, and I think I only cooked dinner twice and made a few lunches. Breakfast was the main meal, and they went into town a lot. Albert liked the restaurant scene. They took me a few nights as well; the tabs were well over a grand each night, and everyone knew Albert. He had the biggest house in Cabo at the time, and he rented it out sometimes as a corporate retreat. Look at the pic—that is a bad-ass pad. I would never go back to Cabo with Albert again; it was too crazy for me.

The last night there, Albert took us to a great seafood place. No one finished their dinner but me.

They all flew out the next day, but Albert asked me to stay behind a few days to get the house back together and take some time off. I thought that was kind of him. Don't get me wrong—he was not a bad guy, just weird and into drugs and whores.

I had some time to do some thinking after they left. I knew it was time to move on. First thing back, I would visit Dora and tell her the truth about the drugs, chicks, and porno all day. I wonder if old Albert is still alive. That would surprise me.

So, I got the house back in order, hung out at the beach, worked on my own tan for once, and had a little peace and quiet for a few days. Then it was time to go back home.

When I returned, Albert and I had a long talk. He asked if I was ok with the trip, and I said, "Yes, I am cool. I had a good time. Thanks for the dinner and the time off down there."

He said he would like me to go to Europe with him and the kids for two weeks next month, five days in Paris and five days in Rome. "I want you to chaperone the kids. I will pay for all your costs and give you some petty cash."

"Sure," I said.

"Ok, I will have the office make all the arrangements. Oh, I have a house guest coming on Monday. His name is Bo Kimble. He played basketball at LMU and is a close friend. He is coming back from Spain, where he was playing ball, and I am trying to get him signed with the Lakers. You will like him, and whatever he needs, see to it."

"Yes, no problem."

The weekend arrived, and the kids came over. They liked hanging out at the beach. I would take them into town and the mall. We had good times. The son and I would play basketball, and the daughter would lie out at the beach with her friends. These kids had a good life; both were smart, the best kids I ever worked with.

I took them back home Monday, and then I had to get a guest room ready for Bo, as he was driving over to the beach house. Albert was taking him to dinner at Geoffrey's in Malibu the first night, and I was to drive them. I would just hang out at the bar and have a coffee till they were ready to go home.

I met Bo at the house around three. I got him a beer and showed him to his room. Albert was in Beverly Hills, doing some shit, and I said, "He will be home soon." Bo smoked a lot of weed, and I am sure he did other shit as well. That's why he did not make it in the NBA—aside from all the ego shit. Bo was ok, but to hear him talk, you'd think he was Jordan.

Albert came home, and they smoked some weed as they caught up. Then it was off to dinner.

Like all of LA's top restaurants, Geoffrey's was a place to be seen, just the place for up-and-coming gold diggers trying to hook a rich fish. LA chicks are the worst.

The food was not bad. They enjoyed their dinner while I sat at the bar and had coffee. When Albert gave me the sign, I got the car. I thought we were heading to Beverly Hills and the Gate, but Albert and Bo were tired and just wanted to head home and chill. I said, "Great, we will be home in five."

Back at the house, I fixed a round of drinks, and then Albert said, "Alan, call it a night. We will see you in the morning for breakfast."

For the next few days, I fixed Bo and Albert breakfast. Then they would head into LA to hang out. They brought whores back a few nights, and I had to wait on them and then and take them back to LA. I hated that. I felt this was beneath me. I mean, don't get me wrong. I fucked a few, but waiting on them and cooking for them was not my deal.

One day, Bo and I went into Malibu to Alice's on the pier to have lunch. He was a cool guy. He told me all about the Hank Gathers story, how Albert would give the kids money, cars, jobs in his business. He said Albert was a godfather to a lot of the players. They were mostly black and poor kids. There was a big investigation about Albert and Hank dying on the court. Like I said, Albert had deep pockets and was never convicted of any wrongdoing, but everyone in LA knew he was involved and guilty as sin.

But that's old news. Bo was supposed to stay a week, but it ended up being a few weeks. I am sure Albert gave him some cash and told him to be on his way, as I heard the Lakers did not pick him up. Kids came for the weekend, and they liked Bo. I cooked, and we all hung out at the beach.

One of his old teammates came by, Per Stumer. He worked at the Gate and did stuff for Albert. He was a real nice guy; I always liked him. He had a lot of class. I think he was from Sweden.

After lunch, we went outside to play some hoops. It was Per and me against Bo and Albert's son. Per and I kicked their asses. How many chefs do you know who can cook for the boss and then go out and play with two of the country's top basketball players and win? Per and I were tough.

Albert was cool about all of this, and we had a great time that day. If not for all the drama, I wouldn't have thought about leaving Albert. We played three games, and Per and I won them all.

Bo and I shot hoops a few times over the next few days. Then he took off, and I never saw him again. Per, I saw every week. We talked about Bo, and that was it.

I took the kids to the promenade in Santa Monica that weekend, and I picked up Brandon and Brody from their place in Malibu. Linda had asked me to take them with us, and I'd agreed. She always gave me a nice tip and was nice to me, and I started working for them part time later down the road.

I was talking to Dora once a week. She told me, "Just hang in there. Something will pop up."

I did not know then why guys left these jobs. I know now—it's because the husbands are assholes, the wives are complete bitched and the kids are brats.

Albert had been on a binge for a few months now, and on Monday morning, he called me to his room. His cousin and the head guy from the office showed up. From out of the clear blue, Albert told everyone that he was going to go straight. He must have flushed a fortune down the toilet, only to buy it all back the next week. That was so funny. Giving drugs up the booze, hiring a trainer, and getting in shape lasted all of one week. The next few days, he was cool, driving himself to the office, eating dinner at the house, no whores—I was impressed. But it didn't last. He did this shit every six months, only to get back on the party train.

One day, Albert's mom called and asked for him.

"He's not here. Is it urgent?"

"No."

"He went to the office to work."

She almost had a heart attack, and she told me not to tell him she'd called. I said, "Yes, ma'am," and that was it.

He went straight about a week this time. Nice to be Albert. Not a care in the world. I think the only thing I did not do for him was wipe his ass, even though he needed it.

A few weeks passed, and it was back to the same routine. I was just waiting for Dora to find me something. I mean, it was not all that bad. Malibu is a great spot, and I had some of the best years of my life there, just not this gig with Albert. One of the best perks was that I got to drive Albert's Ferrara Spider. This was a bad-ass car back in the day. I would take it to the shop, get it detailed, that kind of stuff. Albert was going out of town—I think New York—to take a few days off, but he told me to stay at the house and keep an eye on things. I drove him to LAX, and then I had the beach house to myself for three days. I invited Emilia over for dinner and a hot tub, and we had some great sex all night. Man, was she hot. I miss that shit.

The next morning, she headed home, and I said, "I will call you later. Maybe we can hang at the beach or something."

She said, "Cool. Call me."

Then I thought, hey, I should take the Spider for a cruise up the coast. I decided to call the chick from the Malibu Gelson market, Suzie, the hot-ass casher I'd been banging a few months. What chick would not want to go for a ride up the coast in a Ferrari?

I gave Suzie a call. "Why don't you drive to Malibu? We'll hang out at the beach and then cruise up the coast in Albert's Ferrari. Then we'll have dinner on the coast somewhere."

She said, "Sure, I'll see you in a few hours." She had been there before when Albert was out of town.

I fed the dogs and did a few things around the house just to kill some time till she showed up. When she got there, we had a few drinks, lay by the beach for a while, and then went in and showered together and had the first go-round for the day. She was a Valley girl and hot as balls.

We got dressed, and I said, "Let's cruise up towards Ventura and get dinner on the coast somewhere." I grabbed the keys to the Spider, and off we went. I tell you what. If you want to get laid in Malibu, just buy a Spider and make sure it's red. No chick can say no to a ride up the coast in a Ferrari. Suzie asked if I would like some head. She said she'd never given a blowjob in a Ferrari while driving up the coast. You know me: never say no to a woman in need.

We found a little crab shack on the beach and stopped for an early dinner and a few beers. Suzie was a cool chick. I am sorry I lost touch with her. She was a keeper. We had a nice dinner and a good conversation. She said, "I can't believe you just drive all of Albert's cars."

When we finished, I asked her if she could spend the night. "Sure," she said. "I have tomorrow off as well." I picked up the check, and we headed back to Malibu. If you've never driven a Ferrari, I can tell you there is nothing like it. The sound, the feel, and the looks you get make you feel like Superman.

I was hauling ass down the PCH, way over a hundred. When I downshifted and hit second instead of fourth, man, I nearly lost it. The car almost locked up. I got it back under control, but it turned out that I'd lost the second gear and bent the linkage. Lucky for me, I did not lose the transmission. With the luck of the Irish, I barely got her home. Suzie was so buzzed that she did not even know what was going on. She just thought I'd hit the breaks. Thank God that Albert would be gone for a few more days.

At the house, we got into the hot tub for round three for the day, and then we passed out. I thought, I will deal with the car tomorrow. I will think of something. I always do. I was still the Teflon Kid. Nothing stuck to me. Suzie and I had sex in the morning before and after breakfast, and then she said she had to get back to the Valley, plus I had to deal with the car. We said goodbye, and then I had one more cup of coffee as I tried to figure out what I was going to tell the dealer

As I worked on my story, I called the dealer and had them come pick the car up. I told the salesman it was shifting hard and Albert wanted it checked out and needed it back by Friday. I got a call back at the end of the day, and he asked who had been driving the Spider. I said, "Albert's ex was the last one, I think. I was going to put gas in it yesterday, and it just did not feel right. I called Albert, and he said to call you and bring it in to get it looked at."

He said, "Whoever drove it last tore up the gearbox, and the linkage was bent. Probably missed a gear at high speed. It will be ready Friday morning. Should we use the credit card on file?"

"Yes, and I will pick it up in person."

I have no idea what it cost to fix, but I am sure it was like a month's salary for me. At least I'd dodged the bullet again. I picked the car up on Friday, and when I saw the salesman, he said, "Are you sure it was Albert's ex who drove it last?"

I said, "I think so."

"She has been gone for over a month or so." It turned out that he knew her; Albert had bought her a Porsche from him.

I said, "Albert's been out of town, and we drive the Rover most of the time, or he gets a limo."

We shook hands, and I said, "Albert says thanks, and you will see me soon for a normal service."

He didn't seem to believe my story, but I did not care; it wasn't like he was going to call Albert and question me. I mean, Albert never did anything on his own.

Just before Albert returned, he called me to make sure I brought some weed with me from the house. I knew where he kept the stash. I grabbed some, and then I met Albert at the airport. He was always pleasant and glad to see me. There was the usual small talk: How are the dogs? Did the kids come by? Were there any guests? How had I been? He was cool about things like that and easy to talk to.

I said, "The only issue was with the Spider. When I went to get her detailed, the gears where shifting rough, and there was no second gear. I had them come and get it. There were some tranny and linkage issues. Seems like the old ex must have missed a few gears or shifted at high speed to the wrong gear and bent something. That's what Frank said. It's fixed now and good as new. I drove back from LA, and it's fine now."

Albert said, "Thanks. It sounds like you are on top of things."

If he had known the truth—that I had been out partying with some chick, getting head, and drunk—he would not have been happy. The Teflon Kid got by again.

I took Albert home, unpacked for him, and asked if we were going to the Gate that night. He said, "No, I would like to stay home and have dinner. Can you make me some Mexican food"

"Of course."

"I love your fish tacos and rice and beans, and you make me crazy sauce."

This was one of the few Friday nights that Albert stayed in, but he made up for it Saturday night, back to the same routine. On Sunday, we talked about the trip, and he asked if the kids were ready to go and if I would help him pack and go over what I had planned. We went over everything for the trip: hotel, flights, dinner reservations, what the kids wanted to do, and, of course, Albert's list. I said, "They want to see all the tourist stuff, like anyone going to Paris for the first time."

We arrived in Paris the following week and checked into the Saint James Hotel. If you have not been there, it's high on my list, and if you're in Paris, it's a must, first class. You think there would be a whole lot of cool shit to talk about, but it was just a trip for the kids. They were not old enough to enjoy the great food and wine, but hell, they were teenagers. I took them all over the Louvre for one whole day; that was way cool, and the kids loved that. The next day, we went to the Champs Elysees, the restaurants along the river, Notre Dame, the Eiffel Tower, the Arc de Triomphe—I mean, we did it all. The kids, and even Albert, had a good time. It was the first time I'd seen him straight for more than two days in a row.

I took the kids shopping while Albert went off one day and did his own thing. I am sure he went and got stoned and a piece of ass. I knew he could not make it a few days without getting buzzed. The kids and I had a great time. I hardly remember Albert's ex, but what a good mom. The kids listened to me and were very well behaved for rich kids. This was a great trip for me as well. I got paid to go to Paris, and I did not spend any of my own money; everything was on Albert. We ate at some great restaurants and went to some of the greatest museums in the world, and Albert paid for it all.

There's nothing like enjoying some nice wine and cheese at a cafe on the West Bank. It's pretty damn good. The best thing was that it cost me nothing. It was a nice vacation for all of us. Albert was on his best behavior. It was nice to see him spend some quality time with the kids, as he was usually never around. Life was just about him, the drugs, and the pussy. Pretty shallow.

We ended the trip with a nice farewell dinner. The kids were ready to get back to LA, and Albert was also ready. As for me, I could have hung out a few more weeks—especially with Albert picking up the tab.

We got back to Malibu, and then I took the kids home and got Albert unpacked. He gave me a little tip and a few days off.

I needed to call Dora to see if there was anything out there. I knew it would be a few days and then back to the same old shit with Albert. Then, like a wish come true, Dora called me and told me to see her as soon as I could, that she had something special for me. I knew it had to be something good, as she would not have called me otherwise.

I headed to Beverly Hills to Dora's office to see what was up. I always liked hanging out in Beverly Hills. It's one of the best places in the world to girl watch, and Dora's office was off Beverly Drive. I would go see her and then head over to Rodeo and hang out at one of the restaurants and girl watch. I miss them days. I used to love to see the chicks shopping and spending money like there was no tomorrow. I would hate to be the poor bastard paying the credit card bill for these HMIs, or high-maintenance items, and on top of that, these chicks have been fucked by half of Hollywood. It's true. Don't laugh. I have been there and seen it.

Dora and I talked for a while, and she told me that Rod Stewart and his wife, Rachel, were looking for a personal chef. "They go out a lot and have dinner guests every few weeks. You would have driving duties and oversee the new estate he just built in Beverly Estates. Is that something you would be interested in?

I said, "Yes, of course."

"It would look great on your resume, and you'd have a guesthouse and be living back in Beverly Hills. I've already sent them your resume, and they want to meet you tomorrow at the new estate. Could you be there around two?"

I told Dora I had a few days off and would be there tomorrow. Up to this point, after every interview I'd had, I'd been given the job. She said, "Just be yourself and slow down. They will love you."

After our meeting, I headed over to the Rodeo Cafe to have a drink and some lunch, and oh, yeah, do some girl watching. I hung out for a good part of the afternoon, having a nice lunch, a few glasses of wine, and then a double espresso. Then it was time to get back to Malibu and beat the traffic, as I had a big day tomorrow.

By the time I got home, Albert was gone. He'd left me a note that said to enjoy the days off. He was going into LA for dinner and would be late coming home, so there was no need to wait up. I fixed myself a drink and headed down to the beach, as this might be my last chance for a while. I turned in early so I could get up early and go for my morning run.

My interview with the Stewarts was at two, and I was told they would both be there. I put on one of my black suits, a white shirt, and a nice tie and headed into town. Dora had given me the address the day before and said, "Don't be late," as if I was ever late. Their place was behind the Beverly Hills Hotel, overlooking the city. I mean, bad-ass. At this time, only a dozen or so residents were living there, as they were still building and selling lots.

I pulled up to the gate and told the guard I was there to see the Stewarts. He directed me where to go, and I was off to the house to meet Rod and Rachel. I pulled up to the house and it was just what I expected for a rock star: six-car garage, a few Ferreras, Lambo, Rolls, and a Range Rover. Life had been good to Rod.

I walked up to the front door and was greeted by a hot Spanish housekeeper who asked if I was Alan. I said I was, and she said, "The Stewarts are in the living room, waiting for you. Would you like a water?"

"Yes, of course," I said.

Then I walked in, and the Stewarts stood and greeted me. Rod put out his hand, and we shook. "I am Mr. Stewart, and this is Mrs. Stewart."

"Call me Rachel," she said.

He laughed and said, "Please, sit down. Dora speaks very highly of you, as do the Fords."

He was impressed with my resume, the cooking skills, that I could drive them, and that I was very clean cut and well dressed. We talked for an hour or so about food and service, what they expected, and why I was leaving Mr. Gursten

Then they gave me a tour of the house and asked what I was making, and he was a little taken aback when I told them. He said the job was fifty thousand dollars a year. They would take off a few months and go to Europe, and I would still get paid, but I would just stay and take care of the cars, the house, and a few staff members. I said I could live with that, and they asked when I could start.

"I have to give notice," I said, "but once I do, he will probably let me go." To be on the safe side, I told them I could start in two weeks. I wanted a week off to go back to my house in the desert a chill. They were good with that, and they gave me keys to the Range Rover and house codes on the spot. I had to sign a non-compete and confidentiality agreement. They had a list of things they liked and a job description; that was a first, but I was cool with it. I had a guest house, car, petty cash, house credit card, all the perks, and a hot-ass housekeeper and nanny as well. Now I just had to tell Albert. He would not be happy. We were kind of friends, but I knew I had to move on from him.

Plus, working for Rod Stewart would not look bad on my resume. I liked hanging out in Beverly Hills, and I could drive to Malibu on my day off, hang out at the beach, and still help Linda with the boys.

We said our goodbyes, and I left. They seemed very happy, and I was excited as well. I mean, cooking for Rachel and Rod, and she had those big tits—what could be better?

I headed over to the Ivy for a drink, and then I called Dora to tell her that they'd offered me the job. When she got on the line, she told me that she had already gotten a call from the Stewarts and they liked me.

I told her I was at the Ivy, having a drink, and asked her to join me, and she said she would stop and say hi, that she wanted to talk to me. I thought, oh, shit, am I in trouble?

When she showed up, she had a martini with me and gave me some advice about the Stewarts and Beverly Hills. "You are good and people like your food, so just keep your head down, and you will go far. You are not a bad-looking young man."

She never gave advice like that to the other chefs and estate managers. She really liked me, and I enjoyed her as well. She was a cool old lady, and she knew everyone in Hollywood. She got me many good jobs back in the day; it was not her fault they were assholes.

We chatted about Albert, and she told me not to let him know where I was going or that I had talked to her, just that I was moving on. We had one more drink, and I offered to buy, but she picked up the tab. She had a lot of class, plus I think she liked being seen with a young guy. Who cares? I liked her, and she was good to me

We talked for a while about the trip to Paris with Albert and the kids and the Weintraub job. Then she said she'd put a couple out there and they'd quit the first week. I don't know how I lasted a few years and did not kill one of the kids or all of them.

Finally, I told her I had to beat the traffic to Malibu and I needed a good night's sleep because tomorrow I had to talk to Albert. She said she had to be off and call her after I talked to him. "Make sure you are packed in case he wants me out right away."

I told her thanks and that I would call her tomorrow

That's the one thing that's a bitch about this kind of work. When you live on-site for the people, which I always did, when you quit, your shit had better be moved out, because they can get real nasty.

I headed back to Malibu. I figured I would talk to Albert in the morning, before he got too stoned. My plan was to say it was time to move on and I was going to take some time off. The next morning, I brought Albert breakfast in bed, and he was already burning one. I said, "Albert, I want to give you two weeks' notice. I am moving on."

He was shocked. "Did I treat you badly? Do you need more money? What is wrong?"

"No, you are a great boss. I just need a break, and I am moving back to my house in the desert." I could not say I was tired of the whores, drugs, and late-night shit and hated being around a bunch of stoners.

We talked a while, and he tried to get me to stay. "Please stay two weeks until I can find a new person."

"I will. It's not an issue," I said. I wanted to leave on good terms. I even said, "I could show the guy around and train him, if that's what you would like me to do."

He was thankful, and that was that.

The next few weeks flew by. Albert hired his old butler back, some stick-in-the-mud guy. He must have had some thick skin to put up with all the crazy shit, but I did not care, as I was out of there.

Albert was cool and told me to stop by if I was in Malibu and that I was welcome at the gate anytime, just say that he'd invited me and I would always be on the guest list—pretty cool, I thought. The kids came over that weekend and were not happy with me leaving. They said, "Please stay. We will talk to dad."

I said, "No thanks." I would miss them, but I was sure I would see them around. I just had to move on. We spent Saturday on the pier in Santa Monica. They had a good time; I also picked up Brandon and Brody, and I told Linda I was leaving Albert to take a job with Rod Stewart. She said they knew him and to tell him hi once I got settled in. I told her I would like to keep working for her part time when I was off, and she said that would be cool, that the boys loved me. Wow, what a great day.

When the weekend was over, I was all packed up, and the new guy was moving in. I shook hands with Albert, thanked him for everything, and said I would keep in touch. I saw him around town a few times after that, and when I did, he always said hi.

The Cowboy

Chef, Art, and Max.

Love LA

California Dreamin.

chapter 9

ROD STEWART

MR. EL CHEAPO

WORKING FOR ROD WAS ONE of my shorter jobs. I worked for him for about a year before he fired the whole staff after the divorce, which I will get into in more detail later. At the time, he was married to the supermodel and super stupid Rachel Hunter, but what do you expect? She is a model and fucks rock stars. She didn't have to be smart, but she had other gifts, like those big tits. But after the kids, her ass got big, too. I am sure that is why Rod kicked her to the curb—and I am sure he said, "What am I thinking? She is as dumb as a bag of rocks."

There are a few good stories from my time with the Stewarts. For one thing, he had to be called Mr. Stewart, as if he was royalty. He was not one of the better guys I worked for, cheap, arrogant, and very inconsiderate. Rachel was ok, just stupid. She could not put gas in the car. I did it for her and gave her petty cash as well.

I had a lot of fun working for Rod, from banging the hot Swedish nanny to waiting on Rachel at the pool with her top off and looking at her big tits. She liked me. One time, when she had a little buzz, I thought I might get lucky. I mean, look at Rod; he is no stud by any means, with a limp-fish handshake. I am sure he's had it up the ass a few times as well; he just looks like the type. He doesn't have a great body, with long legs and no ass, and for someone who says he played soccer, I think he was a real pussy. I watched him hit the tennis ball with the nanny, and she kicked his ass. He had no hand-eye coordination at all. He was not in shape, either, with no workout routine. His big workout was getting on the phone with Sotheby's to buy something.

I just laughed. Weintraub could kick his ass and Albert's at the same time. What a couple of wimps. I guess, if you can sing like Rod, you don't have to be a stud. It's all make-believe, just like Hollywood. What a joke.

There were quite a few cool times when I worked there. He would come down in the morning to have his tea, and he'd bring his guitar and sing. He might be working on a new song or just working on some classic. But on the other hand, he might send his tea back every few days if it was not hot enough or too hot or if he thought I hadn't used bottled water. I just said, "Yes, sir," and remade it again. The fucking Brits and their tea. What a bunch of wankers. I should have stirred it with my dick, and if not for the hot water, I would have. He was kind of a shithead about stuff like this. I just sucked it up.

Now I know why he could not keep a chef. The only ones who stayed were the foreigners because they needed the money. I will say one thing about Rod: he knew how to live despite being a cheap bastard. When it came to the chicks and himself, price did not matter, and these super-models, stupid as they are, were not cheap. Cars, clothes, and artwork were all first class. The house in Beverly Park was brand new when I took the job. They were just getting the place fixed up and doing the finishing touches. There was a convertible Rolls, Range Rover, station wagon for the nanny—I think it was a Benz—one Lambo and a couple of Ferraras, one California and one Spider or GTB. Rod sure lived the lifestyle. I won't forget the first day we were in the garage together. He was showing me around, and I said, "Wow! What a garage."

He said, "Yeah, that is a pretty powerful garage."

"That's an understatement," I replied, and he laughed.

The place was bad-ass, with a recording studio and a pool view overlooking LA. I had a great little guesthouse off the back wing, which was also nice.

Part of my job was to pick up Sean, the boy he'd had with Alana, George Hamilton's old flame. I picked him up every week or so. I don't know why these people have kids, as they don't raise them. Most are pieces of shit. They usually end up on drugs and cannot work. They are a waste of oxygen, and Sean was no different. He was not worth a shit back when he was a kid, and nothing has changed since then. Look at him now—he's a loser. Rachel's kids were very young when I was there, so I can not speak about her boys. But I do have a fun story about her.

It was like my third week there when she and Rod came down to the kitchen and wanted to meet with me. I thought, shit, am I getting fired already? What did I say? Turned out it was all good. One of the local morning shows was going to interview Rachel at the house next week, and I was to put a breakfast buffet together and dress sharply, as they might want to interview me as well or just have me on camera. Rod said he would not be there, as it was all about Rachel being married to a rock star and being a supermodel and mother as well.

I would need to have all food out by nine AM: coffee, fruit, water, all that sort. Piece of cake for me. I put out a nice spread and had a quick few minutes of fame on local TV. It was pretty cool. I hung out with the camera crew in the kitchen while she was interviewed. I have never heard such a crock of shit in my life. They asked her how she kept in shape and about being a mother, her marriage to Rod Stewart, her modeling career, running the house, and just keeping up with everything. She said, "I never stop. I just do what I have to get things done, and it's not easy. I put in a sixteen-hour-day most days."

I almost shit. I told the camera crew, "She is never out of bed before ten AM. Never." I had these guys laughing their asses off. "Who is she shiting? We have three housekeepers, one nanny, and me. The kids sleep with the nanny in the back of the house so she won't have to hear the crying. She can't even put gas in the car. I make them breakfast, do all the shopping, everything. All she has to do is get out of bed, and she finds that hard most days. I know. I live here as well. I am not making this shit up."

I had them in stitches for like fifteen minutes. At one point, they almost heard us in the kitchen. I will never forget that day. I am sure most people believe that shit. She never changed the diapers, but she took all the credit. "Oh, I work so hard being a mother and still having my career." What a bunch of shit. She never did anything. Neither did Rod, but you would expect that. I mean, he was already twice her age. People like that should not have kids. If you are not going to raise them or take part in their lives, don't have them. That's all of La-La Land; they're all the same. If she did not have those big tits and looks, she would be on her back in Australia, humping to make a buck.

Rachel thanked me for all the hard work that day and was very happy. If she only knew what I told the crew while she was bullshitting the camera with her sob story about how her life was so demanding.

That was one of the better stories, I think. The rest of the stuff is about some of the guests, mostly Ron Wood. Ron and Rod went way back. He seemed ok, but I am sure he was cheap as well. After all, he's a Brit, and they're known for being cheap pricks.

After about a month, I was settling into the job and getting the house organized. I also took care of the dogs. They had three nice collies, and I took them for walks and fed them.

Ron and Rachel did not have a lot of guests. They went out a lot, and I would drive them. However, they did have lunch at the house every day, and breakfast as well. They took off quite a few weekends, but I still had to stay around the house, so they would take the nanny. I kept an eye on the estate while they were gone. It was a pretty easy job, so I did not mind the lower pay, and I made it up by working side jobs. Plus, I'd take the Ferrari out and cruise around town. That was the best part of the job, besides bringing lunch to Rachel at the pool with her top off and looking at those big tits. I just had to feed the dogs, take them for a walk, and hang out. It was not bad. I helped myself to the wine cellar as well, but it was not great. Same with the booze, but I got by.

Ron came over quite a few times, and they would drink the cheap rum. I would prepare salmon or steak. Rod was pretty easy to cook for, and when he had guests, he was always on his best behavior—I guess to show his friends he was a great guy to work for. As Ron and Rod talked about the old times, I would catch some of the conversation. They would hang out and have drinks, and after a while, Rod would say, "Alan, we are fine. You can turn in." There weren't any great dinner parties to talk about. They were very informal, too—I don't think they knew good food or wine. That was not important to them. I don't think Rod liked parties at the house, as they cost money and he hated to spend money except on him and Rachel.

I remember I had to buy crystal glasses for the house, the whole collection: wine, water, rocks, flutes, you name it. I bought them at Geary's in Beverly Hills, and they all had to have "R and R" on them, the same with all the linen napkins. Nice touch. Like I said, he knew how to live. I think I spent twenty thousand dollars on glasses and linen. He told me to buy it and then shit when he got the bill.

The bad thing is if the next wife does not have a first name that starts with R, that's a lot of money down the drain. I guess you would just give it to the ex and tell her to hit the bricks when it's over. I mean, it's only twenty grand on glasses and a few linen napkins. I wish I had kept a few for my war locker, but I forgot. I am sure Rachel took them.

I liked going into Beverly Hills to shop for the house. I loved just looking at all the hot chicks, but I knew they were a bunch of snakes just trying to bang some rich guy. They were all models or actresses. That is just LA, and it's the same shit in New York, the other city I don't like. But shit, it's still nice to look. Living the life I have, it's hard not to get jaded about these rich pricks and chicks. I mean, they have it all, but they are unhappy and unhealthy, and most don't have but one or two friends. That should tell you something. The kids are almost always a lost cause, too, and that was certainly true in Rod's case.

The job became routine after a few months, which I liked, but I was not meeting any new contacts. I enjoyed taking care of the dogs on the weekend, picking up the kids, and keeping them entertained, and on my days off, I was still doing odd jobs for Linda and cooking for dinner parties, so I was keeping busy and still having fun. Plus, I loved driving the Ferrari around LA. It was not a bad little gig, but I knew it would not last.

One of the things I really did not like about Rod was that he thought he was royalty. I can remember at least three times where he and Rachel walked out of a restaurant without paying the dinner tab. The first time, we were at Dan Tana's. I knew the valets from when I'd worked with Weintraub—he used to go there as well. I had parked in front so everyone would see them, and I was at the bar, having an espresso, when I got the signal that they were ready to leave. I went to the valet and tipped him, of course, and had the car ready when they came out. They seemed to be in a hurry. They got in, and we headed home. I didn't learn that he had walked out without paying until a few days later when I was having a drink at the bar on my off day. It's a great place to hang out for happy hour. I knew the bartender, Joe, and he said the manager wanted to speak with me in private.

I popped over to the back office to see Frank, and he said, "You're Chef Al?"

"Yes, we met a few times."

"You are working for Rod Stewart now?"

"Yes, we were in last week for dinner. He was with Rachel."

"I know. Could you tell Rod that they are no longer welcome unless they intend to pay next time, and you can have him call me if he would like to talk about this. We don't need his business."

I offered to pay out of petty cash, but he said, "No, just pass it on to Rod, and next time, have him make a reservation, and we will see if we have room."

I liked that. If it had been me, I would have thrown the prick out and eighty-sixed him for life. I don't care who you think you are; nobody gets a free ride.

I said, "I am sorry."

"It's not your fault. He often does this around town, and the bills are like a thousand dollars after a bottle or two of Dom. He thinks he is doing us a favor by coming to our restaurants, like Rod Stewart eats here, and he is special."

I could not believe it, but I saw it first-hand a few times more, at the Ivy and then at Geoffrey's in Malibu, where he said he'd forgotten his wallet. Do you believe this cheap prick? Like I said, cheap Brits, stay on your side of the pond. I was afraid to see what my Christmas bonus would be—I might get a bottle of wine and a signed record.

I told Rod what the manager had said about not paying, and he almost had a shit fit. "I can't believe you're telling me this!"

I said, "Mr. Stewart, sir, he told me to pass it on to you. I am sorry, but I thought you should know."

"That place is rubbish, and they should thank me for dining there. We won't be going there again if that's the way they feel. I should not have to pay. I have never heard such shit in my life."

I knew this job would not last long. What a prick, and on top of that, something was up around the house. Things were not going well with him and Rachel. She took off by herself for a few weeks, and he took a few trips by himself back across the pond as well.

I called Dora and told her that I might be giving notice and asked her what she had open. I told her about some of the shit Rod had pulled, and she told me she had heard the same thing.

I said I would not mind taking a break from LA and working someplace else. She told me she got lots of jobs in Dallas and asked if I was interested. I said I was, and she said, "Ok, I will keep my eye out for a job for you."

Dora and I were still on good terms, and I had a few solid references. I'd had some fun working for Rod, from driving the Ferrari around town to living in Beverly Park. I used to go into the sound studio at the house and listen to him record—that was cool. Like I said, Rod knew how to live. I still can't believe he is worth a few hundred million. Maybe it's because he doesn't spend shit, at least, not on tips and staff.

Rod had a right-hand man who took care of a lot of his personal stuff. He came to the house Monday and met with the staff in private, one by one. I knew some shit was coming down. Turned out Rod and Rachel were splitting up, and he wanted to clean house and was letting all the staff go except for the nanny—that was Rachel's call. I was the last one he had to talk to, but the housekeepers had already given me the heads up:

I would get two weeks' pay and have to be off the property by the end of the week. I did not have to work, but I could stay and enjoy a few days off. That was not bad of him, but they were both leaving town anyway, so it did not matter. I had heard he pulled shit like this from one of the old housekeepers—he'd say he would keep you on for the summer while he was in Europe, but then he'd find a reason to fire you so he didn't have to pay you. What do you think of that? Pretty fucked up—that's the Brits.

It had been fun, but I'd always known this would be a short-time job. I was glad it lasted a year, and I'd had some good times and a few good stories. I called Dora to tell her I would be in the desert and ready for interviews in a few days. I wanted to hang out at my house and chill.

She said, "Ok, I will call you. I think I might have something for you. It's in Dallas."

"Yes," I said, "I've always wanted to live in Dallas."

"Well, take a few days off, and we will talk next week."

Neither Rod nor Rachel ever said a word to me, like they were too good to thank me. Not a lot of class. You can put a suit on a monkey, but you've still got a monkey.

This was the first time in my life where I'd been let go. I didn't feel bad, though. As they'd fired the whole staff.

That was the first and last rock star I worked for. I said goodbye to the rest of the staff, and then I headed to the desert, hoping that Dallas would be my next stop.

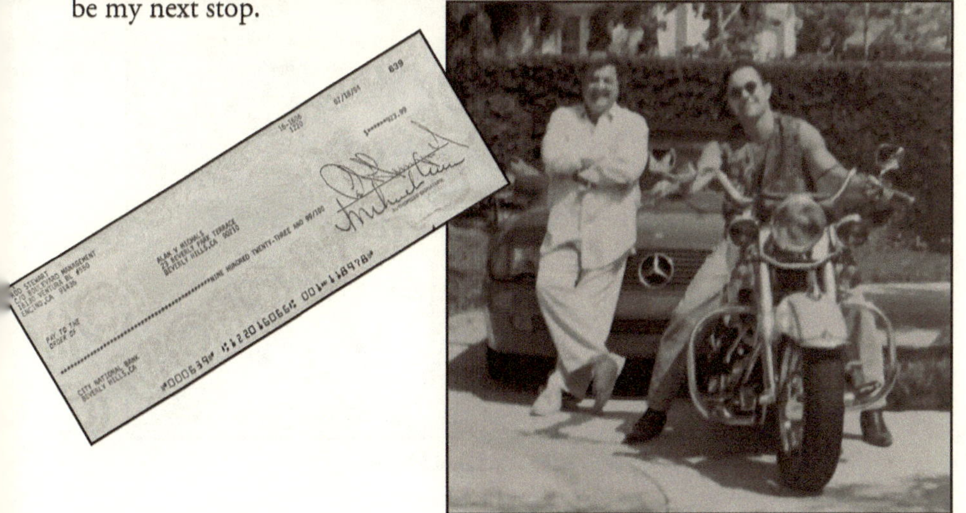

Rods House, Beverly Park

Arts King Air Santa Monica

Chapter 10

THE WOODS BROTHERS
NATIONAL HEALTH CARE, ARLINGTON, TX

I ENJOY HANGING OUT IN the desert. The fall is great there, and I miss the great golf courses. Kevin has since moved on. I heard he is running the Denver field office. I miss my old partner in crime.

Only a few days passed before I got the call. Dora said, "When can you be in Texas for an interview?"

"In a few days."

"Great. I will have the family call you, and you work out the details. Let me know what happens. They will pay fifty-five thousand to start, and you'll have a nice guesthouse and car. They have one teenager at the house, and that's it, and they don't entertain a lot. I've never placed someone there, so I can't tell you a lot about them."

"Cool, I said, but inside, I thought, I need a break from the LA assholes. I did not tell Dora that; she would have been pissed.

I got a call the following day from Paul Woods, not the wife. I liked that. We talked for a while, and then he said, "Would you like to come to

Arlington, just outside of Dallas, for a few days to cook for us and see if it works out?"

"I would love to."

"Fine, I will get a ticket to you, and I will pick you up at the airport."

"Great. See you in a few days."

I hung up and said, "Wow. Dallas, here I come." I had always wanted to live in Dallas. I'd hard the chicks were hot there, and friendly as well.

This seemed like a good reason to go out on the town. First stop, Marriott Desert Springs Resort and dinner at the Italian room. I rolled into the restaurant like I owned the place. That's just how I rolled now that I was a top chef; attitude goes a long way. My old chef pal had since moved on, so I was not getting comped tonight.

I had a great dinner and then hit the club downstairs. I didn't make it a late one, as I had a tee time in the morning. I went home, hit the hot tub, and chilled with a nice glass of red from the cellar.

I got the call the next day in the afternoon from Mr. Woods. He said, "The ticket is on the way, and I will see you Friday at the airport. If you have any questions, call me direct." He gave me his cell number.

"Great. See you Friday." I had a few days to hang out in the desert and catch up on my tan.

The week flew by, and I was on my way to Texas before I knew it.

I met Paul Woods at the airport. He seemed like a nice guy, and as we drove to the estate, we chatted the whole way. He asked about the Fords, Rod Stewart, living in LA, and why I wanted to work in Texas. I told him I'd always wanted to live in Dallas and said I was tired of the arrogant LA celebrities. He laughed and said, "You will fit in here and like the people." We also talked about golf, food, and wine.

When we got to the estate, I met Dottie, the wife, and Beau, the teenager who lived at home. Paul said, "I will show you the guesthouse, and then you can take the night off. We will get started tomorrow."

This was some estate—look at the pics. It had a moat and was around ten acres, not to mention the ranch next door, where they kept the horses. It was built to look like an old-style French villa.

The next day, Dottie showed me around, and we talked about my duties and planned the dinner menu, as I was set to leave the next day. They were big meat-and-potato people, chicken fried steak, that sort of greasy, fattening food. She could have stood to lose more than a few pounds. Let's just say she was not skinny by any means. We decided on pasta with a nice meat sauce and Caesar salad, an easy one for me, and for desert, she said just some ice cream. Wow, really easy first dinner. Beau, I guess, liked pasta.

Dinner went off like a charm, and everyone was happy. I joined them, and we talked about the job, when I could get back to Arlington, and if I would like to come work for them. I said I would like that very much and I could be back in two weeks. "I need to take care of a few things at my house and then drive back."

Dottie said, "Great. We will cover all of your costs to drive back."

We all enjoyed our dinner and had a nice conversation. They told me all about the area golf course, the great restaurants, and that I could ride the horses. They gave me the real hard sale. I said I would love it there, and they really looked forward to me coming on board. I had a glass of wine with them, and then we finished up, as I had an early flight back to LA. Paul said he would take me to the airport in the morning, as his office was on the way. Then I said goodnight and headed to the guesthouse.

Wow, on to the next adventure. This could be a pretty good gig if I played my cards right, and maybe I could have some fun in the process.

I met Paul in the morning at the main house in the kitchen. The other members of the family were still in bed. We had a cup of coffee and then headed out. We had a nice talk on the way about golf, how he was looking forward to my cooking, and things to do around town, and he gave me a thousand dollars for travel money.

He liked the last chef, but he said his wife ran the guy off. I thought, oh, shit. What did I get myself into? Paul said, "Keep Dottie happy, and the world is a better place. She can be tough, but just do your best, and you will be fine."

We arrived at DFW, and Paul said, "Thanks for coming. I look forward to seeing you in a few weeks." We had a nice handshake, and I was on my way back to LA. I was thinking, what the fuck did I get myself into? It's not like now, where you can Google "Paul Wood" and find out everything you want to know in five minutes.

When I got home, I called Dora told her I'd taken the job and had two weeks to get there. She said, "Great. Keep me updated on how the job goes, and don't worry. I can always find you work here." That was nice to hear.

I chilled in the desert for a few days and took care of my shit. Then I thought, what the hell. Let's go skiing on the way. I had friends in Vail from when I worked for the Fords, and it was not too far out of the way, so off I went. I called Kev's old girlfriend and asked her if I could stay with her for a few days so I could go skiing. She said, "Come on over. I will see you in a few days." She and Kev had broken up years ago, but we'd stayed in touch. She lived just outside of Vail in a nice condo. Her mom had some dough and had bought her the place. Must be nice.

After packing up, I hit the road. I had a lot of driving and thinking to do, and I wondered if I should have taken the job. I had a gut feeling it was not going to work out, but what the hell; it was a free trip to Dallas.

I had a week to kill before I had to be in Dallas, and the week before Christmas is never very busy at ski resorts. All locals were out, and the skiing was great. I hung out a few days and ended up in the sack with Kev's ex. We had a great time. I am sure Kevin never fucked her like I did. He was just that kind of guy, and he always had a gut—hard to get on top of, if you know what I mean.

I ran into some old friends, and on top of that, I ran into Emilia Crow. I'd forgotten that she had a place in Vail. She'd gotten it in the divorce, lucky bitch. They always come out on top and take you for everything they can.

After saying goodbye to everyone, I headed for Dallas. I always loved Vail—in fact, I just spent my sixtieth birthday there last year. Now I was on the last leg of the trip to Dallas. Man, I love driving cross-country; you can do a lot of thinking and get your head right. All I could think about was what if it did not work out? Then I said, give it a shot. How bad can she be? Little did I know, she was the meanest bitch I ever worked for, and I only lasted three months.

I got to Arlington with a few days to spare—I like getting an early start on a new job. Paul was glad to see me. Dottie, I think, couldn't have given a fuck, and I felt the same way I had on the first day, wondering when I would get the ax. I tell you, she was the Leona Helmsley of Texas. Everyone I ran into knew her, and they all said, "Watch out," and they were right.

The first month was ok. I just bit my tongue and kept my mouth shut. I liked Paul. He was a nice guy for a crook, just like the rest of the brothers. They were all from Waco, and they had all sued each other and been in fights with one another. But like I said, he was a nice guy—just make sure to keep your hand on your wallet. He's the only guy I ever worked for who had a gun in every room of the house—and also in all the cars, the garage, and safes all around the house. He must have had a few dozen, plus ammo, so you know he fucked a few guys.

Paul's main company was National Health Care, and the main office was in Grand Prairie, but he was into other stuff as well. I will never forget the first trip to the office, and there was a life-size statue of him in bronze. Their kids, Danner, Beau, were just like the ones in the other families I had worked for. They could not wipe their own asses. Danner worked for his dad in the Atlantic office. He thought he was George Clooney and a ladies' man, but he had a gut on him and lacked class. He should have just kept hanging out in North Dallas at the strip clubs.

The youngest son, Beau, was still in high school. He was a lazy piece of shit. He couldn't even get out of bed on his own. Part of my job was to get him up, make him breakfast, and let him smoke weed with his loser friends. He drove a Viper to high school. He was supposed to be some great high school football player, but I did not see it. He was not that big, but to hear Dottie talk, he had a full-ride scholarship to some big Texas school and was going to the pros. I don't think so. One, he did not have the grades, and two, he wasn't that good. I went to a game. Dottie just thought money would buy his way in. Man, was she in for a surprise.

I wanted to quit after the first month, but I really wanted to hang around and see Dallas some, so I hung in there. I did like Paul. He treated me well, and we played golf together. Dottie hated that, and I am sure she said something after the second time we played. He never asked me again until Dottie told him to fire me.

I do have a few good stories from Dallas. I met a few hot chicks and went to the MLB All-Star game and sat in the box with Troy and a few cowboy players. That was a great time, and they were all first-class guys.

I guess I will start with the New Year's Eve party. That was a big event, black tie, at the house. Paul called me aside before the party and asked if I had a tux. I said no. He said, "Go see my friend Ted at Neman's and get a tux. He will take care of you. Just don't say nothing to Dottie."

I strolled into Neman's at North Dallas's high-end mall and found Ted. I did not know it, but Paul had called and had it all set up. I was fitted with an Armani tux—I still have it today—shoes, the whole nine yards. I am sure it cost around four grand. Ted said, "Come back tomorrow, and it will be ready. You know, Paul must really like you. He doesn't do this for just anybody."

I said, "Thanks. I will see you tomorrow."

I had lunch downtown, and that's where I met the blond hairdresser, Linda. She lived in Arlington, and man, was she hot, and nice, too, a real Texas girl, my first. I will never forget her. I banged her the rest of the time I was in Texas, plus I got free haircuts. We had a lot of great times together. I should have kept her.

Dottie always had to be the center of attention. She thought she was hot. I am here to tell you that was one mean, fat bitch. What was Paul thinking when he married that shit? Maybe when she was young, she was skinny, like sixteen or some shit. We worked at the menu, and it was just like I thought: filet, mashed potatoes, broccoli, Caesar salad, apple pie, easy shit. But she still complained after the dinner, even though all the guests were happy, as was Paul. Dottie hated that a few guests had asked me about the Fords, Rod Stewart, LA, the stars, and all that sort of shit. In Dottie's eyes, I was the staff and was not supposed to talk to the guest.

Jimmy Jones was there. He said that if I needed a job, I should come see him. He also said, "Good luck with Dottie." He knew, as they all did. I was new, and I found it out the hard way.

Dinner went off great, but I soon found out you could never make her happy. She had to complain about something. Either the sauce was too hot, the veggies were undercooked or cooked too much. The kids were happy, and Paul loved my cooking. She was just a miserable bitch. I guess if I were fat and looked like her, I would be, too.

That was the first and last big dinner party. The guests included Paul's realtor, his brother Keith, one of the Bass brothers from Fort Worth—a nice person, both him and his wife—and Trammel Crow, the old oil and real estate mogul. What a small world, as I had been banging Emilia Crow for a few years now on and off. She'd been married to the one loser son, the black sheep of the family. I told Paul that, and he got a laugh out of it. He knew who she was. Emmitt Smith also showed up. He was a great guy, and he gave me his contact info. I got a signed Super Bowl football from him, and I still have it today.

It's too bad Dottie was so mean. I liked Dallas, and I was meeting some nice folks, and Paul was good to me. I was playing some great golf courses. He gave me a few of his old drivers, a brand-new set of Cleveland classic wedges, six pairs of custom boots, the shit, Ostrich Snake. And on top of that, he gave me a nice Stetson with a George Strait bend. I did miss the beaches in Malibu and Beverly Hills, but I liked the Stockyards in Fort Worth, Gilley's, and downtown.

I have never seen so many hot chicks in tight jeans and drinking beer out of longnecks in my life, all nice, and they loved to two-step. Man, I miss those days. Then, if you want to put the ritz on Dallas's north end, it's the same deal: lots of hot chicks and all so nice. It's still one of my favorite places to watch girls.

After New Year's, it was like pulling teeth out every day. She was just not a happy person. I felt bad for Paul. He was a nice guy, but he was married to an old hag. They rarely went out. She just stayed at home and ate chicken fried steak, watched TV, and got fatter. I knew my weeks were numbered, so I was saving my pay.

I wish there were some more great stories, but the job did not last that long, and they did not have great parties and guests. I had Sundays off, as that was family day. Dottie would have kids over and have their private family dinner—no guests because they had no friends, as no one liked Dottie, and Paul had fucked everyone out of money—so that was cool.

After my first Sunday off, I'll never forget how I came in Monday morning hoping to find my clean kitchen just as I had left it. What a shock! It looked like a bomb had gone off in the place. I mean, she had not cleaned one thing. She'd left dishes all over the place and grease on the floor, the stove was a fucking wreck, every pot in the house was dirty, the sink was full of food and dirty dishes. I got even, though. One thing is for sure: don't fuck over Chef Al. I will get my payback. Just ask Andy Anson.

I knew the job was coming to an end, especially once I started fucking Paul's realtor. She was an older broad, maybe fifty, but a hot-looking gal and horny as shit, even more than the hairdresser, who was half her age.

Dottie found out. I think Paul slipped, said we'd had lunch and she wanted me to do a charity event with her. I guess she went off, saying all this shit about the staff. I mean, who does she think she is? She did not come from money, but if you talked to her, you would think she was Texan royalty. In reality, she was one step above trailer-park white trash, and that's the truth.

She called me into her little office at the house and told me I should not associate with friends of Paul's or anyone from the house unless it involved house business. I said, "Yes, ma'am," and I thought that was it. She did not let it go.

I didn't care, though. I was still fucking the realtor, and she hated Dottie. She had a life and career. Dottie had nothing; she was just the wife of some rich guy. Her job was running the house. Wow, what a big deal.

Here is how I got even. I am sorry for you dog lovers, especially those of you who love old dogs on their last legs.

I had to make dog food for this mutt. For the first time in my life, I was cooking for a dog. Dottie had it written down, two types, both rice-based, one chicken and one beef with some vegetables and chicken or beef stock. This was something I would serve the crew on a yacht or the estate. One thing for sure, I can make some mean dog food, and believe me, you don't know how evil I got. Poor fucking dog.

After another day of putting up with Dottie's bullshit, I headed back to the guesthouse, poured myself a big Jack on the rocks, and thought how I could get even with this evil bitch before I quit or got fired in the next few days. So, I had a few Jacks and started to think that the piece-of-shit dog was the world to her. I was just about out of dog food, and I made a month's worth at a time. I knew I would be gone by the end of the month. Then it hit me: I'd make some special dog food.

The food was kept in small Tupperware containers for the staff to feed the dog. You just took it out of the freezer, threw it in the microwave, and served the dog. You didn't taste it—who tastes dog food? That's what I thought. I had a new recipe, and the dog was old and had a real weak stomach, so I figured I would spice things up for the little guy. I tell you, this batch would have made a grown man cry and pucker his ass and then run to the head. I put a dozen serrano pepper seeds, the hot ones, a whole bottle of sriracha sauce, a few cups of Ex-lax, cayenne pepper, Visine—it was a good batch.

I heard that dog shit all over the house for weeks, his ass was bleeding, and he threw up like a grown man. I had my payback. Sometimes the fucking you give is the fucking you get.

The weekend was over, and on the clear blue Monday morning, Paul came to the guesthouse to see me and have a cup of coffee. He said, "Let's go place golf at Shady Oaks. We have a tee time in an hour."

I said, "Great. See you in a few," and he headed back to the main house. I knew the ax was coming down Monday morning and had already packed most of my shit, so I was not surprised. It was one of the worst jobs I ever had. I did not know till later that she had triplets, like Jo Jo in Florida and the Slegels back in Dallas. Man, I had a lot to learn. I would leave Dallas soon but return years later, and it was the same shit: one more bitch and fucked-up kids. I guess by now, you see the pattern: these are some real assholes.

So, Paul met me at the guest house, and then we were off to Shady Oaks for the last time. I knew something was up. I could see it in Paul's face.

It was a quiet drive to the course, not like before, when we'd talked sports and shit. We got to the course and teed off, and finally, he broke the ice. He was getting ready to drop the hammer, and I said, "Paul, I know Dottie wants me gone."

He said, "She wanted to send you back to LA last month."

"What's the deal?"

"Don't come to the house no more. You can stay at the guesthouse till the weekend. Then you need to be off the property."

That was fair. I said, "I saw this coming."

He apologized and said, "That is how she is. I tried to talk to her. I have not gotten a blowjob or laid for the last month 'cause of you."

"I am sorry."

"It's not your fault. That is just how she is, a nasty old bitch, but I cannot leave her. She will destroy me. I will be sent to jail, and she will take everything."

I was cool with the whole deal. I hated the job as well, but I did like Paul. However, Beau and his asshole brother, Danner, could take a flying fuck. Couple of pricks.

We had a nice round, and then Paul bought lunch at the club. He said, "Here is five thousand dollars to get home on, and if you need a reference, have them call me, not Dottie. I will call Dora for you."

And you know what he did? Dora told me that he said I was the best chef they'd ever had. It was just that the wife did not like me, but she didn't like anyone. I look back, and I can see now that he was pissed that he had to let me go. I can only say one thing: he needs to grow a pair of balls and kick that old bitch to the curb at any cost. Life's too short to put up with some mean old fat bitch.

I said, "Paul, are we cool?"

He said, "Yes. If you need something, just call me, but do not come to the main house."

We had a nice talk on the way back, and he said, "I am truly sorry. I liked you, and I'm sorry it didn't work out."

We shook hands, and then I headed to the guest house. I called the hairdresser and asked her to dinner, and she said that would be great. "Cool," I said, "I will pick you up at eight."

I pour myself a big Jack on the rocks. I'd just made five grand and gotten fired. That was some cash back then. I said to myself, I will head back to Vail and ski for a month and fuck Kev's old girlfriend and stay for free. That was a good idea.

The hairdresser and I had a nice dinner. Afterward, she came back to the guesthouse with me, as there was a separate entrance to the property. We had a few glasses of wine and then an all-nighter. These chicks in Dallas love to do the wild thing. One more woman I will never forget, a great piece of ass and what a looker. Danner had his eyes on her, but he could not close her. Like I said, he was a prick and not at all what he thought he was.

As she was leaving the next morning, I said, "I will call you later. Let's do something Friday." I had to watch myself, as I was still fucking Paul's realtor as well.

I finished packing and thought about my next move. I had four days before I had to be out, plus I had five G's in cash on top of my petty cash. I knew Dora would have something for me back in LA, so I was not worried about getting a new job. I thought, just take a break and see what happens.

I called Paul's brother Keith to tell him the good news, that Dottie had fired me, and see if he wanted to have a drink and dinner before I headed back to LA. He was pretty cool. I'd met him at New Year's, and we'd keep in touch. He hated Dottie, and he and Paul had sued each other a few times. Like I said, a bunch of crooks.

He said, "Sure, let's get together. I will pick you up in a couple of hours. Let's go to the north end, get a few girls, and have dinner at Turtle Creek."

I said, "Great."

Keith was the brother who started HJ Williams insurance company, a multi-level marketing insurance company. This happened a few years back. Long story short, he stole all the money, left all agents and policy owners high and dry, bought a yacht, and left the country. Years later, he filed for bankruptcy and walked away scot-free. Now he was back in Arlington to start a new business, and he'd just bought a ranch a few miles outside of town. You have to love America.

Keith picked me up, and we headed to North Dallas. He was cool and a nice guy. We'd gone out a few times in the past for dinner and drinks. We had dinner at some high-end steakhouse and had a great dinner conversation. Two girls met us there—Keith had it set up—hot-as-balls strippers. He asked me, "What are you going to do?"

"Head back to LA," I said.

"It sounds like Dottie wants you out of town."

"Yeah, she did not like that I was banging Paul's realtor. Plus, she is just a mean, fat bitch."

"I know," he said. "I have a plan. I just bought this ranch, and I am starting a new company in a few months. I need someone to help take care of the ranch, cook, and help out and drive me into town once a week or so."

"What are you saying?"

"I cannot pay you what Paul was paying you, but you will have a hell of a lot more fun and work half as hard. I can give you four thousand dollars a month, and you will have the guesthouse, but I will pay you cash. I know Paul put you on the payroll."

I said that was cool, and he said, "Move in tomorrow. I cannot wait to see Dottie's face when she finds out."

Paul had just given me five G's to get out of town and go home. He would not like it, and Dottie would be pissed as well. I wish I could have seen her face when she found I was staying in town and working for Keith, whom she hated.

I head back to Paul's finished packing, loaded up, and headed to my new home, a nice ranch just outside Arlington, maybe ten miles from Paul's place. I heard the ranch was Troy Aikman's old place. It was a gentleman's ranch, about fifteen acres with a nice lake in the middle of the property and a guesthouse above the barn. This would be my home for the next several months.

I ended up having a lot of good times there, and Keith was a really great guy and very generous. There were not a lot of dinner parties, and he had pissed off all of Fort Worth and half of Dallas, but a few close friends came by, and his best friend, Wayne Newton, came by once for the annual Silver Spur charity event Paul and Dottie put on every year at their ranch.

All of Dallas's and Arlington's elite would show up. This is a good story, and I will get back to it.

Keith had just bought the ranch a month or so ago. The first morning, I made him breakfast, and he said, "Join me, and I will lay out the game plan." I'd made a nice country breakfast and coffee, and we had a great talk about what he wanted me to do.

I had my notepad, and off we went. First, he said, "You need to go meet Reggie at Mansfield Feed. I know his dad, and Reggie runs the feedlot. Real nice guy. He will be your new best friend. He likes to drink and likes the girls. From what I know of you, you guys are trouble. By the way, you still fucking Paul's realtor and hairdresser?"

"Both of them," I said.

"That's my boy. We are going to get along just great and have some fun. We will tear up North Dallas. Once you and Reggie are on the same page, here is my list. He can get everything I need. We will go to the bank tomorrow and open up a ranch account and get you a credit card and whatever else you need. Let me, and I will take care of it. There is a pick-up truck that's your as long as you are here, a big, brand-new Ford."

I liked it already. We got back to the list.

"I want two longhorns, not real old. I want to keep them for a while and show them off. Six or eight cows, a few goats, chickens for fresh eggs, and we will build a coop for them. That's a new project. You need to get on that. Reggie will know someone who can do it for us. The trees are all newly trimmed. A few have some fungus on them. We need them treated. The fences need to be painted, and the barn as well.

"Then we need to get riding gear for the two new horses I got coming from Poland in a few weeks, plus hay, grain, all that sort of stuff. Again, Reggie can help you with everything. I don't want it done overnight, but I hope, by summer, we got most of these banged out."

Then he asked me, "Now, what days do you want off?"

"It don't matter to me," I replied.

"I always need you to drive me on Saturday into town, but then you're done. You can hang out or drive home, and I will take a limo home. Whatever you want to do."

"Cool."

"Then we're good on days off?"

"Yes."

"Last thing is the lake. It's dirty. We need to get it clean and make it blue again. We need to hire some gardeners as well. As for food, I like everything. Dinner around six, breakfast at nine, and lunch is no big deal unless we got guests or it's Friday or the weekend. I need you to set the bar and wine cellar up as well, beer, sodas, mixers, the whole shooting match. Can you take care of all these?"

"Sure, no problem."

We talked for a while, and then he said he had plans to start a new business and wanted the ranch to be the showplace for his top salespeople. That was his short-term plan. He told me he had a screwed-up daughter. "She's a druggie and a dancer and hooking on the side, so I am raising my granddaughter till she gets clean—if that ever happens. She's not bad looking. You might want to take her for a test spin, but I tell you she is a wild one, and I don't want her around the ranch if I am not there. She is a thief as well, so watch yourself, 'cause she will take a liking to you, I am sure of that. Just some advice. I wish she would be with a guy like you and get straightened out, but that is a tall order."

We finished breakfast, and he said, "Clean up and go see Reggie today and get the list started. You two go have lunch, and I will meet you back here for dinner. Pick up some steaks while you're out. There'll be four of us tonight, including my best friend, who I want you to meet, and the nanny."

I said, "Cool."

"Oh, and buy Reggie lunch. You have cash?"

"Yes, Paul gave me five grand to get back to LA."

He laughed and said, "Good for you. Keep a receipt till I get you a credit card, and I will reimburse you. Does Paul or Dottie know you came over here to work for me?"

"No, I did not say a word, 'cause I wanted the money."

"I will let the word out next week. Now, get out of her. Go see Reggie. See you tonight."

He threw me the keys to the truck. He had a nice Benz SL.

I called Dora and told her what was up and the whole thing with Dottie. She said, "Great. Let me know when you get tired of Texas and head back to LA. And congrats on the new job. It sounds like fun."

I called Reggie and gave him a heads up that I was on my way. He said, "It's almost lunchtime. When you get here, we'll head to downtown Fort Worth."

I met Reg at the feedlot, and he gave me the two-dollar tour. Then we had lunch downtown, a couple of burgers and some beers. Fort Worth is a funky little town. I thought it was way cool, with lots of hot chicks, all nice and friendly, and Reg knew everybody. He'd grown up there, for Christ's sake. We had a great lunch. I told him about the list and said money is no problem. He knew Keith and that he was not a cheap man.

"That's a big list, I know, so let's get started. I will start lining stuff up."

"Cool," I said. "Come by the ranch tomorrow, and we will get a game plan and get the ball rolling."

"I think he would like the longhorns as soon as we can find a few good ones. He likes to get drunk and look at them after he smokes some weed."

I told Reg about the Arabian horses coming in a few weeks and that we needed feed, riding gear, the whole shooting match. That was next on the list. Reg told me that Keith paid half a million for the two from some royal prick in Poland, friends of Wayne Newton's.

Reg and I hit it off from the start. He was a big guy who always wore a straw hat with a George Strait bend. I would have my own by the weekend. We went back to the feedlot, and he told me the best place to buy steaks and produce. I said, "Come by the ranch after lunch tomorrow. I have to go to the bank with Keith in the morning."

"Cool. See you tomorrow."

I stopped and grabbed some steaks and stuff for dinner and then headed back to the ranch. Once there, I cleaned up and got ready for dinner. Keith showed up with his buddy, the Colonel, a cool old guy. I guess they went way back, partners in crime. Then the nanny showed up with the granddaughter. This was a different crowd in a good way. I cooked, and then we all sat down and ate. After the meal, the nanny helped me clean up.

Keith said, "Right after breakfast, we have to be at the bank to open an account and get you a credit card."

Then the Colonel asked what I thought about Reg.

I said, "Great guy. We get along great. He is taking me to get my first straw hat on Saturday, and he's coming by tomorrow. He's already got some longhorns lined up."

We all had a little Jack after dinner. I finished cleaning up, and then it was off to bed. I had a good feeling about this job, and it lasted almost a year. There were a lot of good times. Plus, I learned a lot about running a ranch, tending horses, cows, chickens, and trees, and how to take care of a lake. I even pulled a calf out, along with the cord, my first time helping out with a cow's birth. Keith was simple with food, as most folks from Texas are: meat and potatoes, fried fish, quail in season, regular old salad, and simple desserts. They liked the steaks with stuffed portobello mushrooms, garlic, cheese, and bread crumbs. Simple and clean, and everybody was happy.

I was off to a good start, far from the bullshit over at Paul's place. Nobody I talked to had anything good to say about Dottie. It cost them ten grand to get me there and fire me. She did not care; she just wanted me gone. I was cool with it, and now I was working for the brother a few miles away and had put five G's in the bank. Now I could afford to buy a nice straw hat. Win-win.

I had a nice guest house; just look at the pics. This was one of the better jobs I had. I should have married the crazy daughter striper junky, but who wants to put up with that shit just for the money? Bad way to go. I could have married a few old rich broads in the day. I just cannot fuck old broads or be a dog on a leash. Fuck that. Plus, the daughter was just a wack job; no light at the end of the tunnel for a long time.

I met Keith in the house in the morning, and I made breakfast. We talked as we sipped our coffee, and he said, "We have to be at the bank soon." That was the big plan of the day. In the afternoon, we'd meet Reg and start on the list.

He asked me to drive so he could smoke some weed, and I said, "Cool." Then we headed to the bank.

At the bank, they called us into a private room, and some young, hot banker said, "Oh, hi, Keith. How are you?" She was all over him. "What do you need today?"

Keith said, "I want to open a new account and get a credit card for Alan here, my new chef and ranch manager."

"Ok, how much do you want to open the ranch account with?"

Keith thought a minute, and I almost shit myself—and the chick, too—when he said, "Let's open it for a million. I will probably spend two hundred thousand in the next week or so. I am buying some longhorns, I just spent half a million on the two horses coming from Poland in a few weeks, and the ranch needs some love. Alan is going to get the place in shape."

I thought, wow, that's a lot of cash just to buy some cows and shit, but we spent a good amount of it. When you go big, you have to spend big, and it's not cheap. I've seen guys like that who want to talk the talk but won't spend a dime. I worked for a few, and we'll get to that down the road.

Keith was not that guy. He knew how to live. I heard after he took all the money in the insurance scam, he bought a mega-yacht and lived on it around the world till the shit cooled down. Then he came back to the States and filed chapter 11. He had all his money hidden offshore, and the ranch was in a trust, so it could not be touched. He was a smart guy, beat the system. You have to love that.

We got the shit done at the bank and then headed to Fort Worth to have lunch and a few beers and talk about the list. I said, "Reg is coming over this afternoon, and we are working on it. He has some longhorns lined up and a guy to build the chicken coop, and that guy sells the chickens as well."

Keith said, "Cool. Paul already found out, and I heard Dottie is pissed as all get-out." He laughed. "Don't worry about it. I got you covered. Some folks in Dallas will not hire you if you have worked for a different family. They don't want you telling folks they're assholes or any of their personal info, like money, kids, any of that kind of shit."

I swear, Dottie thought she was like the first lady or some shit, and her kids were going to run the country. In fact, the only things they could run were their mouths. What a crock of shit. They could not even wipe their own asses, the whole lot of them.

Keith said, "Paul will call in a few days, or I will call him and just play along and see if he brings it up. If not, I will tell him I hired you, so don't worry about it. Dottie will just run her mouth like she always does. She hates it when she can't get her way."

I said, "Thanks."

We had one more beer, and then it was back to the ranch. Keith was cool about shit like this. He was funny as well, and he got a lot of pussy. He was a sharp dresser, handled himself well, and had his own style.

When we got back, Reg was waiting for us with his big old Texas smile and his favorite line, "Hoodie-hoo." Every time he saw you or some hot chicks or one of his old buddies, that was the line, delivered in his big voice, "Hootie-hoo." It's been over twenty years, and I can still hear him. What a character and a first-class guy. We sat on the patio, I got some beers for us, and then we got right into the list. I was having a great time.

Reg said he had found a great pair of longhorns. "You can breed them as well, and they're a bargain at fifteen thousand dollars. The guy needs the money."

Keith didn't even think about it. "You and Chef go look at them, and if you think they're a deal, have Alan write a check and let's get them here. I want to see these big-horn bastards."

We all had a shot of Jack and one more beer. Then Reg said, "The guy will start on the chicken coop Monday. It'll take a few days, and we will have that wrapped up, with hens and roosters by the weekend. Reg had one more shot, and then he said, "I hope these old fucking hens lay some eggs." He laughed and threw a "Hoodie-hoo" in there.

It was Friday night, so Keith said, "Take the night off. I am going to Dallas on my own. You and Reg go tear up the stockyards. Don't worry about breakfast tomorrow. I might not be here. We'll catch up in the afternoon."

I never felt more at ease with a boss than with Keith.

Reg said, "Ok, let's hit the stockyards. I will be back around six, and we'll grab a steak and head to Gilley's. We can stop on the way, and I'll get you a new straw had.

"Cool," I said.

Keith and I made small talk, and then he said, "Are you happy?"

I said, "Yes, I love working for you."

We had a drink, and he told me about suing his brother. Then we talked about the horses coming next week, and he said, "Go, have a good time, and if you want to, bring some ass back to the ranch. It's no big deal. Reg knows all the pussy in town, and you will hook up tonight, so don't worry about bringing her back home. It's cool. Just keep them in your guesthouse unless you got two one for me."

I laughed. He was a hoot.

I headed back to the guest house to have a beer and get cleaned up. I already had some nice boots from Paul, some jeans, and a few nice shirts. I just needed the new straw hat, and I would be ready.

Reg showed up in his truck, and then we had a beer, said goodbye to Keith, and headed to town. First stop was a western store to get me a new straw hat. Reg, "It's my treat. Pick out whatever you like." We were downtown in the stockyards. What a cool place. After walking around for a while, I found a hat, a Charlie Crazy Horse. Reg liked it, and we asked the guy to put the George Strait bend on it. I've still got the hat, and it's one of a kind; that's how he makes them.

For dinner, we had a couple of steaks and a few Lone Stars, and then it was off to Gilley's. Man, was I in for a surprise. I should have known it. Everywhere we went, they all knew Reg. We walked to the head of the line, and Reg shook the bouncer's hand and said, "Alan is running Keith Wood's ranch, so show him the same courtesy. He used to work for Rod Stewart in LA but now lives in Fort Worth."

That was it. I was golden from then on, but most of the time, Reg and I were together. I did fly solo once in a while, and I got the same VIP treatment, no cover and front of the line. It was pretty cool, just like at the Gate in LA when I worked for Gersten.

I bought the first round of beers and shots cause Reg had gotten my new straw hat and dinner.

This had to have been the biggest bar I had ever seen, with live music and tons of hot chicks in tight jeans. I loved the place. We had some drinks and a few dances—Reg was a pretty good dancer, and I could hold my own. Then we picked up a few girls Reg knew. We bought them a few beers, and the next thing I knew, we were headed home. One drove me, while the other went with Reg. She took me back to the ranch to do the wild thing, and then she said goodbye in the morning. What a life. Reg called later that day, and I filled him in on what went down.

"She was hot and good in the sack," I said.

"I know," he replied. "I had her before." I just laughed.

This was our weekend MO. We might go to Dallas sometimes or to the lake to hang out, but we got laid every weekend, sometimes with the same chicks and other times with new ones. Man, was Fort Worth good to me. The only bad thing was that I was not meeting celebrities and high-powered people, just hookers and Keith's drinking buddies, the Colonel, Reg, and his druggie daughter. But I was making ok cash and having a good time and not killing myself. Plus, I was getting a lot of pussy. I went to some baseball games with Keith, sat in his box, met a few Cowboy players, and got to meet Nolan Ryan, so that was kind of cool, but mostly it was strip clubs in North Dallas and hookers, kind of like Albert only in Texas.

After cooking for first ladies and presidents, it's kind of hard to wait on and cook for whores. Don't get me wrong—I fucked many whores. I just don't invite them to stay for dinner. You pay them to leave. Keith, though, wanted them to hang out. They'll drink your booze, eat all your food, and still want some more cash. It's easy—fuck them, pay them, and kick them out.

This went on for about six months. I could go on and on about whores at the ranch, the stripper pole in the barn, getting head in the hot tub, Reg and I switching off on some chicks. At the end of the day, it was all crazy. We all drank too much, but it was a real good time.

When the horses came from Poland, that was a big week. The list was getting banged out, and the ranch was looking good. The one stud was named Bachelor. I have never seen a prettier horse. Just look at the pics.

Keith hired a trainer to help me with the horses till I got the hang of it, and she gave me riding lessons as well. I would go on nightly rides with Keith and bring the horse over to the girls to pet. Then they'd watch me ride around the arena. I was getting pretty good, but the horse was amazing to ride. I didn't have to do anything. He was a well-oiled machine, like a Ferrari.

One day, Reg and I went to get some riding gear: saddles, reins, blankets, all that sort of stuff. Keith said to get whatever I needed, so I got some bad-ass chaps, a pair of boots, and a work straw hat. I think we spent ten grand on saddles and riding gear. That was a lot back then. It was all custom. I mean, you don't buy a two-hundred-dollar saddle for a half-million-dollar horse. Just ask Wayne Newton. He has Arabians, too. That's how Keith got into them.

That was a great day, one I will never forget. One of the best things about my job was spending the other guy's money. I mean, how many guys walk into a grocery store and drop three grand or a western store and drop ten grand. As Reg would say, "Hoodie-hoo. Living the dream."

The horses were out of this world, and I had all the bad-ass riding gear. Keith did not blink an eye when I told him I dropped ten grand on gear. He just asked, "Is it nice shit?"

I said, "Yes, the best," and that was it.

I was riding just about every day, not counting the lessons I was getting. We had cows now, some longhorns, chickens, and a few goats. I hired gardeners and bought a tractor. We were looking good. I just had to get the lake cleaned up. It had an algae issue.

The place was looking good; just check the picks out. I hired an arborist to work on the trees. They had issues, including some disease, but the guy got them all cleaned up and did the trimming, and man, they came out nice.

Keith spent the weekends and evenings on the patio, having dinner with the nanny, his granddaughter, and the Colonel, drinking beer and eating steaks. A few strippers would come by on Sunday—or they were still there from the night before. Reg might stop by for a beer. Keith was of the few bosses I worked for whom I joined for dinner almost every night.

He liked for all of us to sit down and join him, the nanny as well. He and I had a lot of long talks. He was a friend as well as the boss. He asked me about growing up in Ohio, the Marines, and my house in California. Lots of good times and all the strippers and hot tub parties.

This went on for months, and the list was almost done. We had fresh eggs, cows, all that shit. I like it when a job gets to be routine. You know your days off, dinner guests, all that. Keith bought me some nice boots and a bad-ass belt. He let me take the Benz once in a while if I had a hot date—only Keith and Art let me do that. He liked the hairdresser I was banging; she was a hottie. He even tried fucking her. She told me he asked her out. I was not crazy about that, but that's how some of these rich fucks roll. They've got cash, and they think they can buy anyone, and sometimes it's true. No big deal. I just laughed about it.

My last big job was to get the lake cleaned up. It was shit brown and full of algae, and the aerators did not work. Plus, we had Wayne Newton coming in a few weeks, so Keith said, "Get it done at all cost. By some ducks and fish as well, get a pontoon boat and a few kayaks, and have the dock refinished."

I liked that: "Just get it done. I don't care what it costs." Weintraub was like that: "I don't care, just fix it. If you have to ask, you cannot afford it." I like that line.

The next morning, I called Reg and gave him the last of the list. "Let's get the lake cleaned up," he said. He knew a guy right off the bat and said, "He will be by tomorrow, and he will take care of the boat." He had a friend who had one for sale, like brand new.

The same guy who did the chicken coop was on the dock detail. He showed up in the morning and was all over it. He said, "It will take a few days, but it'll be done by the weekend." He knew a guy who had ducks and a friend who would take care of the fish as well. It's funny how quickly things get done when you have cash.

The fish came from a guy who worked for parks and recreation. He called and asked when I needed them, and I said, "I have a guy coming today to start to clean the lake. I need them next Friday."

"Done deal," he replied. "See you next week."

A guy showed up to replace the aerators and clean the lake. By noon, he had the new aerators in and working, and he was out there in a small canoe, adding chemicals and a net all around the banks. When he was done, he said, "I will see you tomorrow. It will take all week to get the lake clean, but it will be done by the weekend and be crystal blue again."

I cooked dinner that night for Keith and the Colonel, and I gave him an update. He saw the dock getting done and the aerators and lights all working, and he asked about the nets. I said it was to drag all the weeds and algae out tomorrow morning. All the shit was floating to the surface, and the guy would pull it all in. Keith said, "The place is looking good."

I said, "Everything but the fish will be done by the weekend, and that's 'cause there might be some shit in the water still."

We had a nice steak, as usual, and a few beers and called it a night. I was beat; I'd put in a long day. I was learning some cool shit: how to take care of livestock, clean up a lake, feed horses, chickens, cows, and the longhorns. Not to mention what I learned from the arborist. He got all the trees looking good in a few weeks, and I fed them and nursed them back to health with his help.

By the weekend, the lake was clean, and you could see the bottom on a sunny day. The guy gave me one hell of an education, showed me what chemicals to put in the water every weekend, what to look for, how to turn the aerators on and off, and how to operate the fountain. He said, "To keep it clean, you need movement, so run the aerators at least twelve hours a day, and twenty-four hours on the weekends." There was also a dye to make the water blue. Golf courses use it. He told me that this had to be added every few weeks, depending on the rain and weather, but it needed to be done in the morning when the water was moving. Man, was he right. By the next morning, the lake was crystal blue. I almost shit myself.

The next step was to add the ducks and fish, which I would do the next week. I'd never felt so proud about what I had done. None of the shit had to do with running an estate or being some celebrity chef, but I'd learned a lot and had the time of my life in the process.

As usual, on Sunday, Keith had a few strippers show up. He had a few he liked, and they were regulars. I would cook for them, and then they would retire to the hot tub. Sometimes I would bang one, or the nanny if she was around; she was always up to throw it down.

I had the list just about done. I'd spent a shitload of money. The lake alone had cost around twenty-five thousand dollars, and the trees around fifteen thousand. Arborists are not cheap. I tell you what, this was a gentleman's ranch, and the grounds looked bad-ass.

Wayne was coming into town the next weekend and would be staying at the ranch. We were all going to attend the Silver Spur charity event, and he was the guest of honor, and he would sing as well. I had the rest of the week to get the place dialed in.

Over the week, I finished up the final touches. The bar was stocked, and the wine cellar was full. This was a true bachelor pad, with everything you could ask for, and the chicks just kept coming back.

Late in the week, a guy showed up in his truck with more coolers than I could count. They were full of fish, and he dumped them in the pond. I gave him a grand in cash, and that was it. He said, "Don't ask where they came from." I did not ask.

Wayne showed up that evening, and I made a great steak dinner for everyone. We talked about the ranch and Keith's new horses and how the ranch looked. I guess Keith and Wayne went back a few years. I thought Wayne was a great guy, first class. Keith said he had a limo lined up for tomorrow night and that I was going as well, and we worked out the details and schedule.

Keith and Wayne mostly talked about horses. I think they'd done some business together years ago, but I am sure Keith hadn't fucked Wayne over, or he would not have come around. We drank some nice wine and just shot the shit for a few hours. Wayne knew my old boss Weintraub, and he asked how old JW was. I said it was a great job and he treated me well, and he told me that if I was ever in Vegas and needed anything, to give him a call. Then we had some cigars and after-dinner drinks and retired. We had a long day ahead of us.

The next morning, I was up early to do my chores, and then I fixed a nice country breakfast for everyone. After breakfast, Keith and I showed Wayne the horses. I think he helped pick them out for Keith. They were beautiful animals. Then we showed him around the place. He liked the Longhorns and told Keith, "Nice touch." That made Keith's day.

Later in the day, everyone headed to their rooms and got ready for the big formal event. I am sure it was the main one for Arlington. I mean, the guest list was impressive, including the Bass brothers Trammell Crow, a few Cowboy players like Emmitt Smith and Troy Aikman. There is a saying in Dallas, "Go big or go home," and this was a big event.

We had a few drinks at the ranch before the limo showed up. Keith was smoking weed, as usual, with a hot little stripper. I was still going out with the realtor, Ann, and she showed up looking like a million bucks.

We all met on the patio, and I fixed some drinks. Wayne was hanging out as well, a real cool guy. Keith told everyone the story about Dottie and me and that he'd hired me just to piss her off. They all knew what a king bitch she was. I could not wait to see her face when we rolled up with Wayne. She knew he was staying at Keith's but had no idea I would be joining them as well—and, on top of that, with Ann.

We rolled up, and there was Paul and Dottie, greeting all the guests, and a waiter was giving everyone a glass of Champagne. The guests were all over Wayne, taking pitchers and shit. Keith looked at Paul and Dottie and said, "You all know Chef Al."

Then Ann said, "Chef is going to be my new business partner, and he'll run the ranch as well."

Dottie almost shit. Paul was kind of pissed, but not really. He liked me, and I am sure he missed my services. I had this shit-eating grin on my face. I said, "Hi, Dottie," and shook Paul's hand, and then in we went. It was truly a great day, and I got the last laugh this time.

Inside, the Oak Ridge Boys were playing, and Wayne was the final show. He sang a few songs and was the guest speaker, and then they had the silent auction. Keith and I got a good buzz on, and Ann did, too; she liked to party as well.

We all had a great time and then headed back to the ranch. Wayne said he had to leave early, as he had a show back in Vegas. Keith said to me, "Take the next day off. I will drive Wayne. He wants to talk some business. Have Ann stay the night and enjoy yourself. You have earned it. The ranch looks great."

Ann liked to fuck, and she showed me her thanks for getting her into the event. The next morning, I made her breakfast and coffee, and we went one more time around. Then she said, "I wish I could stay all day, but I have clients to see today. Call me, and we will get together later in the week."

I just chilled the rest of the day and went for a ride in the afternoon. Keith came back and banged a stripper for the rest of the day, and he got drunk and stoned as well. What a life. He and Albert would have gotten along great. But Keith had more charm with the ladies. Let's just say he had some game, plus a shitload of money, which doesn't hurt.

The next few weeks flew by. I had the list pretty much done and was fine-tuning the place and cooking for Keith, the Colonel, the nanny, and the strippers. I was getting used to it, and the strippers were not bad chicks, not like the LA bitches. I had learned a lot about longhorns, chickens, goats, cows, you name it, even putting up with Keith's drug-crazed daughter, whom I had to call the cops on one weekend and escort her off the property.

Keith had to leave town for the weekend, and he told me to never let her on the property if he was not home, as she was a thief. It was a Sunday afternoon, just me, the nanny, and the granddaughter. I was out doing something in the barn, and the nanny was at the store. I went up to the main house to check on it, and there was Keith's daughter, going through his desk. As she yelled at me, I could that she had one of his watches in her hand. I called the cops, and they were there in five minutes, as Keith had a few friends in the department. When the cops pulled up, along with the nanny, Keith's daughter tried to get past me. I cut her off, but I did not touch her. Keith had a court order that she was not to be on the property without him present, and the cops knew this. I said, "She has a watch that is not hers, and I want it. It's Mr. Woods's."

The cops told her to hand it over. One said, "You need to leave the property now or be arrested."

She called me a few names, and the nanny as well, but she left without a fight, as I am sure she was high as a kite. One of the cops said, "If she comes back, just call, and we will take her in next time."

What a freak show, and she was not a bad-looking chick, just fucked up. I heard her boyfriend was a tweaker as well. What a waste of oxygen. That happened a few times, and one time, they took her to jail, but she had been there many times in the past. I would be surprised if she is still alive today. Just a waste.

Keith got home, and I told him the whole story. He just asked, "Did they take her in?"

I said, "No."

"Thanks," he said, and that was it.

I heard she even tried to kidnap her child to blackmail Keith into giving her some money. Keith had custody of the grandchild, as she could not take care of the baby—or herself for that matter. So much for that. Don't want to beat a dead horse.

I had a feeling my days in Texas where numbered, with no news on the business and talk about it quieting down. To tell the truth, I missed my home in the desert, and cooking for strippers every weekend was getting old. I was not meeting any interesting people, just Keith's drunk friends. I had been in Texas for close to a year now and I have been talking to Dora, who'd said she could always find me work in LA. Paul had given me a nice reference letter, and I was sure Keith would as well. I'd really enjoyed my time there, but I was ready to go.

A few more weeks passed and we were having our Sunday afternoon cookout with Keith, the girls, and the Colonel. After dinner, the girls retired to the hot tub, and the Colonel saw himself out, so was just Keith and me.

He said, "Go get the Jack, and let's have a drink."

I knew something was up. I got the Jack and a few Lone Stars, and we sat down with our drinks to talk.

He said, "Alan, the business is not going to happen. I have some issues with some state agencies, and they found out I am involved in the business and won't grant the license because of my past. So my new plan is just to stay here, raise my grandchild, stay drunk, and fuck some strippers every Sunday for as long as I can."

You have to admire Keith's honesty.

Then he said, "I just don't need you to cook, and there will be no work for you in the business. I will give you a month's salary to get back to Cally and a reference and whatever you need. You worked your ass off, and the ranch looks great. Hang out for a week or so. Take some time. You and Reg go tear it up one last time. Hell, let's all go out and do it one last time."

"Cool," I said, "and many thanks for everything. It's been a fun ride. I really enjoyed your friendship, and I hope we can keep in touch."

"I sure as hell hope so."

We got into the Jack pretty good that night, and he let me have one of the strippers. That was the ending of a really good run and a great guy to work for, one of the best. Keith, you are the man. I will never forget his stories; no matter how many times he told them, they were great. He would say, you know, you've heard of the guy who would say, 'My partner took all my money and fucked my wife and left me high and dry'?" Then he would just smile and say, "Yeah, that was me."

Reggie, I will never forget you. Thanks for all the good times, man. I miss the Stockyards and hanging with you. I will never forget the "Hoodie-hoo."

We all went to Gilley's one last time/ Keith lined up some strippers and picked up the whole tab, easily a couple of grand. Of course, I had one, plus a great steak dinner. Keith, many thanks again. I hope you are alive and fucking. Hope some old partner did not put a few rounds in you.

We had a few more lunches, but that was the last big night on the town. Soon I was on my way back to LA. It had been a little over a year now or close to it. I had saved a nice bit of cash as well. I'd been paid twice to leave, and I'd saved around fifteen thousand dollars, plus all the shit I picked up, hats, boots, all that shit. It adds up. It was a great year. Keith was sorry to say goodbye, and I got my payback with that old bitch Dottie.

I had already spoken to Dora, and she was cool. Keith gave me a great reference, and Paul did as well. Dora called them and did a follow-up, so

I was still was the golden boy in her eyes. I told her, "I need a month off once I get back to California. Then I will be ready to get back to work, and I can come see you for a sit-down.

After all was said and done, I drove back west with a pocketful of money and some great stories.

Chef and the General Panama

Cowboy at heart

Chef and Tina Ferrari, model

Chef and Kev Special Agent La Quinta

Chapter 11

BARRY DILLER
THE QUEEN

LOOK UP "ASSHOLE" IN THE dictionary, and you'll see a picture of Barry Diller.

I got back to the desert house, and everything was good, just like I'd left it, except now I had a pool and a hot tub, as I had been making good money for the last few years and saving it. The strippers had moved out, and I had some MILF living there to keep an eye on the place. She paid some rent and kept the place clean. It was a great arrangement. Nancy had been there for quite a few years. The best part is that she would lie by the pool with her top off, and man, did she have a big set of tits. I never banged her—I did not want to fuck things up—but she hooked me up with a few of her friends, whom I did bang. She was great at that, and we were good friends.

Man, it was nice to be back in Cally. I missed my house. I called Dora the following week, and she asked me to see her next week for lunch. "I might have a great job for you, the best in the country. It's in Malibu. I will tell you about it when I see you."

I met Dora the following week, and we had lunch at the Ivy. She said, "The job is with Barry Diller. It starts right away. He wants to meet you this week, and he already has your resume."

"Tell me about the job," I said.

"It's for his beach house in Malibu, but you will sometimes cook in Beverly Hills as well and run errands and entertain guests on the weekends. The salary starts off at six thousand dollars a month. He is a very private person and eats very simply. Here is his direct number. Call him today and get out there as soon as you can. You are the only one I am sending. He asked for my best, so don't let me down."

I called Mr. Diller later that day, and we spoke for a few minutes. He asked if I could come to the beach house this Saturday to see the place and meet him, and he gave me the address in Malibu.

"I will see you then, sir," I said.

"Eleven o'clock sharp. Don't be late." That was kind of a sign already. I had no idea who this prick was, but Dora had said he was very wealthy and powerful, just like Jerry Weintraub, only so I had to be on my best behavior.

I got to Malibu an hour ahead of schedule, found the house, and then parked around the corner to kill some time, think about the interview, and tell myself to slow down.

There was no gate but a long driveway to this nice little beach house on the cliff, which you could not see from the rear of the house. There was no one there to answer the door except Mr. Diller. He invited me in and asked me if I wanted a coffee. I said, "No, but a water would be great."

It was the only time I ever saw him get something. Then there was the handshake, the dead fish. I could tell he was as queer as a two-dollar bill, and that wimpy voice—I will never forget that.

He asked about the Weintraubs, Rod, and what happened in Texas. I told him the job had ended and my services were no longer needed. He said I would have to stay every weekend at the house even if he was not there. I said that was fine, as I was used to working weekends. He then said he might need me to cook in the house in Beverly Hills. I said I was fine with that as well. He had a list of all this petty shit, like how to answer the phone and make his coffee, and how the newspapers had to be set up when I gave them to him. I should never have taken the job. I could tell this guy was an asshole. I guess nice guys don't make the *Forbes* list.

Plus, I could tell this guy was just weird. I don't care what Diane Von Furstenberg says. Once you take it up the ass, you just don't change. I am sure he is still the catcher in some form or other. Back to the interview. He asked when I could start, and I said, "Next week will be fine."

"I look forward to having you on the staff." He gave me the number of his assistant, who would give me the rest of the details, petty cash, and all the little things. Then he gave me keys to the house and the Range Rover, showed me my little guesthouse, gave me the tour of the property, and explained how to work the elevator to the beach, the hot tub, and all the alarms and cameras.

He said, "I will not be here Monday. Find your way around, and I will need to have the house ready for the weekend, with food, drinks, and all the beach towels down at the beach."

I had to call him Mr. Diller as well, like he was royalty or some shit—well, maybe a queen. I had no idea what I was getting into with this dickhead. I am glad the job only lasted six months before I quit, and believe me, it was a long six months.

It's funny. Months later, I ran into Jim Belushi. We used to have a few beers together at the Gate. He asked what I'd been and been up to and if I was still working for Albert. I said, "No, I just left Barry Diller, and I am freelancing till I find a new gig."

He gave me a crazy look and said, "Yeah, Barry, I bet there was a lot of dick-sucking going on over there." Jim had a way with words.

I said, "Yeah, you are right about that."

We threw a few back and had some laughs. He was one crazy fuck. I liked him, a good guy and funny as shit.

I said goodbye to Barry, grabbed the keys and my notes, and was on my way back to the desert after one more dead-fish handshake.

I stopped by Alice's to have a few cold ones, but first, I called Dora and told her the news. She knew he was going to hire me; I was batting a thousand at this point. Now, years later, I know I was not that great; it was just that these assholes could not keep staff because they're pricks.

At Alice's, I saw my favorite bartender.

"Hey, Chef, what's up?"

"I just got a job with Barry Diller. Do you know him?"

He laughed and said, "Everyone knows Barry, the queen. What a fucking asshole."

"Thanks. That's my new boss."

I guess everyone knew he was gay and an asshole.

I had a bad feeling about this job, but it was good money, and I would be living in Malibu again. However, I knew the job would not last long, so I had to make sure I saved some dough. I was sure it was not going to get easier.

Back in the desert, I enjoyed seeing some old friends, staying at my house, and visiting Cecil's at the Marriott in Palm Desert. It was chick heaven, and Bob was still the head pro. He was an old friend, so I got to play golf for free. The days flew by, and I soon found myself back in Malibu.

I sat down with Barry's assistant to fill out confidentiality agreements and W2 forms and get the list of all the dos and don'ts, and was it a list. I wish I had kept it, just crazy shit that only a prick would request. When I answered the phone, I was to say, "Hello," and that was it. And I was not to say he was there.

Oh, and the newspapers in the morning, all three of them were delivered by a driver at four in the morning: the *Wall Street Journal*, the *New York Times*, and the *LA Times*. When he was in, I had to put them by his door at six and have his coffee ready. If he was not there, I had to put them on his bed, but they had to be in this order: the *Wall Street Journal* on top, followed by the *New York Times*, and then the *LA Times*. Everything had to be perfect for the queen. His coffee was a blend of three kinds: espresso, French roast, and Colombian dark roast. I did it right the first time, and then, after that, I just winged it, and he never complained. Sometimes I would just use two, and he never knew. These rules were all on the list. The craziest one was that pens had to be laid on all notepads at a forty-five-degree angle, and there were notepads all over the house: on his desk, at the bar, in the kitchen, and by the pool. He would move them around, and I had to go back and fix them. Is that not some crazy shit?

I filled everything out, and then we chatted for a while. She was cool. I am sure he treated her like shit. Everyone was scared of him, but he was a pussy. If you raised your voice back at him, he would probably cry. I would love to run into him in LA. I would love to say, "Hey, Barry, what's up, asshole? Are you still taking it up the ass, or are you now the pitcher? Or does Diana strap one on for you and put it to you? That would be cool as shit.

She took off, and I was on my own to buy food, beverages, and all that sort of stuff for the house. The Rover also needed to be detailed. Barry would drive out in his Porsche when he came. I just had to put gas in it for him, as he could not wipe his ass. I am sure he had the young boys do that for him. Of all the guys I had to work for, he was the biggest prick, right up there with Jordan Zimmermann—more on him later.

I don't have a lot of stories about this job, as I was only there a short time and he did not entertain much, but I have a few. Mostly I would have to drive his young boyfriends to the airport Monday morning after a weekend of hard fucking up the ass. He would head back to Beverly Hills, and I would have to drive the fucks to the airport. For the life of me, I cannot figure out why these fucks think they are special just because they have money and means. At the end of the day, you are still some dirty old gay fuck who likes little boys. Everyone in LA knows you are a prick and taking it up the ass, you and all your pals, Geffen, Gallen, Kline, Beatty, and all the rest of the fudge-packer gang. Let's start with the only lunch party I did for these fucks.

Barry told me he was having some guests over Saturday and just wanted soup, sandwiches, and a pitcher of iced tea. I said, "Yes, sir. I can do that," and that was it.

The following Monday, I got a call. A wimpy voice said, "Alan?"

"Yes, may I help you?"

"This is Warren."

"Warren who?"

"Beatty."

"Oh. How can I help you?"

"Please tell Barry that Annette and I will see him on Sunday."

"I will, Mr. Beatty. See you on Sunday."

I got off the phone, and all I could think was, why is this guy coming over here to hang out with a bunch of gay guys? But by the sound of his voice, I was not far off on my thinking. I mean, he had a pussy voice. I would know for sure come Sunday. The rest of the fucks did not bother to call and confirm.

The week flew by, and the big day arrived. These would be my first guests, except for a few young boys who'd spent the night. I was told to see the guests to Barry's room and bring lunch to the patio off his bedroom. Don't you find that a little weird? I just did what I was told.

Geffen, Kline, and Gallen showed up. They all had dead-fish handshakes, and you could tell they were all queer as fuck. Kline is married; who knows who is banging his old lady, but I am sure it's not him. I showed them all to Barry's room, fixed a few drinks, and then the last guests showed up, my idol Warren Beatty and Annette. He asked, "Are you Alan?"

"Yes," I said. "It's a pleasure to meet you both."

"I heard great things about you."

"Thank you," I said, and I put out my hand. Then I almost shit myself: what a pussy of a handshake. I almost broke his hand. I was crushed. I mean, come on, Warren Beatty—*Shampoo*, *Bonnie and Clyde*. He's supposed to have fucked half of Hollywood—and he did, only it was guys, not chicks. I couldn't believe it. Just ask Jane Fonda. She knows, to say the least. I was at a loss for words. I am sure he read my face. I took him to Barry's room, and then I served lunch.

Mr. Diller said to me, "We are not to be disturbed, and see to Mrs. Bening. Take her down to the beach."

I said, "Yes, sir," and he closed the door.

I headed back to the entry hall and greeted Mrs. Bening again. She said, "What are the boys doing?"

"They are in Mr. Diller's room, and I was told not to disturb them. I am to take care of you."

"Please, call me Annette." She was very pleasant.

"It's a beautiful day. Would you like to have lunch down on the beach?"

"Yes, that would be nice."

"I made some club sandwiches and soup, and I can serve you down on the beach."

She smiled at me and said, "Yes, that would be nice, Alan."

I took her down on the tram, gave her a towel and sunscreen, and took her lunch order. She wanted some iced tea and "what the boys are having," as she put it. She knew about these gay fucks, I am sure. I returned with her lunch, only to be surprised: she had her top off, and what a nice set of tits.

"Excuse me," I said.

"It's fine. You can bring my lunch over."

"Yes, ma'am."

"It's Annette."

"Fine."

I asked her if she needed something else, and she said, "No, I am fine."

"Yes, you are," I replied, and she laughed.

I turned away, and she said, "Alan, what are they up to back there?"

"I have no idea, but if I were Warren, I sure as hell would not be up there with those guys. I would be down here with you."

She smiled again and asked, "Are you gay?"

"No." I am sure she knew this, as I could not keep my eyes off her tits.

She then asked, "How long have you been here?"

"Just a few weeks."

She laughed and said, "That's a long time."

"Yes, I don't know how long I will be here."

"Alan, you can do better. Keep in touch," she said, and then she gave me her personal number.

I am sure that if the guys had not been up there talking, I would have fucked the shit out of her right there on the beach. She is one cool chick. I don't know what she is doing with Warren. The only thing I can think of is for appearances—what a waste of a really nice piece of ass and a nice chick as well.

The afternoon passed, and I brought Annette back on the tram and led her into the living room just as the boys were done with their meeting. Annette and I said our goodbyes, and then she told me to keep in touch. I said goodbye to all the guests and got one last handshake from Warren. I still can't believe it to this day. I have told that story a hundred times over the years. Now everyone can read about it. It's the truth. What would he be doing hanging out with all the gay fucks who like young boys if he was not taking it up the ass as well? From the way Annette looked at me, she was not getting any action.

I lost my respect for Warren that day. As for the rest of the guys, everyone knows they are gay as shit, so who gives a shit. They all left, and Barry said lunch was fine and he liked the soup. He told me he was going back to Beverly Hills and that I could take the night off. I had to carry his briefcase to the car for him, as he did not want to strain himself. It didn't upset me, though. I'd had a great day, staring at Annette's tits.

The house cleared out, and Queen Barry headed back to LA. I had survived the week and the first party. Man, did I need a drink, so I headed to Alice's. The other big story was, a week later, Keanu Reeves and the other queen, Geffen, met at the beach house. I was told to take the night off once I let them in and showed them to Barry's room. I was also told to make sure the hot tub was on and come back after midnight. I knew something was going on. I told Rob at Alice's about it, and he said I should have hidden in the bushes and taken a picture of them, that it would be worth some big money. I laugh now, but I wish I had. Keanu was on his way up, and I guess he had to give some ass up, or maybe he was gay as well. Who knows? Nothing in this town makes sense.

The only good thing about this job was that I was back in Malibu, and on my off days, I was working for Linda and her family. I liked them; Brandon and Brody were way cool, and I still saw the little Weintraub brats and Gersten's kids. But I knew this would not last, so I had better talk to Dora.

At about the time, I ran into a new agent. She was like Dora in many ways and had a nice agency as well, just not as big. It was called the Continental, and her name was Kathy. She got me a few gigs, as Dora thought

I was being fussy. I told her I was just trying to find a normal family to work for, but I guess that's just something you don't find in LA, especially in the entertainment business. I just kept my head down, saved a few more paychecks, and waited to see what would happen. I had to quit, but I wanted to line up a new gig first. I asked Linda, but she did not need me full time, and she did not have a guesthouse for me, either. I knew something would come up; it always had. I had a few bucks put away, so I would be ok till something good came along, but I was learning that there is no perfect job in this business. Either the wife is a bitch, the old man is a prick, the kids are little shits, or all of the above.

I thought about going back to the hotel business, but my ego would not let me do that. I had been cooking for all the A-listers and been on corporate jets, so going back to the hotel business and working with a bunch of losers wasn't an option anymore—fuck that. I would stay put. I still had some big plans, and I knew I could find a job better than this one.

I will say one thing about Barry: he knew everyone, or they knew him, from Murdock to Katzenberg to Eisner, all the heavy hitters. Except for Murdock, I think they all went both ways. I met Murdock at the beach house for lunch, and he was cool, self-made and not a guy to take lightly.

Barry had a lot of clout. I mean, the whole entertainment business is run by a bunch of dirty old gay fucks who fuck little boys, and if you want the job or to get ahead, give up the ass. Weintraub was the same way with the young actresses: "Read the script, and while you're at it, take down your pants or give me a blowjob." Look at Weinstein. It's the same shit, and it's been going on forever.

Now you know why I had to get out of the job. I mean, who in their right mind would put up with this shit? I knew my days were limited. Every day was like doing hard time. Just hearing his whiny voice was enough to make me want to put my Marine foot up his ass. My saving grace was helping Linda around the house and cooking for her, David, and the kids on my days off. Now, that was a normal family—if you take Bruce out of the picture. That is one weird motherfucker. I knew he was fucked up back then, and now what is he, transgender?

As you can see, I've got a hard-on for the shitheads, but I did meet and work for a few nice folks. I loved Linda and Mrs. Weintraub. I'd had some good times with them. Linda was fixing me up with some of her friends, married and single. I would cook for them, and the next thing I knew, I was like the American gigolo, banging all the old broads. They were in their fifties, and I was in my early thirties, so that was old for me. I got paid as well. I was having a ball, and once in a while, I would go see Emilia and bang her as well. Life was good, and Barry did not come to the beach house for a few weeks. He was in New York, which was great for me. I was out moonlighting, making extra money, living in Malibu rent-free and getting laid and paid.

I was becoming good friends with Linda—and David, too. They were not married yet, and I was spending a few days a week there doing stuff and cooking on my off days. I am sure a few of her friends said I was pretty good in the sack, as they all kept coming back. I had just dropped Brandy and Brody off at school and was putting the groceries away when Linda called me to help her in her bedroom.

"What do you need?" I asked.

"Can you zip me up in back?"

"Sure."

"I think it's stuck."

I walked over to zip her up, and she turned and let the dress hit the floor. She had no bra or panties on, and there was just a little thumbnail of hair above her pussy. She grabbed me, and I said, "Are we sure we should be doing this?"

Then she grabbed my cock, dropped to her knees, and gave me one of the best blowjobs I ever had. We must have fucked all afternoon. I had her every way I could. Man, was she great in the sack for an older broad. That was some good pussy. I will never forget that afternoon, and I still think about it. I still can't believe Bruce had that shit. Needless to say, this never happened again. I think she just wanted a young, hard dick, and I was the guy for the job, but I never saw her the same way again. Every time I saw David after that, I just smiled and thought, man, I had that ass as well. What a great feeling.

Life was great except for the shit I had to put up with at Barry's freak show. The good thing was that I knew my days were limited—the new agent from the Continental had something in the works. Barry had not been spending much time at the beach house; he had been in New York, hanging out with Von Furstenberg, I think. The two Miller sisters were coming to spend the day at the beach that Sunday, and I was to serve them lunch and drinks. I had little idea who these two chicks were till months later. I knew that one of the sisters, Pia, was marrying Christopher Getty, but I did not know anything about the other, Marie.

They were both rude and nasty. I knew who the Getty's were, but I'd never met Christopher. I felt sorry for the poor bastard. They were hot, but you know what they say: for every hot chick, there is a guy tired of fucking her. They're always a pain in the ass, and these two sisters had to be the biggest bitches I ever met. I am sure that if I had not quit the next week, I would have been fired. They thought they were so much better than anyone else. What a couple of losers. The only good thing was I got to see their tits, as they were just flaunting them—bought and paid for, of course. I heard later they both got divorced. I don't know how many times, but I am sure it was a few.

Christopher woke up and got rid of Pia. I think he got caught cheating. I am sure the pussy was no good. With those types, it never is. They were bred to marry money at all cost. Even though their old man was rich, it was all about image and money. They reminded me of Albert's old girlfriend. One of her friends had once told me that her mom had been prepping her to marry a rich guy since grade school. She was in beauty contests and all that shit. Then she told me that the girlfriend had fucked so many guys trying to get to the top that she did not even enjoy sex anymore. She just wanted the money. Man, is that shallow or what? I bet the same is true of the Miller sisters. I would love to have a beer with Christopher and ask, "Hey, how was Pia in bed?" I bet I am right.

Finally, after a long day, the two pains-in-the-ass were on their way back to LA as if they had not ruined my day enough. Just plain nasty chicks. It's true—money can't bring you happiness, and I am sure these two have no friends. By that, I mean true friends, not the ones who hang around with them to make them feel big, like they are someone special. I would never see them again—thank God for that—or Queen Barry either. I was out of there. I had an interview with a big developer the next day in Brentwood. The guy's name was Richard Selby. I was told the job was mine if I wanted it. I was not worried about giving Barry notice. Guys like that just fire you on the spot when you quit. Plus, he was a prick.

Selby's house was in Brentwood. I'd never worked there before, or for a developer, but he had a bad-ass house around the corner from OJ's old place. We had a cup of coffee, and he asked why I was leaving Mr. Diller. I thought long and hard before I answered. Then I just said, "It's his lifestyle. I don't like being around him. He looked at me long and hard."

"That's what I thought," he said. "I have heard that about him and his perv buddies. I think all of LA knows. They just don't want to say anything."

"You got the picture."

We both laughed. Then he said, "Over here, there will be nothing but hot chicks. I have some good friends, and we have a few parties a month, ten guests max for dinner and maybe a big one every few months, but then we will hire a caterer and staff. I would want you to supervise."

He showed me the guest house, and he had a Suburban for me to drive. "How does a grand a week sound to start?"

"Sounds great."

"When can you start?"

"I will give Mr. Diller notice tomorrow, and I am sure he will fire me on the spot and tell me to be off the property. I need a few days off so I can get organized again, and I can start next Monday. We can work out a schedule and the rest of the job duties."

"Great. I look forward to having you working for me. We're going to have a great time, and you will like my friends. They're all nice people."

We exchanged cell numbers, and I said, "I have to get back to Malibu."

"Here are the keys to the guesthouse and the gate codes. Move in whenever you want. Just call me and give me the heads up when you are coming."

"Sounds great."

This sounded like a cool gig, and he seemed like a nice guy. He was a bachelor, and we were about the same age. He might have had a few years on me. Not many, but a few. He was also a good-looking guy and a very smart businessman.

I returned to Malibu to pack my stuff up and give the queen notice. What a relief. I was so glad to be done with this job. I did not have a lot of stuff at Barry's, so it was a quick pack. Then, after calling Barry in the morning, I headed off to Alice's for a drink with Rob.

I had already called the new agent, and she was happy, too. She said that Mr. Selby really liked me and was looking forward to me working for him.

I told Rob about the new job. He picked up my first round, and we bashed Diller's ass and had a few laughs. The next morning, I called Barry's secretary and gave her my notice. Just as I thought she would, she said, "He is in New York, but you need to be out by tomorrow.

"Sure thing." I knew he was a prick.

I thought I would drop my stuff off at the new guest house and head to the desert till next week. I called Mr. Selby, told him what had happened, and he said, "Great. I will see you next Monday."

"Yes, sir, and I will be dropping a few things off at the guest house before I head to the desert."

"No problem. Have a great weekend. What a nice guy."

Just like that, I was on to a new chapter and living in Brentwood. That was a first. And on top of that, I had a great new boss. Thank God. I needed a break from working for assholes.

Dinner in LA

Chicago vacation, when fur coats where in.

Chef, Sam Behrens , Shari Belafonte, friend Sherwood CC

Chef and John Weintraub's old butler, Lake Tahoe

Chapter 12

RICHARD SELBY
THE DEVELOPER

AFTER A FEW DAYS IN the desert, I had a new outlook and was excited about the new job. I just needed a few days to relax and enjoy the time off. I loved that house in La Quinta.

What a great place to just chill and recharge. Though the summers are hot, it's hard to beat the weather there in the winter. I just hung out by the pool and relaxed—a nice way to spend the weekend. Before starting the new job, I had a good feeling about this guy.

I got up early Monday and headed to LA. Traffic always sucks on the Ten. I called Rick to tell him I was on the way, and he said, "Make yourself at home, and I will see you for dinner. Pick up some fish."

"I've got it covered. See you for dinner."

I had never heard of Rick until the interview. The agent had told me he was a big-time real estate developer in LA, had a good reputation, and was a playboy and nice guy to work for. I cooked some salmon, wild rice, and veggies, and he was impressed. I forgot to say he was a bachelor, never married, and enjoying life to the fullest. He had a nice Benz and a bad-ass house in Brentwood with tennis courts—he was an avid player—and pool like you'd find in a hotel. I joined him for dinner that night, and we talked about what he wanted me to do for him. It was pretty much what I had been doing at my last jobs, taking care of the cars, running errands, shopping, overseeing the gardeners and housekeepers, taking care of the estate, and cooking.

I liked this guy. He was easy to talk to, and he had some class, unlike Diller. He was a real ladies' man, tall and good looking, and he knew how to dress. This was going to be a good fit. I could tell right away, and he felt the same way. We shared a bottle of wine as we talked. He told me he liked to eat healthy, lots of fish, greens, salads, and grains. I told him that was how I ate and we would get along fine. He was in great shape; you could tell he took care of himself. I liked that, as I have always stayed in shape.

As it turned out, I worked for him for a few years. The only reason I left was that he got a girlfriend, a serious one, and she was a royal bitch. She only wanted Rick because he had money, a real LA gold digger. Trish was her name, hot as balls, just a royal pain in the ass.

Rick was one of the best guys I ever worked for. He enjoyed life and took care of himself. He didn't not a lot of drugs. Some of his friends smoked a little weed, but they were mostly drinkers. They were cool guys, too, all business owners, brokers, and attorneys. Sometimes I wish I would have taken a different path, but I had a good run, made ok money, got to see the world, and had some great times and met some great people. I met some assholes, too, but that is life. You cannot live it looking in the rear-view mirror.

Rick and I hit it off from the first week, and we soon got into a routine. Every Friday was happy hour at the house. A few of his friends would stop by sometimes, some girl,s or his neighbors, OJ Simpson, Sugar Ray Leonard, or Arnold Schwarzenegger. If girls were coming over, Arnie would be there for sure, as he was a whore dog in a good way. He came by quite often. He and Rick were pretty good friends, as they both had houses in Sun Valley and liked to ski.

I would always have some appetizers for the guests, and I'd make my kick-ass margaritas and guacamole sliders. I looked forward to these little events. Everyone had a great time. Afterward, they would go home and clean up, and then they'd all go to a club or dinner, or I might cook for the guys and a few of the girls. Once a month, Rick would have a party, not crazy, just ten to twenty guests—tho9ugh he had a few parties a year with over a hundred guests. I would hire staff and caterers for those. Rick was cool about that and did not mind spending money. I liked that about him; he was not cheap.

My job was pretty basic. I oversaw the gardeners, pool guy, and house-keepers, made sure Rick's Benz was detailed once a week and gassed up, did all the grocery shopping, made sure the bar was stocked, and just made sure the house was in good order.

After a few months, Rick and I became better friends. He took a liking to me, and we had a good working relationship. I started helping out at the office, filing paperwork, running errands, picking up and dropping off plans, and going to his attorney's office. He paid me a little extra for this, and it got me out of the house. I also got to wear my nice suits. He liked that I was a sharp dresser.

On top of that, I was meeting the girls at the office, and I started banging one. Before I asked her out, I asked Rick, and he said, "Cool, go for it." Rick was a class act. He never fooled around with any of the chicks at the office, and there were some hot ones, and I am sure he could have fucked any of them if he'd wanted. Me, I just sacked Becky for a while. She was a hot Valley girl in her late twenties with a rockin' body. She loved to do it rodeo style, and man, she rocked my world. I would tell Rick stories, and he loved that sort of shit.

This was a great job, and I was having fun again. I did miss hanging out at the beach in Malibu with friends, and I hoped I might get to throw one more shot into Linda, but it never happened. Then she married David Foster. They offered me a job to work for them and run their new Malibu estate, but I turned them down, as Rick was a nice guy, the job was pretty easy, and I could never look at Linda the same way after fucking her that one day. On top of all this, I was treated well by Rick and his friends and getting used to living in Brentwood. Going to Venice and Santa Monica Beach was not bad, either. Becky and I were starting to become an item, too, so life was good for the time being.

Our first big event arrived, the annual YPO celebration. I think Rick was the president or something like that, but he hosted the party every year. There were 150 guests, and we had valet parking and caterers—I oversaw the whole thing. I liked that, running the show. This was not your typical LA party, with drugs, hookers, and wannabe actors, where everyone's full of shit and themselves as well. These were all professionals, no one you would know unless you were doing business in LA, builders, owners of companies, that sort of thing. You always get a few pricks and bitches who think, because they have money, their shit don't stink, but all of Rick's good friends were nice. I have learned that nice folks usually don't have assholes for friends, and if they do, they will tell you he is an asshole but is their attorney or doctor or some shit like that.

The party went off flawlessly, and Rick was happy. He gave me a few days off and a nice tip. Rick was a popular guy around LA and making a lot of money, and a lot of people at the party kissed his ass. I am sure they wanted to do business with him, which is just how it is, tit for tat. After the party, Rick and I had a few drinks together. He told me, Thanks for the hard work. You did a great job." Then he gave me one of the best compliments I ever got from a boss: "You looked like a YPO member, not the guy running the party."

"Thanks," I said. "That means a lot."

"Take a few days off. Go down to the beach and hang out. Use my cabana at the Santa Monica Beach Club and have some drinks and lunch on my tab."

That was cool of him. The next day, I headed down to the Santa Monica Beach Club. It was a pretty swank place and had a great restaurant. I'd been there with Rick and the guys but never on my own. They treated me like a member. Rick had called ahead, I am sure, and told them to hook me up.

Most of the guests there were snobs. If you live in LA, you know the place and what kind of assholes go there—lots of movie types doing deals and having meetings—but still, it was cool for me. I just hung out, drank some beer, had a nice lunch of oysters on the half shell, Champagne, and a nice piece of fish, worked on my tan, and watched all the hot chicks come in and out. They were way out of my league. This was what I call living: you got a towel boy and your own cabana waiter.

I hung out there the whole day and then headed over to Gladstone's for happy hour, an LA landmark and great place to watch girls, have a few more oysters, and pound down a few beers. It's right on the water and a cool place. I talked to a few chicks and waited for my girl to show up. Becky arrived and had a glass of white wine, as always.

I said, "I missed you. The last few days, I've been busy with the party."

"I know," she replied.

We had a few drinks and decided to go back to her apartment. It was close in Santa Monica. I said, "I have tomorrow off, too."

"Great. Let's get out of here."

I knew she was horny, as I had not seen her in a week.

We headed back to her place, and not even five minutes later, we were at the rodeo, if you know what I mean. I just love young chicks. They are always so horny and ready to fuck. The old broads, you've got to get lubed up, and they never get wet. These young chicks, you just reach down there, and that thing is sopping wet. You gotta love that.

We had crazy sex all night and in the morning, too. Then she had to get to work, and I needed to get to the gym and check on Rick to make sure he was ok. So, we had coffee together, and then I bent her over the kitchen table and gave her one more orgasm. She left with a smile on her face, and me as well. What a great few days off.

I hit the gym and then went back to the house to enjoy the rest of my day off. I needed to get some rest after a hard night of fucking. She'd worn me out; I liked that about Becky. I called and checked on Rick to make sure he was good. He said he was and to enjoy the day off. Then he asked how the club was.

"It was a great day, and they treated me well," I said.

"Great," he replied. "I will see you tomorrow. I need you at the office, and let's have fish tomorrow night."

"Cool. Have a great day, and I will see you tomorrow."

Next, I headed to Venice beach to watch all the weirdos, get some sun, go for a run on the beach, and just chill. If you've been to Venice, you know what I mean. It's one of the best places to people-watch. You will see everything—just some weird shit there.

This was my life for the next two years. I banged Becky all this time.

The job was great, and I got into a nice routine, skiing Sun Valley a few times a year and cooking for Arnie on my days off. I won't bore you with the daily shit at the house and the YPO parties. Instead, I will tell you about Arnie and the nasty Maria Shriver

Arnie would sometimes stop by for the happy hour parties on Friday, along with OJ and Sugar Ray. They were all nice guys, but OJ, talk about arrogant and a real piece of shit. Well, we all know that now. He is the kind of guy who, as soon as you leave the room, if you have a white wife, especially a blond, you can bet he'll hit on her. The man had no class, and on top of that, he is a murderer. Arnie and Sugar Ray were the total opposite, both classy and nice guys. Don't get me wrong—Arnie was no angel when it came to women, but he would never hit on another man's wife or date, and neither would Ray.

After meeting Maria, I knew why Arnie cheated on her. She was right up there with all the king bitches I worked with, nasty, and I am sure the pussy was cold. Poor Arnie was fucking the housekeeper even back then, a cute little Latina chick. Believe me, if you'd met her, you would feel sorry for Arnie, as he was a nice guy and deserved better than that. I would not wish that kind of shit on my worst enemy.

I would come over to the house every few weeks and work for them on my off days, run a few errands, get the Hummer, Ferrari, and Maria's Benz detailed, do the shopping, and cook dinner. Arnie always tipped me well and gave me Cubans all the time. Rick was cool with me making a few extra bucks, and they were friends. We went skiing together in Sun Valley. Rick had a condo there. The first year I went there, it was with Rick and a few of his pals. They took me to cook, bartend, and lug all the ski shit. I was cool with that, and I got a few days of skiing in as well. Sun Valley is still one of my favorite mountains to ski and a great little town. There are a few too many stars there for me, like Aspen, but not quite as bad. I had a great time every year. I just tried not to get caught up in the bullshit.

Rick and his pals were all good skiers, and all they wanted to do was ski, party, and get laid in that order—not a bad plan. These guys had chicks every night in the hot tub. Man, I envied these guys, all young, rich, good looking, and getting tons of hot pussy. What else is there in life? I mean, if you've got money, the hot chicks come. I don't care who says differently. They're full of shit and only kidding themselves. All hot chicks want a dude with money. They don't want to work; they want to sleep in, spend your cash, and maybe give you a blowjob once in a while. It's true; ask around, or maybe you know first-hand what I am talking about.

We went for a week at a time and might do two trips a season, depending on the snow and Rick's work, but it was always a great time, skiing with the guys, hanging out with Arnie, and cooking for the whole gang. Plus, I cannot forget all the hot chicks in the hot tub with their tops off.

I met Arnie's personal ski instructor and long-time friend from back in Austria. His name was Audie. I can't remember his girlfriend's name. She was American and very nice. Both were great skiers. Audie was a great carpenter and did a lot of work on Arnie's home and his office in Venice. The house looked like something out of an Austrian fairy tale. It was pretty sweet, and everything was imported. I got the tour with Arnie, and I will never forget that day.

Audie and I became pretty good friends, and when he came to LA the next summer, we hooked up and went out for drinks and a nice dinner. We always had a good time together. I also liked his girlfriend, first class, not like these chicks in LA.

Rick and I were becoming good friends, and I was accepted into the gang. We had a lot of good times, from going to clubs to skiing in Sun Valley, and there was always lots of hot ass around for the taking. The last few days in Sun Valley, the guys rested up and got ready to go back to LA and work after a week of drinking, hard-core skiing, and fucking. I was the only sober one, and I did bang some of the stray leftovers. One of the best things about being a private chef for the rich and famous is that you kind of live that life but on their dime. Not a bad gig. I mean, you have to put up with a little shit now and then, but at the end of the day, it's a job with some nice perks.

The first Christmas with Rick was cool. I spent two with him before the dumb-ass broad fucked my shit up. We had a small party at the house for office staff and a few of his pals. I did a nice buffet with apps, the whole deal, prime rib sliders, roast potatoes, Caesar salad, and roasted veggies. It was a nice spread, with some very nice wine and a full open bar. Rick was impressed. I went all out.

After the guests had left and while the staff was cleaning up, Rick said, "Come to my office. I want to talk to you."

I thought, shit, did I fuck up? Am I getting fired?

When I got there, to my surprise, he pulled out the Louis 14th for a Christmas toast and handed me a small present in a box. "Open it now," he said.

I opened it, and inside was a watch. I'd never heard of the brand: it was a stainless-steel Breitling Colt Chronograph with a blue sapphire face. Rick knew I did not have a nice watch, and he was a watch guy. He said, "If you're going to hang out with the gang, you need a nice watch."

"I don't know what to say."

"You earned it. Merry Christmas."

I will never forget that night, the watch, the Louis—it was a great Christmas. Ever since that night, I've been a watch guy. I still have the Colt today, and it's still a classy timepiece, thirty years later. Thanks, Rick. You are the man. Wherever you are today, you are a prince. I will never forget our talks and your business and real estate advice.

Next stop, Cabo San Lucas. I'd been there before with Albert, but Rick said he was planning a fishing trip, guys only, in February and wanted me to come and cook for the guys and take care of the gang. I said, "Sure! I would love to. Cool."

"I am putting the trip together, renting a big sport fisher and a few villas. I will work it out where you can stay on the boat or get you your own room at one of the villas. It will be a six-day trip."

"I am good to go," I said. That was how he rolled.

I liked Cabo. It was cool back then; now it's too commercial. It's like LA. Everyone is from Southern California, and it's filled with working girls.

The Cabo trip would be in February, and until then, I helped out at the office and went to Arnie's every week or two to cook and help them out. I was also still banging Becky, the Valley girl from the office, so life was good. Nothing new with Arnie; it was still the same old shit. Maria was just as nasty as ever, and he was still banging the staff—and I am sure anyone else he could find to fuck, poor guy. I turned them down a few times. I'd say, "Arnie, I love cooking for you. Let me know when you get rid of the bitch, and I will work for you. Otherwise, please don't ask me again."

He'd say, "That's fair." He liked how I was so upfront. I've always been like that, even today. Don't ask me what I think, because you might not like it. The truth is hard to deal with. Arnie was miserable for many years, and it still cost him millions. Rick was paying me well, and I really didn't need the extra cash, but it was nice hanging out with Arnie, and I liked having some pocket money. We did one more ski trip the next year, and then I never saw Arnie again after I left Rick. That was history.

Rick was busy with work, always working on a new project. When the fishing trip drew near, we had a pre-party at the house for the guys to go over the plan and the trip: girls, fishing, dinner, clubs, all that stuff. I helped set up dinner reservations and club VIP passes. I always took care of that stuff. Rick would say, "Just make it happen," and I did. I had all the best restaurants and hottest clubs on speed dial, and they all knew me from working for Weintraub, Albert, Art—the list was pretty impressive. Rick liked that about me. I had some bad-ass shit going on. Ivy, Dan Tana's, Wolfgang's, Valentino's—I'd just pick up the phone and make the call, and I could always get a table. Not bad for a high school dropout from Ohio.

The pre-party was at the house, and the guys were ready to go fishing, making bets on who would get the biggest tuna and the hottest chick. Rick's friends were as bad as balls. The Three Kingsmen, I called them. What a bunch of crazy fucks—in a good way. I wish I had their money, but I'd taken a different path. I felt out of my league. I mean, I was making sixty grand a year, had a house in the desert, and had just bought a lot in Breckenridge, Colorado, for thirty-three thousand, so I was ok, just no millionaire. These guys were all making big-league cash, but now I know it's all relative.

They all got a buzz on, and then I drove the gang to go clubbing, and we made the rounds. One more crazy night in the books.

Then came the Cabo trip. A few days before the gang arrived, I flew down to get the boat and villas all set up with food, booze, that sort of stuff, and meet the boat Capitan. This was not my first trip to Cabo, so I knew my way around. I got all my shit done in one day, buying fresh fruit, breakfast stuff, plenty of beer, tequila for margaritas, chips, avocados, all the basic stuff. Then I headed to the marina to meet the captain and buy some things for the boat, like beer and all that sort of shit. The guys were going to fish for just three days. One day would be a golf outing, and the rest of the time, they'd just lie by the pool and pick up girls.

By the end of the first day, I was looking good. All my shit was in order, so I could go out and get a little crazy before the guys came. I knew I would have a busy week, but I would stay an extra day when they left, so that was cool.

I treated myself to a nice dinner and headed into town to see what kind of trouble I could get into. Cabo has some great restaurants if you like Mexican food and fish. After dinner, I went to Cabo Wabo, Hagar's place, to see if I could grab something to go, if you know what I mean. I headed to the bar, grabbed a cold one, and started scoping the place out, looking for what I could pick up and take back to the villas for the night. It did not take too long. I had a few dances with a chick from the Valley I bought a shot for and two of her girlfriends as well. It was like shooting fish in a barrel. After a few shots and some dances, I dropped the bomb: "Let's get out of here and take a dip in the hot tub." She loved the idea, so we said goodbye to her friends and were off. I still got that swagger and plenty of game in the tank.

We went back to the villas, got undressed, and had a drink in the tub. What a great set of tits, all natural. You have to love the young chicks, with their hard asses and perky tits, and they love to do the wild thing. We did it in the hot tub, the kitchen, all over. She had one hell of a buzz on, and I did as well. We had sex a good part of the night and in the morning as well. Just like Becky, she could not get enough.

I fixed her breakfast, we went at it one more time, and then I took her back to her hotel. After exchanging phone numbers, we shared a little moment, and she said, "I had a great time. Let's get together and do this again."

"Sure, I would like that. See you back in LA." She was going to Cal State Northridge.

We said our goodbyes, and then I went back to the villas to lay by the pool and rest up for the busy week ahead. Wow, what a great fucking night. Great dinner, a hot piece of ass, what could be better? The trip was off to a great start. I hung out by the pool the whole day, resting up and getting some sun. Man, she was a hot little spinner. I did my rounds later that afternoon to make sure the guys' rooms were all set up. Then I checked the flight and at the front desk to make sure they had a driver to take me to the airport. The flight was on time, the driver was lined up, the dinner reservation was set, and everything looked good. Rick and the boys would be happy.

I headed to the airport to pick up the guys, and they were glad to see me. "Chef, we got beers?"

"Of course. I've got it all set up for you guys."

When we got to the resort, the guys were doing shots and drinking beer before they'd even unpacked. Rick and I went over the schedule for the next week.

The first night, I cooked for the guys, and they didn't get too wild; they knew they had to be up early, as we were going fishing, and they did not want to get sick out there on the water. I prepared one of my great Mexican buffets, beans, rice, fresh beef fajitas. The guys were happy, and they all turned in early, as we had to be at the boat at six the next few days.

The next morning, I was up early, making box lunches, icing down the beer, and loading the van up, and then we were on our way to the marina to meet Captain Jeff, aka the Colonel, and the '72 custom Cabo, *Boomer*.

What a nice boat. I had met the Colonel a few trips back, as he was friends with Albert and he'd used him a few times. He was a great guy and one hell of a fisherman.

We loaded up and were underway with the help of the mate, FT, better known as Fat Bastard, and yes, he was, but one hell of a first mate. It was a beautiful morning. I always liked the Pacific. The water is almost always calm, with great tuna and marlin fishing, which was what we were looking for. Plus, we had a few extra guests, some hot Mexican hookers— what a great way to go fishing. We hadn't even left the dock before beers were cracked open and Bloody Marys and shots were flowing. Man, these guys knew how to do it right.

The Colonel hooked them up with a school of tuna right before noon, and the boys caught a few nice ones. Then we went to find some marlins. Meanwhile, the girls were doing body shots in nothing but G-strings, and blowjobs were for the taking. I said, "I will have one of those, and Rick said, "Go for it." A few of the guys spilled their lunch, if you know what I mean.

We cruised around for a while, and then all hell broke loose when we hooked a big marlin. Rick took the chair for an hour of fighting and brought home a five-hundred-pound fish. Then it was time to head home, with some nice tuna for dinner and bragging rights on the marlin for Rick.

When we returned to the villas, everyone was drunk. The chicks came back, too, and we all had our way with them and then some. The great thing about hookers is you don't pay them to stay; you pay them to leave. The guys took a nap while I got dinner ready, as they were all pretty pissed. They decided to stay in that night, as we were going fishing tomorrow as well.

I cooked some black and blue tuna, garlic mashed potatoes, black beans, and roasted red pepper salsa, a nice spread, and the boys killed it. Then they sat around bullshitting about the one hooker's nipples, which were the size of silver dollars. Rick said, "What a day. Let's go back out tomorrow, but let's leave the strippers home and get some fresh ones tomorrow night." The gang agreed, and then we all turned in. One more for the record books.

The next day was pretty much the same. The boys were not that hungover, and no one got sick on the boat. We had a fresh couple of strippers, which always makes for a great boat ride. Throw in a few fish and beer, and it was the perfect day. Nobody caught a marlin, but they did get a few more tuna and some wahoo.

They guys were a little tame. Rick said, "Save it for tonight, as we are going clubbing." We got back around sunset, and I told the Colonel I would be back tomorrow with his tip and to settle up for the beer. I had already taken care of the strippers. We kept some fish and gave the rest to the boat.

Back at the villas, I had the night off. It was our last night, and they would all leave tomorrow afternoon. I would leave the day after, as I had to take care of a few last-minute check-out items. Rick was taking all of us to dinner, and then the guys were going out hunting for the last night. I told him I would pass on the clubbing, as I had to drive to the airport the next day and help the guys pack, but I would join for dinner. I fixed up some nice ceviche and cocktails before dinner, and the guys all reflected on the week and made a toast to Rick, great boss and one hell of a cool guy.

Sometimes I wish I had gone a different path in my career. Chefs don't make the big money, and I was always a little insecure around these guys. They all had money, beach houses, Benzes, and tons of hot ass, although I got my share of ass, too, so I cannot cry about that. I was always in good shape and had great health and not much stress, and I had places in the desert and Breckenridge, Colorado, more than the average fuck, so life was not all that bad.

We had a great dinner, and Rick took care of the tab. Then I dropped the boys off at Cabo Wabo downtown and headed back to the villas to take care of business.

From the sounds that night and into the next morning, they had one hell of a last night. I am sure no one got much sleep from all the fucking and drinking going on. They picked up a batch of college chicks from Michigan who wanted to let their hair down—as well as their panties. That's what they do in Cabo on spring break. I got to see a few of the chicks in the hot tub, and they all had nice tits and asses. I needed a break, as I'd fucked the shit out of the strippers the last few days and was tired. It's hard to believe, me turning down hot ass, but I had a busy day, and it was hard to sleep with all that shit going on.

Morning rolled around, and I fixed breakfast for the whole gang, chicks as well. They were all pretty beaten up from the drinking and the hard fucking the boys had given them. After they'd eaten, I sent the chicks in a cab back to their hotel, and the guys packed and talked about how horny these young Midwest chicks are. I said, "I know. I grew up in Ohio."

We headed to the airport, and on the way, Rick asked how I was on petty cash. I said I was low, and he gave me five hundred dollars to take care of the staff and the Colonel. I got the boys to the airport just in time. They were still drunk from last night, and they all high-fived me and said thanks for a great time. Then Rick said, "I will see you in a few days," and thanked me, too. What a way to end a perfect trip. The guys had plenty of fishing and fucking. I was glad just to be along for the ride, and I got a free trip again as well.

I headed back to the villas with my list of things to do and people to see and pay. As soon as I got back, I cracked open a cold one and started on my list. I had some time to kill, so I decided to hang by the pool, work on my tan, and see if there was any leftover pussy to be had. At the end of the day, I had to meet the Colonel; he was out on a charter with some LA stars. I took care of all the hotel staff and the bill with Rick's card and arranged a ride to the airport for tomorrow. They were all happy at the big fat tips I gave them. Me, I was loving life. I got some sun and had a fantastic lunch, large shrimp right off the grill and a top-shelf margarita—is there any other kind.

I hung out by the pool, checking all the ass out. It was all couples—no loose stuff running around, or I would have grabbed it. My last stop was to meet the Colonel at the boat at the end of the day to square up and say goodbye, and we might have a few beers together.

In the afternoon, I finished packing and was off to the marina to meet Colonel. When I arrived, I saw John Travolta walking off the boat with some young kid, and they were pretty close. He acted like he did not see me, but I called out, "Hey, John. Chef Al from Weintraub's." I'd met him a few times at Jerry's house in Malibu, and I'd fixed him lunch at the Warner Brothers lot a few times. He said a quick hello and then gave me the dead-fish handshake. I knew there was something weird about him, besides the Scientology shit. I had a feeling he was playing both sides. I hate to ruin it for you girls, but it's true—one dead fish. He doesn't introduce me to the young kid—barely legal, by the way—and just rushed off.

The Colonel walked up and said, "What was that all about?"

"I know John from LA and was just saying hi."

"Shit, I did not know that."

"Yeah, I know a lot of these fucks. They're all full of themselves and mostly assholes. I've been working in LA off and on for over eight years now."

He asked about Travolta, and I said, "I think he goes both ways. I know he likes young men."

He looked at me and said, "Yeah, that's what I thought."

The two fucks never came out of the master till the end of the charter. I am sure someone was getting their ass pounded.

As for the Colonel and me, we pounded down beers, had a shot of Don Julio, and laughed at Hollywood assholes. Living a double life—I never got that. If your gay, that's cool. Just don't get married and try to pass yourself off as some great dad and think you're all of that when you are really just one fucked-up dude. Don't get me started.

The Colonel could not stop laughing. He said, "Chef Al, you are one crazy fuck, and I mean that in a good way. You call them like you see them. That's what I like about you. Must be the Marine in you."

"Yeah, let's have one more shot and a beer and go get some dinner. I have to be in LA tomorrow."

"Cool. Dinner's on me. Let's hit it."

I helped wash the boat down, and then we were out of there. We headed to these little taco dive in the marina and had some fresh fish, great beans and rice, and the coldest beer in Cabo. As we ate, we told a few stories, talked about shit, and laughed at Travolta and his little boyfriend, whose ass was probably sore as fuck. I will never forget that night. We drank a shitload of beer and talked for hours. It was a great last night in Cabo.

After we were good and hammered, we said our goodbyes. "One more shot"—I must have heard that ten times that night, but you never say no to the Colonel. I made it home alive, and yes, I made the flight the next day. Thank God it was an afternoon flight.

I was back in LA that night. Rick was glad to see me, and he asked me how I was and if I'd taken care of all the folks down there, and I said I had. He told me this was his last big show, as he was getting serious with a girl, and I could hear wedding bells and my great job coming to a screeching halt.

"Take a few days off and rest up," he said. "You look like shit."

"Yeah, I know. Me and the Colonel hit it hard last night."

"I can tell. Get some rest. I am glad you had a great time." He was cool with shit like that. I knew the line and never crossed it with Rick; that's why we got along.

I took a few days off and hung out at Santa Monica Beach. I also got back with my girl for some make-up sex; that's always a good thing. Rick was planning a ski trip with the new girl and wanted me to go and cook and take care of them while they were there. Arnie was going to meet them up there and have dinner one night as well. This would be my last trip to Sun Valley and with Rick. The friendship was still good, but the job was not the same with the new girlfriend. What a bitch. I don't know what he saw in her. I think he wanted kids and a trophy wife, you know, LA lifestyle, the perfect couple, and all she wanted was the money. I am sure she fucked his socks off for the first few years and then nothing, not even a blowjob. That's how it is. Ask any guy who's been there. It's the same shit every time.

I did the ski trip, saw Arnie again, and we went skiing together. I cooked some great dinners, and it turned out to be a nice trip. I would miss Sun Valley. I'd had a great run with this guy, went on some fun trips and made lots of good friends along the way, but I knew it was coming to an end.

When we got back to LA, Rick invited Audie down to LA to stay a few days, and I drove them around LA and to Arnie's office, where he had to do some carpentry work. This was down by the beach in Santa Monica, where Arnie had started at the gym in Venice Beach. We all had lunch that day at Wolfgang's place.

After lunch, I took them to the airport, and then I returned to Rick's to plan my next move. The new wife was moving in that weekend, and I had to help. What a bunch of shit. I told Rick that and I was not happy, and he said, "Just chill. It will be cool. I will talk to her, and don't worry. I don't want you to leave."

I agreed to give her a chance, and we shook hands.

Things didn't go well. Rick threw me under the bus. I am sure he didn't do it on purpose; she was just a real bitch and wanted to have things her way, and I hated taking orders from a money-grubbing bitch. I knew the days were limited. I just needed a plan if the worst happened. I had plenty of cash socked away, so I could go to the desert and chill till a new gig came along. I'd had a great run with Rick, but it was time to move on. No more Friday happy hour parties with Arnie and the gang. No more guys' night out, clubbing. It was all over. Poor bastard Rick was about to have his nuts cut off. That was on him. I wouldn't be around to watch it.

A few days passed, and she called me into the living room to have a talk and go over next week's plans for a party and my schedule. She had told Rick she needed me at the house and I should not be going to the office. There were things she wanted me to do for her that would keep me busy. She wanted me to drive her once in a while and help with changing things around the house. Then she said I would be reporting to her and not Rick. They were not even married yet.

I tried to control myself, but I could not. She asked me if I had any questions and if she'd made herself clear, and I said, "Yes, I understand, and you can find someone else to wipe and kiss your ass. I am done, effective now."

She did not know what to say, as if I were going to let her walk all over me. I stood and said, "Now, do you have anything else for me? I have to see Rick at the office and give him my keys and say goodbye. Have a nice day."

She had no comeback for that.

By the time I got to the office, she had already called Rick. She said

I'd called her a bunch of names and she'd had to fire me, and I should not be getting any severance pay or reference. Rick knew the truth. He knew I would not do that, though the thought did cross my mind, and she deserved it. I just told him that I could not work for her and we could not work it out.

Rick said, "Let's go have a farewell lunch at the club. I will take the rest of the day off, and we will hang out like old times."

We headed to a club in Santa Monica, had a great lunch and a few drinks, and talked about the ski trips, the last trip to Cabo, and all the good times and pussy we'd had. He said he would miss me and was sorry it didn't work out, but he was in love. I mean, what do you say to that?

I told him what I felt, as we were close. "I think she just wants your money and the status of being with you and getting into the inner circle."

"I know," he said. "I just want her for the ass and maybe a few good-looking kids. I have to admit, she is one hot piece of ass, and she fucks like a champ and gives it to me whenever I want it and however I want it."

"Fair enough. All the best to you, then. I will miss you and the gang. It's been great working for you, and I will never forget all the good times."

We laughed and threw back a few more beers, and then Rick asked, "What's your plan?"

"I'll head to the desert and take a few weeks off. Then I'll look for another Rick to go to work for."

He laughed. "I will give you a great reference. Don't worry about it. I might know a friend in Newport who might want you. I will check it out and let you know what he says. Go to the desert and get some fresh ass."

"That's the plan."

"I will tell everyone at the office you said goodbye, and if you are in town, stop by anytime. They all like you. I know Becky will miss you." I had quit fucking her a while ago after we had a little falling out, but we were still friends—kind of.

We said our goodbyes, and I was off to the desert.

I had a great time with Rick and met some of LA's business elite. It was a hell of a run, but all good things come to an end, and I always come out smelling like a rose.

I hung out at my place, got some fresh ass, played some golf, and waited for Rick to talk to his friend in Newport. I had plenty of money socked away and a rental property, and my car was paid, so I was doing ok. Plus, I was still in demand and had a good reputation in some circles. In others, not so good, especially if I had fucked the boss's wife, girlfriend, daughter, or all of them. I had no shame.

Dinner Party Pacific Palisades

Last Call Tony G and the gang. Atlantis 2

Chef and Sam, Riviera CC. LA

Saunders Ritz Carlton, Palm Beach

The Boys Vero Beach

Vacation in Ohio. Mom, favorite cousin Lisa, and Roger.

Chapter 13

GOODBYE, LA

THAT WAS MY LAST FULL-TIME job in LA. I had, had enough of the rich bitches and celebrities, who were so full of themselves, and all the money-hungry whores, and I couldn't wait for Rick to get back to me about his friend in Newport.

Throughout my years in LA, I remained friends with Sam and Shari. We played golf regularly, and I would get work from them once in a while. We had a lot of good times and became very good friends. I miss those days. They were a lot of fun and treated me well. I did a birthday party for Shari's dad one year, the legendary Harry Belafonte, what a great guy, and her mother was there, too. They were both very nice. I wish I had taken more pictures back then, but I had no idea that I would be writing this twenty-five years later.

Back then, Shari and Sam lived in the Valley, in a nice house up in the hills, I think Sherman Oaks. I did a buffet for the party and made my famous seafood salad, with all the best seafood poached with my you-make-me-crazy sauce. It was always a hit, and Shari loved it. So did Harry. I got to meet the whole family, and it was truly a fun event.

That's when I met Shari's half-sister, Gina. Why do I always get the sisters? Gina was hot, with a great ass, and she loved to do the wild thing. I banged her off and on for a few months. She was busy as shit. I think she had a gig on the old *Hill Street Blues* drama back in the day. Shari was cool with it. She and Sam really liked me, and I liked them as well. She hooked me up.

After I left LA, I never saw them again.

They came down to the desert once, Gina as well, and spent the weekend. We played golf, hung out on El Paseo Drive, and lay by my pool, and the two sisters had their tops off. Sam said, "Now there are two nice sets of tits," and he was right. They both had nice racks. I will never forget that. Sam was cool as shit. Sam, this one's for you. You are the man and the best in my book. Love you, man. That was the last time they came to the desert. I miss those days.

Here is the shortest job I ever had, about two weeks. What an asshole, one of the worst. The estate was in Beverly Hills, on the same street where Jimmy Stewart lived, and the turd's name was Henri Lazarof. He was some famous Bulgarian composer who married an older heiress. She had quite a few years on this fuck; I'm sure he married her for the money. I will have to give credit to the shit. He did own one of the great art collections of his time: Passoc, Van Gogh, Rodin sculptures. I mean, he had the shit. Part of my job was raising and closing the blinds in the room where the artwork was kept, depending on the time of day. That seems easy, but believe me, it was not, and he was a prick. If one painting got direct sunlight for even a minute, he would go off, swearing at me. He complained about everything and was mean to the old lady as well.

The only time he was nice was when we had guests. The rest of the time, nothing was right. The food was too hot or too cold, it needed more salt, or there was too much salt. The guy was just a prick. One good thing about the job was that I got to meet Jimmy Stewart a few times. He was a few houses down the street, and he and Henri were friends. I don't know why, because this guy was an asshole, but Jimmy was cool. We had a few great chats. They don't make actors like him nowadays. These new actors are a bunch of spoiled little shits who cannot wipe their own asses and make way too much money. The old actors had class and knew when to keep their mouths shut and do their job.

Another great part of the job was that the old fuck had a nice wine cellar and loved Italian wine, and I mean the good shit, too good for this mean old fuck, cases of it lying in boxes. Still, I knew I would be quitting any day, so when they went out to dinner one night, I helped myself to a few cases and some nice vintage port, twenty-five years. I felt it was severance pay for putting up with these fucks for two weeks, and I mean two long weeks, so I did not feel bad about helping myself.

Besides all his whining about the food and the blinds and being mean to his wife, he wanted me to start bathing his two dogs. Like, what the fuck do I look like, a dog groomer? These were two big shepherds. That was the last straw. I said nicely, "Sir, I don't wash dogs."

He looked at me like we were going to go at it, and I was prepared to knock the old fuck out. I had taken enough of his shit, and I was not going to put up with it anymore. He said to me, "You will bathe the dogs, or you can look for employment elsewhere."

I looked at this fuck and said, "Yeah, and you can take this job and these fucking dogs and stick them up your ass, and if you got a problem, I will gladly kick the shit out of you. You are nasty to your wife, treat the staff like shit, and think you are something special. Go back to Eastern Europe and get your ass kicked around back there, and maybe get fucked up the ass. That's what you need."

He started to make a move at me, and I said, "Bring it on, you old fuck. I am going to make you wish you were never born."

He thought for a minute and then tried to grab me. I grabbed the fuck by his shirt collar and put his ass right on the floor. I should have put a few shots into him, but I didn't. I just held him there with the Marine death grip around his neck and said, "Yeah, you fuck, what are you going to do?"

I held him there a few minutes just to let him know I could really fuck him up. He cooled down, and when his wife came out, I let him up. He said, "You are finished in this town. You will not work again. I am calling Dora, and I am pressing charges."

"Fine, you nasty piece of shit. If you like, I will drop your ass right now. Then you have something to press charges for."

"Come on," he said. "I was not ready last time."

That was it. I dropped this fuck like a bag of potatoes right in front of his wife, and I said, "If I hear that you were nasty to the missus, I am going to come back and really kick the shit out of you, and furthermore, if you want to press charges, I am going to call Jimmy and a few of the neighbors and tell them what a real piece of shit you are, and on top of that, I am going to the tabloids."

I looked this fuck right in the eyes and said, "Are we done? If not, I am going to make you wish you were never born."

From out of nowhere, the wife spoke up and said, "Henri, he is right, and if you don't start treating me better and the staff as well, we are getting divorced, and you will leave with what you came with, nothing. Do you get that through your thick Bulgarian skull?"

I'd never heard her talk like that. She was pissed.

I was at a loss for words, and he just stood there like his world had just been rocked and his rule was over. Good for her. Then he stormed off, saying, "This is not over."

"Yes, it is," she said. "I don't want to ever talk about this again, but changes are happening, starting now, or you can pack your bags."

That was it. He knew he had no place to go. I am sure she owned everything, the artwork as well.

When we were all alone, she looked at me and said, "Alan, I am so sorry you had to put up with this, but don't worry. He will not press charges, and I will call Dora myself and tell her that you were great. We just don't need a person like you at this time. I will give you a reference."

She walked over, gave me a big hug, and said, "Thanks. No one has ever stood up to Henri before. Now I really see what an asshole he is. If he doesn't clean up, I am kicking him out. I made him sign a prenup."

"Yes, ma'am. He has no reason to treat you like that."

She gave me another big hug, one I will never forget, because this Marine got all choked up inside.

As I was on my way out, she handed me an envelope and said, "Take this, and thank you very much. If you need anything, just call me." She gave me one more big hug, and we said farewell.

On my way back to the desert, I opened the envelope, and there was a thousand dollars, all hundreds, with a note saying, "Thanks. God bless." Wow. What a cool old broad. She finally stood up for herself. Henri never pressed charges or called Dora. Case closed.

The next little gig started off as a catering party from some other agent. She said, "If they like you and it works out, they might hire you full time." If you are a young chef and you hear this, stay clear. These jobs are shit, and the owners are assholes, cheap, and pains in the ass, and they don't pay. I learned this the hard way.

This job was for the Deutsche family. I think they were related to the German bank family and the husband was a producer of some sort. They lived in Beverly Hills, and the job was a Sunday brunch. I was to go to the house and meet the wife and get the final details. This was a week's gig. I cannot believe the gall of some of these fucks. Who do they think they are?

I met the wife at the house on Friday to get the details and menu for Sunday. It would be an all-girls brunch, catered by Jerry's Deli in Beverly Hills, a New York-style deli for all the Jews. I was to pick the food up, serve, bartend, and clean up. I said, "Yes, I can do that. I need two hundred dollars for the day." I thought she was going to have a heart attack. She said, "That is a lot of money for the day."

"That's my rate."

She told me who I would be waiting on: Nancy Reagan, Betty Ford, Mrs. Firestone, and a few other old broads I did not know. She said, "I will pay you a hundred and fifty dollars." That was her budget. I should have told her to piss off, but I wanted to see Betty again and meet Nancy. Mrs. Firestone was a cool old broad as well, so what the hell. It was cash.

I showed up early at the house and headed to the deli to pick up the food, get the table and bar set up, and attend to all the last-minute details. The old man went out to play golf. He was a pretty cool old fuck, kind of like a Sam Houston. I think they were friends, old-school guys. I wish I could have hung out a few weeks. I am sure he had some cool old friends and good stories.

All the women arrived on time, with their agents driving them. Betty and Mrs. Firestone saw me, came over, gave me a big hug, and asked how I'd been. Betty waved Nancy Regan over and told her that I used to work for her and President Ford and I'd left to work for all the stars in LA and Jerry Weintraub. What a feather in my cap that was. I brought them up to speed on my life and told them I'd left Mr. Selby and was looking for a new home. I said I might have a new job in Newport next month, but the owner was out of town.

Brunch went off perfectly. I fixed some drinks, and they all dug into the deli lunch I served. As they ate, they talked about politics and their vacation trips. When it was over, the ladies said goodbye to me, wished me good luck, and said how nice it was to see me and that they were glad I was doing well. Mrs. Ford was a class act, but as for Nancy, I could tell she would be nasty to work for. She was kind of a pain in the ass at the brunch, very demanding, and needed special treatment, like she was all that, and she was no spring chicken at this time. I would never see this crew again. I would miss my talks with mom, aka Betty. What a great first lady. One for the storybooks,

Miss Deutsche, on the other hand, was a real bitch. After I cleaned up and was ready to drive back to the desert, she called me into the dining room and asked me to buff the entryway marble floors. I almost shit. Was she fucking nuts? What a set of balls this old broad had.

I thought a minute. I did not want to blow this just yet. I might want this job for a few weeks till the builder in Newport got back and I had that job in the bank. She had a buffing machine out with all these pads and shit, plugged in and waiting for me. I kept my cool and said, "Ma'am, I have plans, and I have to get back to the desert, but I can come back next week and do the floors."

She said, "That will be fine."

I told her I could start on Tuesday, and then I left for the desert.

What a crazy old piece of shit. Come over, cook and serve, do the dishes, and now wax and polish the floors? I don't think so.

When I got home, there was still no word from Rick's friend in Newport. He says he was sure the guy was going to hire me. He just had to get back home and meet me and work out salary and living arrangements. I thought, what the hell. I will work for this mean old bitch a few weeks and make a few more bucks. Then I'll tell her to fuck off when I get the gig in Newport. Not a bad plan. I liked working, and I liked making money.

I went back to Beverly Hills on Tuesday. The couple had one of the old mansions looking down on the city, I think off Beverly Glen. We talked, and she laid out my weekly duties and the schedule for the week, polishing silver, the floors—those fucking floors again—and driver duties. I was just about to walk out on the first day. The only good things were that I had a killer guesthouse looking down on the city and a Rolls to drive around in. I prayed every day for Rick's friend to get home.

Cooking for these two old farts, who complained about everything, was a pain in the balls. Just when I thought it could not get any worse, I was driving the old hag on Rodeo to get her hair and nails done, and she started yelling at me about the wrong directions and how she was going to be late and it was all my fault and can't I do anything right? She told me to turn left, and I said, "It's one way, ma'am."

"It's not," she insisted.

"Look at the sign again."

"Don't argue with me."

That was it. New job or not, I had taken enough shit from this old hag. I turned around and said, "Are you finished barking orders?"

"Don't talk to me in that tone of voice," she said.

"Who the fuck do you think you are? You are just some ugly old rich cunt who thinks her shit don't stink. Fuck you and this job, and you can walk from here."

She got on her high horse again and said, "You will drive me to the salon or else."

"Or else what, you will fire me? I have news for you. I fucking quit. Take this job and stick it up your tight Jewish ass."

She barked back, "I am calling Dora, and you won't work in this town again!"

Do you know how many times I heard that in LA? It's just like, "Do you know who I am?" What a bunch of assholes. I told her to shut the fuck up before I wrecked the car. Then I pulled halfway into the intersection, rolled the windows up, threw the Rolls in park, turned back to the old bitch and said, "Fuck you. Have a nice day." Then I got out of the car and threw the keys as far as I could. This was in the middle of summer, a hot day, during rush hour in Beverly Hills. When I tell the story to the boys, they still laugh their asses.

I might still be the Teflon Kid, but Dora would never get me a job again. I knew I was done with LA and the phony fucks.

I called Rob, my bartender buddy, who lived nearby and said I needed to get back to the house to get my car. He was there in a jiffy and took me back to the house. He asked, "What the hell is going on?"

I told him what I'd done, and he busted a gut. He could not stop laughing. "You crazy fuck. Chef Al, that is just way too cool."

"I will be out of here in ten," I said. "You want to go have a drink at the Ivy?"

"Sure, see you in thirty."

The old man met me halfway to the guest house and said that his wife had called and said to stop me and call the cops. "What happened?"

"She started yelling at me, and I will not put up with being talked to like that."

"Is it true about the car and the keys?"

"Yes, sir."

He laughed. "Maybe that will teach her. I've been married to her for thirty-five years, and I still wonder why I put up with her shit. I am just too old and tired to argue with her. I know she can be nasty. Not one of my friends likes her, only the other nasty old hags. They all stick together like the plague."

He looked at me, and I thought, oh, shit. Here come the cops. I am fucked. Then he said, "Alan, get out of here. I will make sure she does not press charges, and for what? Losing car keys is not a criminal offense. I will stick up for you and make a call to Dora as well. I know my wife can be nasty. You have not seen what she can really be like."

"Shit, how mean can the old bitch be?"

"Alan, you have no idea. Take care, and all the best." He slipped me a few hundred for the few days I'd worked. That was cool of the old man. He was not a bad dude as long as she was not around. I would give anything to have seen that bitch's face when I threw down the keys, but I never looked back, just kept on walking. People were blowing their horns; it was some scene. I can still hear the nasty voice, "Alan, you come back here! Get those keys and get back here!"

I met Rob at the Ivy with a few of the guys I hung with. Rob had already told the story a million times to the guys, and they were all in tears. They just said, "Chef, is it true?"

I said, "Do you have to ask?"

"Holy shit, that is just way too cool. You are truly a legend. They broke the mold with you, Chef." We had some shots and some beers and laughed for hours.

To this day, when I see Rob, the story still comes up, and we laugh. It's a good reason to have a few shots for the good old days.

I have one last LA dinner party to tell you about. There was an attorney I did a few parties for. I also did some part-time work around the house for him: taking care of the cars, shopping, buying flowers, honey-do list, and let's not forget fucking the guy's wife. That wasn't my job—I did that for free—but they always gave me some gifts, usually clothes, and once in a while, they would give me a few bucks and say, "Go have a nice dinner on me."

I met Glory in Gelson's in the Palisades, the same store where I'd met a few of my conquests. She asked me how to make good hummus and if I did private parties. I gave her a good recipe, and we exchanged numbers. She was having a party next weekend, and she asked if I could do it. I said I could, and she said, "Call me Monday, and I will give you my address. Stop by, and we will go over the menu and work the details out."

"Of course. See you Monday."

Man, did she have an ass on her for an older broad. Nice tits as well. She worked out; you could tell. That's what these rich broads do—spend the old man's money, go to the gym, and fuck the trainer or the tennis coach, or in my case, the chef. Oh, I forgot, and go shopping. That's what really hurts. Rodeo Drive is not cheap, so you had better open up that wallet with these bitches, or they just move on.

Back to Glory. I met her at the house up in Hollywood Hills, a bad-ass modern-style place with a great view of the city. She invited me in, and we had a cup of coffee. Then she showed me the kitchen, and everything looked fine.

"Everything is here that I will need," I said.

"I don't cook often, but the kitchen is well set up."

Next, she gave me the guest list: Vidal and Ronnie Sassoon, Don Johnson, and one of her girlfriends, Stephanie. Don was just getting out of the Betty Ford Clinic for like the third time or some shit, but I still love the guy. He just has issues with drinking. It turned out that Glory's husband, Ron Litz, was a big-time divorce attorney to the stars. That was how he knew Don; he'd probably done the divorce for Don and Melody.

We started on the menu, and I told Glory, "I've cooked for Don before, and I know he loves a good veal chop with a rosemary demi-glace and a dollop of fig jam. I love that sauce. Roast potatoes, charred Brussels sprouts, and baby carrots." She was getting wet as I talked about the menu. I told her we'd have a simple house salad with a Champagne vinaigrette, crème brûlée for dessert, and for starters, some fruit, caviar, and pellinas.

"That sounds great," she said.

"I'll need a credit card for the food, or you can just reimburse me."

"I will get you a credit card." Then she asked me if I could recommend some wine.

"A cab would be nice, and Champagne to start."

She headed to her office, came back with a credit card, and said, "Just bring back the receipt."

We worked out the times and picked out the china, placemats, all that, and then she asked me what else I needed

"I just need to look at what you have in the fridge, spices, that sort of stuff. Then I'll make my list, and I will be out of here."

"Fine, I am going to be at the pool, getting some sun. Just come out and get me when you are finished, and I will see you out."

I helped myself to a beer and worked on my list. Then I went through the fridge, saw what she had and in the pantry, and looked at all the cookware to see what I needed to bring. She had every gadget I could think of. I was all set and had my list, so I finished my beer and was ready to hit the road—at least, that's what I thought.

I headed out to the pool and said to Glory, "I am finished."

"Ok," she said. "Would you please bring me a glass of wine?"

I could tell she had her top off. "What would you like?" I asked.

"The pinot grigio. That's the preferred wine for Beverly Hills cougars."

Glory was probably in her early forties, if that, and as far as I could see, she had a kick-ass body as well. I returned with her glass of wine, and she was just sitting there, showing off her nice, store-bought set of tits.

"Thank you," she said. "Do you have to work tonight?"

"No, I am between jobs, but I have to drive back to the desert this afternoon. I drove in just to see you."

"That was so kind of you. Why don't you take in some sun with me and have a beer before you head back?"

"What if your husband comes home?"

"Don't worry. He is in New York till Wednesday."

I took my shoes off and headed to the kitchen to get a cold beer, thinking this could be fun. I returned to the pool, and she said, "Take your shirt and pants off, and let's swim. Her top was off, and she was wearing this little black G-string. I could not keep my eyes off her, and she knew.

She said, "Do you like what you see?"

"Glory, you are one sexy bitch."

"Al, you are just saying that."

"No, you are fucking hot."

"Yeah, not bad for forty-year-old cougar."

She jumped in the pool, and I followed her in. Next thing I knew, she took her G-string off, ripped my underwear off, and grabbed my dick. "Wow! Nice package. It feels like you are glad to see me."

"But of course."

For you guys who have never had a sex-deprived woman, you don't know what you are missing. All I can say is, they're horny as hell, so grab your hat, because you are going for a ride.

We kissed like two high school virgins. She had my cock in her hands, and I was grabbing her ass and fondling her pussy. We got out of the pool, and she climbed on top of me on the chaise lounge, and man, did we fuck like champions all afternoon. When we finally made it to the bedroom, we were both out of breath. I got her a glass of wine and a cold beer for me, and then we passed out.

When I woke up, it was already ten. I said, "Shit."

Glory said, "Don't worry. Spend the night and leave in the morning. I want to have sex in the morning."

I looked at her and said, "Why wait till morning?" I got on top of her again and just wore that shit out till I could not go one more thrust. We passed out again while I was still inside her warm, wet pussy, with that nice little black thumbnail of hair going right to her warm little spot. What a great night of sport fucking.

I got up the next morning, and she had already made coffee. She said she had to get to the gym and to let myself out. "I will see you Friday, and if you need something, feel free to call."

"What about the sex in the morning?" I said.

"I am running late."

I pulled her toward me, yanked her yoga pants down, bent her over the kitchen counter, and got her from behind until she was sopping wet. She was almost in tears and panting like she had just lost her breath.

"See what you did?" She said. "I am all wet, and I have to change now."

"Is that a good or bad thing?"

"Good, now put that thing away, finish your coffee, and I will see you Friday."

I gave her a nice, long, wet kiss, and I was on my way. I have banged a lot of chicks in my day. Models, wives, daughters, housekeepers, nannies, I have had them all, but I will never forget Glory. What a hot piece of ass.

I went home, chilled by the pool, and took a nap. After all, I'd had a hard night of fucking and was beat. Then I played a few rounds of golf. I had a few days to plan the party, and it was only six guests, easy for me. Rick's friend would get back this weekend, and I would know if I had a new gig on Monday. I could not get Glory out of my mind, and I hoped I would get to fuck her again.

A few days later, I called her to let her know I was all good for the party, and she told me she'd had a great time and would like to get together the next time Ron was out of town. "Sure," I said. "I had a great time as well. See you Friday. I'll be by around noon to set things up."

I picked up the veal chops at Gelson's and had the butcher trim them up nice. Then I grabbed the rest of the produce and went to the house. I called Glory to tell her I was about an hour behind and would see her around one. "Ok, see you then," she said.

When I got to the house, I rang the bell, and holy shit, she answered the door in just the black G-string that I could not get out of my mind and said, "Come on in. I am getting some sun."

She asked, "Do you need a hand?"

"You're going to help me carry groceries in dressed like that?" I said.

She laughed. "I was just being polite."

"I got these. See you at the pool in fifteen."

She had already set the table—that was a big help—so I put all the food away, chilled the wine and Champagne, and then headed out to the pool to view those nice tits.

She said, "What took you so long? I've been waiting a week to suck your cock."

Before I knew it, my pants were down, and I was getting worked over. I came in two minutes; she gave the best head. I got my second wind and fucked her right there on the chaise lounge.

Afterward, I got up and said, "That was nice, but I have to get dinner ready and clean up."

"Me, too," she said, and we both laughed.

I still had plenty of time till dinner, so I got cleaned up, grabbed a beer from the fridge, and went over my checklist. The lamb was prepared, the salads made, and the veggies prepped, so I was in good shape. Oh, and the caviar was on ice.

Glory popped into the kitchen and made me a cup of coffee, still half undressed. What a horny chick. Chicks like that, they just can't get enough. She said her husband would be home late, as always. Don would be there first, as he was coming in a limo straight from the Betty Ford Clinic.

"He will be here at six, and my friend Stephanie is on her way, and no, you cannot fuck her. I am trying to fix her up with Don. If he doesn't like her, then maybe."

What a crazy bitch, as I know they all are.

Stephanie showed up as Glory was in the shower, getting all dolled up. I answered the door, and she walked right in. Before I could say anything, she said, "You're Chef Al."

"Yes, and you're Stephanie, Glory's friend. She has told me all about you. It's nice to meet you. Glory is getting ready, and I am cooking. Come in, and I will get you a glass of wine till she comes out."

"Can I help?" She asked.

"Thanks, but Glory set the table, and now I have dinner all prepped. I just have to cook the veal chops and veggies. The salads are made, and desert as well."

Glory came in as if on cue, and she said, "I see you met Chef Al. He is great."

The doorbell rang, and Glory said, "I'll get it."

Like clockwork, it was Don at the door, and she showed him into the kitchen and introduced him to Stephanie. He saw me and said, "Hey, Chef Al. It's been a long time. What's up? How is your game?"

We shook hands and gave each other the cool LA hug, and then I said, "I've been good, and you look great, as always."

He turned and looked at the girls and said, "I know I am going to have a great dinner tonight with Chef Al in the kitchen, and Glory, how do you know Chef Al ?"

Thank God she did not say, "I've been sucking his dick for a couple of weeks." Instead, she said, "I met him at Gelson's."

Don said, "I met him at Arthur Annarico's. He was pitching *Tin Cup* with Kevin Costner, the golf movie. Al's a golfer, and we played a few times. Then I ran into him at Jerry Weintraub's when I was looking at a different project. So, I know dinner will be great."

I butted in and said, "It's one of your favorites tonight, Don. Veal chop Tuscany style, saffron risotto, charred Brussels sprouts and red peppers, and a nice custard for dessert."

He said, "Sounds great."

The bell rang again, and it was Vidal Sasson and his wife, Ronnie. Glory showed them in and made the introductions while I poured everyone Champagne, even Don, though he'd come right from the Betty Ford Clinic. And on top of that, Stephanie was hot as balls, with big tits, and she was all over him like Glory was on me.

Then Ron, Glory's husband, came in. He said to me, "Chef Al, nice to meet you. Glory has told me so much about you. I am so glad to have you in our house, cooking for us. I am sure it will be great."

We shook hands, and I said, "The pleasure is all mine." It's hard to look a guy in the eye when you fucked his wife a few hours ago. She'd told me he couldn't get it up, and when he did, the sex only lasted for two minutes. What a shame.

He did not have a clue. Ronnie and I talked about Ohio and how I ended up in LA. What a first-class chick, and Vidal was a great guy. You could tell he worked out; he looked in great shape and had a great style.

They all sat down, and I served dinner. I came out and told them the menu and said, "It's one of Don's favorite dinners, and it has been prepared with lots of love." They all laughed, and I returned to the kitchen. One more for the records.

Don's limo showed up right after coffee, and he asked Stephanie, "Do you want to join me at the Beverly for a nightcap? I just hate riding in a limo alone, but Paramount comps it, so it's free."

"I would love to," she said.

Then Glory said, "Just leave your car here."

Don said goodnight and thanked Ron and Glory. Then he said, "Chef Al, great dinner. Good to see you. Stop by the studio or call, and let's go tee it up."

I said, "Sure. It was great to see you as well."

Vidal and Ronnie came over as well and said, "It was good to see you again, Don. Good luck with *Tin Cup* and keep in touch."

That must have been a cool night for Don Johnson. Get out of Betty Ford, go to your attorney's house for dinner, the guy's wife hooks you up with a hot piece of ass, and Paramount sends you a limo. Not a bad gig, and I am sure Don fucked the hell out of her. I would have, little LA groupie.

Glory was still in awe that I knew Don that well. I never told her we played golf together and he gave me a private tour of his office and Paramount. I'll say one thing: DJ knows how to live. He has a bad-ass office, drinks the best wine, and fucks chicks half his age. He's still a damn good-looking dude, with lots of class and style. I never will forget Don. We played golf a few more times, but when I got the gig in Newport, I did not come to LA much except to fuck Glory for a few more months.

I did not see Ron again or much of the old gang, Linda, David, and the kids. I was glad to be done with LA. I'd had a good ride, banged tons of hot pussy, and cooked for all the A-listers. It was a time I will never forget. Goodbye, LA. Hello, Newport.

I would never work in LA again. You could not pay me enough to go back. Tony Gonzalez wanted to hire me a few years back when I met him on a yacht. He asked what I needed for a salary, and I said, "Seventy-five thousand dollars and a car and living quarters."

He looked at me and said, "That is a lot of money."

I almost laughed in his face, cheap fucking jock. I said, "Go through an agency and look what it will cost you." I am sure he hired some illegal Mexican and paid them shit. If you pay peanuts, you get monkeys. Tony G, man up, you cheap fuck.

I saw Shari and Sam a few more times. We played golf, and they came to the desert one last time. I miss them. They're a great couple and really good friends. We had some great dinners and rounds of golf.

So long. It was not meant to be.

The Snake Perscio, Chef at Stoweflake Resort, Stowe VT.

Paul's House

Ski Bums, Stowe VT.

Chef Als LA. Crew

I WENT BACK TO THE desert and chilled. Rick's friend would get back from the honeymoon this week, and Rick told me he wanted to meet me and would call me around midweek. He wanted me to come to Newport and meet him. I said, "Cool. I will wait for the call. Thanks, Rick." We were still friends. Like I said, he was a first-class guy.

I was doing ok. I had over a hundred grand in the bank, two houses, and was still having fun. I wasn't rich like the folks I worked for, but I was a few up on the average Joe's. Plus, it helps not having a wife and kids to support and spend my hard-earned money on. That's how I really got a leg up. I didn't spend much, either. I'd eaten for free for years, driven the company car, and gotten a lot of nice perks. I'd had roommates pay my mortgage while I lived for free in guesthouses. Not a bad life. I was in my mid-thirties now, so I still had a lot of miles left in me.

I got the call a few days later from Mr. Dopp, and he said, "I have heard all about you and want to meet you Friday at my boat in Newport."

"Fine," I said. "See you Friday."

I hung out a few more days, got some sun, and then called Rick and said I was meeting Bryan on Friday. He said, "Don't worry. I gave you a great reference. You will like this guy, and it's a pretty good job. He needs someone like you to do just what you did for me."

It looked like the plan was coming together. I'd been to Newport a few times, a cool little beach town, not as crazy as LA. I met Mr. Dopp at the boat on Friday, a real nice Sport Fisher, thirty-eight or forty-two feet, called *Pacifico* after the beer and West Coast. We had lunch at a little seafood shack there.

He said, "Please call me Bryan. I am too young to be addressed as mister." He was probably forty or so, and he'd just gotten married for the second time—no kids yet. He asked me to tell him about myself and how I'd met Rick. I told him about the Marines, quitting school, the hotel business, working for the LA A-listers, and all that. Then said, "I met Rick through my old agent, and we had a great run. I just did not get along with the new wife."

"I know," he said. "Rick told me, and he speaks very highly of you. I need you to be more of a personal assistant than a chef. Would that be ok?"

"Yes, whatever you need."

"Great. I don't have a guesthouse, but you can live on the boat. I have a Rover for you to drive when you are working, and you can take it to the desert if you need to. I will start you at five thousand a month. How does that sound."

"That sounds great."

"Can you start Monday?"

"Sure."

"Great. Let's have a beer and a shot to celebrate our new friendship."

We hung out for an hour, had lunch and a few beers, and he said, "You will meet the wife next week, and I will get all the keys for you. Meet me at my office Monday at nine. I have one more meeting this afternoon, or we would take the boat out, but we will do that next time. Welcome aboard, and I look forward to you coming to work and being part of the team."

"Thanks," I said. "See you Monday."

Just like that, I was back on track, with a new gig, good cash, and living in Newport on a nice Sport Fisher. All my life, I have been lucky. I just fall into shit like this.

I had one more beer and was on my way back to the desert to beat the traffic. What a great day. I called Rick and told him that Bryan had hired me and I would start next week.

"Congrats," he said. "You will have a great time. Bryan is cool, and I will be down to check on you. I will leave the wife at home, as I know you just adore her. Have a great week, keep in touch, and I'll see you in Newport. And tell Bryan to call me when he gets a chance."

Will do, and thanks again for the reference."

"Don't worry. It's my pleasure. You are a hell of a hard worker and a loyal and honest guy. That's hard to find in LA, or anywhere, nowadays. You will go far. Just keep it up. Best of luck."

Back home, I called Sue, a little Asian I'd been fucking for a few months, and told her about the new job. I said, "Meet at my place at six for drinks."

"Cool," she said. "Where are we going?"

"El Paseo."

"Wow! I will look my best."

Sue was one of the pastry chefs at the Marriott Desert Springs. She was a hot little mess who liked it up the ass and loved to talk dirty. I like that sometimes. She arrived on time, as usual, and I made a couple of martinis and told her about the job. She just said, "You are living the dream."

"I am blessed," I said.

We toasted and then caught up. I told her we had reservations at seven thirty at Sullivan's. "Oh," she said. "I love that place."

"I know. That's why we are going."

She came over, grabbed my dick, and said, "Make sure the hot tub is on before we leave."

I said, "It's on already, a hundred and three degrees."

"Great. Then let's go. I am hungry."

Sue was a real cool chick and a good golfer. I banged her on and off for a few years. She was a career girl with Marriott, had been there like ten years and had her own house as well. She had her shit together and was a real keeper. I should have held on to her, but I fucked it up as usual.

Over dinner, I told her about the new job and what I had been up to in LA, and she talked about the hotel and said my name still came up once in a while. I thought that was kind of cool. We went back to my place, and the hot tub was steaming, so we got undressed and wore each other out. She spent the night, and we had great sex in the morning. I liked hanging out with Sue—no strings and nice pussy.

On Monday, I was on my way to Newport for the first day. I was excited. I'd had some time off, and now I am ready to get back at it. I was to meet the new boss at his office at nine, and I ended up being early—you never know with traffic in California.

Bryan showed up around nine and introduced me to the staff. Monica was his personal assistant. Bryan told her, "Alan and I have a few things to go over. Then I have to take off, and I will send him to you." Then he asked me, "How was your weekend? I have a place in the desert, too."

"Cool," I said. "Where is it?"

"Desert Falls."

"That's a nice complex and has a great golf course."

"Yeah, we will have to go play there sometime."

"I had a great weekend. I saw my girl, had dinner at Sullivan's, relaxed by the pool. Everything was good."

"I like Sullivan's, too. Great rib-eye."

After that little exchange, we got right into what he needed. I would help him in the office, deliver documents, go to the bank and escrow companies, cook at the house sometimes, run all his and his wife's personal errands, cook on the boat, make sure the boat was clean, help with the lines and stuff when he went fishing, and make sure cars were detailed and gassed up.

I said, "I can do all that."

"Great. I have to run. Go see Monica, and she will get you a credit card, keys to the boat and Rover, and some petty cash. Whatever you need, just ask her. She is great and has been with me for ten years. Just don't tell her what you and I do when we are out or if Rick is in town. Keep that to the boys."

"Sure."

"Cool. I will see you tomorrow. Get organized on the boat, and tomorrow I will take you to the house to meet the wife, and Friday, you can cook dinner for us."

I went to Monica, gave her my driver's license and bank info, and got all the keys to everything. Then she took me around the office to meet the rest of the staff, and just like that, I was in. I had a good feeling about this job and Bryan as well.

I was right. I worked for Bryan for the next five years, my longest job since Marriott. We had a lot of good times: ski trips to Squaw Valley, Aspen, and Tahoe; fishing trips to Cabo, Ensenada, and Catalina Island; trips to the desert. Bryan knew how to live and had it all at a young age. He treated me great. I could not ask for a better boss—and friend as well. There were no stars at his dinner parties, which was fine with me, mostly family and business colleagues. Most of my job was around the office, being the gofer. I did a fair share of cooking as well, holidays, weekends, things like that. They went out a lot.

I really don't want to bore you, so I will only tell you about some of the trips he took me on and the boat life in Newport and Huntington Beach.

Bryan knew how to live, and he was the only guy in all my travels who liked women more than me. He was a real playboy and a great-looking dude, and it helped that he had lots of money as well. He even flew his own plane, kind of like a Stone Barrington character, bigger than life. His wife was hot, too. I knew she was a pain-in-the-ass trophy wife, just like Rick's. I did not have to deal with her too much, just a few days a week. She sold real estate till she got pregnant with Ryan after a few months.

This was one of the best jobs I had, with something new every day. I did quite a few lunches for the office staff and dinner parties at the house. I was on the move the whole day, picking up and dropping things off. I liked that, and living on the boat was nice, right in the middle of Newport. After a few months, I had it dialed in, and Bryan and I became great friends. He always bought me lunch and drinks and picked up the tab at Fritz's, our hangout. It was a great strip club, and Bryan liked that scene. I was cool with it—it just wasn't my scene. I don't like to look at it and not have it. You get a few lap dances, get a little stinky finger, and go home and jerk off, but Bryan had money. He took a couple of them out—paid them, I am sure—and got some ass. Not my style, but we still had lots of fun over the years.

I was hanging out with his partner as well, Doug Irvine, owner of the Irvine Pacific Company. Doug was one crazy guy, older than Bryan by ten or fifteen years but sharp. He loved the chicks, too. That's why we all got along. They were building hotels and commercial buildings and just hitting it out of the park. They took care of me, and I never felt below them. Doug had been married a few times and had a new young wife.

Most of the trips I went on with Bryan were family trips, like skiing and going to the desert. I would cook, drive them to dinner, arrange stuff for the nanny, get ski passes, all that sort of stuff. I got to go on some nice trips, but nothing crazy, as Sonya was with us, and it was not long before the second kid came around, a son, Colby.

Things were starting to change. The wife wanted me to help out more at the house, and I'd had enough of these spoiled kids, but I managed to hang out for one more year. I hate taking orders from wives. They don't do shit, just spend their old man's money, order the staff around, go shopping, and do yoga. What a bunch of shit. That's why their kids are all messed up these days. The parents spend no time with them, just throw money at them. The damn nanny raises the kids. They don't know right from wrong, and they're just spoiled rotten and feel entitled to do whatever they want. The parents wonder why their kids are lazy and worthless, but it's their own damn fault. Last I heard, Ryan was still living with Sonya, and he is around thirty now. If he were my kid, he'd be paying rent or out on his ass.

I told Bryan I would stay till after the holidays, but I would be out of there the first of the year. I had a few hundred in cash by now, and I thought I would just take some time off and figure out my next move. Bryan was cool. He knew Sonya could be a bitch, but he'd made his bed.

He was cool and did not say a word to her, but he really needed me at the office more than the house.

The rest of the year was tough, but I'd made a promise to hang till the first of the year. About this time, I started banging one of the office girls, Hope, a little surfer girl from Huntington Beach. I thought, I will be gone in six months, so what the hell. She was a little hottie and cool as shit, a little pothead, and liked it cowboy style. I was all over that. She would come over to the boat on her lunch break, and we would have a quickie. We had some good times partying at the Hurricane and hanging out at the beach. She was around eight years younger than me. One more I won't forget.

Some of the trips we went on were pretty cool, just the guys going fishing. I am surprised Sonya was cool with that, but we did quite a few. They were all the same: Cabo, Ensenada, Catalina Island. Bryan and Doug liked to fish. I caught my first blue-fin with these guys and took a bite of the heart. That was in Cabo. We went there a few times, and it was the same old crazy shit: hit Cabo Wabo and the Giggling Marlin for shots and beers, grab a few hookers, and then off to the races to smoke some weed and switch off on the girls or just go get a new batch. They were cheap enough. We always stayed on the boat and in nice marinas.

The year was coming to an end soon. It had been a good five years, and I'd made some good friends along the way, including my mentor, Mike Gayner, who lives on Lido Island and is a hedge fund guy. I met him while living on the boat. We became great friends, and he treated me like a son, gave me lots of good advice, and I did a few dinner parties for him on his boat in LA and the house in Newport. I had a lot of Mondays off, and Mike would have these football parties on the boat, and I would cook for him and about six of his good friends, other hedge fund guys. One of the guys owned a chain of restaurants in LA. He was also longtime friends with Robert Shapiro, one of OJ's attorneys, who told us that getting OJ off was the worst mistake he ever made. He knew OJ killed her. He was a real stand-up guy. He just fucked up, and now he has to live with it. Another big-time guy was Kurt Concordean's brother. I did an interview with him, and he was a real prick with some young wife, and I did not take the job. I was happy with Bryan.

All the guys had their mistresses come with them, or call girls or whores. They're all the same. You are paying for that shit. I only knew these guys from Mike, and it was none of my business. I could have made some money blackmailing some of these guys with the whores, but I never thought about it. Not my deal, but I could have made some good dough. I miss Mike, and we still keep in touch to this day. I will never forget him from smoking those damn Pall Malls with no filters while drinking vodka and Diet Coke.

We had some great talk and dinners, and Kris, his wife, aka Beaver, what a great woman. They'd been married forever and still are today. Mike was the father I never had. I love my dad, but he was just a drunk and lazy fuck. He never did shit, never had shit, and died owing me money. I know it's hard to say, but Dad was a deadbeat. He was never around and never did anything.

My mom would kick him out for months at a time when I was young, telling him he could not come back till he had a job. He smacked me around a little bit, but I am sure I deserved it. He was just never around never did anything with my brother or me. Ron wrote him off as soon as he left home and never talked to him again. I was bitter for a long time after seeing the relationships my friends had with their fathers.

I told Mike all this, and he said, "Yeah, but he's still your dad."

I got over it and made peace with my dad about five years before he died of cancer, and I am glad I did. He passed away in my arms. Now I can sleep at night. I thank Mike for that, and I will never forget his good advice.

I love Mike, but some of these cheating guys were real pricks, or as Mike would call them, some of his asshole college buddies. Mike's deal was eatin' ain't cheatin'. That's pussy, of course. I always liked that one. Mike, thanks for all the good times, advice, laughs, and friendship. I will never forget you. I am a better man because of you.

Bryan was cool with me leaving. He knew kids were not my deal. We had a great run that Christmas, and he gave me a Rolex GMT for Christmas and a going-away present. Bryan, I miss all the good times in Catalina, including the one time when I fell out of the dingy—man, we were hammered—all the great trips, skiing, Mexico. You were good to me and treated me with respect, unlike some of the LA assholes.

And with that said, let's close that chapter. Love you, buddy.

See you in Panama

Best Friend Bryan, Huntington Beach

Bryan and sons Ryan and Colby, Huntington Beach, Ca.

Cigar night, Cubans of course

Love Panama

Love Panama, that's me with the girl smoking Hookie

Chapter 15

PANAMA BOUND
ABOARD THE *SEA ROOSTER*

I WAS BACK IN THE desert, planning my next move. I had almost two hundred grand and two houses, and I'd just bought a penthouse in Panama on Balboa Blvd, right downtown. I was in control and sitting on cash without a care in the world.

If I'd had a wife, I would have been broke and fucked, and she would have been saying, "Get back to work. I need a new car." Fuck that. That's why I never got married. I am not going to have some bitch stay home, spend my hard-earned money, and tell me what I have to do and still have to beg for some pussy. All you guys know that once you give them a ring, the pussy starts to go away a little every year till, finally, you don't even want it. That's why I have been on the rental plan for years—less money and no hassle. It's the best, and I get the fresh stuff. You have to love that.

I took a few more trips back to Newport to see Bryan and my mentor, Mike, and to LA a few more times to throw a shot into Glory. I could never get enough of that ass. Bryan was living large and did not plan for the slowdown. I had a few long talks with Mike, and he said, "Sell every-thing. Shit is going to hit the fan in the next year. A recession is coming, a big one. Sell your real estate and all your stocks." Best advice I ever got. Mike said, "Do your dream. Buy the sailboat that you've been wanting and head to Panama. Take a few years off and then sell it. Do it now while the market is high. You will double your money on the houses in the desert and take your cash to Panama. You're young and single, so take off. I got a boat lined up for you. One of my clients is selling his, and you can steal it."

"What is it?"

"It's a 44 Morgan, center cockpit, one owner. It's in great shape, like new, and has never been used except around San Diego. You will love it."

"Cool. Let me get back to the desert, get my house in order, get the two houses on the market, and start making some plans. What does he want for the boat?"

"A hundred and twenty-five thousand dollars, but I am sure, for cash, you can pick it up for seventy-five."

"I got that lying around. Let's go look at it next week."

"Cool. Let's talk this weekend."

The real estate market was hot in the desert, and I put both houses up for sale. Then I called my buddy in Breckenridge, and that market was off the chart. I said, "I want to sell my lot. I bought it for fifteen thousand dollars quite a few years back. What can I get for it?"

He said, "Let's ask for a hundred and twenty-nine thousand and take a hundred and twenty."

When I bought it, I did not know they were putting in a ski lift chair down at the end of the street. It was a big home run. We had an offer in a week, a full-price, cash deal. There was the money for the boat without touching my savings. I sold both houses in the desert by myself in the next two months and made two hundred thousand dollars. That was three home runs in one year, a great run. I had almost half a million in cash—and I mean cash, like, in the bank, take it out tomorrow. All my friends were saying, "Don't sell. It's going to keep going up. Take the money and buy a few more units." They all said I was stupid. Well, who is laughing now? We all know what happened. I took a pass, stayed on the sidelines the next four years—not bad for a high school dropout.

I called Mike on Saturday, and he said he would be in San Diego, staying at Bowe's son's house. "Come on over. We got room for one more if you will cook, and Monday, we will look at the boat and take her out for a sail."

I said, "On my way. See you tomorrow. How does southwest sound? Carne Asada, rice beans, chicken enchiladas."

"Sounds great. See you at Bowes."

I liked Bowe. He was the youngest of three nice guys. We got along and had a lot of good times together. Bowe's house was in La Jolla, a nice place. That's what you would expect with his dad's connections. Still, Bowe was all right in my book.

I showed up with some cold beer and put together a nice Mexican buffet. Then we all caught up, did a few shots of Patron, and had a nice dinner.

Afterward, the boys headed to the patio overlooking the bay to have a few more shots and fire up cigars. Mike pulled out the info on the Morgan. Bowe knew the boat as well and said, "It's a great boat. If you don't buy it, I am. Plus, I have a captain friend who needs a ride to Panama. He will sail with you for free and teach you the ropes. Just feed him and buy him drinks. Plus, he is an engineer and can fix anything."

I said, "Shit, that sounds great."

"I am free in the morning," said Bowe. "We can all go for a morning sail."

"Sounds great," I said. "Let's have one more shot and call it a night." Mike was in as well.

The boat was at Harbor Island, not too far from the house. We were up early, had coffee, and were at the boat by eight to meet the owner, Bob Buzzard, a client of Uncle Mike's. He gave us the rundown on the boat. Bowe and Mike already knew everything; it was just for me.

Then we cast off and headed out to the bay for a morning sail. I will never forget that day. It was a nice day in the spring. The sun was shining, and there was a nice breeze. It was a great day for sailing. At that moment,

I knew I was buying this boat and heading to Panama. It had always been my dream to own a sailboat and sail the Pacific. I was at the helm and just got a huge hard-on. This was the life, my dream, and I was buying this boat today.

When we got back to the dock, I did not want to seem too interested. I told the guy I had to think about it and look at my financing. I also needed to survey the boat, and I would get back to him in a few days. He said, "Let me know as soon as you can. I want to make a deal, and you're a friend of Mike's, so we can work something out."

It was after lunchtime, and we were all starved and thirsty, so we headed to a little bar on the harbor to eat, have some drinks, and talk about the boat. It was in great shape, hardly any miles on it, with a new sail. It needed some updating, but that was it. I knew I had to have that boat. I told Mike and Bowe, and they agreed. It was a great sailboat, a 44 Morgan Perry Design blue water cruiser with a walk-in engine room and a great layout.

I said, "Bowe, are you sure about the captain? If I buy the boat, will he help me get it updated and get to Panama? Let's call him."

Bowe got him on the phone and lines up a meeting for dinner that night. Mike loved the boat and said, "Don't even think about it. Just buy it. Offer him seventy-five thousand in on cash Friday, and that's it."

"You're right," I said. "I am in. Let's meet with the captain and make sure I've got a crew lined up, and I will make an offer tomorrow."

We finished our lunch, had a few more shots, and toasted to my new boat. Mike had to head back to Newport. He said, "If you have questions, call me, but rest assured, this is a great boat at a great price, and you will get a lot of years out of her."

Bowe and I headed back to his place to see his old lady and check in and freshen up before our meeting with Captain Greg.

We met Greg at Harbor Island and showed him the boat. Then we went out for drinks and a bite to eat—mostly for drinks. Bowe told Greg about the boat, that it had been well taken care of and needed new electronics, autopilot, dingy, all minor stuff.

"When do you want to go to Panama?" Asked Greg.

"I have to be out of my house in thirty days," I said. "I am selling everything and moving to Panama. I will be living on the boat in a few weeks, and I would like to take at least six months to get there, sail the whole Pacific, all stops in Mexico, no rush I will pay all your expenses, and you can have the forward cabin and stay long as you want. I will buy all the food and beer and provide the girls in port."

Bowe laughed and said, "I told you, Greg, that you would like Chef Al. He is one crazy fucker. He's never sailed before, never owned a boat, and he buys a 44 Morgan on the spot. You have to love this guy. And now he is on his way to Panama with you, the trip of a lifetime."

Now we just needed one more crew member, and Bowe had someone else lined up, Peter. I had met him before, a guitar player/singer and mate on sailboats who was always up for an adventure. He was one more crazy fucker. This was going to be great. I hadn't even bought the boat yet, and I had a crew and plan all set up. Bowe said, "Buy it. I will tell Dad to talk to Bob and get him to put the offer in tomorrow. We will do a haul-out this weekend to make sure the hull is good, and then we'll start the refit and get ready to set sail south in a month or so."

More shots, and we all toasted to the Morgan.

At noon the next day, Uncle Mike called me and said, "We have a deal. You just stole a 44 Perry Design Morgan center cockpit. I call Bowe and the rest of the gang. Bowe says he will handle the hull. Just pick up the lunch tab for the guys."

On top of all this, the dock rent was paid up for two more months. Man, I was on a roll. The house closed on time, and I sold all my shit. The survey also went well. The hull was great; it just needed some updating. Besides that, the boat was in great shape. Greg moved into the boat a few days later. I still had some shit to take care of, but the plan was in motion. Greg was working on his punch list from the first day, and we soon became good friends. We were free spirits, just living for the moment.

Over the next month, I moved into the boat. We bought charts, fishing rods, a dingy, electronics, a TV, a sound system, Bimini cushions, and a new autopilot. I spent about twenty grand on the refit, but I bought the best of everything. I had this Morgan tricked out. I even had a water-maker installed. She was my new girlfriend, and I wanted her to look good when I came into port.

The gang had one last blowout on the boat, and I told everyone we were setting sail Sunday evening for Ensenada to do some final work on the boat. We could hire some cheap day workers there, get the work done, and then sail to Cabo. That was kind of our shakedown cruise.

The guys could not believe I'd sold everything I owned and called it quits. Mike said, "Listen to me. You did the right thing. Just wait and see. Next year or sooner, you will be glad you took my advice."

Bryan and a few of my friends were still flying high, thinking the market would keep on going even higher and spending and spending like there was no end in sight. Me, I was sitting on a nice paid-for Morgan, with a paid-for penthouse in Panama and shitload of cash. I just said, "Yeah, you guys are probably right. I just need a break and some new adventure."

They all wished me luck and brought me bottles of rum for the voyage. Mike and I had a heart-to-heart, and he said he was damn proud of me. I damn near broke down. He was my first real father figure, and I have never forgotten him. I love that man. He made me the man I am today. It's just too bad I did not meet him when I was growing up. I could have done so much more and made a difference in this world.

Unfortunately, we cannot change what we are dealt in life. We have to play the cards we are dealt and make the best of it. I'd been dealt a shitty hand and had done the best I could to get out of that hole back in Ohio full of deadbeats, crackheads, and losers.

We left San Diego the following night around midnight to get to Ensenada the next day around noon. It's a great little town, with cheap booze and plenty of pussy. We hung out for about a month, getting the wood done, the bottom cleaned, and just having a damn good time. A few of the guys came down to see the boat and visit our favorite little whorehouse, Club Paris. This place was the shit. If you have not been there, you don't know what you are missing. I will just leave it at that. I will get back to Club Paris later.

Before we knew it, the boat was shipshape, and we were ready to head south. We had one last blowout, and then we were off. I could write a whole book about this trip, and I plan on it if you guys like the first book. So, be on the lookout for *Tales of the Sea Rooster: Chef Al Returns.*

It took us almost a year to get to Panama. We were all tired and had done our share of fucking and just plain raising hell. I told the guys that once we got organized, I would buy them airfare back to California. I gave them the grand tour of Panama and took the guys to my favorite whorehouses, and we had a few dinners at my penthouse on Balboa. The boat was at the Flamingo Marina. I was friends with the owners, two brothers and another dude, all from well-off Panamanian families. Lots of dirty money, if you know what I mean. But who gives a shit? It's Panama, the money-laundering capital of Central America.

The crew hung out a few weeks. They were burned out and wanted to get back to the real world. We had been living a fantasy for a year, sailing to Mission Bay, Acapulco, the Sea of Cortez, Costa Rica, Nicaragua, Guatemala, Colombia, and that's just a start. So, as you can guess, they were ready to get back to the real world. Me, I was just getting started. This was what I was made for and what I lived for. But I could use a short break. Plus, I'd just spent around fifty grand. I needed to be a little cool; I was no millionaire.

We had one last blowout, just us three and a few girls I'd lined up. We took the *Rooster* out for a dinner cruise. It was the last time the three of us would ever be on the boat again and a night I will never forget. We switched off with the girls and had a nice steak dinner with some great red wine, '74 Saint-Emilion grand cru, a great year, out of my private stock. We finished the evening by drinking shots of Zacapa rum off the girls' bellies. The next morning, I put their asses in a cab.

I soon had the *Rooster* cleaned and ready for her next adventure. I had a great slip at the Flamingo, and I was all dialed in to Panama, with a bank account, credit card, penthouse, Porsche Cayman—I was living large. I was just planing my next move. Should I buy a bar in Panama or just keep sailing the *Rooster*, drinking and fucking whores for the next ten years, or maybe go back to work? I did not like the way that sounded. So, I stayed drunk a few more months and bagged a few more locals, some working, some from the bank, some from my complex. I really did not care. They all wanted something, dinner, cash, to go sailing. Pussy is never free, and don't let anyone ever tell you that.

Then the shit hit the fan. The stock market took a big shit, the worst since the Great Depression. My CPA lost it all, and my attorney did, too. I emailed my old boss, Bryan, and he'd had a run of bad luck as well. It seemed he'd lost it all. The money had run out, and Sonya had taken him to the cleaners once the gravy-train money ran out. I'd told Bryan that he was making a big mistake, but he had not listened. He'd wanted a hot young chick for the image. The marriage had lasted a few years, and they'd had a few kids, but now that the money had run out, she was looking for a new meal ticket.

She ended up fucking one of Bryan's friends, Ed Grech, owner of Crystal Couch Limousine in Orange County, a big-time guy. She was back in business, and the poor bastard married her. What the hell was Ed thinking? I know the pussy was not that good, but Ed was not much to look at and was kind of an asshole as well. He was boring, with no hobbies, just work, and all the world was about Ed, but Sonya did not care. She was living in a mansion in Villa Park and just setting Ed up for the taking. I heard it lasted about seven or eight years before Ed had to write her a check for five million. She went through that in no time. Sometimes, the fucking you give is the fucking you get.

Me, I couldn't have cared less what people thought of me. I was doing what I wanted when I wanted. I had a nice boat and a few bucks in the bank and was still young, with no stress. I had all I needed, and like I say, you have to be able to look in the mirror in the morning and like what you see, and I could do that with a big smile.

I was glad to be in Panama, just enjoying life, but I was getting bored. I had always liked being busy, working on a project or something, and I'd just taken a year off and fucked everything from San Diego to Panama in seven countries—I lost count after fifty or so. Plus, I had been drinking too much and smoking too much weed. I needed to get back to work to dry out again.

I was sitting on the back of the *Rooster* one Sunday afternoon with a couple of hotties and my English mate Luke, one more crazy fucker, when *Boomer* pulled in a few slips down from me. I heard the Colonel shout, "Chef Al, grab some lines. I need a hand."

What a small world. Luke and I went over and helped them tie up, and I introduced Jeff, aka the Colonel, to Luke. Then I brought over some beers and invited them over to the *Rooster* for dinner and drinks. Jeff said, "We have to clear. See you in a few hours."

Luke and I fucked the two tramps and told them that they had to leave, that we would do dinner next time. I gave them cab fare and said, "Hit the road." That was how we rolled in Panama.

Jeff and his mate, Fat Bastard, showed up a few hours after they cleared. I brought out some cold beers and a few shots of rum. I said to Jeff, "It's great to see you. What the hell are you doing in Panama?"

He said, "I heard rumors you were down here and was in to Panama, the banking and the chicks. I heard it was your town."

"Yeah, you're right," said Luke. "Chef is dialed in. You got to see his penthouse. He has the hook-up. You saw the two bitches we just fucked and kicked out when you guys pulled in? That's like an everyday deal for us. Well, it is for Chef. I have to work all week, but you guys are in good hands with him. You will have more pussy than you can handle. Trust me. I know for a fact he and his pal Ethan, who just left, bagged ten girls last weekend, two threesomes. It was crazy as shit. I saw the pics, and everyone at the marina was going nuts. I hope you guys got plenty of the little blue pills. You will need them."

I cooked us all a nice pasta and shrimp dinner and uncorked a great super Tuscany red. It was a great evening with some old friends. I never thought I would see the Colonel again, and sure as hell not in Panama. Jeff told me he was taking *Boomer* through the canal and needed a few deckhands and asked if I could help.

"Sure," I said. "When are you passing through?"

"A few weeks, no rush."

"Cool. Don't worry. I've got an agent for you, and Luke and I will go with you through the canal. Where are you going?"

"Fort Lauderdale. I bought a penthouse on Las Olas, and I'm going to keep *Boomer* there. The hell with Cally. It's going to shit, and the recession killed everything there, so I'm giving it a shot in South Florida. I am going to buy a few places, and you should do the same. It will be a home run. I am sure of that. Everything is pennies on the dollar. You cannot go wrong. Now is the time to buy again, or within the next year or so, but it's dam near the bottom."

"Cool. I will think about that."

We spent the next few days catching up. He told me that Bryan hit rock bottom. That little whore Sonia took everything and really fucked him, and now he was living on Pacifico, trying to regroup. I was glad I'd quit when I had. Jeff had bought a bunch of shit in Vegas, sold his Cally shit, and was off to Lauderdale, and I thought this might not be a bad plan. I still had half a million in cash lying around.

I lined Jeff up with my pal Pete, the legend of Panama and the only agent you need there. If you have a boat and need anything, Pete will make it happen. I was banging one of his daughters. She worked at the Marriott downtown. He never knew, or he would have killed me, I am sure of that. Jeff, Fat Bastard, and I did the Panama bar hop, and then I took them to my favorite whorehouse: Golden Time. For seventy bucks, you get two free beers and any girl you want, all Colombian and smoking hot. I always got two—I needed the extra beers. Jeff and Fat Bastard were in heaven. It beats the hell out of Club Paris in Ensenada. All the chicks are super hot, not some fat Mexicans. We hit it up every day for happy hour for a whole week, clear up to the day they were leaving. I showed them around town to some great restaurants and showed off my pad downtown. I mean, you can only fuck so much and put up with these whores for so long. You need to go to a nice restaurant and relax once in a while.

We also hung out at the Flamingo Marina, which had a great little bar, Cayuco. It's still my go-to bar before I get some pussy. All the guys meet there. The owner is my friend. She is from Spain and has been in Panama for a long time. I never fucked her. I wanted to, but her old man would have had me killed.

Beer was cheap, and the rum was nearly free. We would get a bottle of Abuelo every day, kill it, and then head to Golden Time. What a life.

I thought for sure I would never see fifty if I kept this up, but I'd leave a good-looking corpse and die one happy motherfucker. By the way, I made it to fifty. Now I'm sixty and doing the same shit, just a little slower, and no more than three at a time.

We got the Colonel through the canal, and he was on his way to Lauderdale. I went back to the *Rooster* to plan my next move. I stayed drunk a few more months and went to Golden Time and banged Panama sluts. I was cooking on a yacht for the two brothers who were partners in the marina. They were big real estate developers, but they were a couple of real fucking crooks, just dirty motherfuckers. They took my friend to the cleaners, never paid him for the install on some elevators. He was from Argentina and just got bent over. They treated me ok, but I was just the chef on the boat.

I thought about what Jeff had said about Lauderdale and decided to fly up, check it out, and buy a few units. I ended up buying three, all cash. I did ok on them and still own one.

Back at the Flamingo Marina, I knew everyone and was making money as a line handler going through the canal, seventy-five a day, and it was always two days. I did that once a week; that was my beer money, plus it was easy work.

Luke and I would meet damn near every night at Cayuco for drinks. It was a pretty good life, but I was getting bored and spending money like crazy. Then, just like always, shit fell into my lap. A new yacht came in and berthed right down the dock from me, on the end, a Westport 102 named *Rapture*. It was a nice boat, a little old but clean as a whistle. The captain was a fat guy, Doug, a real piece of work, just like most captains, who think they know it all. The only worse fuckers are private pilots. What ego complexes. They all must have little dicks.

Doug was cool with me, but he could be a real asshole if you were a deckhand. This was his first time in Panama, and I met him at Cayuco. He did not speak a word of Spanish and was not much to look at if you were trying to get some ass. Thank God he had money to pay for it. Plus, he was pretty fat. I don't think he could even see his dick, so I am sure the chicks had to get on top. Don't get me wrong. I bought my share of pussy in Panama, but I had several hot chicks, including a hot attorney who wanted to marry me. She just wanted a free ride, but she was smoking hot, and man, did she like to fuck. Latinas are all horny. You reach down there, and that pussy is just sopping wet. They cannot get enough. I must have had a dozen threesomes down there.

Doug took a liking to me. He saw chicks coming off my boat and saw that I knew all the right contacts. He needed someone to show him around and get him laid, poor fat old bastard. He was already in his mid-sixties and did not have a pot to piss in, with a fat old lady at home and a piece-of-shit old house in Port St. Lucie, Florida. I was up there a few times. He never saved any money, but to hear him talk, he had it all. Loser. I took him under my wing. He could be ok sometimes, and he always bought, so that was ok. I just do not like hanging out with fat old fuckers who are not very good looking, to say it nicely. Plus, he had no game.

We hung out together for a few months. The owner would come down, and they would go fishing for a week. Then he would leave, and I had to hook his boss up with some pussy. He had a pretty cool crew, and I took them out a few times. The chef he had was a drunk and real piece of shit from Michigan. He said he worked for the CIA, but I did not believe him. He could not cook for shit, but the two deckhands from South Africa were nice guys and hard workers, as all the guys from there are.

Just as I was about ready to close on one of the condos in Lauderdale, the chef on *Rapture* was drunk when the boss was on the boat for the last trip before they headed back. I guess he couldn't get out of bed, said he was sick so the mates had to cook. What a crock of shit. You have three weeks off every month, the boss only comes once a month for six days, and you can't keep your ass sober for a week? What a piece of shit, but one man's bad luck is another man's good luck—in this case, mine. It looked like I was going back to work, so I said goodbye to all my girlfriends, Luke and I tore it up a few more times, and I made one last visit to Golden Time.

Boat, La Buscadora. BVI

Panama 2011

Chef and Arts Pilot, Santa Monica

Chef Art and Lacy

Panama. Rapture, Freeport

RVA. Paul's Jet

chapter 16

ANDY ANSIN
CHANNEL 7 NEWS, MIAMI
MOTOR YACHT *RAPTURE*

JUST LIKE THAT, I WENT back to work. Before *Rapture* and crew headed back to Lauderdale, Doug came by the *Rooster* with a bottle and said, "Let's have a drink, and I'll buy you dinner tonight. Do you know a good steakhouse?"

"Only the best in Panama," I said. "Gaucho's. It's been there, like, a hundred years or some shit. First class, and not Miami prices."

We had a few rums and then headed downtown. I had a nice Porsche Cayman I'd picked up in a real estate deal. First stop, as always, was Golden Time. Doug was up for a couple of fresh ones before dinner. My MO was to get there before they opened and wait for the girls to get them while they were fresh. I taught all my pals that trick. You don't want sloppy sixths or sevenths.

Doug and I got all tuned up, and then I took him to Gaucho's. I brought a nice Saint-Emilion grand cru, 1975 estate. That's just how I roll. I knew the crew at Goucho's, so they never charged me corkage and took care of me. This was one of my go-to places. I took all my little chicks there; after that, I knew I would get some pussy.

We had a few drinks before dinner. I had my Knob Creek; they'd been buying it just for me. After some small talk, Doug said, "What are your plans? Do you want a full-time job on *Rapture*?"

"It depends on the pay and what the job entails," I said.

"It's cooking for the boss and the crew. You also gotta learn how to be a deckhand. You need to get your STCW, and we will pay for that if you take the job. It costs about eight hundred dollars. And you have to agree to a year. You will learn how to drive the tender and help with the lines. You don't have to help the guys clean the outside. You will be in charge of the inside and doing the boss's laundry. This boat moves. Unlike most yachts, we are in Panama every year, Mexico, the Keys, the Bahamas, Costa Rica, and the yard for two months for repairs."

"Cool. What's the pay?"

"We will start you at four grand plus bonuses, and the boss tips a few hundred bucks every trip as well. We are headed to Lauderdale in a few days, going straight to the yard, and we'll be firing the old chef once we are there. It will be great for you. You can get signed up for the school. I will take care of that for you. Just get back to Lauderdale in a few weeks and start class."

"Ok," I said. "I just bought the condo there, and I'm closing in a few weeks, so I will have a place to stay. Sounds great."

We had a great dinner, a couple of nice rib-eyes and an excellent bottle of wine. Then I drove us back to the boat.

They were leaving the next morning, and that was it. I was back to work again, my first real yacht job. I was excited. It sounded like a lot of fun, and the money was not bad. I made plans to get back to Fort Lauderdale. I had to close on the condo and start school, plus I was new to Florida. I had to buy a car now, too. They told me they would take care of the expenses.

I started school, and there were lots of young chicks in class—lots of dumb ones, too. What do you expect for South Florida? I also worked on the boat. We would be in the yard for two months, so Doug taught me how to drive the tender and tie lines. He also went over what the boss liked, and he put me in charge of the crew. They had to share a cabin, and I had the junior VIP suite to myself.

The boat was getting some major work done, as we would be heading to Mexico, Panama, and Costa Rica and would be gone about eight months. Meanwhile, I got to know Lauderdale. The Colonel showed me around. He had a place on Las Olas, so I had one friend there. I also started fucking my realtor, this little Jewish yentel, about forty years old, so I was back to my old tricks as well. Plus, there was a school teacher in my complex in the rotation as well.

We were set to leave right after Christmas, spend New Year's in Miami with Andy and his wife, then head to Key West, Mexico, and Panama. I had finished my STCW, and I was good to go. Doug liked that I was a diver, and I was learning to be a deckhand. We had a new crew, too. We'd hired a young kid, Brandon, as one of the deckhands. He was from South Africa and a good worker. First mate was a Texan, Cole. He's a great guy, and we are still friends. He runs his own boat now.

This was an all-guy boat. Andy wanted no chicks. They would only cause problems. I had to agree. If I am not fucking them, I've got no use for them. They always want something.

I think this is a good time to tell you who Andy is. Everyone seems to think these rich fucks have it all. They may have power and money, but there is more to life than that. Most people just don't get that. I have seen it all first-hand, so I know for a fact that most of them are all screwed up. Andy's family was no exception. He never had to work a day in his life. His old man made the money, Edmund Ansin.

Edmund was a Russian immigrant who made it in real estate and owned TV stations in Boston, New York, and Miami. Andy was the oldest and set to run the empire. His younger sister was gay, a real piece of work, and his younger brother was the same. When I was on board, the old man was on the *Forbes* 400 list. Andy fucked that up, lost half the empire in five years. The brother and sister could not wipe their own asses. I am sure the old man is rolling in his grave, thinking, "These three cannot be from my loins. What happened to my legacy? I got news for you, Edmund. It died with you. You should have made these fucks do some work. Rich kids are usually pieces of shit, and Andy was no exception. They never learn the value of a dollar or the importance of discipline. So, Edmund, what do you think? They're not going to work. Why should they when everything has been given to them?

Andy ran the real estate division, while Edmund still ran Channel 7 in Miami. I won't forget the first time I met the old man. We were getting flu shots at the TV station. Andy gave us a tour, and we got to meet Edmund. He was an ok guy, cheap, just like Andy. The station was the worst I've ever seen, with dirty carpets and peeling paint. I could not believe Edmund's office, just shit furniture. I don't think he ever spent a dime.

Andy was married to some Russian whore, as all the girls in Miami who were worth a shit told him to hit the road. Even though he was supposed to be this big playboy, he was cheap and had no game. He tried screwing all the weather girls at the station, but they shut him down. What a loser. He met this Russian whore online and ended up marrying her. He tried to pass her off as an attorney from Belarus. She was just learning English when I came on board. The crew knew better. She was only on the boat two times a year, and all she did was play video games on her phone while the two Russian nannies took care of the kids. Andy knocked her up right away, and they had three girls back to back. He was hoping for a son to carry on the legacy, and I'm sure the old man wanted it, too. Like I always say, the fucking you give is the fucking you get. Three granddaughters and gay daughter and son, and with that, the old man's legacy is dead. I say it's poetic justice.

Back to the *Rapture*. We were on our first trip, and our first stop was Miami to have Andy and the Russian bimbo on for dinner. Then, in the morning, we would head to Key West. I had spent all week provisioning, buying thirty cases of water and thirty cases of Gatorade. We had a huge, custom-built freezer, and I filled it to the brim. I also bought first aid supplies. The first trip would be nine months, Key West, Isla Mujeres in Mexico, Panama, through the canal, Las Perlas Islands in Costa Rica, and we would return home by the same route. Andy's hobbies were freediving and fishing, and the boat had about ten world records.

It was an all-guy boat, all about sport fishing, hookers, and blow, and it was always moving. Andy came once a month, staying on the boat at every port. He would fly in with one or two friends, all free divers, and they would fish for a week and then head back home. It was a pretty cool gig except for putting up with Andy's shit. I was in charge of getting the girls, as that was my strong suit and part of my job, and some blow as well. We towed a thirty-two-foot CV tender, which Andy and his guests fished from.

I did two trips like this with Doug and the same crew and one short one for four months in the Bahamas, as the boat was getting painted that year. The trips were great, but we did the same shit every time: girls, blow, fishing and just partying our asses off, so I will just cover the first one.

After that first night's dinner with Andy and the Russian, they hung out for a while and then went home. Andy liked my cooking, but the wife did not know shit about good food, so that was easy. We made it an early night, and the next morning, we headed to Key West.

The first part of the adventure was on. I had never been to the Keys, so this was a first. We were going to be there for three weeks or so. Andy was coming for five days, and he would be bringing the wife, the three young girls, and two Russian nannies. Then we would head to Mexico for a month or so. We had a week to prepare and a few days off to enjoy Key West.

The diving was great there. We dove the wreck of a Coast Guard cutter—I can't remember the name—and did all the tourist things. The Hemingway Museum was kind of cool, as I am a big fan and read his books. There were great restaurants, cool bars, and lots of weirdos, but it's Key West—what do you expect? I did not know Florida is the swinger capital of the USA. Crazy shit, but it's all good. It takes all kinds. I just don't think I'd like to watch some guy give it hard to my wife or girlfriend, but what the hell. Key West has it all. It's not my favorite spot, but there's lots of good fun to be had, and it's a great place to people-watch.

You can see all of Key West in a weekend: Mallory Square, the Hemingway Museum, Truman's Little White House, the southernmost point in the continental US, and that's it. The pink shrimp are great, and the oysters, too. Eastwood's bar is a cool little spot. It's not cheap to drink and eat there, and that's my deal. There's not a lot of pussy walking around Key West, and you might not know what you've got till they drop their panties. You might find a big surprise. Thank God we were never there during fantasy week. That's when all the crazies are out. All in all, though, it's a fun place.

The week flew by, and the next thing we knew, the boss was coming the next day with his wife, the two Russian nannies, and the three little girls. I had no idea what I was in for. They were supposed to be there for five days, but I changed that.

The trip started off great the first day, but it went to shit after that. The nannies were worthless. For one thing, they spoke no English. I hate that. You are working in the USA, and you cannot even try to speak English? The wife did not speak English, either, except "Roll over," "Get on your back," and "Bend over." She had Andy trained like a dog. She would sit on the couch all afternoon. The kids would cry, but she wouldn't do shit but play video games on her phone all day. This went on for a few days. The nannies did not do shit, either. They wanted me to cook for the kids and help watch them, too. I said, "No way. I don't do that. It's all on you." What a fucked-up deal.

Doug came into the galley and started giving me shit, saying that I had to cook for the kids and help watch them. I said, "Fine. Fuck you. I quit. I am out of here."

I packed my shit up and was on the dock when Andy returned from fishing. He and that asshole Doug come running after me. Andy said, "You can't leave."

I told him, "This was not part of the deal. I don't watch kids and cook for them, too." It would not have been so bad if this bitch had gotten off her fat ass and helped. They were her kids, after all. What a worthless piece of shit. She just had the kids for the money. Sad.

Andy said, "Listen. We are going to leave tomorrow, a few days early. I will take the family out tonight and tell the wife that bad weather is coming in and we have to get the boat out of here and head to Mexico. She won't be back on the boat till next Christmas, so don't quit."

"We need you and want you to stay," added Doug.

"Ok, I'll stay," I said, and we all shook hands.

Then Andy said, "I will get the deckhands to take your gear back to the boat, and you can take a night off."

I thought that was pretty cool of Andy. He had some balls after all. They all left the next morning, the worthless wife, the Russian nannies, the three little girls, and Andy, too. What a nightmare it had been, but just like that, things were back to normal.

Doug took the crew to dinner, and Andy gave everyone a few hundred dollars. We all had a great dinner that night, and we laughed about the Russian wife and the three kids, not to mention the two nannies.

At the crack of dawn the next morning, we were on our way to Isla Mujeres, the island of women, Mexico-bound. As we passed the Dry Tortugas, the weather was great, and the sea was calm and flat. I just love being out at sea, with the dolphins and whales. It's just so peaceful out there, watching the blue horizon, and the sunsets are spectacular on the ocean.

A few days later, we rolled into the Villa Vera Marina on Isla Mujeres. If you have never been there, it's a great little spot, still one of my favorite stops. I have been back many times over the years. It's old-time Mexico, right across from Cancun. It's small, maybe two miles long and a quarter-mile wide, if that, but what a cool little town. It's got a great beach, the water is just mind-blowing, and there's great fishing. The big deal is the whale sharks that come every year. It had been on my bucket list for years to ride one, and yes, I finally got to do it here.

We would be here for a month and then head to Panama. Andy would be coming in two weeks with a guest, and they would stay six days, so we had time to get the boat ready and for me to pick up fresh fruit and produce. Once the boat cleared customs, we got our game plan ready for the next month. You can see the whole island in one day. Cancun, though, takes a few days, if not more; it depends on what you want to do.

Within a few days, I had the island wired thanks to Helena. She ran the office at the marina, and we quickly became friends. She is from France and her mother lives in Spain, and she showed me around the island. Then we went out to dinner and over to Cancun. She is one cool chick, and we are still friends to this day and keep in touch. Her mom came into town the next week, so I met her. We all had dinner, and she told me about Spain, saying that once I came to visit, I would never want to leave. She gave me an open invitation to come, which I took her up on the next year, and she was right. I fell in love with the country and visited a few years in a row till I bought my own place in the south. I love that place. I still keep in touch with her, and she has some great stories. She used to run with Churchill's wife and was married to a spook, MI6. She is one hell of a lady. We had a few good laughs and great dinners. They were really nice to me, and I'll never forget our time together.

The rest of the crew was out banging whores and getting drunk every night, but I'd cleaned up my act some. I got back into running and working out, plus I had Helana to go out with, and she was a lot of fun. The crew and I did some great diving and took a few trips to Cancun to watch bullfights. Doug and I did a road trip up to the largest of all the Mayan ruins, Chichen Itza. It's close to an old colonial town called Meredith, with lots of great shops. I still like going to the bullfights and drinking cold beer and tacos.

Back on the island, we got ready for Andy and his guest. This would be a week-long trip, no wife, just Andy and one of his buddies from Miami, a world-class freediver. Doug would always pick up Andy and his guests at the ferry in the tender.

The trips ran like clockwork after the first few. The first night, steak was served for dinner. Then we'd either go to a whorehouse or I would have a few delivered. I would hand-pick them myself the day before. Andy and his guest would party on the boat, bang the girls, and get a little crazy. After the first night, they would go to bed after dinner, and there would be no drinking except a glass of wine with dinner or maybe a beer. It was all about the fishing and trying to get more world records. The last night was the same as the first: grab some chicks and rock and roll. Even the crew would participate.

The boat already had a few dozen world records, but Andy was looking for more, and so were the other divers. I'll say one thing about Andy: he was one hell of a free diver. He could go down well over a hundred feet for some time and caught some big-ass fish. I have to give credit where it is due, even if he was a cheap prick and an asshole as well.

We would all be up at six am to have a light breakfast of oatmeal. I would pack lunches for Andy and the guests, as they would be gone all day. They would take one crew member with them to drive the boat and help with the fish. The crew members would trade off every other day. One would stay back help, clean fish from the day before, and wash down the boat. I would take care of the inside and work on dinner, laundry, and whatever had to be done. Doug, though, would go back to bed for a few more hours. He was the laziest captain I ever worked for and a pig. He would get the real young hookers, like teenagers. He was a real piece of shit.

The guys would be out fishing all day. If they got a world record, they might come back early. If not, they would stay out all day. When they returned, we'd take pictures of the fish. Then everyone would clean up, I'd make a nice dinner, and then we'd all go to bed early. So, there were really only two days of madness.

No world record on the first trip, but there was lots of fish to eat and freeze for the crew. Before I knew it, the trip was over. We all were so busy we just lost track of time. Andy gave us all a tip of a few hundred bucks. That was nice, as we'd busted our asses. Andy thanked us all, and then Doug took him to the airport.

Now we had the boat to ourselves again. We spent a few more days in Mexico to fuel up, recharge, and wait for a weather window, as we were towing a thirty-two-foot CV. I took Helena out a few more times, as we were becoming good friends, while the boys tore up the island, spending their whole paychecks. I was just saving everything, living on the tips and not much more, but I was older than the rest of the crew, except for Doug, who had about fifteen years on me. Doug did not plan for the future or save shit. Instead, he spent tons of cash on these young whores. I mean, he had three kids, one of whom was still in college, and lived in an old shack in Port St. Lucie. He put the young girls ahead of his family—pretty fucked up, I think.

Finally, we had a weather window, and it was time to get underway. On the last night, the young guys tore it up with Doug, and Helena and I joined them for one drink, and then we were off to our favorite place on the island, Roland's, which had the best salt-crusted snapper I've ever eaten. If you find yourself on the island, it's a must-stop for dinner. There is one on the mainland as well. Man, I miss that place. Real old school.

The next thing we knew, we were casting off and underway to Panama. Our first trip was under our belt, Andy was happy, and we wouldn't see him again for a month. The trip from Cancun to Panama was great. I ended up doing it a few times, and I later took the *Sea Rooster* from Cartagena to Isla Mujeres, but that's a whole other story. The crew was all rested, and there was no drinking while we were underway, except for my nightly glass of wine with my dinner.

At night, the crew would take turns standing watch. I did not have to, but I would make some snacks and coffee for the guys, check the engine room, and keep an eye on the tender we were towing. To me, there is no better feeling than being underway on a nice yacht and waking up with only the sea in front of you. It's so calm and peaceful; you just can't describe it. Unless you have done a trip yourself, you have not a clue. Trust me.

This was our longest trip so far, and it went off without a hitch. We arrived in Panama and docked at Shelter Bay. It's on the Caribean side, where you cross through the canal. I once took the *Rooster* through and kept her at Shelter Bay for a season. That's how I knew the owner and the staff there. Russ was the owner, a retired Navy commander who'd married into a wealthy Panamanian family. Lucky bastard. He had it made. He was a real nice guy, and we became good friends. I almost took over the restaurant at the marina. Thank God I did not. Panama is no place to own a business unless you're Panamanian or connected. There are a bunch of thieves and crooks, so stay clear.

We hung out for a day as we waited for Pete to get us cleared to go through the canal, and I got ahold of Juan to help us go through, as we needed one more line handler. Finally, we were set to go the next morning, so we just hung out at the marina. I fixed a nice dinner, and we had a few beers and went to bed early. We had to be on our game while going through the canal, as we had the CV tied up to us.

It was not an easy task, but we got through in one day without a hitch and were pulling into the Flamingo right about dinnertime and happy hour. It's so cool to go from the Caribbean to the Pacific in just one day. There's a big difference—for one thing, the tidal surge on the Pacific side is easily five feet.

Pete met us at the boat with the customs guy, and we were all cleared and checked in before dinner. For me, it was like coming home again. The owners of Flamingo were my pals, and yes, I had a few girlfriends. One of them, I liked a lot. She was my banker at Bank General. We still keep in touch. We had a nice run, but she wanted kids, just like the attorney. I was like a sailor—I had a few in every port, and when they started to get serious, I kicked them to the curb and got a new model. Nothing was going to tie me down. I'd rather be single than married with a life of misery. How true this is. Ask any married guy, and he will tell you the same.

This was Cole's and Brandon's first time in Panama, so I showed them around, taking them to all the good restaurants and watering holes and the old city, Casco Viejo. But I always liked the Flamingo. It was a cool place to hang out and a cheap place to drink and eat. Plus, my favorite spot was there, Kutakas. They all liked it as well

Brandon did not go out much. He hated to even spend five bucks and thought he could just bang these girls for free, and he did not speak a word of Spanish. Cole spoke some, and he was nailing a few locals, but still, you have to give them cab fare, food, stuff like that, no different than in the States. It's the nature of the beast. Doug was up to his old shit, getting the underage ones. He was lucky he did not get in trouble or his ass kicked.

I took Cole to my penthouse, but I never took Doug or Brandon. They were not worthy. Doug would have just wanted to use it, and he was a slob on top of that. Cole and I doubled-teamed a few up there, even switched off a few times.

We had three weeks till Andy and one of his guests showed up for the next trip. We put fuel in the boat, and I bought provisions. The guys kept the boat clean every day, and I did my part to keep the interior tidy. I also fed the crew three squares a day, and I mean nice stuff.

We all took the same days off, and on those days, the galley was closed, end of story. Brandon was so cheap he did not even want to go out after being on the boat five straight days. Doug told him, "The galley is closed. If you want something to eat, buy it. Don't be in the freezer. You have a fridge in your room, so buy a few things." I thought Brandon was going to cry. What a cheap little fucker. Buy a pizza or some cereal and milk. Spend a few dollars.

Once I laid the law down, that was it. I ran the crew and the inside of the boat. The buck stopped with me. I was good to the crew and a super-fair guy. I just cannot put up with lazy fucks and cheap bastards. Doug was pretty cheap as well. I can count the number of times he took the crew to dinner on one hand. That sucks. I took care of the guys more than that. Andy only did it a few times. That was his MO. I'd heard from past crew that he'd tip the crew in the States and buy a few lunches or dinners, but once he had you out of the country, the tips stopped and no free lunch. That's why, every year, he had a new crew. They quit. No raise, no more tips, and you worked your ass off, and if you drove the tender, he always gave you shit: too fast, too slow, or you cost him a fish. It was never his fault. He also yelled at the crew.

Brandon left as soon as we got back to Lauderdale. He needed to save money, and if you quit, you had to pay your way back home. That sucks, but it's maritime law. Cole and I stuck it out two seasons. He needed the sea time. Me, I was saving some cash as well. Plus, Andy never fucked with me. He knew better, as I had already quit once, and he loved the way I cooked fish and took care of the crew, not to mention that I got the pussy for him and some coke on every trip.

The day arrived, and we sent a driver to pick up Andy and one guest, Sue. She was from Boca and worked for IBM, and from what Doug said, she was one hell of a free diver and had a few records. Plus, she was not bad looking. The trip was going to be a little over a week. The first stop was the Las Perlas Islands. A season of the reality show *Survivor* was filmed there, and it had great fishing. The area is remote, with nothing but fishing and islands with no one living on them. Truly undiscovered and very pretty.

Andy and Sue boarded on time, and I showed Sue her room. I told her all the dos and don'ts, but she knew, as she has been on *Rapture* several times. There would be no girls or blow this trip. The first night, I did a nice surf and turf, served with a bottle of red, as they wouldn't be diving tomorrow. On the first night, the crew and I always had dinner with Andy and his guest to talk about the trip and the plan, kind of a welcome-home dinner. It was a nice touch; I will give Andy credit for that.

After dinner, everyone turned in early, as we had a long trip and a busy week ahead. I liked these trips. We always went to a great spot, and I was so busy every day that they were over before I knew it and we were on our way back to our home port. I always got a break in the afternoon to catch a little sun and swim to one of the islands and go for a run, hike, or just a little exploration.

A typical day would start with feeding the boss, guest, and crew. I would already have lunches made for Andy and his guest to take with them. Then I would go clean the rooms, do some laundry, vacuum, straighten up the interior, that kind of stuff. Once that was done, I would fillet some fish from yesterday's catch and feed the crew lunch. I was usually finished with everything by one. They would fish till dark, so I had all afternoon to plan dinner, take a break, and explore. Dinner was the same every night, whatever they caught that day. The crew ate the same, so I only had to do a salad, starch, veggies, and fruit for dessert, nothing heavy, very clean—as I call it, spa or moderation cuisine. When they got back, we would unload the fish. If any were world-record size, we would take pictures, get the scale out, and do all the documentation needed. Then, if there was a grouper or a nice snapper, I would filet it up and serve it that night.

We never had a shortage of fresh fish. That is the one thing I miss about that gig. We ate the best fish all the time. I cooked more fish on that boat than at any other time in my career. That's how I learned to perfectly prepare and cook fish in many different ways. I can go on for hours about my fish recipes. We will get back to that later, and I will tell you some nice dishes I like doing.

We went out to Las Perlas a little after sundown and dropped anchor, and I got dinner ready, as it would be an early night again. We always got to the fishing spots around this time.

Sue was a real cool chick. I think she was Thai, with a little island French Polynesian blood. She was hot, with one hell of a body, and in great shape. I would say she was in her mid-forties and smart. The next morning, they were off early. Quite a few islands make up Las Perlas. They're remote, and there's some great fishing. All the tuna from Mexico come down. I took *Rooster* there for a while to explore the islands.

They got back at dusk with a few nice red snappers, about six tuna, all about a hundred and fifty pounds each. It was a good day's catch, but no records. Cole and I filleted the snapper for dinner. We would do the tuna tomorrow. That's a job; it takes a few hours. We took some pics, and then everyone cleaned up for dinner by yours truly. I made one of my island favorites: house salad, pan-seared red snapper with roasted red pepper salsa, sweet potatoes mashed with banana and dark rum, grilled asparagus, fresh berries and lemon sorbet. It's a nice dinner—always a hit, that one. Andy and Sue had a nice glass of wine, and then it was off to bed.

I cleaned up, did the turn-down service, and set up for breakfast the next morning—always a step ahead. Then I ate and had my glass of wine. The crew had already turned in, so it was quiet and I could enjoy my dinner and wine by myself. That was the best part of the day. I miss those days; lots of good times.

The rest of the trip was pretty much the same: up early, fishing, nice dinners, and that was pretty much how the trips were once we got to the fishing spot and dropped the hook. It was all on autopilot unless the fishing was shit. Then we might move the big boat. That did happen a few times on some of the trips.

Before I could blink an eye, we were pulling up anchor and heading back to the Flamingo with a shitload of fish. Andy was happy, Sue had had a good time, and we all got tips. We made it back to the Flamingo about dusk, tied up, and Andy said they were going out. Sue wanted to see the historic part of Panama, Casco Viejo, so I cooked for the crew that night. We could not leave the boat, as Andy was still kind of on board.

That was one of the rules—it's the same on most yachts—and there was no drinking, except for the chef. That's my rule.

When Andy and Sue returned that night, I fixed them a drink, Sue and I exchanged emails, and then they turned in, as they had an early flight back to Miami. Just like that, the first trip was in the bag. We still had a lot more, and we are heading to Costa Rica, to a place called Los Sueños. It was a big sport fishing marina about a three-day trip from the Flamingo.

The best thing about this job was that Andy only came every month or six weeks, so we had plenty of time to grab some chicks and drinks and explore the places we were visiting. We had a week till we took off again, as we were waiting on a weather window. I made one last provision stop, loading up on food and water, and once the weather looked great, we were off on a new adventure.

We traveled up the coast to one of the few still-unspoiled places on the coast and dropped anchor off a little island about half a day from Los Sueños. We wanted to get there in the afternoon—I guess the marina is a bitch at night; I think they all are—so we dropped the hook and spent the night. We all stood anchor watch that night and kept an eye on the tinder, as there are thieves up and down the coast.

At the crack of dawn, we pulled anchor and started the final leg of the trip. We planned to be here for a month. Andy was coming in two weeks with Jose, his friend from Spain. They would spend eight days here, and we would stay on a week or so, depending on the weather, to take on fuel, food, all that sort of thing. Plus, we always did a day trip somewhere, and I was always exploring, hiking, checking out the locals.

I'd taken the *Sea Rooster* here a few years back, so I knew the area. It was a great spot to chill and fish, Jaco Beach, with tons of chicks and cheap drinks, an old surfer town. There is a Marriott resort close by as well if you want to spoil yourself, which I did. The place has a great spa. If you have never been to Costa Rica, I highly recommend it. It's the Eco capital of the world, with great hiking, beaches, rain forest, water-falls, monkeys, birds—especially the toucans; they are so cool—and of course, lots of chicks.

We pulled in, cleared customs, cleaned the boat, and were ready to go ashore and get into some trouble. At least, Cole and I were. He had never been there, so I showed him around. We had plenty of time until Andy and Jose arrived. We did a few day trips, went diving off Cocos Island, a natural marine garden that's off limits for fishing. Time flies by when you are having a great time, and the next thing I knew, it was the day before Andy was supposed to show up. The party was over, and it was show-time. Eight days straight and then a month off again, with one more check to throw in the bank.

Andy and Jose arrived at the boat about noon, and the party started. We planned a day trip to town to get some girls to bring back to the boat, have some drinks, and fire the hot tub up. Then we'd hit the beach town sideways. We drank all afternoon, grabbed a half-dozen ticas, and headed back to the boat. After fucking and sucking all night, we sent the girls back the next morning. That was the drill: you pay them to leave. Most guys still don't get that. I fixed breakfast for the boss and crew. No fishing today, but we had to get ready for tomorrow and the next few days. We got the tender all fueled up and hired a local guide to take the group to some fishing spots. I served a nice local corvina fish dinner, and we all turned in early.

The next day, the game was on. Now it was all about fishing. The first day, the group caught a half-dozen tuna and a few groupers, just small ones for dinner. It was the same the next few days, except for some dinner-size snappers and some big amberjacks. The locals love them. I think they're good for smoking and fish dip, but that's it. This is where I learned how to smoke fish and make dip. We had a smoker on the boat, and Andy loved smoked fish. The dip I made was a great snack, clean and all protein. It's still one of my go-to snacks, a great starter.

We must have had a few hundred pounds of tuna by the third day. I told Doug we were out of freezer space, and then I gave the extra away to some of the sport-fishing guys and crew, as we had tons. At dinner, I told Andy, "Don't shoot no more tuna unless it's a record. We are full, all fridges." So, what happened the next day? He shot a goliath grouper, five hundred pounds or some shit. It was a world-record-setting fish. Look at the pics. We had to use the crane to get it onto the boat.

That night, we went into town, drank, and brought some girls back to the hot tub. This was the last day of the trip, and it seemed fitting to get a world record and a hot tub full of naked hot chicks. Andy was in a great mood and tipped us again this time.

The next day, he and Jose headed back to the airport. They were happy, and one more great boss trip was in the bag. We had six weeks to meet Andy back in Panama before we started the trip back to Lauderdale, and the boat had one more world record to its credit. All in all, it was a great trip.

So, we hung out a few days, waiting on the weather to clear before making our way back to Panama. We would stop at CoCo island for an overnight and then go on to Panama. We had about six weeks till we met Andy in Panama for the next trip, and Jose from Spain was coming back.

We made it back to Panama in a few days after the stop in CoCo and were back at our home port, the Flamingo Marina, home sweet home, where the girls were plenty and the beer was cheap and cold. What more could a guy ask for? Maybe some weed. We still had almost a month till the next trip.

There is always plenty of work to do on a yacht, like cleaning and polishing the steel. There is always something, and then you have to start over again, and the same is true with the interior. The good thing when we were in Panama was that we could go out every night and grab a few chicks or beers or just hang out. We stopped working at about five every day in port. I fed the crew, and then we were off till seven the next morning.

We had one more trip in Panama with Andy and Jose before we made our way home. This last trip was going to be ten days, and we were going to hit a few places, La Perlis Islands, Pinas Bay, the Gulf of Chiriqui, and Ciba National Park. These are all great and remote spots; you have to have a boat to get there and plenty of fuel and food for ten days. I hope you enjoy the pics. I did this trip three times: once on *Rooster* and twice on *Rapture*.

We still had a few weeks till Andy arrived, so we partied like rock stars in Panama. Cole and I were fucking everything that moved. Oh, and of course, we were drinking lots of rum in the process. Cole loved Panama and was having a great time. Brandon just stayed on the boat, jacking off every night. Doug, the fat old captain, was out trying to get some pussy, but he was cheap and a fat old fuck and not great looking on top of that, and he had to have teenagers. He was a pig—barely legal was his MO. He's lucky he did not end up in a Panamanian jail. I hope his wife reads this book. I will be sending her a copy and pictures of Doug with these whores. He was a real piece of shit, or I would not think about doing this, but what an asshole, and he thought he was the shit. The first time he introduced me to his brother, he said, "This is my chef."

I said, "I don't think so. Your name is not on my check, and it's not your boat."

He thought he was as all that—all the pricks do. I let him know I worked for Andy and Doug was the captain. What an ego for a fat piece of shit. I still don't get it.

The next few weeks passed by. Cole and I had a few good times, and we had the boat ready for the next trip. Andy was due the next day. If you like to move, this was the yacht to be on. We were on the move all the time, and I loved the all-guy crew—no one crying over petty shit and no drama. It's just too bad Cole was not the captain and we had a better owner, but that's life—would have, should have.

Andy and Jose showed up, and I grabbed a few girls for them the first night. The next morning, we were off to Las Perlis, and the fishing game was on. This trip was the longest, ten days, and we moved the boat three times. The guys were killing it. We had the freezer almost full after the first few days. We hit a few more spots for a day or two each, and there were no records this trip, but they caught a lot of fish and had a really great time. We did not see another boat for days.

We went ashore in Cherokee, hit a few bars, grabbed some girls, and had a hot tub party again. Nothing new there, just some new faces, or should I say, new ass. I will never forget these trips. We hit all the best spots on the Pacific coast of Panama and damn near Colombia. We did not get a world record but did get tons of pussy, and to me, that's better than some record waiting to get broken.

We fished and fuck all week long, and when we got back to Flamingo, we were all beat, including Andy and Jose, who were ready to go home. We hit the dock, tied up, and got all squared away. It was the last night, and somehow we all got our second wind. Oh, shit is right.

Andy wanted to take us all out, and I put it together. The first stop was my favorite: Golden Time. That's a nice place to start. What's better before a nice steak dinner than getting your dick sucked and throwing a few shots into a little Colombian honey? Nothing. If you have something better, please let me know. We all picked out our numbers. If you have not been there, the girls each have a number on their bra, and you just pick a number, and she is all yours. We all had our two free beers, did the wild thing, and worked up an appetite. I made a reservation at Gauchos, the steakhouse. Andy liked this place as well. We ordered bottles of wine and a bottle of rum and talked about the girls we'd had and the numbers. We all asked about number seven—had anyone grabbed her? No one had. We all laughed. "Let's go back and all fuck her," someone said, but now we were already into a few bottles of wine and had just polished off a bottle of Abuelo. We talked about the trip and the fishing and how we would see Andy in Mexico in a month. That was the next stop.

We finished our steaks, got into the Knob Creek, and fired up a few Cubans, and the next thing you know, we all got our second wind. It was still early, so Andy said, "Chef, grab some girls and get them back to the boat."

"Ok," I said. "I am on it. See you back at the boat. Give me an hour or so, and give me a few hundred to start with to get them there."

I made one stop, Cohibas, across from the new Marriott. It's like a shooting gallery. I knew the owner and bartender there. I grabbed a handful of girls, told them I'd pay half now, half later, and cab fare, and we were on our way, one more hot tub for the ages. We all switched off on all of them. Andy took the hottest one to his suite, but the rest of us stayed in the hot tub and had our way with the girls. They loved it, too. Big yacht, hot tub, rum, what is not to love? And they all got paid.

Jose had the best time in Panama. He did not come back the next season; this was his last trip with Cole and me. I liked him. He was a really nice guy and one hell of a diver, with many world records. He was a fireman back in Spain and was in great shape. Andy was, too, but not in the same league. He thought he was, but it was not even close.

The next day, I cleaned and drained the hot tub, and we sent Andy and Jose to the airport with our driver. Andy did not tip us this time. He just said, "Goodbye, and I'll see you in Mexico." That was it.

We got the boat buttoned up and ready to pass through the canal again, stocked up on food, took on fuel, and waited for a weather window. We tore up the town a few more nights, and then I said goodbye to all my girls. We also picked up one of my pals, as we needed an extra line handler to go through the canal. Then, early one morning, we were on our way. By the end of the day, we were through the canal and heading north to Mexico. The next stop was Isla Mujeres, and Helena was waiting for me.

We had all had our share of Panama and were ready for a fresh port, some fresh pussy, and some good Mexican food. I love Mexico; I've had lots of good times there. I love the beaches, and it's still very affordable to eat and drink there. The diving is great, and it's got some world-class golf courses. Oh, and there's lots of hot ass all around. What more do you need?

We were at sea few days and getting close. You don't want to go into that marina at night in a yacht; it's pretty damn tight. So, we spent the last night on the hook and pulled in first thing in the morning. We cleared customs and immigration and were drinking by noon, and now we had three whole weeks until Andy arrived.

Helena was glad to see me. We had dinner that night at my favorite place, Rolando's. I always have the salt-crusted snapper, the best I've ever had, and a nice bottle of Spanish red. We played catch-up, and she said her mom was fine and couldn't wait for me to visit her in Spain. I said, "I will next year when I quit this job. I will plan a trip in the spring or fall." That's the offseason over there in the Med. We took a few day trips down to Tulum to the south. It's got the best ruins of the whole coast, and there is a cool little town that reminds me of Islas Mujeres as well, a very laid-back place. We spent the night at a great little beach cabana and had dinner on the beach. It was a nice evening.

The next couple of weeks, we did the guy thing: going to bullfights and grabbing a few girls. I had to watch my back as Helena ran the office at the marina and lived next door as well. I played golf a few more times, dove a wreck, and did the wall at Cozumel one more time. That's always a great dive. The highlight of the whole trip was the whale sharks. It had been on my bucket list for years to swim and ride a whale shark. I'd even flown to the Bay Island, as they used to spend the winter there, but now they congregated off the coast of Cancun, halfway between the island in a kelp garden. We got wind of it from one of the locals we knew from the bar, who said he could take us there. Doug said, "Cool, we'll go early the next morning."

I packed a cooler full of beer and lots of food: grilled shrimp, baby squid, guac, salsa, chips, and grilled grouper fingers. We loaded up the CV, our tender, and were off to ride the sharks. After a short boat ride, we reached a small private reserve with no fishing. We came around a little rock point, and there they were, thirty or forty—I mean, a whole shitload—just hanging out, eating the plankton. There were some big-ass ones, too. I'd never seen such a sight in my life; it was right out of some TV wild kingdom show. We sat around and watched them and then sorted out our snorkeling gear and dove right in the middle of all of them. It was just spectacular. I petted one in the mouth, and I got on one and rode him for a few minutes. Then he got bored and dove to the bottom with me on top of him, cool as shit. I got off, got some air, went back down, and got on a different one.

This went on for a few hours, and then we started to get bored. I mean, after I rode three or four, the thrill was over. We were getting hungry and thirsty as well. Cross one more off the bucket list. We talked about the experience for the next few days. Man, that was a great time. Only once in a lifetime will you see that many in one spot.

Now we had to get back to work. Andy was due in a few days, and I had to get the galley ready, line girls up, clean the inside, and plan the menu. When in Islas, we didn't move the big boat. For trips, they took the CV out to the top fishing spots they liked. I enjoyed living in a marina, and it didn't suck to be on a hundred-foot Westport. Doug left me alone, so that's why I stayed two years. I also liked the spots the boat went to.

Plus, Cole and I were pals. He was a real good dude. We had lots of laughs.

Andy showed up with one guest, a Cuban guy named Roman from Miami. He had quite a few records and was one hell of a diver. He was one of the very few friends of Andy's who were nice. They came on board, and it was the same game plan as before: I had some girls lined up for them the first night, and then it was down to business for the rest of the week. They wear shooting lots of tuna, snapper, and mahi-mahi. It was a good week, and there was one new record for the boat.

Andy shot a twenty-five-pound porgy. They're ok to eat, but normally, they're around five pounds, so that was a big one. We all gave Andy shit about the porgy. He hated to be teased. He thought he was a tough guy. Come on, water polo in college? Give me a break. Oh, and the debate team, I think. It turned out that he beat the record by around ten pounds. We got the scales out, took the pics, did all the documentation, and it was a record for the boat and Andy, too.

They shot a lot of fish that week and had a really good time. They decided to take the last day off and go to Cancun and hang out and then have dinner on the boat and Mexican ass for dessert. I lined up two hotties for them after dinner, as they had an afternoon flight and Andy was known to rush in the morning. I fixed a nice salt-crusted snapper with pico de gallo, yellow rice, roasted green beans, and a nice caramel flan for dessert. All parties for happy. It was a nice dinner, and the fish was oh so fresh. It was a good send-off dinner, and the girls on the dock would be a great nightcap. I fed the crew and turned in. I was beat.

The next morning, the girls were gone. We never let them spend the night—boat rules. We got Andy and his guest loaded up, and Doug took them to the mainland and put them in a cab. Andy stiffed us again, saying he did not have a chance to get to the bank and would make up for it in Key West. I didn't believe it. For all we knew, that fat bastard Doug had kept it. I would not have put it past him. We would find out when we got to Key West. I planned on confronting him and saying, "Hey, what's up?" The rest of the crew was pissed as well. Cole and I knew Brandon was done soon as we got back to Lauderdale, but we did not say a word to Doug, as he was an asshole and he'd fucked Cole on a reference, too, so no favors for Cappy Shithead.

The next few days, we get the boat ready to make the last big leg to Key West. We had half a month to get there, as Andy wouldn't be there for weeks. That was par for course, which was good for us, as it meant time off. We still had daily duties but not like when the boss was on board.

Helena and I had a few more nice dinners, and Cole and I got fired up a few times as well. Islas is such a cool little spot. It's on my list of favorite places. I miss Tiny's bar. My dear, old friend, the bar, is no wider than ten feet and about forty feet long. The owner, Tiny, is about 350 and can hardly fit behind the bar. What a great guy. My money is never good there, even to this day. I gave him so much fish. Man, what fun times Cole and I had there. We spent a few afternoons there while waiting for the weather to be in our favor for the trip. Finally, we got a nice report and were underway again. I said goodbye to Helena, telling her I would see her in about six months.

We returned to Key West, where we had a great time. We did a couple of dive trips—there are a few cool wrecks there—and the Mallory Square thing again. That never gets old. A little Cuban bar there makes the best mojitos in town. It's a great place to look at all the hot chicks and, of course, all the freaks—and there is more than a fair share there. I say, whatever floats your boat. As long as you don't invade my space, I don't care what you do. There is plenty of pussy to go around for whoever wants it.

We had a few weeks till Andy returned, so we cleaned the boat every day and went diving and drinking. I played a few rounds of golf as well. After you've been to the Hemingway Museum, the treasure hunter Fisher deal, Mallory Square, the Hog Breath Saloon, and the Truman place, that's it. The beaches are nice, oh, and the farthest place south in the USA, like ninety-two miles to Cuba. And if you have a boat, there's Tortugas Park. There are some great shops as well and a few good, though overpriced, restaurants. It's a tourist trap, you know, but it's all good.

The best time I had was with Carolina, my little Polish hottie from the golf course. She was the beverage cart girl. She knew the meaning of full service. What a little spinner. We had a few nice dinners and went a few rounds together. That was one hot little mess in a good way. Time flies by in places like that. I'd get up, clean the boat, feed the crew lunch and then dinner, and then the day was over, and we'd go out for a few beers. Then it was time for bed, and the cycle would start all over again the next day. I had some of my best times on these yacht jobs.

Andy was driving down from Miami the next day, and the vacation was over. Now it was time to earn our pay. Andy's guest had canceled, so he was coming down solo. He would only be with us for five days, but he wanted to fish every day. We got him unpacked, and he told me that he wanted to meet for my annual review on the last day of the trip, as it had been a little over a year that I had been on board. *That can't be good*, I thought, I knew that he would not fire me, but I was worried that I might not get a raise. As it turned out, I was not far off.

Five days passed like nothing. Andy canceled his meeting with Cole and me and left early in the morning, right after breakfast. Doug called Cole and me to the bridge. He told us what our raises were, a measly three percent, and said, "Andy is sorry, but that's all he can afford. He is having a rough year, and he will make it up next year."

I looked at Doug and said, "What a crock of shit. This cheap fuck just stiffed us again on this trip, and on top of that, we get a three percent raise? That's bullshit."

Meanwhile, Andy was building an estate on Singer Island in Miami for around twenty million, so I knew he was full of shit. The good news was that he was not coming back for the second trip and we had one more week in town before we headed to the yard in Lauderdale. For two months, we would get paid and really didn't have to do shit, so that was a bright spot, plus Doug was home in Port St. Lucie and only came down every few days. Cole and I oversaw the painting and work.

Cole was still staying on the boat, and I stayed at my condo. We had beers every night and ate well on the boat. Brandon had already quit; he'd had enough, and I don't blame him. Andy was a prick to the deckhands. Cole and I were planning to get even with him and that fat bastard Doug.

We hired a new deckhand, and when the boat was done, we headed back south for one more trip: Key West, Isla Mujeres, and Panama, but no

Costa Rica this time. We were only gone for six months, but we tore it up everywhere we went and ended up back at the Lauderdale Marina Center.

The new deckhand, Peter, was South African. He was a nice young man, a great diver, and he liked to drink, so he fit in with Cole and me. He wasn't cheap like Brandon, so now there were three of us tearing it up. We hardly ever invited Doug. He was too old and fat, and he dressed like shit. On top of that, he was a cheap fuck; he'd been working for Andy too long, I guess.

So, back to the yard. Toward the end of our second year, we just quit counting on the extra beer money, so I just started buying booze for us on the boat's credit card. Not every week, but a bottle of rum, vodka, tequila—call it severance pay—every few weeks and started buying better food for the crew: crab cakes, shrimp, steaks. We were eating pretty damn good, and I was buying better wine for the boat and drinking more of it. Cole was not a wine guy, and neither was Peter.

We were having a great time in the yard. As usual, Doug was gone half the week, so we oversaw the refit again. Cole and I had a plan we were working on, and we brought Peter in as well, as he thought Doug was an asshole, too, and was looking for a new boat. The next trip was going to be a long one. It had two parts: the Bahamas from January to March and then on to Key West, Mexico, Panama, and Costa Rica. It was the same trip we did the first year except for the Bahamas, and it would last a little over a year, give or take. None of us had been to the Bahamas, and we would only have three trips with the boss, so we decided to do the first part of the trip till we got our plan together. The Bahamas would be some fun, with lots of rum, but as I found out, the pussy is not so great unless you like them big, black, and sweaty.

Doug hated that we never invited him. We'd say we were just going out for a quick beer or not going out at all, and once he went to his room, we would bolt out on him. The next day, we'd say our plans had changed. He would see us in town sometimes and come over for a beer, but then we would leave and just blow him off.

Lauderdale is a yachtie town and not a bad place to hang out. I had lots of good times there. I would have Cole and Peter over to my place for dinner and drinks every few days as we worked on our plan to do in *Rapture*. Peter and Cole planned to hop on a yacht heading to the Med for the summer. I was heading to Spain to visit Helena and her mother and look for a place to buy over there. We all had something planned, but it sure as hell did not include another yearlong trip on *Rapture* with no tips and shit raises again, plus putting up with Andy and Doug's shit.

The boat was getting close, so I got my list banged out: food, wine, water, and the provisions we needed. I had been told that everything over there is just crazy expensive and I should stock up on what I could. It turned out that my sources were right. I'd never thought about it. Everything is shipped in—and it's the same for the rest of the Caribbean—and you get shit produce, so stock up, my fellow chefs, if you are planning a trip. Fish and conch are the only two cheap things, and we caught all our own fish, so we were cool there. I learned the trade system over there. Most locals were too lazy to go fishing, so I would trade fresh fish for conch and veggies at local markets. We got a weather window, Doug had the trip planned, and we would be off in a few days.

We had a few last blowout nights in Lauderdale before we cast off. First stop, Freeport. This was going to be a great trip. Peter, Cole, and I had become pretty tight, and our plan was coming together, but first we'd enjoy the Bahamas, bang a few girls, and drink lots of rum. Not a bad way to go out. Doug had no clue what was coming, and man, was he going to get rat-fucked.

I had the guys over for one last dinner at my condo, and we got into the rum, as usual, and laughed and talked about our plan to leave Doug helpless and ruin Andy's trip. Finally, we got the green light, and the weather looked good for a smooth ride to Freeport. Two days later, we rolled in, hung out for a week, cleared customs, got some supplies, and took on some fuel, as we would be on the hook for a week when we got to Moore's Island. It's a little island just a half-day from Freeport, but they had an airstrip, a few stores, and one little bar. Andy would be flying in and out of there.

There was great fishing around this area and some decent diving as well. It was the same drill as Panama: we would be on the hook most of the trip, which was cool. Andy brought a new guest, some young hotshot. Man, was this kid a diver and one hell of a spear guy. We had so much mutton snapper, grouper, and mahi-mahi, and we got some tuna as well. There were no girls this trip, not because the guys didn't want them but because there were none to be found. Moore's Island is really nowhere, and it's only good for fishing and just plain doing nothing but chillin, and that's cool once in a while. We were so used to just tearing it up everywhere we went that it was nice to relax for a bit.

The week flew by, and I served fish, stone crabs, conch salad, and cracked conch ceviche. I tell you what. I'd never had mutton snapper till that week, and OMG, what a great fish, tender and light, and hog snapper, too, really tasty. We were stocked up on fish for weeks, not counting the lobsters Cole and Peter caught. I had never eaten such great seafood as we did on *Rapture*. We all had a great time, and there were only two guests. It was an easy week, and there were no whores to clean up after. Like I said, we had plenty of fresh fish for us to dine on; it's too bad we could not trade the fish for pussy.

When Andy and his guest flew back, we returned to Freeport for a week to take on fuel and get the boat cleaned and ready for the next trip. We had three weeks to get to Harbor Island and get ready for him again, so we could enjoy a few days off. Freeport was a cool little spot, with a funky little downtown, lots of bars, and a casino with chicks. When we got back, we tied up the boat and cleaned up. I cooked up some of that fresh hog-fish and cracked open a nice bottle, and then we were off to the casino to find a little action.

We ran into some of Cole's buddies from Texas, there on a Sport Fisher, so we really got into the rum that night. They were on their way back to Lauderdale after spending time at Harbor Island, our next stop. We would be there a few months and then head back to Lauderdale, check in at the yard, and make sure the boat was all good before heading to Key West and beyond.

Freeport is where I learned how to make cracked conch ceviche. I found this little hole-in-the-wall café, nothing special, but the cook made great conch dishes. I bribed her with twenty-five pounds of snapper. She was a very big woman but had one hell of a personality and what a laugh to go with it. Cole, Peter, and I would hang out there, drink beer, eat cracked conch, and watch girls. She showed me how to clean the conch and pound it out, which I would never have figured out on my own. The only way you learn these tricks is to watch, or better yet, have someone show you how to do it, and that's just what I did. I tweaked the recipe a little, but she showed me all the shortcuts and how she made her sauce. She was cool. She would have some rum with us. She liked us, plus we were good customers, and I gave her a hell of a lot of fresh fish. I look back at her little place, which puts a smile on my face.

We hung out with Cole's friends for a few days, and then they headed home. We tore up the casino one last time and grabbed some girls, as there would not be much action for the next two months. Cole's friends had told us that the only pussy on Harbor Island was on other yachts. Maybe you'd get lucky and grab a tourist, but it was tough. We all thought, what the hell. We'll save two months of pay and do lots of diving, fishing, exploring the smaller island, riding the jet skis, and just having some guy fun, and that's what we did for the next two months. We went to Thunderball cave, where they filmed the Bond movie, Staniel Cay, all the small islands around, even Johnny Depp's island, which was around the corner. We had some great day trips the next few months and did some great diving. I hope you like the pics. Words cannot describe the water. It's just so blue and clear.

We had our last lunch at Mom's place; that's what we called her. She made us a big batch of cracked conch and some whole fried snapper, and we drank lots of cold beer and rum. We said our goodbyes and gave her some more fish and a big hug. Then we were off to Harbor Island for the next few months.

When we got to Harbor Island, Doug had to hire a private pilot as he could not get us in. I suppose there are some real shallow spots and you need local knowledge. What a crock of shit. Eventually we made it into the marina with no problems. I fell in love with this little island. It's really a special place, and I have made many good friends there over the years. If you have been there, you know what I am talking about.

Andy could fly into the airport on the other island, a short boat ride away. We had a few weeks till the first trip. The island had a few nice restaurants, a pink sand beach, and a nice marina with a great bar, and we had a golf cart to take to town, but you could walk as well. There were a few stores to buy supplies, and you could get conch down at the pier. In fact, you could get pretty much everything you needed except pussy. Wayne Huizenga had a huge place there on the water. It's still there. I am sure someone in the family owns it, but it is gorgeous, and it's right by the marina. There are some other nice homes as well and a few world-class hotels. The beach is beyond words, and we had a great time there as well, from day trips to just lying at the pool and drinking cold beer.

Andy only did two trips, and he only brought one guest, Jose. We had lots of time off, so we would have a great dinner then take the tender out for a cruise, ride the jet skis, or just hang at the bar at the marina and talk to the other yachties. This was not my style; I did not care for their type. The chicks were always stupid and acted like they owned the boat. It's like, "Hey, you're a stew, a seagoing waitress. Give me a break, and you can't even do that job right." I had to get that off my chest. Sorry about that; they just get under my skin.

Andy flew in for the first trip, and it was the same routine. We got stiffed again, but at this point, we never looked for a tip, so none of us went out of our way to do anything special for him. For the guest, it was a little different, but fuck Andy. One day, he could not find his sunglasses. We helped him look, but they did not turn up. A few days later, I found them with his fishing gear, and I just tossed them overboard. Let him buy a new pair of Costas. Asshole.

There was not a lot of big tuna there, but they shot some big mahi-mahi and snappers. No world records on these two trips, but this was a warm-up trip for the rest of the year, kind of a boat shakedown. The trip went off flawlessly, and he was back on his way to Miami, and we were all happy that he was gone again. You know it's a bad boss when the whole crew does not look forward to them coming on board—that's an easy one to figure out.

We only had to put up with his shit one more trip, and then it was back to Lauderdale. It was worth it. We had some great times in the Bahamas, and Doug said that after the last trip, we were going to Atlantis for a few days before heading home. We were back to our routine again, diving, fishing, riding the jet skis. These activities kept us going, including taking care of Doug. I still cannot get over that fuck. He had a wife, three kids, and a mortgage but was still spending money on underage whores. He'd tell his kids he was broke and could not send more money home. He was paying one whore's cell phone bill in Panama. What a fat piece of shit. I will never forget the shit that guy did. He should be ashamed of himself. How he could look at himself in the mirror in the morning, I don't know.

The whole crew felt the same way about Andy as I did. Don't get me wrong; we all grabbed our share of whores, but none of us were married or had wives, not even girlfriends, so we were not hurting anyone, and none of us grabbed the underage ones—that's just not right.

We were enjoying our last few weeks there. What a great place to spend the winter. We'd all saved some money as well. The nightlife was nothing to speak about, and we used the boat's toys. We did not even pay for gas, just did the upkeep and cleaned the jet skis and tender after we used them, and we did the same with the dive gear. We really had it made when the boss was gone, and we only had one trip left. Andy was due back next week for his last trip before we headed back to Lauderdale and was bringing one guest again. The crew had been meeting in private, and we had our plan almost all worked out; we were just putting the final touches together.

I would be heading to Spain to meet up with Helena and her mom and do a recon of the country to see if it was a place I could live. My idea was to retire to a little cafe with some bicycles for rent and a nice flat above, work six months a year and travel the rest—not a bad plan. I had been setting aside some money, plus I still had some cash in Panama, more than enough to buy a small building along the coast. Then I would just enjoy the rest of my life in the sun and the Mediterranean lifestyle, cooking for a few guests and my close friends, small and simple. If I could just break even, that was the plan. As long as I could eat and drink for free and have a free place to live, that was all I needed. In fact, what more does any one person need in life? Money is way overrated. Sure, you need some, but letting it control your life and soul is no good. I have seen it first-hand with worthless trust-fund kids and cheating wives. They have no sense of right and wrong and don't live in the real world. They are not truly happy and have no real friends. I have seen it up close. Set some life goals and live life on your terms.

Andy was due tomorrow, and he would be bringing a new friend. No one had met him yet. They were only going to be out for six days, and we were all in a good mood, as we would be heading to Nassau when the trip was over for a week. That was going to be fun. None of us had ever been to Atlantis. We were all getting tired of harbor islands. It gets boring after a while. I call it island fever, same shit every day and a shortage of pussy walking around. We all just wanted to move on.

Andy had a great trip. He took us all to dinner; I guess he thought that was enough of a tip. They got lots of fish, just no records again, but they had lots of fun and seemed very happy when they left. Andy said, "See you in Key West, and safe travels," and just like that, we were underway to Atlantis, our last stop.

Doug took Andy to Standel Key, where they have a small airport, and he was on his way to Miami. We were all grateful to be getting out of there. If you have never pulled into Atlantis by boat, you have no idea what you are missing. It's bad-ass, with lots of megayachts. We were one of the smaller ones at 103, but we didn't care; we were going to have a good time. We had a week to take on fuel, wait for weather, and take a few days off and relax. That meant casino, rum, and chicks in that order. There were tons of hot chicks everywhere. Peter was a great wingman: young, good looking, and with an accent that chicks loved. I was the old man of the three, not counting Doug.

It was Friday night when we tied up—we'd planned it that way. We got the boat washed down and had an early dinner, and then Peter, Cole, and I made plans for the night. Doug was on his own. They have a hot nightclub inside the casino, and that was the plan. One of the dock guys got us three free passes and a few drink coupons. We gambled a little and had a few drinks at the real cool lobby bar. Then we headed to the club, where we grabbed a table, started a tab, and began to pound down some rum drinks. Me, I like mojitos. The other two wear drinking painkillers and beers, two-fisted. I just wanted to keep pace and not fade early.

I needed to get laid—all of us did, in fact. It just so happened that there was a bachelorette party going on with some drunk chicks from Ohio. Peter took control and brought three of them over. All he said was, "Which three of you want to get naked and get in a hot tub on a yacht?" Just like that, we were hooked up, and they were hot, drunk, and ready to get down.

This was not our first rodeo. We bought the girls some more shots and danced to a few songs. Then the girls asked us if we really had a yacht. Peter told them that he and Cole were the crew and I was the owner, as I looked like I could be. I had my Rolly on and was dressed pretty sharp, as always.

"What yacht?" They asked.

"*Rapture*," Peter said, "with the blue lights right at the end of the dock."

"Yeah, we saw it. Let's go party."

They were from Ohio and had never left their dads' farms, let alone soak in a hot tub in the Bahamas on a yacht. We closed out the tab and returned to the yacht at a dead run. Doug was in bed already. I grabbed some champagne, and the show was on. The girls were not shy at all. They had their clothes off before we did. They chose which guy they wanted to hook up with. They were hornier than we were and probably had not been laid in months.

We were all in the tub, drinking Champagne, making out, and grabbing tits and ass. They were in heaven. I grabbed the one I was with and took her right down to Andy's suite. We fucked like badgers, and the other guys did as well. I bent the girl I was with over the master tub. It had a big mirror, so she could watch while I got her from behind.

The girls left before dawn, as they had to get back to their friends. We walked them down to the end of the dock. The deckhands on the other yachts were up, starting their morning wash-down as we strolled along with three hotties at the crack of dawn and gave them all big kisses goodbye. We also grabbed that ass one more time; they loved every minute of it, and so did we. The other yacht crews were just kind of like, "The guys on *Rapture* rock," and we did. What's really cool is when the stew bitches checked us out, and we just threw it in their faces, like, "Yeah, we just got laid in the hot tub. Fuck you."

We were an all-guy boat for two years, and Rapture did get around, unlike some yachts, which don't move much. We got tons of pussy wherever we went; that was just how we rolled. Doug was cool with shit like this as long as I cleaned up and they were gone first thing in the morning. He knew that we carried his ass, so he did not want to fuck with us.

We were out washing the boat down later when the girls came by with the whole bachelorette party, like ten chicks. Doug said, "Bring them all on board," and just like that, we were back at it again. The whole afternoon, I fixed them all some appetizers and drinks. It was one hell of a party. The girls hung out till dark. Then they had dinner plans, as it was their last night there. We got to bang our girls one more time as Doug made drinks for the rest of them. I told the girls I was a real estate developer in Miami. That was my first and best weekend in Nassau.

We all had a great time, but Peter hooked it up. Peter, wherever you are, you rock. Chef Al loves you, man. That was one for the record books.

We hung out a few more days, playing tourist and just getting drunk again, waiting on our weather window, as always. Atlantis is one really cool property, with a large, walk-through aquarium, pools, great girl watching, and restaurants. It's first class in my book.

The other crews did not know what to think of the *Rapture* crew. We just did not give a fuck. We did our own thing and were a great crew. *Rapture* was always in great shape; we had our shit together. Finally, we had worn out our welcome in the marina, and the weather was looking good, so we cast off and headed home. As we said goodbye to the island, we all had a good laugh about the girls from Ohio. "I like them corn-fed Midwestern girls. They like it rodeo style," I said to the guys, and they busted up.

We'd been gone all winter and were looking forward to getting back to Lauderdale. We had to put the final touches on our exit plan, and the guys had to work out their new starting dates. Me, I had to book a flight to Spain. Plus, *Rapture* was heading back to the yard, which worked well for us, as there would be no Andy till we got to Key West, one month away, but we would still get paid.

We had a smooth ride home, flat sea all the way, an easy two days. By the time we pulled into LMC around dusk, we were beat. We tied up, washed the boat down, and decided to go out for Sammy's wood-fired pizza and lots of beer. It was close, and I had left my Extra at Tong Lu hangar, so we had wheels. We all talked about the great trip to the Bahamas, the girls from Ohio, and all the small islands we'd seen. I knew I wanted to go back there again one day on a yacht trip for the winter.

Peter's and Cole's new jobs were coming together; they were just waiting on start dates. We had the plan almost worked out; we just needed the dates and someone to drive my Extra to Key West to pick us up. The latter would not be an issue. Cole and Peter knew lots of deckhands in Lauderdale. Our pizza came, and we dug in and pounded down some beers as we laid out the rest of the plan. The boat would be ready in a few weeks, and we would head to Key West. Andy would come down with his wife and kids for a week and then head off to Mexico, Panama, and so on. The trip would last a year.

The plan was to have Cole's friend drive down to Key West in my truck and get a hotel suite, which I would pay for. The day Andy showed up, I would walk off and tell him and Doug to stick it up their asses, so they would have to find a chef in a day or cancel the trip. That was part one.

The next day, Cole and Peter would just walk off, and we would party for a day in Key West. Then I would drive us all back to Lauderdale, leaving Doug without a crew and chef and really just fucked. They would have to hire all new crew, a real pain in the ass, and the trip would have to be pushed back or canceled. We would have our payback and day in the sun. We all laughed and had a few shots as we finished our pizza. Cole said he would take care of the driver, and we headed back to the Marina for a nightcap.

It's no fun being in the yard on a yacht, but we made it fun, and I fed the guys like kings. As soon as Doug was gone, we would get out the good wine and turn it up a notch. We only had a few weeks left, and a free ride to Key West was in the future.

The day before we were supposed to leave, Peter and Cole had dinner at my condo. Cole had invited his friend Roach to come along with them. Roach was going to drive down and get us. I'd met Roach a while back. He worked as a dive-master at a scuba shop in Lauderdale. I gave him the keys to the Nissan, and that part of the plan was done and in motion. Roach finished dinner and had to take off. We said, "We'll call you in a few days and see you in the Keys." The three of us had some nice Zacapa rum after dinner and spent the night at my place, and then we were back at the boat at the crack of dawn to beat Doug back.

We were set to leave mid-afternoon. I had already spent thousands on food, water, and wine for the boat, as this was a yearlong trip, so whatever space we had was filled. I was also running low on wine at the condo, so I'd bought myself a few cases as well as some rum and Grey Goose. After putting up with Andy's shit for the last two years, I thought I deserved it. The plan was coming together, and we were about to leave LMC for the last time on *Rapture*. That boat would never be the same.

We cast off and were bound for the Keys. Cole called Roach and said, "We are on our way. Chef Al made a reservation for you at Parrot Key under his name. It's a suite. We'll all be staying there for a few nights."

Roach was on his way, and we would be pulling into the dock tomorrow about dusk. Andy would be there the day after tomorrow, so we had a day to get the boat ready, fill up the tender, and get everything squared away. The plan was that as soon as the guest arrived, I would confront Andy, tell him what a cheap fuck he was, and just walk off with dinner not prepped and nothing done. The next morning, the guys were going to get up and just walk off without a word, and we would meet at the Parrot, party for a few days, and then head back to Lauderdale.

For extra payback, I put some used small panties in the wife's dresser. I also hid some tampons in different places where she could not miss them and put a used condom in the trashcan in her bathroom. I also put an open pack of condoms and some lubricants from Panama in one drawer and a bunch of black hair in her shower drain—she was a blonde.

As for Andy, he kept some Johnnie Walker Blue and Remy XO in his private bar, and I took both of them and put a bottle of water with a note saying, "Go fuck yourself, you prick. Thanks, Chef Al." We drank them at the Parrot. In fact, we took all the rum and left them high and dry. I also took all his sunglasses and cut the lines on his spear guns—I really broke my foot in his ass, I would say.

The day finally arrived, and they were on their way. Doug told us, "Be here for dinnertime. Make sure you have all your list done. I am going to take a nap, so wake me around five."

I said, "Sure, we got this." I felt like saying, "Get off your fat ass and help," but we were past that. He headed down to his cabin, and we had four hours or so to finish up. We checked what we had left. Cole sent Peter to take their bags to the Parrot, so all they had were backpacks, and all my shit was already gone. While Doug slept, we loaded up on party supplies. I also went around and unplugged all the freezers and refrigerators and turned off the ice makers. We would see who would have the last laugh.

We met in my room, and I said, "As soon as they walk down the dock and we go help with the luggage, that's when the shit is going to hit the fan. I will confront Andy and just walk right off the dock and tell Doug to fuck himself. I will see you guys tomorrow at the hotel. Call me when you guys talk to Doug, as he will be kissing your ass. Andy will have to take you all out to dinner, as I did not fix shit. See you guys tomorrow. At least you guys get one free last meal on Andy."

I did not bother to wake Doug up until we saw Andy with the Russian and the three little girls walking down the dock with tons of luggage. He managed to walk up just in time to hear me tell Andy, "I wish I could say it's been fun, but you stiffed me for the last time. Stick your three percent raise up your ass, you cheap fuck. Take the cash and go buy some more hookers in Panama. That's all you do on every trip anyway."

He was in shock. He told me to get off his dock and said that I could not talk to him like that. "Do you know who I am?" He asked.

I just laughed in his face and said, "Yes, a spoiled little rich boy who can not wipe his own ass."

He backed down then. Doug started to say something, but I just looked at him and said, "Don't start, or I will drop you right here, you fat old fuck. And you go back to your underage whores. Don't even talk to me."

The last thing he and Andy said was that I would never work on a yacht in Florida again. I just turned and said, "Fuck the both of you. You're lucky I don't kick both your asses." Then was it over. That was the last time I saw *Rapture* or those two assholes. I did help myself to a nice bonus and took care of the crew as well. Andy and Doug had just gotten their first setback. The next morning, they'd get the next one when they found out they had no crew at all.

I went to the Parrot and partied with Roach. We had dinner at Hog's Breath, and when I told him what had gone down, he was in tears, just busting up, saying, " Chef Al, you crazy fuck."

"Just wait till tomorrow," I said, "when she finds the panties, hair, and condoms. Shit is going to hit the fan, and when Cole and Peter walk off, that will be the icing on the cake."

Later on, Cole said he would never forget what went down. The crew, even Doug, was in the galley, having some beer and waiting for Andy and the family to come up. As soon as Cole cracked his beer, all he heard was shit breaking and loud, nasty words in Russian and what few words she knew in English. It sounded like one hell of a fight, with her yelling, "You fucker, asshole, cheating fuck!" Turned out she found all the evidence sooner than we thought. The guys had a clue, but I did not tell them. I wanted it to be a surprise

And man, was it. Cole could hear bits and pieces, like, "Whose panties are these? They're not mine!" Andy was fucked. The wife grabbed the three girls and said, "We are leaving and going back to Miami! Find some other whores to fuck on your yacht, you asshole. And find another ride home!" Then she walked off the boat and drove off in the SUV.

Doug was at a loss for words, but Cole and Peter could hardly hold back their laughter. Andy thought he was fucked, but it would blow over. She was going nowhere. She was just a dumb Russian hooker, but she would still make Andy pay. All in all, it was one hell of a payback.

Andy said to the crew, "Hey, guys. It's just us, so let's go get some dinner and have a drink together."

He headed down to his stateroom, grabbed his box of Johnnie Walker Blue and four glasses, and then returned to the galley. He said, "Guys, here is to crazy

Russian wives and to a great trip this year." Then he opened the box, and there was the bottle of water and my note. He was so pissed that he threw the water at the window and yelled, "That fucking chef! I am going to get him back!"

He took the crew to dinner, but all the time, it was, "Chef Al, that fucker!" After a few drinks, he calmed down, and that was it. He knew it was over and he would have to do some ass-kissing on the home-front. The night was still young, and he had no idea what tomorrow would bring. He picked up the tab, and they returned to the boat.

Doug asked the guys if they knew about any of this, and they said, "No, but it was pretty cool of the chef." Doug did not want to hear that and let them know, saying he would blackball me, as if he had any clout. Everyone in Lauderdale knew Doug was a fat, lazy captain and Andy was cheap and an asshole. Andy went right to bed, as I am sure he was just burnt out. Doug turned in, too, after he gave the guys a little shit.

Andy was still planning on fishing for a few days until he woke up to no crew, and I am sure Doug overslept, as I was not there to wake him up. Cole and Peter were gone before light and at the Parrot having coffee with Roach and me. I got a call from Doug, and I did not answer the first few times. Then I finally took his call. I said, "Good morning. What's up, Cappy?"

He said, "You crossed the line, and you are fucked."

"Really."

"Yeah."

"You better check to see if you have any crew left," I said, and then I hung up.

He called back around six times. Finally, I answered. "What's up, asshole?"

"Where are Cole and Peter?" He asked.

"I have no clue."

"You are going to pay for this."

"Go fuck yourself, you fat fuck."

I hung up, and that was it. He blew all our phones up for the rest of the day. Even Andy called the guys. We took no calls. Instead, we hung out at the Parrot all day, and then I drove us all back to Lauderdale. Cole's new job started in a week. He was the first mate on a 130 Palmer Johnson for some family out of Venezuela and based in St. Croix. Peter was heading to the Med on a new boat after a few months in the yard. They were all set, and I was on my way to Spain for a few months.

When we got back to Lauderdale, I invited the guys to the condo—Roach, too, as he was part of the plan—for one last dinner together and to share the stories about the Key West trip. I wished I could have seen Andy's face when his wife found the panties, condoms, and hair, but Cole said he was in deep shit, and that was good enough for me.

I cooked a nice pasta dinner, the guys' favorite, and then we drank Andy's Johnnie Walker Blue. We all had new plans, and the guys had better jobs for more money. Cole and I still keep in touch. We lost track of Peter, but he was one solid and cool dude I will never forget.

Cole says he sees the boat once in a while, always with a new crew. *Rapture*, what a joke. That was it for the bullshit of Doug and Andy. I pulled some pretty good shit there with the help of Cole and Peter. I am sure this story has been told many times over many beers in many ports when my name comes up.

There's a lesson to be learned: never piss off the chef and crew.

Chef and Bryan on the way to Catalana, on-board the Pacifico, Long Beach Ca.

Yacht Dealership

Chef, Bryan and Peter, Boys Night, Huntington Beach.

Yacht Last Call

Chef and Piero Selvogio, Valentinos, LA

Vail. Not bad flying First Class

chapter 17

DOUGLAS CRAMER AND HUGH BUSH
THE TWO QUEENS IN MIAMI

I SPENT A MONTH IN Spain, staying with Helen's mother in Nerja. It's a small beach town about an hour north of Málaga. Man, did I have a great time. I loved it so much that I went back again the next year. I was looking for a place to call my retirement home, my little getaway outside the States. I was tired of Panama.

Eventually I found myself back at the condo in Lauderdale, looking for a new gig. Peter was on his way to the Med, Cole was in St. Croix, and I was looking for a short-time gig, or as they call them, a freelance chef job. I was trying to get up to New England and out of Florida for the summer and see the old gang in Stowe.

I don't know how, but some agent got ahold of me. She said she was a friend of Dora's from California and had a dream job for me. I should have known to stay clear after Dora said Barry Diller was one of the best jobs in the country. The job was winter in Miami, summer in Martha's Vineyard, and trips to New York. They had a place in the city, the job was live-in and paid big money, and they wanted specifically me, as she'd told them I'd worked for Weintraub and the Fords. They wanted me to meet them and cook a trial dinner, and they said they would pay me.

I said, "Sure." If I just worked the summer, that would get me twenty grand more in the bank towards the Spain project. I'd also get a free trip to the Vineyard and the city. It'd been years since I had been back on the East Coast, and it would be fun to see the old gang and do New York one last time.

I put on a nice suit and headed to Miami for the interview. The next day, I arrived at a nice place on an island right on the Inter-coastal, a real cool pad. It's easy when you've got millions to spend on a house and decorator. Cramer was a lot older than Bush, but neither was good looking. Cramer looked like some old pervert who liked little boys or young men, and Bush looked like a fruitcake, but they were nice enough in the interview, and I thought I could make it through the summer without kicking one of their asses. Man, was I wrong.

We chatted about LA, the Weintraubs, Rod Stewart, and the Fords, and they seemed impressed and asked if I could cook for six Saturday night. I said, "Yes, of course." They wanted a fish dish, and I told them, "That's one of my specialties." They also wanted a nice tossed salad, healthy food, and light desserts, like fruit sorbet, stuff like that, right up my alley. They said that if all went well, they wanted me to start the following Monday. They would be heading north in a few weeks, and I would be cooking here in Miami until they left for the Vineyard. I would drive my car or fly, and they would pay all my expenses and travel time. Sounds good, I thought. Man, was I in for a huge surprise.

The trial dinner went off just how I planned: grilled grouper with a lemon caper sauce, couscous with grilled peppers and asparagus, a nice arugula salad with dates, walnuts, and lime vinaigrette, and a fruit torte. It was easy, and they were impressed; the job was mine if I wanted it. I took the job, thinking that if I could make it a month in Miami and the summer in the Vineyard, I would get a free trip up there and a few bucks in my pocket for the rest of the summer. Turns out I did not make it through the summer.

Who the hell are these two queens, anyway? That's a good place to start. Douglas Cramer is best known for his TV shows with Aaron Spelling;

that's where he made his fortune. He did *The Love Boat*, *Dynasty*, *Vegas*, *The Brady Bunch*, and the list goes on and on. He was head of ABC and married to some gossip columnist, Joyce Haber, I think. They divorced, and he came out of the closet years later with this new lover, Bush, some would-be writer and artist who did not do shit and was half the age of the old man. He probably just gave him blowjobs; I don't think Cramer's hips could take a good ass fucking.

Like I said, all these rich fuck are messed up. Cramer's daughter killed herself at thirty, and his son died at forty-eight. I'm not sure from what, but I heard he OD'ed on drugs. I would say that is a good bet. Like I said, one screwed-up family, now all dead, so the old man is getting his payback.

I don't know much about Bush. All I can say is that he is one big asshole and a flamer. If I see him on the street, I will break my foot off in his ass, but he might like that. So, now you know the two queens. Rumor has it, when Cramer left Spelling, he fell on his ass, but he already had tons of cash—I had heard around four hundred million back then, plus his art collection, one of the largest contemporary collections in the world. I thought it sucked, but to each their own. I liked a few pieces, but they sure as hell were not worth five million or so, but that's Hollywood, where everyone has money to just piss away on some bullshit artist. Bush's stuff sucked. I've never heard of him selling a piece; it was shit in my book. Like they say, beauty is in the eye of the beholder. So, now you are up to speed on these two queens.

I was supposed to do lunch and dinner in Miami and brunch once in a while. I would show up around nine in the morning and get ready for lunch and plan dinner. They went day by day; I could not plan a week's menu. They wanted everything bought that day. This was a first. I don't know how I made it past the first week with these assholes. They would text me at six in the morning about today's lunch and let me know that they wanted to have this, that, and the other. It was crazy. It was mostly Bush, the young boyfriend—I'm not sure if they were married back then. On top of that, half the staff and all the service providers were gay as well.

I made it through the first month, and I would be on my way north in a week or so. Up to this point, I had not beaten up any of the staff, though

I wanted to badly. I was hanging in there, but it was tough. Bush would complain about every meal: it was overcooked, there was not enough salt, there was too much salt, it was too dry, there was too much sauce, etc. He was just a real pain in the ass, and he thought he was some food guru. I had to hold myself back every day from kicking his ass.

Cramer was a harmful old man. He had already done his damage to these young boys years before. He will rot in hell, I am sure, along with Dillard and the rest of those guys. The only time things were great was when we had guests. The best thing about the job was Bush's dog, a purebred Vizsla from Hungary named Linus. He was one great dog and well trained. He ate better than I did, but he looked great. I fed him, so you know who his favorite was. Bush hated that. If I was in the kitchen and Bush called for Linus, the dog would not leave my side until I looked at him and said, "It's ok to go to the asshole." That dog made my day.

This was the first time I'd worked at an estate in Miami, and I knew in a few weeks that the city was just like LA, full of liberal actors and a bunch of rich assholes, and the chicks were just like in LA, gold diggers. It was not for me. I felt like I'd never left LA.

Finally, it was time to go to the Vineyard. It was hard to believe; I'd made it through the trial, and a month had passed. I was allowed three days to get up there and a week before they arrived to get the place ready. They had a houseman there, a kind of a butler and handyman. He was gay as well. I kept wondering if the job was worth it. I'd get a trip up to the Cape, but I had to put up with too much abuse.

I arrived at the house in the Vineyard and met Rafael, the houseman, a real limp dick. Then I immediately unpacked and got organized. They had notes for all the farmers' markets, fishmongers, and a butcher. I was cool with all of this, and I had a garden I was supposed to tend. That was new to me. I said, "What the fuck. This might be fun." I got the house ready with flowers and set up for the first week when they arrived.

I thought I was prepared. It turned out that Bush, being the asshole he is, did not like the menu I had planned for the first few days. I said to myself, "What the fuck is wrong with this gay fuck? You show up to your summer home, you have a chef preparing great food, and you have a stocked fridge. You don't have to do shit, and you are still unhappy. It makes me think I would love to bend this fuck over and fuck him hard up the ass, but he would probably like that.

The next few weeks were the same as in Miami. I made it through two dinner parties, more like lunches, as they went to bed early. Cramer needed his rest before he took it up the ass. Carly Simon came by a few times. She was ok. She'd put on a few pounds and was a liberal, but she was ok and was open to new ideas, unlike Rosie O'Donnell, that fat lesbian bitch from hell. What a pig. Rosie only stopped by the house once, thank God.

It had been a long few weeks, and I was ready to quit any day. I'd had enough of all these weird fucks; it was like I was working on Mars. I only had a few days left before I pulled the trigger and headed to Vermont to see the old gang, and then I would head back to Florida. It was Sunday, and we had no guests, and Bush wanted a Mexican brunch for him and Douglas, just the two of them. I thought: *How romantic for a couple of perverts*. I already had my car packed. I did not have much: golf clubs, a few suitcases, and that was it. I'd also filled my gas tank up and bought a case of beer and some food for the road on the house credit card before I gave it back. I had my exit all planned out; you have to when you live on-site. I was not sure how this was going to go down. I just knew I could not last one more day of Bush's petty shit and all the drama. It was like two women having their periods every day.

I made my roasted red pepper salsa, fresh guac, and my famous Baha fish tacos. I had the table all set, put the water down, and was getting ready to serve them. Then I would give them notice and just walk away. Bush and Cramer come to the patio for lunch, and Bush asked in his feeble voice, "Chef, can you make us two skinny margaritas?"

I said, "Of course." Then he proceeded to tell me how to make them, which was pretty close to how they are supposed to be made. I said, "Give me a few minutes to squeeze some limes, and they will be right out with the chips, salsa, and guac."

I told them the brunch menu and then headed back to the kitchen to make the drinks, classic margaritas: silver tequila, Cointreau, agave nectar, salt, lime wedges, give it a good shake, pour, and serve. Keep it simple. I brought them out with all the sides and was heading back to the kitchen when Bush called me.

"Yes?" I said.

"You did not make the margarita like I wanted. How did you make it?"

I told him, and he looked at me like he was always right and said, "It tastes too tart. Too much lime. Take it back and make us two more."

That was it. I'd had it. I looked at him and said, "Hell, no. I will not make you a new one. You can either drink that one or stick it up your tight ass. If you don't like that one, you wont like the next one I make. I have had enough of your petty shit and complaints, from the toast being too dry to eggs being overcooked or not cooked enough. You complain about everything. You think you are the queen bee. I have had the last of your petty gay shit. You both can go fuck yourselves, but you two might like that. I quit. Go get your own fucking lunch."

Bush was almost in tears. I think he thought I was going to kick his ass. He just needed to be bitch slapped. He might have liked that.

Creamer was at a loss for words as well. "Alan, I am sorry for Mr. Bush," he finally said. "I will talk to him. Please don't leave us. We want to work with you. Let's try to sort this out."

"Were you not listening? It's worthless. He is the biggest pain in the ass I have had to put up with, and I am done. It's over. Have a nice day."

He tried to convince me one last time as I walked to my car. Bush said he was sorry, but only because he was scared that I might hit him. What a pussy. Not even a man.

Just like that, I was out of a job again, but at least I was free from the bullshit of these two assholes. I also had two months of pay in the bank, so I was ok. I'd hoped to spend the summer on the island, but I would have killed Bush or at least given him a good tune-up the Marine Corps way. They were the first and last gay couple I ever worked for; I will never do that again.

An agent called me and asked me why I'd quit, and I told her it just did not work out. I guess Cramer did not tell her the whole story. That was kind of cool of him. He probably did not want to look bad, and I am sure he knew Bush was a real prick.

Life goes on. I never worry about the small shit. On the ferry, I could not have been happier. You cannot let these rich fucks walk all over you, or they will give it to you, as you can see. I don't take any shit, even to this day.

So long Martha's Vineyard. Hello, Stowe, Vermont.

chapter 18

JERRY AND LEE KATZOFF
NEW YORK AND ISLESBORO, MAINE

I GOT TO STOWE, ROLLED into the Sunset Grill, Haab's place, and we got the old gang together for a steak dinner and toasted to the old times. Persico was there, and so were Wilbur and the whole crew from the Stoweflake. Man, it was a great reunion. I hung out for a few days, staying at Rich and Nancy's place. It'd been over twenty years since I'd left Stowe. It was great to see everyone, and I promised I would get back again and it would not be twenty years this time. We all said our goodbyes, and I was on the road again to Lauderdale. I wanted to get back home and try to get on a boat or just out of Florida for the rest of the summer. It's the worst time of the year to be there, hot and hotter.

A few days later, I was back in my condo. I made some calls, and it did not take long before I had a few job offers. One of my yacht agents emailed me and asked if I wanted to go to Maine for September. It would be one week of work, but I would get paid for a month plus travel.

I said, "Sure."

She said, "You have to feed the staff while you are there, but the boss will only be there one week. You'll work seven days. The total number of guests is seven: the owners, their son, his wife, and the grandkids."

"Sounds pretty easy," I said.

I'd never been to Maine. She set up a phone interview, and the boss's wife, Lee Katzoff, called. We chatted about food, and she asked if I could cook like Alice Waters. She said they were friends.

I said, "Yes, I know who she is." I felt like adding, "Some bitch who thinks she is Paul Bocuse." Instead, I said, "I know her style, clean and farm to table."

"Great," she said. "We are on the same page. What do you need?"

I said, "I need half up front for deposit and travel money."

"Of course," she replied.

We agreed on the dates and the pay, a grand a week, and that was it. I would be on my way to Islesboro, Maine, a small island for the wealthy. This was the first week in August, and the Katzoffs wouldn't be there until the last week of the month and would stay through the holiday week. Then I would be done. It sounded easy enough, but man, was I in for a surprise. I got a check through Fed-Ex the next day for two grand.

The Katzoffs were pretty rich and powerful, assholes, too, and she was one crazy bitch. What was cool was that I really only cooked one day for the boss, and I don't count feeding the staff of three as working, as that was just for fun. I got paid four grand to work one day, along with a free trip to Maine and a few more perks, like the hundred-year-old bottle of cognac I took as a tip.

Who are the Katzoffs? Old money. Jerry owns malls, lots of real estate, the Reno Aces baseball team, and the Mulino chain of restaurants in New York and LA. Lee started Montessori schools. They had houses all over the country and political ties, too. I am pretty sure he is a dirty businessman.

The estate in Islesboro was the old gray mansion. I heard it sold recently for thirty million. Travolta has a place there, and Kirstie Alley used to live there. Stuart Woods, the author of my favorite guy, Stone Barrington, has a place there, and one of the novels was set there, *Dark Harbor*, I think. It was a good one.

So, now you know about Lee and Jerry and have a feel for the island. Summer is great there, but I'd hate to be there in the cold months—you freeze your ass off. I loved going for runs on the island. It's a special place, but you need lots of money. There are a few nearby towns on the mainland that are cool, like Rockland, with lots of charm.

The first two weeks, I cooked for the staff, explored the island, and started to provision. They did have one hell of a garden, and the seafood is hard to beat up here. Lee had accounts open all over the mainland, so I just signed for everything. I would take the morning ferry to the mainland and then go shopping. There were lots of great little seafood places. I learned my way around pretty quickly and had met a few folks on the island. They all said the same thing about the Katzoffs, that Lee was crazy and no one lasted a week with them. I had not met them and had a few grand in my pocket and a free trip. How bad could they be? I found out the following week.

Even the girl at the ferry office knew the Katzoffs were nasty. She said that she had me all the chefs over the years, and none of them had lasted a week. She would know—they all had to board the ferry and buy a ticket. I heard this story many times. One time, I was on the ferry, coming back from the mainland. I had my chef's coat on when an older gentleman asked me where I worked on the island. I told him the Katzoffs. Lee had told me that I was not supposed to tell any local that I worked for them, and now I know why. She was worried about what I might find out. He told me what I had already heard several times: no one on the island liked them or talked to them. They were rude and just nasty. He had met several chefs over the years, and none had made it through the summer. Many had quit the first week. He did not have one good word to say about them. He also said they were always trying to change the zoning on the island to benefit themselves. I had heard this story many times, too.

It turned out that everyone was right. I only lasted one day. She Fed-Exed one more check, which had me all paid up except for the last week. So, whatever happened, I had my money. Then I got lucky. Lee called and said they would be a few days late and I would only have to cook for them for five days. The same guests would be coming, but they would be late as well. This was great news. I took off a few days and went to Bar Harbor, a few hours away. It'd been on my bucket list, a cool little town north of where I was, by Arcadia National Park. I had a great few days off, and then I returned to the island. They were coming the following Monday.

When they arrived, I helped them carry their luggage in. Lee said that she would like to talk to me in one hour. I said, "Yes, ma'am, thinking that she wanted to give me some rules—more like demands. I was like, fuck, how bad can this be? I was about to find out.

She sent the housekeeper to get me in the kitchen. I was told to meet Lee in the dining room. This fat, old broad couldn't even walk into the kitchen to get me. She really thought she was that important. I walked into the dining room, and she told me to sit down. She didn't even ask, I knew I was about to explode on her, but I waited to hear what she had to say.

She said, "Alan, these are the ground rules. Do not talk to us or other members of the family. If we need you, we will ring the bell during service or send the server"—aka the housekeeper—"to get you. The food must be on time and cannot be late at all. You can tell the server what we are having, or I will tell you what we want for lunch and dinner, so you don't need to make a presentation about the meal. We don't have time for that and don't care." Then, with a condescending attitude, she added, "Do I make myself clear?"

I said, "Yes, ma'am. I will do my best."

"I hope so," she replied.

I felt like saying, "Fuck you, you ratbag." What a pain in the ass. Everyone on the island said the same thing: what a couple of pieces of shit. The son and his wife were just as nasty to me. They were some of the most arrogant folks I ever worked for. Money can't buy class.

This went on for about half an hour, telling me who they were, ordering me to give them their space, the whole spiel. I almost got sick. Thank God they were leaving the island the first night. Then she told me I was excused and ordered me back to the kitchen. I was pissed.

She was not a good-looking woman, downright ugly, in fact, and fat on top of that. I wondered why her husband was still with her. He was not a bad-looking old man. He was a prick, but he had money. She must have had something on him and, if he left her, would rat him out and take him to the cleaners. Like I say, the fucking you give is the fucking you get. So true.

The next morning, I was in the kitchen and she came in and started ranting about how to make her eggs, basted, not tossed, and then patted dry. They both wanted them the same way. The kid was sleeping in, thank God, that little prick. I prepared breakfast like she asked, with sliced tomatoes and avocados, roasted potatoes, and bacon. I can cook. I've been doing this now for a long time, and I can honestly say that anyone who complains about the breakfast a private chef makes for them in their home is an asshole. Take that to the bank.

The bell rang almost as soon as the housekeeper put down the food. I was like, what the fuck? Already?" I didn't know if I was supposed to go or if the housekeeper was wanted. The bell rang again, and the housekeeper came into the kitchen and said, "The miss wants to see you right away."

I walked out there, and the first thing Lee said was, "Did you hear the bell?"

I said, "Yes. I did not know if it was for me or the housekeeper."

"I told you that if the bell rings, you are to come to the table."

I was cool. I said, "I am sorry. How can I help?"

"I cannot believe you would serve this meal."

"What is the issue?"

"The eggs are overcooked, there is a spot on the avocado, the potatoes have too much salt, and I did not like the presentation."

It was all I could do not to just take that plate and throw it at her. Jerry just sat there and did not say shit, but his plate was clean. She hadn't touched anything. I bit my tongue and said, "I am sorry. I will never do that again." If I had been packed up, I might have told her to stick it up her ass. Looking back, I wish I would have, but I got my payback in spades.

I was stuck on an island, and the ferry only came every two hours, so I was trying to figure out how the hell to get out of there before I killed this bitch. Then, lucky bastard that I am, I got a break. The grand-baby was sick, and they had to go to the doctor's office in Portland and would be gone all day. The bad news was that they would stay a few more days and had two more guests coming the next day, but I would not be around to put up with her insults and the shit from both of these shitheads.

She called me into the kitchen and said, "We will be here for dinner, but it will be late. We want lobster thermidor for six, and it had better not be overcooked." I was thinking, *Not only will it not be overcooked, it won't be cooked at all,* and there was nowhere to eat on the island at that time.

The moment they left for the doctor's office, I packed my shit. I had two hours before the housekeeper returned, and the next ferry was and hour away. I was packed in thirty minutes. Then raided the fridge and the bar, grabbed some food and beer, and took all the petty cash. It was mine, as they owed me gas money back to Florida and a few days' pay as well, not to mention the fact that I'd had to put up with their shit. Finally, I was out of there.

I passed the housekeeper and her husband on the way to the ferry. They knew my car was the white Benz with "Chef Al" plates. I had already paid for the ferry and had a space so I would be sure to make the next one, and I was in line about four cars back. I was just about to make a clean break when the husband walked up to my car and confronted me. He and his wife were Mexicans, not legal, so they had to protect their job. If you're ever interviewed and the wife says, "Oh, the staff has been here forever," there are two reasons. One, they are truly nice people, or two, the staff members are not legal and have no place to go. It's sad but true. I have seen it first-hand. You do what you have to survive, so I don't blame them.

He said, "Where are you going? You cannot leave."

I told him to just get out of my face, that it was not his concern. These went on for five minutes, and then they started to load the ferry. He tried to stop me again, and I said, "If you do not get out of my way, I am going to kick your ass. Now, get out of here."

He left, and I got on the ferry. Soon I would be on the mainland and on my way south, and I'd never have to see these assholes again.

Just when I thought I was home free, my cell phone blew up. I was still on the ferry but almost to the mainland. There was no way I was going back. If I did, things would get nasty. I would for sure kick this guy's ass. He needed it—him, the old lady, their son, the whole lot of them. I did not take any of the calls. It was childish. Every five minutes, they called and texted me. I wanted to wait till I was off the ferry and out of Maine. I knew they were hated on the island, but they might call the cops and say I'd stolen something. You never know. Like I said, this was one crazy bitch.

I got off the ferry, put my phone on airplane mode, and headed south. I would deal with this tomorrow once I was out of town. I drove almost nonstop to Boston, where I stopped and had a few beers. I figured I was far enough away from this fucked-up family, so I turned my phone back on and there were ten messages and the same number of texts from both Jerry and Lee. I think they took turns. It was some juvenile, crazy shit. They threatened me with jail and said that I would never work again. I had heard that last line before, so that was not new. They ordered me to return, saying that I would be sorry if I didn't, that they had guests coming and I had to be there. I wish I had saved those messages. I could not believe how desperate they were to get me to come back. This was truly the family from hell.

I decided to make them wait until tomorrow morning before I called them. I drove all night to get through New York and all that traffic along the way, which was a good call. They called every hour until late in the evening. I just turned my cell off again. I even got a call from the agent, Linda, who said to call her back right way.

I called her first to hear what she had to say before I called the Katzoffs back. I wanted to know what they had said about me. She said they would report me to the police for stealing coffee and food and not returning the petty cash, about two hundred dollars. The agent wanted me to give them the money back. I said, "Are you fucking crazy? I drove all the way to Maine and back to work for some mean and nasty people. There's no way in hell I'll give that money back."

"I cannot place you ever again," she said.

"Fine. Who needs to take shitty jobs like this on? Don't call me again. I will call the Katzoffs and give them my side of the story, and that is it. Let them try to sue me. We have no contract. I don't care who the hell they think they are."

I waited a few hours, as I am sure Linda called Lee and told her I was not coming back and would not be giving the petty cash back. To this day, I cannot figure out who the fuck these people thought they were. I made the call just to hear what she had to say. Lee picked up on the first ring. I was cool at first; that's just who I am. She started in, saying, "We demand you get back here today and finish this week. We have house-guests and have made plans, and we deserve more."

I said, "Ma'am, I am not coming back. You owe me for a few days' pay. I will keep the petty cash as gas money to get home, but we are done, and I am not coming back. As far as I am concerned, we are even. Send me a bill for the coffee and snacks I took, if you are that cheap, but we are done."

She started in again, calling me names, but I cut her off. I said, "Listen. I have the right to quit a job if I want to, and I am not going to be treated like shit and talked down to buy some fat, old Jewish bitch, so go fuck yourself, lady."

There was no comeback then. Jerry got on the phone, and it was the same shit. I said, "Listen, you fuck. I don't care about your guests or your spoiled little son, who couldn't wipe his own ass without his dad there. It seems like the apple does not fall far from the tree, as it seems you are a grown man and still cannot wipe your ass. Does Lee lick it for you?"

"You can't talk to me like that," he said. "I will have you arrested. I have connections."

I just said, "Fine. Kiss my ass, you Jew prick. Go back to New York with the rest of your rich asshole friends."

He started to say something, but I just said, "Fuck off," and hung up.

They called the rest of the day, leaving nasty messages saying that the cops were looking for me and I would be sorry for the way I talked to them, that no one had ever done that and gotten away with it. Like, are you kidding me? What a crock of shit. I sent one last text the next day, one of my favorite lines: "The fucking you give is the fucking you get." I hoped I ruined their plans. Assholes. They deserved worse. I guess I can cross them off my reference list.

I enjoyed the DP and brandy. Thanks, Katzoffs. They are at the top of my list for assholes. Never work for a New York Jew. I made that mistake twice, but I'd never make it again.

chapter 19

JERRY CONRAD
LAST CALL IN FORT LAUDERDALE

I FOUND MYSELF BACK IN Lauderdale, hanging out at the beach and enjoying the South Florida lifestyle. I never heard from the Katzoffs again. Linda, the agent, never called or emailed, either. That was a good thing. Now it was on to the next gig, and I was looking to get on a boat again.

It's always nice to come home after being gone, and I liked my little condo in Lauderdale. I thought, what the hell. I'll take a few weeks off and chill. Something will come up. It always does. I'm still the Teflon Kid. It must have only been a few days when, from out of the clear blue, Captain Cole called me and said, "Let's get a beer at the Elbow Room at the beach. I just got in town."

I said, "Cool. What time?"

"Six for drinks. Then we can go grab some dinner."

"Sounds great. I just got home, and I am looking to get back on a boat, so I am not working at the moment. I've got all night to catch up. See you at the Elbow Room."

Cole had been on the boat for some time now and was really doing well and dating some hot island swimsuit model. Turned out it was the chef's daughter. Only Cole gets pussy like that.

We caught up at the Elbow Room and then swapped some old stories about Panama, including the panty story. He said, "I will never forget that morning. I am sure Andy won't, either." He told me that he loved St Croix and the job was working out great.

I said, "I am looking for a new gig myself."

We pounded down a few beers and a couple of shots and headed over to the Quarterdeck. It's right around the corner, and the boat was at Berhi Marina, all within walking distance. When we got to the Quarterdeck, Cole ran into one of his captain buddies, Pete. We exchanged greetings, and he said, "Yeah, I've seen you around, Chef Al."

I said, "You look familiar, too, Pete."

Cole said, "Want to join us for dinner?"

"You cool with that, Chef?" Asked Pete.

"Yeah," I replied. "Cole and I are just catching up."

Pete asked Cole, "How do you two know each other?"

Cole told him about how we worked on *Rapture* together, but he left out some of the stories. Some captains would not have the balls to do what we did—they kiss the owners' asses—so we just left that out.

We had a few beers at the bar and then grabbed a table and ordered some burgers, a few more beers, and some shots. Then we started talking guy shit—you know, who has the biggest dick, shit like that. Most captains are full of shit and themselves. Cole was not like that; that's why I liked him and hung out with him. He was a first-class guy and a nice young man.

Pete asked if I was working, and I said, "No, I just got off a freelance land job in Maine, and I'll start looking for a new boat in a few days."

He said, "Shit, I can use you all winter in the Bahamas. It's an easy gig and great owners."

As if I'd never heard that before. I said, "Give me the game plan and tell me about the owners."

Pete said, "They never charter. The first trip is one month, and the owners come twice. The first trip is to Nassau and Pig Island and then back to Lauderdale. You get a grand a week and your expenses."

"I can do that."

"The missus will have to meet you, but I am sure she will like you, and the job starts in a few weeks. I will need you to help with lines and drive the tender as well."

"I can do that."

"I will call you tomorrow and set up a meeting with you and Yvonne."

"Sounds good."

Our check came, and we were out of there. I said goodnight to my old friend Cole and thanked him for the hook-up, and we were good to go.

I got a call the next morning from Pete. He said, "Hey, can you come by the house this afternoon and meet Yvonne? I will show you around the boat."

"What time?"

"Three."

"Cool. See you there."

I knew the house. Jerry had the premier pad, right on the Inter-coastal and next to the bridge on Las Olas. I mean, shit, five minutes, and you are in the ocean. He had a Mediterranean-style house, a Ferrari, and a big Westport, *Last Call*, which I had seen around town. I pulled up in my Alfa and a nice suit; that's how I roll. Pete met me at the front door and took me in to meet the Conrad's. They had just finished a late lunch and were having drinks.

Pete introduced me and said, "When you are finished, come by the boat. It's right next to the house."

Jerry put his hand out and said, "Hi, Chef Al. We've heard all about you. Great website. This is Yvonne." She said hi as well, and we all sat down on the patio. We hit it off right from the get-go and talked about food and wine. They had a place on Lido Island in Newport Beach and knew my mentor, Mike Gayner, so I guess you know I got the job. Jerry liked everything, Yvonne as well, as long as it was clean and fresh. I said, "That's all I do." I told them about a few of my dishes, and they were getting hungry: fish tacos, eggs Benny with crab, cracked conch, red snapper; they were in love.

Yvonne asked if I minded cooking at the house once in a while and maybe for a dinner party or two. I said, "Sure. I would like that." Just like that, I got a new gig and one that would last for a long time. They were a nice couple, one of the best I ever worked for, first class both of them. Jerry was the best, and Yvonne was just a sweetheart. We still message each other on Facebook once in a while.

Yvonne asked how soon I could start. I said, "Pete says the boat is leaving late next week depending on the weather window."

"Yes, but can you cook at the house this weekend for us two days and for two couples one night?"

"Sure. What do you feel like?"

"Fish one night."

"Let's do some nice red snapper one night and then a flat iron steak the next."

"Sounds great."

Yvonne and I would start getting the boat ready on Monday. Jerry said, "It's great to have you on board, and I look forward to some nice dinners."

They had to run, so I said, "I will come by tomorrow and go through the kitchen and see what I need for the weekend."

We all left with smiles on our faces. I had a good feeling about them.

I went over to the boat, parked right next to the house. I saw Pete, and he waved me in and said, "You got the job. I knew they would like you. Let's have a beer. I am ready to knock off anyway."

I said, "They want me to cook at the house this weekend for a small dinner party. Then, on Monday, I will start getting ready for the trip."

"Sounds great. I told you that you would like them. They're nice people."

We chatted a bit and had one more beer, but then I had plans with a Jewish woman I'd been fucking for the last few weeks, so I had to cut out early.

The Conrad's wanted me to make dinner on Saturday and brunch on Sunday. I was down for that. Yvonne wanted to do something fun Saturday. I said, "How about Mexican fish tacos, and the guests can build their own?"

She said, "That sounds great. Let's do that, and on Sunday, let's have eggs Benny."

"No problem."

It would be just four adults on both days. On Sunday, Jerry's son and his wife were coming over. Saturday was a breeze, and everyone loved my roasted red pepper salsa, Mexican street corn, and Southwest coleslaw mahi-mahi tacos, the best with all the sides. Sunday went well, too. Jerry's son and wife were great, and they wear going on the first trip as well. The weekend went well, and everyone was happy. They could not say thank you enough. It's nice to feel appreciated. Brunch was first class: Bloody Marys, champagne, eggs Benny, grilled asparagus, roasted Chef Al potatoes, fresh fruit with homemade whipped cream, tomato and avocado salad on a bed of mixed greens, always a hit, jumbo shrimp grilled with Jamaica-me-crazy sauce, chips, salsa, guac. It was a hit. I was asked to join them, which was a nice gesture. I had a busy week coming up tomorrow, and I started provisioning for the trip. Nassau, here we come.

I worked for Jerry and Yvonne on and off for the next year. The first trip was a fucking nightmare, not on my account but Captain Peter's. What a mess. Cole had suggested him, but he did not tell me he was a coke-head, and his girlfriend was just as bad and lazy as shit, the worst stew I ever worked with. The trip started off well, but they all did. There were going to be three trips this season, so the boat would stay in the Bahamas, and guests would fly in every month for a week or so. Then we would go island hopping, always the same ones, Pig Harbor, Staniel Cay, all cool places. Then the boat would come back to Lauderdale for the summer and stay behind the house.

I got all the provisioning done, and we were set to leave at sunset. We got a nice weather window and were underway, bound for Nassau. If you haven't been there, it's a cool spot. We got there two days before the guests arrived, and I lined up some fresh conch, lobsters, and fish. We were looking really good. The first trip was with Jerry and Yvonne, his son, his son's wife, and their kids. It was a ten-day trip.

The day before Jerry, Yvonne, and their guests arrived, I was all ready for them, but Peter's girlfriend, aka the stew, had not done shit, so I went ahead and vacuumed and cleaned up some. By the way, Pete was new to this job. This was his first trip with the owners, and it would be his last. He was the worst captain I ever worked for. He was a nice guy, just a loser and coke-head, and his girlfriend was worse. That's Fort Lauderdale for you, or as they call it, Snort Lauderdale.

All the guests were great. Jerry and Yvonne would get up early, and they liked their breakfast on the back deck. Every day, it was the same thing: eggs over easy, well-done bacon, and sourdough toast. Get that right, and they were happy. Pretty easy, if you ask me. Yvonne was a few years younger than Jerry, but there was not a crazy difference, and you could tell she cared about him and Jerry cared about her. They were a nice couple. I think Yvonne was good looking for an old broad. I would have fucked her back then, but she'd be past her prime now. But back in the day, she was a catch, and she had lots of class.

On the second day of the trip, Jerry came down first and entered the galley. He got a cup of coffee and said he would like to eat as soon as I could fix it. I said, "Give me five minutes. Tell me when Yvonne comes up, and I will be on it." Then I did a double take. Something did not look right about Jerry. I gave him a hard look, and then I realized he had his wig on backward, and I mean to tell you, it looked like a shit wig taped on. I could hardly keep myself from laughing out loud. Dumbest thing I ever saw.

Just as I was going to say something to Jerry, Yvonne came up and fixed Jerry's shit. She looked at me and knew I was ready to bust a gut. She just smiled and said, "Alan, we are ready." Jerry couldn't have given two shits. I fixed him a Bloody Mary, and he was all good. You could tell she really loved him.

That's kind of how every morning started. Then the kids would come down and have drinks and breakfast. Jerry took us all out the first night to Nobu, inside the resort, first class, and we had a great dinner. The next morning, we headed for Pig Island. If you've never heard of it, it's a small island in the Bahamas not too far from Nassau. There's not much to the island except the wild pigs. The beach people come there to feed them, and it's a great anchor spot and a nice beach if you don't mind the pigs. They want food and are quite spoiled. I saved all the food scraps for the last few days so the kids would have something to feed them. They'll eat anything.

We dropped the hook, unloaded all the toys and jet skis, and tied off the tender, and then the party started. The kids, and even some of the adults, went ashore to feed the pigs. Some of them even swim. It's the damnedest thing I have ever seen. All the guests had a great day feeding the pigs, jet skiing, and just having a great time. I served some cracked conch with my pineapple martinis before dinner, and I grilled some fresh grouper with Jamaica-me-crazy sauce, coconut rice, and grilled asparagus.

Jerry and his son had a little buzz on, and they asked me to join them for a toast. I said, "Of course. My pleasure." I had one drink and said, "Good night. I have to be up early."

Pete and his crazy girlfriend were nowhere to be seen. I knocked on their cabin door, as it was right across from mine. He said they were tired and would see me in the morning.

She had not done turn-down service, and he should have been on anchor watch, yet they had retired to their room for the night. I thought that was a little strange, but what the hell—I was just the chef.

I turned in and woke up to the sound of horns going off. I got dressed as fast as I could and banged on Pete's door. They didn't answer after five minutes of knocking, so I went on deck and found all the guests. Jerry's son was at the helm, and Jerry was at the bow with fenders. I grabbed one and joined in to help. Jerry asked me, "Where the fuck is Pete?"

I said, "I banged on the door, but there was no answer." We got the fenders out just in time, and the yacht in front of us had its crew on deck with all fenders out as well. We came within a few feet of hitting them. Jerry's son and I pulled anchor, which we had been dragging, moved the boat, and dropped the hook again. Everyone was pissed. Jerry asked again, "What the hell is Pete doing?"

I don't lie for anyone, so I threw them under the bus. Jerry's son knew something was up; he knew what I was about to tell them already. I said, "They're drunk and passed out and worn out over coke."

We got everything under control, and then Jerry came over to me and said, "Thanks. Go to bed. We are all good. See you in the morning."

It was around three in the morning now. I got a few hours of sleep and then was back on deck for breakfast. Jerry and Yvonne were first up as always. I served them breakfast, and Jerry asked me what I thought of Pete and his girl. This was their first trip with them. I said, "Look at last night. No anchor watch, no turn-down service. They were drunk on top of that, passed out. There you have it."

He said, "I want to ask you for a favor. I will let them go as soon as we get back to Nassau. Could you help Dan and his son, Taylor, bring the boat back to Lauderdale?"

"Sure."

"I want you to stay on with us and help us find a new captain and stew."

"It would be my pleasure."

Pete and Nancy didn't get on deck until about nine, and they acted like nothing had happened. I thought Jerry would let him have it, but he was way cool about it, as he knew he was letting them both go in a few days and he did not want to ruin their trip. He just asked, "Where were you last night, and why was there no anchor watch or turn-down. Chef is cooking and serving as well. What does your girlfriend do, and why do we need her if she is not doing her job?"

Pete was at a loss for words. Then he said, "She has been sick, and we were sound asleep last night and did not hear anything."

Jerry stayed cool. "I don't want this to happen again. I want you guys up on deck at eight, and I want turn-down service and for Nancy to clean and help Chef Al serve. You got that?"

Pete said yes and offered a weak excuse again about her being sick. Jerry was not buying that.

A few hours later, Pete came into the galley started to give me some shit. "What did you tell Jerry? I hired you, and you report to me."

I said, "I would if you could get your drunk ass out of bed and do your job. I told Jerry that I knocked on your door and you didn't answer. That was it."

He started to same some shit, but then Dan walked in. "What the fuck happened to you last night?"

Pete started to say something, but Dan cut him off. I thought Dan was going to kick his ass. Jerry walked in and calmed Dan down. Pete knew his days were numbered, and I am sure he knew I would tell Cole what had happened.

By the end of the day, cool heads had prevailed. Nancy was cleaning, and Pete was sober for the time being. We hung out at Pig Island for half a day and then traveled on to Staniel and Compass Cays. At Staniel, we would be at the marina, so there was no chance of dragging anchor. We would spend a few days there and one day at Compass Cay. We get to Staniel around sundown. It's got a small marina, but they have a nice little bar and a great restaurant there. I've been there a few times. There is some history about the owner, whose son runs the place. Rumor has it the old man invented or had something to do with AC for yachts or a cooling system. I can't remember the whole deal, but anyway, he made a shitload of money with his patent and bought this place. Then, a few years later, he cleaned out the bank account—I heard it was in the millions—and took off in his plane out of Lauderdale. The plane crashed, and he and the money were never recovered. It makes you wonder. Me, I love shit like that. Good for him, wherever he is at.

Back at Staniel, we got tied up, and Jerry took us all to dinner the first night. It's a great little spot, but the service is typical for the Bahamas. Wherever you go, it's not great; it's island time. I have been all over, and the Bahamas has the worst service anywhere. We all had a nice dinner of fresh fish and drinks. The plan for the next day was to go to Thunderball Cave, where the filmed the Bond movie *Thunderball* with Sean Connery. It's kind of cool, and there is some great jet skiing through the mango groves. There are a few other islands nearby, but the Bond stuff is cool.

The next day was spent at Compass Cay. It's the same. You don't want to spend the whole day there, but it's a good place to hide during the hurricane season. It has a small marina, and there are always nurse sharks to feed, and that's kind of cool. Plus, my friend owns the place. It's cool to spend a few days there, but you will go stir-crazy after that. There's just nothing to do. I am sure I walked every foot of that island. We spent one day there, and everyone had a great time feeding the sharks and fishing. The guys caught some fresh mahi-mahi, which I cooked up.

We were heading back to Nassau the next morning. Pete knew he was on thin ice, but he had no idea how pissed Jerry still was, and Nancy was still not holding her own. Just worthless, the both of them.

On the way back to Nassau, Jerry came to the galley and asked if I was still good with taking the boat back to Lauderdale. I told him I was, and he said, "As soon as we get tied up, I am firing both of them. They have one hour to get their shit off my boat. Book a flight and get the credit card back to me. I want you to help them get their stuff off, and I will tell Pete to give the petty cash and credit card to you."

I said, "Sure, I can do that."

No sooner had we docked and tied off than Jerry told me to get Pete to meet him on the aft deck with Nancy. I did, and then Pete and Nancy went out to talk to him. Dan entered the galley with his son, a pretty good-size kid, and said, "We will stay here to back you up until they get off the boat. Once they're off, we will meet Jerry for dinner. Make sure you get Pete's keys. We will pay for their hotel one night, and then they're on their own."

Jerry brought the hammer down. I was not there, but he didn't take any shit. I was in the crew lounge when the two came down. Pete was like, "What the fuck?" And his girlfriend was like, "I don't believe it. They won't find anyone better than us."

They looked at me, and I almost laughed in their faces. I said, "Are you two really serious? You are a couple of drunks, and you are the worst stew I've ever seen. You did not do shit, and you wonder why you got fired? Get real. I am supposed to help you get your stuff off, and I need the petty cash back and the credit card. You've got one hour. Jerry will pay for tonight's hotel, and that's it, so book a flight for tomorrow. I will go get you two a room here for tonight, but that's it."

Pete said, "Who is taking the boat back?"

"Dan, his son, and I will."

He laughed and said, "Good luck," like he thought he was Captain America. What a piece of shit.

Dan came down to check on me, and he said, "Pete, is there an issue?" Pete backed right down, and Dan said, "Now, let's get your gear off the boat. We have dinner plans. Give me your keys to the boat, and where is the petty cash? And give Chef the credit card."

Nancy would say something, but Pete cut her off, which was a good thing. She did not have a clue. Dan and I gave them a hand, and we got the two deadbeats off the boat. I wonder how some of these captains and stews get these jobs. Never hire a captain and stew who are a couple; it's a no-win situation. Trust me on this.

Dan and I had a shot and a beer, and then he said, "Let's go meet Jerry and Yvonne." He thanked me and said, "Dad likes that you were a Marine. You're a stand-up guy who takes care of shit. Now, let's go eat."

"Thanks," I said. "Give me five so I can change." We were going to Nobu, and I wanted to look my best.

I got squared away, and then we were on our way. Jerry already had a table. As soon as we got there, the first thing he asked was, "Are they off the boat, and do we have the keys?"

Dan said, "Yes, Chef and I took care of everything. They're gone. I got the petty cash and the credit card, so we are good, thanks to Chef."

Jerry said, "thanks."

"I am glad I could help," I said.

"We are going to hang out one more day. Then you and Dan are on your own. As soon as you get a weather window, bring the boat home. I want you to help hire a new crew and captain, too."

"I can do that."

We had a great dinner and some drinks and then headed back to the boat for an early night.

The next morning, I made breakfast and cleaned the main saloon. Then Jerry, Yvonne, and I had a small chat about the old crew. We all agreed it was time for them to go, and that was it. The subject never came up again. Dan and his wife and son went fishing, while Jerry and Yvonne went to hang out at the pool for the rest of the day. I went out and got some lobsters for dinner.

This was the last night for Jerry and Yvonne; they were heading out right after breakfast the next morning. Dan's wife would join them, and Dan, his son, and I would be taking the boat back to Lauderdale. Dan was a captain, and the trip was only 180 miles. We got Jerry off, and then I fed Dan and his son. He checked the weather and said, "Shit, it's flat. Let's take off after breakfast. Chef, take the credit card and pay the dock bill, and let's get out of here. Chef, you drive the tender. Taylor and I will get the lines and tie it up once we get out of the channel,"

"Cool," I said. "Let's do it."

Just like that, we were on our way home. The trip had gone off like clockwork. When we got back to Lauderdale, Jerry was waiting for us at the dock. The boat stayed behind the house when not in the Bahamas. We got her backed in and all tied up, and Jerry said, "Let's have a beer."

I did one more trip with Jerry, Yvonne, Dan, and his family, only this time we went to Harbor Island and hung out there for a week. If you have never been to Harbor Island, put it on your list. It has a nice marina, a few nice restaurants, and a local weekly market. It's a diamond in the rough was a nice trip.

Back in Lauderdale, I was doing a few dinner parties for the Conrad's, not too much. Then, from out of the blue, Jerry called me and asked if I could come over that afternoon. He had something he wanted to talk about. I said, "Sure. See you in a few hours." I wondered what he could want. I got cleaned up and headed over. He and Yvonne were in the dining room, and they asked me to join them.

He asked if I wanted a drink, and I said, "No, I am fine. What's up, guys?"

Yvonne said, "We want to hire you full time and want to see what kind of salary you need and what services you would provide. If you want, you can stay on the boat or the guest house."

I said, "I will take care of all the cooking and shopping and do errands that you need done, post office, dry cleaning, that sort of thing. Cars gassed and detailed, serviced as well. I can travel to California if you want me out their dinner parties and oversee the gardeners and general maintenance of the property."

Jerry said, "Great. How much do you need?"

"Six thousand a month to start."

I thought he would have a heart attack right there on the spot. He looked at me and said, "That's a lot of money."

"That's a grand less than I would charge someone else because I like you guys and we have a history together."

Yvonne was cool with the price, but not Jerry. He asked me, "Can you change the oil on the boat and do maintenance?"

"I can't do that," I said, "but I can make sure it gets done. I have lots of key people in Lauderdale to do the work for me."

He did not like that. He wanted me to do the work. Come on. How many chefs do you know who can change the oil and maintain a 112' Westport? Not many, you can bet your ass on that. Jerry wanted to pay me three thousand a month and have me do all the maintenance and everything else. What an insult. Yvonne thought so as well, but Jerry was the boss, and he had the money. I said, "I am sorry, but I can't work for that. But I will still do the trips on the boat and dinner parties when you need me." We agreed, had a beer, and shook hands.

Yvonne walked me to the door and said, "I'm sorry. Jerry is cheap with things like that."

I said, "It's cool. Don't worry about it." I still like Jerry, and Yvonne was great. He was just cheap. Lots of these rich fucks are. After that, I went back to my old rate of three hundred a day. Money is money.

I did one last trip on the boat that year. It was my last trip on *Last Call* and the last time I worked for them. I just hated being around cheap fuckers. I am sure that if I wanted to hire Jerry for his services, he would not give me a break, and God forbid I try to cut the price. I will never forget that day: "Alan, that's a lot of money." Bullshit. Tony G said the same thing to me just a few months later in the Bahamas. Do you think I work for free? Where do these rich fucks get off on trying to get services for free? I think Tony G's contract was way too much, forty million to catch a football. Give me a break. That's robbery, if you ask me.

Back to the last trip. It would be to the Bahamas again, only this time with the daughter and her LA friends. It would be a ten-day trip. I quoted three hundred a day to the daughter, and she fought me till I gave her the old price of 250 a day. I should have known better than to do the trip. Nowadays, I just say, "No, I am not your guy. You better hire someone else." But I like the Bahamas, and I wanted to go back one more time, as I was looking for a land-based job after this trip. Plus, I hired Cole's friend Richard as captain, and he was a cool guy, so I knew it would be a good trip. I just had to put up with the daughter and her LA guests. I would just put my head down, keep my mouth shut, and do the job. The guests were Jerry's daughter and her husband, Tony G and his wife, Stacy Keibler and her new husband, Jared Pobre, and their teenage kids.

Like I said, easy trip, ten days, a few good stories, hanging with Tony G. The guests would fly into Nassau, spend a few days there, and then we'd head to Pig Island for a few days over, and then to Staniel and Compass Cays, and back to Nassau for the last few nights. Then they would fly back, and a day or so later, we would take the boat back, and the trip would conclude. That's kind of how most of their trips went. It's nice, but it gets old after a few times. However, the water in the Bahamas never gets old. It's just so blue. It's some of the prettiest water in the world.

I got all the shopping done and loaded up on booze, and we were off on one more adventure. We got to Nassau without a hitch, and I hired two stews to help with the trip. Stacy wanted first-class service. There are only two really good stories from this trip. I mean, I could go on and on about the two Stacys, how they thought their shit didn't stink. They could not keep themselves from looking in the mirror every five minutes, and these were not two young chicks. I mean, they'd both seen better days. They needed some more work done, but their personalities could not be fixed. They were just nasty bitches.

They got to the boat late afternoon, and I had the snacks ready and the beer iced down. I knew they were drinkers. The first night, they started drinking, getting loud, and just acting like high school kids. They all got buzzed pretty good. Then they said they were going out for dinner and wanted to take the crew, and they told me to make reservations at Nobu and get a big table at the nightclub. I said, "I can do that." Then they all went for a nap before dinner and going out.

I fed the crew a late lunch, and then Cap and I talked about the rest of the trip. It looked like we would have great weather all week. Next I headed to the casino to make reservations and get a table at the nightclub. Once that was done, I had some petty cash, so I tipped all the right guys and we were dialed in for the night. Then it was back to *Last Call* to take a break and clean up.

I took an hour's break and then returned to the deck just to make sure all was good. The gang rolled up a few hours later, and they started drinking again. Stacy asked, "What time is dinner?"

"Just like you asked," I said, "Eight thirty at Nobu and a table at the nightclub for ten."

Dinner was great, and the girls were on their better behavior, but the night was still young, and they were just getting started. Tony G and his wife were nice. I think they were a little embarrassed and didn't like hanging out with this kind of crew. I'm not sure how they fit into the mix. He might have been friends with Stacy Keibler's husband, as he was in the movie business—a producer, I think. I'd never heard of him. He wasn't a bad guy, just a little full of himself. Poor bastard had to put up with Keibler's shit. All she talked about was how she used to be George Clooney's girlfriend. I am sure Clooney fucked her a few times and said, "What am I thinking? What a bitch," and kicked her to the curb. She had no class at all. The new guy, Jared Pobre, the poor bastard, has to put up with her shit. What a train wreck. He's no Romeo, so she's the best ass he ever had; I am sure of that. He must have some money, or I am sure Stacy would not be with him. LA chicks—living proof of why tigers eat their young.

We had a nice dinner and then made our way around the casino. Everyone was stopping Tony G for a pic, and he was cool about it. Stacy was not happy about that. She thought she should be the center of attention. To tell you the truth, I had no idea who she was. Someone had told me she was a wrestler who had fucked Clooney, but that was all I knew about her, and I couldn't have given a rat's ass anyway.

Mom was buying the girls drinks, even though they were only around fifteen, I think, and they were drunk—and high on top of that. We got to the nightclub, and they wouldn't let the girls in because they were underage. Stacy started to make a big scene, so I told her, "Cool it. Let me take care of this."

I grabbed the manager and threw him a hundred, and he said, "Cool, but the two girls cannot drink, and they have to leave by midnight. If I catch them drinking, they are out of here."

I thanked him and then returned to Stacy and told her the deal. By the way, Tony G's son went back to the boat, and he was around the same age. They were good parents, and Tony's wife was really nice and showed some class. I asked Stacy, "Are you cool with this?"

She said, "Yes, and thanks."

I mean, they did not even have fake IDs, and they were fifteen, anyway, and looked it, too.

Everything was under control for a few hours. Stacy was letting the kids drink from her glass, and soon after, she started buying them drinks. Just as it was getting close to midnight and the girls had to go, the manager came over, grabbed me, and said, "Who is in charge?" I pointed to Stacy, and he said, "Chef Al, you know they broke the deal."

I said, "Yes, I am cool with whatever you have to do. It's your call."

He headed over to Stacy. The kids' drinks were in plain sight. He asked about them, and she said they were virgin piña coladas. He said, "No, they're not. They were rung in as regular, and it's now midnight. You broke our deal, and now they must leave. But the adults can stay if the kids leave now."

You'd have thought Stacy was being raped. She started laying into him about how the kids were of age but didn't have their IDs on them and how dare he accuse her of buying drinks for minors." I'll say one thing. She had a set of balls. No class, mind you, and no tact. Then Keibler hopped on the bandwagon, too, saying, "We're not leaving. You will have to throw us out."

And that's just what they did. He said, "I am asking you to leave. If you don't, I am going to call security and have you removed."

Tony G hopped in and said, "Come on, guys. It's getting late. Let's head back to the boat. Pobre said the same, but the two nasty bitches were not going to leave.

"How dare he embarrass us and accuse us of giving drinks to the kids." Stacy called him a few names and said, "Do you know who we are? We could buy this place. I will have your job tomorrow."

He finally gave up and called security, and a staff of about six guys walked over. I am sure Tony wanted no part of this bad PR, if you know what I mean. They escorted everyone out and said they were eighty-sixed for the entire trip.

I told the manager I was sorry, and he said, "Chef, we are cool with you. Just don't bring them back. They are not welcome here."

Do you know how hard it is to get kicked out of a bar in the Bahamas? You have to be really stupid and fucked up, and they were. I mean, really, "Do you know who we are?" I still laugh when I think about that. I was glad to see them get kicked out. They deserved more than that.

When they got back to the boat, Stacy still had not had enough. "How dare they kick us out. Wait till I tell Dad. He will have their jobs." I thought Jerry would tell his daughter to shut the fuck up. He drew the line, something I liked that about him.

I went ahead and turned in. Tony G and his wife did, too, but the others kept partying. I am sure they got into the coke. Stacy could not shut up and let it go. Her poor husband. I hate to think of the shit he had to put up with and the fat daughter who thought she was America's next top model. Maybe for Duluth Underwear, if she got lucky. What a joke.

Just as I got into bed, I heard a knocking on my door. "Chef Al, we want breakfast." It was around three in the morning. It was Keibler and the two kids, drunk and high. I said, "Give me five, and I will be up." Just when I thought it couldn't get any worse.

I headed up to the galley, and they wanted eggs Benny. I said, "That's not going to happen. I can do eggs and toast. It will take five minutes, and then I am done."

They gave me a little flak, but I just went ahead and scrambled eggs and cheese, made some toast, and then went back to bed. I was pissed. That was not called for. Like I said, no class. That was one screwed-up night and what a way to start the trip off. I thought, *Man, I hope this gets better. If Jerry were here, this shit would not be happening, but what the hell. It's my last trip with these screw-ups. I will miss Jerry, Yvonne, and their son, but the daughter and her nasty LA gang can pound sand.*

The rest of the trip was not bad. At least they did not get kicked out of anywhere else. That's hard on Pig Island and Staniel Cay, but I am sure they could have found a way. But things were ok, just lots of drinking and boring conversation about how rich and good looking they were, that kind of shit. Pretty shallow for adults, but they did live in LA, which explained everything. The next four days just flew by. They went jet skiing, fishing, and snorkeling, and I cooked some nice fish dinners, cracked conch, lobsters, the whole nine yards. They were all blown away, and I made the pineapple vodka, also a big hit. The next thing I knew, we were on our way back to Nassau, one more trip in the bag. I got to talk to Tony G a few times in private. He's a really nice guy and a great football player, but I don't think he will make it as an actor. Good luck, Tony G.

We got back to Nassau, and they partied some more. The girls were just getting drunk and acting stupid again. Stacy wanted to take the crew out. It was the last night, and she wanted to play the big shot. We were going to Nobu again—just to be seen, I am sure. What the hell—it was on her dime. Dinner was nice. It's is one of the best places to eat in Nassau, though overpriced. De Niro was there that night, and Stacy had him come over. I am sure the only reason he did was that Tony G was at our table. De Nero is a real piece of shit. I did a charter with him a few years later, and he thinks he is something special. What do you expect? He is a New Yorker, the biggest assholes in the world. What a dick. I almost got up and left due to the shit coming out of his mouth.

Thank God this was the last night and last trip with these fucks. They all had early flights, so it was not an all-night drunk-fest. We got back to the boat by midnight, and everyone was soon out for the count. As it turns out, Stacy knew my old boss Bryan Dopp, and I think his third wife, Kimberly Church, was in the mix, one more Newport Beach whore. I heard the girls talk about how Kimberly cleaned Bryan out: stole a diamond ring and sold it, cleaned out the bank account, sold the furniture and left with all the money. If that's not a whore, what is?

The next morning, I was up on deck early to make coffee, muffins, and egg sandwiches for the road. The girls were hungover, which, I am sure, was an everyday thing for the hoes. Cap and I helped with all the gear, got them loaded in the van, and said our goodbyes. I got a photo of me, the guys, and Tony G.

We got stiffed, of course—no tip—but I had seen that coming. I'd told Cap this would happen, so he was not expecting anything, either. We decided to just clean out the bar and take it all, and we did. We got lucky on the weather. A front was coming in, so we had to stay a few days till we had a weather window. Jerry hated that he had to pay for the dock and only us crew. I loved Jerry, but he was just one cheap guy. With power and the dock fee, it was five hundred dollars a day plus the crew's salary. We ended up staying two extra days. The stews were cool. They got paid, and they met some young deckhands from *Wheels Up*, a yacht next to us.

Cap and I met a few tourists from Boston, filled the hot tub, popped some champagne, raised a glass, and toasted to Jerry. Then we laid into these two chicks. They were in heaven, getting fucked in a hot tub on a yacht in the Bahamas.

For the next two days, I fed the crew steak and lobster, drank their best wine, and killed all the Grey Goose. Did I tell you we were getting paid, too? We get the weather window on the third day, and Cap said, "We better leave now, or Jerry will be really pissed, as I am sure he is looking at the weather as well." The last two days had been kind of borderline. Now we had a clean shot home.

While we were underway, I packed up all the good stuff for Cap and myself, fifty-fifty. When you don't tip the staff or take care of them, they help themselves. I made sure we did not leave shit. I told the girls the check would be transferred electronically this week, and they were cool with that. I also gave them each a few bottles of nice wine and some food, and they were really happy. I said, "This makes up for the tip we did not get." I felt bad because I had brought them on board and they'd done a great job.

The stews took off, and then Cap and I washed down the boat, doing a half-assed job. Then it was time for beer and unloading our bounty: a few cases of wine, a case or two of beer and liquor, and all the shrimp and steak I had in the freezer. We cleaned it all out, loaded up, and that was it.

Cap called Jerry and said, "We are home, and the boat is back behind the house. Call me when you need me."

Jerry said, "Thanks. I'll be home in a few days. Checks will go out tomorrow, and everyone will be paid."

A few days passed, and I got a call from Jerry. He said, "I am back in Lauderdale. Can you come by to talk?"

I said, "Sure. What's up?"

"Stacy has some issues with you, and I want to talk to you in person."

"No problem. I'll see you this afternoon."

I rolled up dressed nicely, as I like to clean up. Jerry asked if I wanted a drink, and I said, "Beer is fine."

He got right to the point. "Stacy felt you were rude and was not happy with the service she and her guest received, and Tony G was not happy about taking a pic with you and the guys. She never wants me back on the boat again. What do you make of that?"

"Wow," I said. "I was about to tell you the same thing, that I will not work for your daughter and friends again. If you want to know the truth about the trip, I will tell you what happened."

Yvonne said to Jerry, "I told you there are two sides to every story." She knew the daughter was a piece of shit, and her friends, too. Jerry just did not want to hear it or believe it.

So, I told him what had happened. First, I asked, "Did she tell you that they all got kicked out of the nightclub at Atlantic?"

"No."

"Call Omar, the manager. He had to call security to have them removed. Stacy was buying drinks for the underage girls, and they told her they would let them in but no drinking and they had to leave at midnight. Stacy lied and then went nuts and said, 'Do you know who we are?'"

I told Jerry the whole story. Then I said, "Come on. You know me. That's the truth. I will not be back. If you and Yvonne want to hire me, that's cool. Stacy, no way, and on top of that, I cut my price by fifty dollars a day at her request and got no tip. That is just pure bullshit."

I looked Jerry dead in the eyes and said, "What else did you want to talk about? Do you have any more questions about the trip? I feel I have been insulted by this. I don't like being around drugs and drunks. I don't need that."

Jerry said, "You know that's my daughter."

"Yes, and I am sorry. I wont be back."

Tony G was cool with the pic, and if you ever run in to him, ask him what happened. He will tell you he was very embarrassed to be with them, and I bet he will not be hanging out with them again. You can take that to the bank.

We had one more beer, and Jerry said, "Thanks for being honest, but she is my daughter."

I said, "Cool. Don't worry. I don't need the money that bad."

We shook hands and finished our beer. Then Yvonne walked me to the door. She said, "Alan, if you need a reference, call me," and she gave me five hundred dollars. "Here's a tip from me. Thanks for telling Jerry the truth. He needed to hear that. I will see you around town."

I liked Yvonne. There was a lot of class in that woman.

I got two tips, all the bounty, and five hundred from Yvonne. It had turned out to be a good trip after all. I saw Jerry and Yvonne around town a few times, and they always said hi. I heard that they sold *Last Call* and the big house. We had some good times. I will miss them.

Stepping out in LA

Guest Dealership

Always liked the blondes

Jojo's Circus 2

chapter 20

DR. GREKIN
GROSS POINT YACHT CLUB, MICHIGAN

THIS WAS SUPPOSED TO BE a summer job, from June to September. Then, if it worked out, they would hire me for the next summer, too. I thought: *Cool. Summer in Michigan, winter in Florida. Not bad. Work eight months and take the rest of the year off. Good plan.* I lasted two months before I almost put my foot up the old lady's ass and bitch-slapped her daughter.

If you live in Michigan, you have heard of this prick. He is on TV and has a skincare line, a big-time dermatologist with offices all around the country. My job was to cook on the boat when they used it, clean the inside, and cook at the house a few days a week. It was a small yacht, an eighty-two-foot Lazzara.

So, it did sound ok, and I would live on the boat at the Grosse Pointe Yacht Club. It was supposed to be one of the oldest clubs in the country. It had its share of nasty owners, but all the yacht clubs do. You always have the stuck-up wives who married into money and think their shit doesn't stink, just like Tara, Dr. Grekin's wife. She was a nasty bitch.

This was the first time I took a job without an agent or a friend. I'd heard of DayWork123 for jobs on yachts, but be very careful when you take jobs off there. Most of the time, the job sucks. The owners are cheap and don't want to pay a fee to hire good staff. I never took a job off that site again. I should have known that coming in.

We talked on the phone, and they seemed nice, so I went for it. The job started with me picking up an SUV at Tara's parents' house, along with a credit card, and driving it to Michigan. At the end of the summer, I would drive it back. It sounded easy. I should not have gotten in that SUV. As soon as I met Tara's mom, she was giving me orders: don't stop to eat and make sure of this and that. I was like, "Shut the fuck up, you old hag." I should have turned right back around. I finally got out of there without losing my cool and was on the road. I spent the night in Ohio to see my favorite cousin, Lisa, who lives outside of Columbus. We had a nice dinner and caught up. I also got to say hi to my mom, who lives there, too. The next day, I had a long drive up to Bloomfield. That was where the house was. The boat was in Grosse Pointe.

I was supposed to meet them at the house, and then Doc would take me to the boat to pick up keys and all that sort of stuff. I rolled in about six. They immediately asked if I could cook dinner for them. I should have known better. That was how the next two months went—a pain in the ass. They had no food in the fridge, but they wanted steaks. I had no clue where to buy food, so he took me to Costco. We were there for an hour, and it was already eight by the time we got back. I was there until ten, and then he said that he couldn't go to the boat with me. He would call the gate and tell them to let me in and take me to the boat. I had no clue where I was going. I'd been driving a few days now, yet they had no respect for me. It was all about them: cook them dinner on the fly, find the boat on my own.

Late that night, around midnight, I found my way to Grosse Pointe. The security guard welcomed me and took me to the boat. I got unpacked and crashed. I was beat. The first day had been shitty, and the job only got worse. The best thing about it was that I had the boat to myself except when they were on it some weekends. I also enjoyed my morning run along the lake. Grosse Pointe is a cool little spot, with lots of great bars and young people.

The only bad thing is the bugs, and they have every kind. Black flies are everywhere for six weeks, and they are nasty. You cannot walk anywhere around the lake without them getting in your hair and clothes. I would never work in Michigan again that time of the year. They covered the whole boat, and you can hear them crunch when you run over them on the road. That's how many of them there are. Mosquitoes are even worse. Who would want to live there in the summertime? You can't even go outside.

What was bad about the job? Well, let's start with the kids. There were two of them, one boy one girl, both worthless, just like their mom. They better pray that their dad never runs out of money, or they will all be fucked. Between the three of them, they could not screw in a light-bulb, let alone wipe their asses. The boy was a little punk. He had no hobbies, unless you call playing video games a hobby. He didn't play sports and had no girlfriends. He might have been gay. All he did was jack off and play video games all day. He never went outside to the lake or the yacht club. He only had a few friends, and they all just stayed inside and played video games.

I ask you, is this normal? Since the kid was ten, they'd had him on meds. One was to make him grow. Both parents were short. So am I, but I never thought about taking drugs to make me taller. They also said he couldn't focus, so he was on some other shit as well. No wonder he was all messed up. That is just not normal, but Doc and Tara were far from normal. They were one fucked-up pair. That's why the whole family was screwed up. I tried for a few weeks to get him out of the house to play golf, shoot some hoops, come to the yacht club to hang, go sailing, but never once did he take me up on any offers. He just stayed in his room, jacking off and playing video games. If I'd been his father, I would have taken the games away, but they spoiled the little prick. And he would talk back if he did not get his way. I would have kicked his ass all the way down the hall and put his games in the trash, end of story.

The daughter was not much better. She was the older one by a few years, maybe sixteen or just a year older. She was not a good-looking girl.

Like her mom, she had no tits and a tiny ass, and she was just as nasty as her mom. She had been on the same drugs to make her grow, and her tits, too, but it did not work. At sixteen, she had hairy arms and a mustache and sideburns. Doc had already been working on her face with plastic surgery, and it had not helped. She still looked homely.

Neither kid had any direction, not a clue about life, and on top of that, not a lick of common sense. One weekend, Tara's mom came up—my favorite person. I will never forget the conversation she had with the kids. She asked them what they had planned for the future, and they did not have a clue, so she went on and on about how her kids grew up to be heads of state, doctors, and attorneys. This was all bullshit. She only had two daughters. One was a teacher in Florida and weighed two hundred pounds, and the other marred Doc and never worked a day in her life. I almost laughed in their faces. Tara's old man was a teacher as well. There's nothing wrong with that, but it's a far cry from being a doctor or attorney.

The daughter had all kinds of shit wrong with her, not just the peanut allergy, but she would eat M&Ms. Both kids had issues. One would not eat these, and one would not eat that. Tara and Doc were no better. They were like a couple of little kids: "I don't like the texture of that." Neither drank, so he would just serve the cheapest wine he had when we had guests. Most of it was bad. He'd say, "We don't drink, and the guest will just drink what we have. It will be fine."

We were getting gas one day, and I was driving the Bentley. It was the same shit again, fighting over what lane to get in. After a few lane changes, we got to the pump, and I proceeded to fill the gas tank with high test. He looked over and said, "What are you doing?"

I said, "Filling the car up."

"With high test?"

"Yes, it's a Bentley."

"Stop the pump. There is no difference. Never use the high test again for any of the cars. Just use regular." He made me stop the pump and finish with regular. We're talking a 500 Benz, Bentley, Jag, and a GMC Suburban with a big V8. You have to be shiting me. That was one cheap fuck.

For one of the few dinner parties I did, the CEO of Fiat North America and his wife came over. She was a singer, and he was a frog. I poured them a glass of chardonnay that I knew was bad on purpose. I mean, it was just like vinegar and cheap on top of that. They both took one sip and never touched it again. I looked at them and said, "That's all I have." They drank water for the rest of the night. Doc couldn't have cared less. I am sure the guests were like, "What the hell is he serving us?" I never saw them again. Nice couple. I am sure they were not good friends, and if they did come back, I bet they brought their own wine.

Mostly, I just cooked for the family, his dad, that sort of shit. Tara would have me drive forty minutes a few times a week just to make her lunch. I was supposed to be cooking on the boat and keeping it clean, but what the hell. I only put up with her petty shit a few months before I quit. The kids wear just as bad, and Doc was a prick and a type-A personality. He knew it all and was always right. I hated it when they came over to the boat for the weekend. It was like pulling teeth. She had to have the bed made a certain way, the pillows, everything. She thought she was the royal queen, for Christ's sake.

Right before I quit, the weekend started badly. First, she was in one of the kitchen cupboards, saw some peanut butter, and went nuts. "What is this doing on the boat? I told you my daughter cannot have contact with nuts in any shape or form."

I said, "It's mine."

"I don't care. I don't want it on the boat. There can be cross-contamination."

I laughed. "Are you serious?"

She got nasty and said, "Yes, this is not funny. Throw it in the trash."

I was ready to bitch-slap the whore. Who the fuck did she think she was? And the little hairy-arm, mustached daughter just set there and said, "I told you, Mom."

I only lasted a few more weeks. That was almost the last straw. I had a talk with Doc, and he said, "Don't quit. I will talk to Tara." But I was sure she wore the pants in the house and a talk would only make things worse.

I told him, "I am not happy."

"I know. She is tough, but don't worry. We will work it out."

I think he just wanted to get through the Fourth of July weekend. We were going to the Old Club on the small island, a private club about an hour and a half away. I knew it was going to be a long weekend.

Early that week, I made dinner at the house. After the kids left the table, Tara and Doc said, "We want to talk to you."

I said, "Sure. What's up?"

Tara started right off, and Doc could not get a word in. "Alan, we don't like you wearing the chef coats to work at the house or on the boat. I bought you some polo shirts, and I would like you to wear them from now on."

"Sure. No problem. Can I ask why?: I looked her dead in the eyes as I waited to hear what the hell was up. What I heard was such a crock of shit.

She said, "We don't want the neighbors and the people at the yacht club to think we have too much money and a private chef."

"Ok, I am cool with that. Whatever you like."

She gave me like six polo shirts. I cleaned up that night and headed back to the boat, thinking about what she'd said and how it did not make sense. They had a house in Bloomfield Hills. He drove a big-ass Bentley, and she had the big Benz plus a bad-ass Jag. They had the biggest boat at the yacht club, a eighty-two-foot Lazzara, a little overkill for the lake, and a thirty-two-foot Grady-White. He had just sold his jet before I'd come along. His partner with the jet had been Joe Dumars from the Pistons. He lived around the corner and was an ok guy, a little full of himself but not a bad guy. Doc said he was a crook and not paying his fair share and he had to sue him over the money he owed him for plane expenses. I wondered about this; it sounded like the pot calling the kettle black. I only met Joe once, or I would have popped the question, "Hey, what happened with you and Doc over the plane." Unfortunately, I never got the chance.

So, what Tara had told me was bullshit. She spent like crazy. It cost around three hundred a week to get the dog's hair done. I poured myself one more Woodford Reserve at the boat, and as I sat in the saloon, thinking everything over, it did not add up. I mean, by this time, I was pretty sure she was full of shit. What was the deal with the chef coats? I thought about this long and hard, and I could only come up with one thing. It sounds crazy, but that is how this bitch was. She did not like people to know me as Chef Al, the celebrity chef from LA. It made me sound too rich and famous, and she did not want me to have that image. It was always about her. She had to be the center of attention, and she hated the thought that people at the club liked me. They could not stand her. No wonder. She was a cunt.

A few of the guests at the club asked how long I had worked for them. I would say, "It's just a summer gig," and they would reply, "It's going to be a long summer." They were right. What a bitch. She wanted to strip me of anything she could to make herself feel better. Five minutes after meeting her, you'd know exactly how much of a bitch she could be. And it would only take another five minutes to know that the kids were a lost cause. Doc was full of himself, and five minutes after meeting him, he would already be telling you how he was the best in the business and the only doctor who really cared about the welfare of his patients. That was the furthest thing from the truth, and I will tell you why.

On the Fourth of July weekend, we were at the old club. I got up at six, and there was Doc in the galley, sending texts to some of his office managers and staff and leaving them voicemails. "We need to see more customers. You should only spend so much time with each client and move on," he told them. It was all about numbers. They needed to see a certain number of clients a day and spend a certain amount of time with them, and that was it. It was all about the bottom line. For all you folks who think Dr. Steven Grekin cares about you, he only cares about the money. Just look at how he lives and how many offices he has. He doesn't care about you. It's all a bunch of bullshit. I would not trust that fuck as far as I could throw him. His skin care line is the same. Check into it. It's way overpriced for what you are paying, no better than most products.

I've worked for a lot of guys like this, and they're all the same. They drive like they're the only ones on the road, so just get out of the way. We were in line to get gas at Costco one day. I was driving, and he told me to change lines. I pulled behind an old lady, which is ok—that happens. As we waited, he got pissed and said I should have stayed where we were. I felt like yanking him out of the car and kicking his ass. He needed it, and it would have been fun.

He was like that every day. The world revolved around Dr. Grekin, and Tara was even worse. I am really surprised he has not gotten his ass kicked. Pull that shit with me, and your ass is getting tuned up. She was the same. Everyone else drove too slow or didn't know what they were doing. I really hope I see her again one day. She is the only woman I would hit. I would just bitch slap her; she needs it, and I would not feel bad about it at all. Everyone who knows her would say the same. She deserves that and even more.

I survived the weekend at the old club, but I knew my days were limited. We got back to Grosse Pointe Yacht Club for the fireworks on the Fourth, and we had a few guests for drinks and appetizers. It was a pretty easy evening. They went to the club for dinner, so I was off the hook, thank God.

The next morning, I was mopping the galley floor, and Tara came in and asked me what I was doing. I said, "Cleaning the floor."

She had this nasty look on her face and said, "You won't get it clean that way."

"Really."

"Yes. You need to get a towel and get on your knees and clean it."

I gave her this look from hell and said, "Are you kidding me? You can't be serious."

"Yes, I am, and you will do it."

"I don't think so. You had better find someone else to bark at and put up with this shit, because I am done. I have had enough of your shit."

She was at a loss for words and stormed off the boat as they were all heading back to the house. Doc came back and said, "It's all cool. Great job for the weekend. Take a few days off. I will come see you in a few days, and we will work this out."

I said, "Ok, I will be here if you need me."

That was the last straw. I was not going to put up with this bitch anymore. As soon as they were gone, I poured a big glass of Woodford, neat, cracked open a Stella, and said, "What the fuck do I need these shit for?" I got a little buzz on and headed down to a little bar down the street on the lake to see if I could find some stranger and have a few cold ones to get me in a better mood.

What do you know—I ran into one of the wives from the club. We had a few drinks, and I told her the boat was empty back in Bloomfield and I had it to myself. That was it. We drank up and went back to the boat for a long night of sport fucking.

So, as you would guess, I was in a better mood now—a good piece of ass will do that for you. She left before light so no one would see her leave. We said our goodbyes, and she said, "Thanks. I needed that."

The next morning, I went for my run and got a good workout. I was sure Doc wouldn't call for at least a few days. When I got back from the gym, I had a message from my old captain friend John Herman from Lauderdale. He'd grown up in Grosse Pointe, and his kids lived there. I'd told him I would be up there for the summer and to call if he was in town. The message said, "Let's meet for beers if you are free. I am in Grosse Pointe at my daughter's a few miles from the club."

I called him and said, "I have the next few days off."

"Cool. Let's have lunch in Greektown. I will pick you up in an hour."

"I will be ready."

I had known John for a few years. He was a really great guy and a first-class captain. He rolled up, and we headed to Greektown in Detroit. If you find yourself in Detroit, this place is a must: great food and a really cool spot to hang out. We went to Pegasus; it's been there forever. Everyone at the bar knew John, so we drank for free all day. We just paid for lunch, and not that much, as John knew the owner.

We caught up, and I told him that the job sucked and I would probably be done in a week, as the wife and I had had words over the Fourth of July weekend and it had not been pretty. John just laughed. "I told you about the Jew bitches."

We had a shot and laughed about it. Then he told me he wanted me to meet his kids, one son and daughter. They were grown up, married, had kids, that kind of shit. He asked me what my boss's name was and said, "I will make a few calls and find out about this prick for you."

John showed me around Greektown all afternoon. We hit a few cool bars. This was his old stomping grounds. We had a great day together. Later, he dropped me off at the club and said, "Seven. Dinner. I will text you the place once I talk to my kids."

I said, "Cool. See you tonight."

I took a short nap and then a dip in the hot tub at the club. Then I got cleaned up and ready for round two. I had forgotten all about the fact that I was probably out of a job. This was a good thing, as I had plenty of cash in the bank and had put up with enough of the Grekins' shit.

John texted, saying we were having dinner at the Hill Seafood & Chophouse, his treat. I had heard about it, but I'd never been there.

I met John's kids, and they were just what I thought they would be, very nice and kind. I could tell they were very hard-working. John was a hard-ass when it came to rules, work, and education, and it had paid off.

We all had a few drinks, followed by a great dinner. John bragged about me to his kids, said I was famous, worked for the elite, and was one hell of a chef, world class. It made me feel good. Thanks, John, back at you. You are first class as well, and that place is on my return list if I am in town again.

We finished up with a few espressos and some port, and then John said, "I asked around about this Dr. Grekin, your boss, and it seems you were spot on. All my friends say he is a cheap prick and fucked over a few guys in town." It turns out that Grekin paid his bills late, if he paid them at all, or he paid what he felt was fair. I knew I would be gone in a few days, so I couldn't have cared less as long as I got my last check.

John was heading back to Lauderdale in the morning, and he said, "Call me when you get back home, and I will see you in Tarpon Bend." That was our hangout.

I said, "Sure. Thanks for dinner." Then we all finished our port and said goodnight.

I knew that the doc would be calling or coming around the next day. I had already packed most of my shit in case he kicked me off the boat. You never know with these pricks, so plan for the worst. He called first thing in the morning and said he wanted to buy me lunch. That wasn't a good sign.

He hadn't done one thing for me up to this moment. I knew Tara wanted me gone, and I was cool with that. I hated the bitch, too. He took me to a nice place over by the hill. I was very surprised. He was very nice. Maybe he'd gotten a blowjob that morning. I am sure that was rare for him. He said that Tara wanted me gone and he was sorry.

I said, "I feel the same way. I am not happy, and there is no need for me to stay if it's not working out."

He said, "Have a drink. I am buying."

"Cool. I will have a Stoli martini."

We made some small talk, and then he said, "I need a favor, and I will lay it out for you. I will pay you the rest of the month in cash plus five hundred petty cash. Keep the credit card and drive the SUV back to Tara's parents in Florida."

I said, "Ok, deal. When do I have to be off the boat?"

"I am taking the family to Asheville this week, and we will be gone five days, so you have a week from today to pack and hang out on the boat. Just keep her clean. Take a few days to get to Florida. Don't kill yourself. Put it all on the card and give the receipts to Tara's dad."

I looked him dead in the eyes, shook his hand, and said, "That's fine, and I am cool with all of that. And thanks for lunch."

"Sorry it didn't work out. I know my wife can be a pain in the balls. Trust me. I've been married to her a long time. Sometimes I want to kill her. She is a crazy Jew." He laughed, and I thought that was cool. He knew, the poor bastard, that if he got divorced, she would take him to the cleaners.

I said, "I can tell," and this time, we both laughed.

"Give all the keys to the boat to the security desk and text me when you leave town and when you get to Florida so I know you got home safe."

"Will do. It's been real."

And that was it. We shook hands, he gave me an envelope full of cash, and I was good to go. I was impressed. The doc stood up. He could have stiffed me, but he did not. Pretty cool.

I had five days off and a fridge full of food and beer. What more did I need? Maybe a few strippers or the member's wife to come by again for some more sport fucking. I looked for her, and she did turn up for one more round. It made my summer.

I hung out for a few more days. Grosse Pointe is a cool spot in the summer, except for the bugs. There are good restaurants and lots of nice people when you get outside the yacht club. It's too bad the family was all screwed up, or it could have been fun.

All my friends in my travels say I have a dream job and live the life. I tell them they have no idea of the shit I have to put up with. Nasty wives, spoiled kids, asshole owners, it's a lot of shit to put up with, but there are some perks, and the money is not bad.

I had a nice rode trip back to Florida, and I stayed in a few nice hotels along the way and had some nice dinners. I did not want to beat him up too badly on the credit card, but I did not want him getting off easy, either. I would be back in Florida for all of August. All the yachts are gone, and there's not much work that time of the year.

I dropped off the SUV at Tara's dad's place and gave him the credit card receipts, and he drove me to the Tri-Rail station. Then I was back home in Lauderdale, and one more adventure had come to a close. Now it was time to take a little break. I needed one after the shit I'd put up with for the last few months.

Crew. Jojo's Circus

Prowler. Las Vegas.

Jojo's Circus

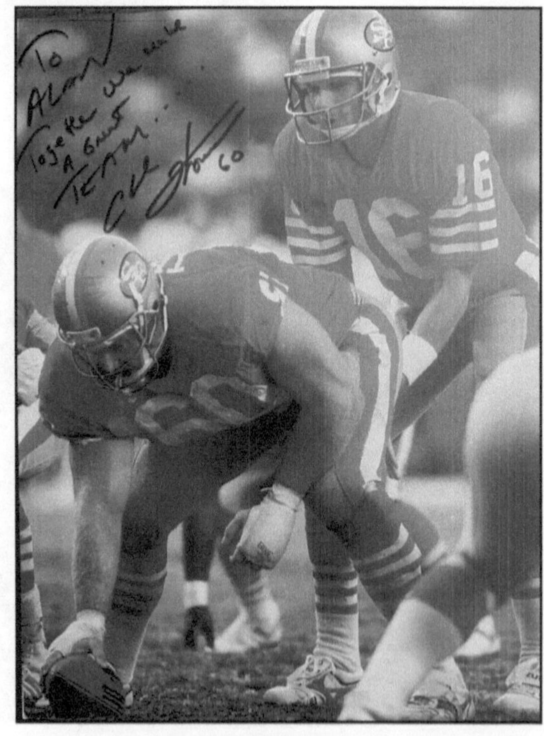

Chef and Gary, Rascal Flatts Las Vegas

Chapter 21

BACK TO DALLAS
THE SCHLEGELS
THE ROYAL FAMILY OF DALLAS

I FOUND MYSELF BACK HOME, thinking about my next move. I had been getting emails from some new agent, PCI, Private Chefs, Inc., out of Dallas. The guy's name was Dan, and he was a chef, too, worked for some big-time people, like Mark Cuban, who, he told me, was the king of pricks. I sent him my CV, signed up on his site, registered, all that bullshit.

One day, he said, "I've got a great job for you if you want to come back to Dallas. They pay well and are one of Dallas's big families. It's an estate manager-chef job combo, with a nice guest house, eighty grand to start, a car, the whole deal. They got your CV, and one daughter saw you worked for Rod Stewart. They want to meet you and said they would fly you to Dallas."

I said, "Cool. I am in. Looks like I am flying to Dallas next week. I am down for this if it works out."

I flew out the following week, and they didn't even pick me up at the airport. I took a cab to the hotel, and the room was not paid for. I called

Mr. Schlegel, and he said he forgot to give them a credit card so I should give them mine. I said, "I am sorry. I don't work that way. If you don't want to give them your credit card, I will just head back home, and that's it."

He said, "What if we don't like you or do not hire you?"

"That is your choice."

He was unhappy, but I couldn't have given a rat's ass. He took care of it and said he and his wife would pick me up in the morning and take me to the house for the interview.

I was thinking: *We are getting off to a bad start. This guy didn't even have a room booked and paid for.* I should have told him to fuck off and then spent the week in Dallas, grabbed a few hookers, and had a good time before heading back to Lauderdale. But the next morning, when I met them, they seemed ok. They wear on their best behavior. I did not meet any of the kids this trip.

They hired me on the spot. We talked about food, and they said they wanted me to run the estate, take care of the cars, and oversee the staff. There were only two housekeepers, but to hear them talk, they had a whole staff. They were so full of themselves. New money is always like that. I could use the work, and I did like the idea of living in Dallas again. The women there are so hot and nice.

They said they had to check my references, and if that worked out, they wanted to know when I could start. I said, "The first of the month, but I have travel expenses to get back first." He almost balked at that. I should have never taken this job, but I am always up for an adventure.

He said, "We are all good. I will call you in a few days, and I look forward to having you on board."

That was it for the interview. They said they had a few big parties a year but hired a catering company, so I would oversee everything. The kids came over once a week or so for Sunday dinner, and they rarely had house-guests. It was pretty cut and dry. I knew this was too good to be true. I would soon find out the real deal.

I returned home, and a few days later, I got a call from Mrs. Schelgel. She said, "We checked your references, and we would like you to come work for us."

I said, "I would like that."

"We are sending you a credit card to get here, and we will see you the first of the month."

"Thanks, and I look forward to it. See you in a few weeks."

They stepped up. This must have been a big deal for them. As it turned out, I was the first chef and estate manager they'd ever had. I look back now, and it all makes sense. But at the time, I was up for an adventure, and it was good money. Even if I just lasted the summer, I would make enough cash to get me through the winter, so I rolled the dice.

I got to Dallas after a few days on the road, stopping in New Orleans for a day and having a good time along the way. It was a grand estate, a really nice place. I arrived in the afternoon, and they greeted me, showed me to the guest house, and said we would talk tomorrow. They seemed nice, but that was soon over. Myrna, the wife, was one nasty bitch, and so were the daughters. They were all peas in a pod, some of the worst people I have ever met. If you know them, you know I am right.

Now, where to start? There are a few good stories, and I met a few interesting folks, not like the LA crowd but businesspeople and a few Dallas Cowboys players. That was kind of cool. The biggest VIP was George W. Bush. He and his wife, Laura, came over for dinner one night. It was the first month I was there, so this was the first big dinner party. It was just Rob, Myrna, and the Bushes. I think Rob wrote a big check for them and that's why they came over. I could tell by Laura's face that she did not like them. Who would? They had no class and were so full of themselves, and they were not even Americans but Canadians, for Christ's sake.

And on top of that, they were cheap as fuck. It was a regular dinner party, and they talked policy and business, but George and Laura left early. I don't blame them. Dinner was simple, just a nice flat iron steak, chimichurri roast potatoes, veggies, and flan for dessert, simple and clean. Everyone was happy.

I got George W. alone in the kitchen, and we started to chat. I said, "I know your father and mother, and they are really great people." He asked me how I met his dad, and I said I used to work for Jerry Weintraub. "He and your father are good friends, and I have been to Keen Port and met them in Malibu at Jerry's place."

Then Myrna entered and cut right in. Laura said to her, "Chef Al knows Mom and Dad."

Myrna was blown away that I knew George and Barbara and worked for Jerry Weintraub. She had no clue who he was or that he and the Bushes were friends. It was a big feather in my cap. To hear Myrna talk, you'd have thought they were the first family, the same with the rest of the litter. I told George W. to tell his dad hi. Laura said she would. I thanked her and said goodnight. She was one hell of a first lady. Super nice. She never got the credit she deserves. They were a really nice couple and a great family. I will never forget them. They were kind to me.

The rest of the stories are about the family, the shit they pulled and the shit I had to put up with, and a few nice Dallas women I had the pleasure of banging. For the most part, I just want to tell you what pieces of shit the Schlegels are, from scamming insurance companies to not paying their bills and just putting on this whole front that they are charitable in the community when they only do it for their personal gain. I know first-hand, as I heard them talk about these things at dinner. It was always what they would get back in return.

Now, where to start with their worthless offspring? Let's begin with Kirby, the only son. The only thing true about him is that he is a good-looking guy and chicks who want a rich prick would like him. But what an asshole, and he cannot wipe his own ass. He had no friends, and if not for his dad, he would have flunked out of SMU and had a DUI on his record, among other shit as well. That's why there is a small street at SMU named Schlegel Dr. The old man gave them a bunch of cash to cover up the DUI and fix his grades so he could pass. I heard this first-hand, and the housekeeper also heard it, and she told me. She had been with them for years, poor woman. She put up with a lot of shit. I became close friends with the controller at the office, Michael Bently, and he told me the whole scoop on the family, and I will share it with you.

Back to the little prick. First, he had to buy his way out of school. Michael told me he took over Pavestone and almost lost everything, ran it into the ground. That's why the sale never went through. He screwed the books up, and the old man took charge and bailed the shithead out. He still did not sell the company; there were too many issues. Then his dad bought him a few minor league teams—Schlegel Sports, I think. To hear Kirby talk, he bought them with his own money. Turns out this was short-lived. The last I heard, Kirby's next great deal was with some sneaker company. That was about the time I left.

The only thing he had going for him was that he was good looking. I don't know where he got them from. He would show up at his dad's house with some hot young chick, probably underage, show off the place, and take them for a ride in his dad's Aston Martin. That's a sure way to get laid. If not for his dad's money, he would have been just some average, good-looking guy trying to make a living, and he would have had a hard time, as he was one lazy fuck. He slept until noon and could not even balance a checkbook. That was dad's fault. He bought all the kids' houses, paid all their credit cards, paid for their housekeepers, gardeners, and car insurance, and bought them all their cars. No wonder they could not wipe their own assed and had no clue. They better hope their dad does not run out of money. Not one of them could make it on their own. Everything you read about them is fake news, or dad paid to make it look good for them.

The last thing about shithead is that he always bragged about the condo he had in New York in Trump Tower and how he hung out with Donald Jr. I know for a fact that they're not even close to being alike. Kirby thinks he knows it all and is smart, when, in reality, the only thing he can run is his mouth, while Don Jr. is a hard worker, smart, and willing to go out and make it. I am sure they have nothing in common. Kirby did have one bad-ass penthouse that he shared with his sister on the top floor of the W. Of course, his dad paid for it. The shithead did not work, let alone make any money.

On top of that, in an interview, Colby said he remembered working at Pavestone in the yards and that his dad paid him nothing. What a crock of shit. He never worked a day in his life, and that went for the rest of the pack, too.

Compared to his sisters, though, Kirby was a prince. Let's start with the youngest, Krystal. When I worked for them, she was in college, living downtown in a great condo that her dad bought for her. I only had a couple of dealings with her except for the weekly dinner on Sunday at the house. At the time, she was not bad, but I am sure, now that she is older, she is like her older sisters, queen bitches who think they own Dallas. Like her sisters, she didn't have any tits, unlike their mom, who had big fake ones. I always said they had no tits and no brains.

The first time I dealt with the little brat, I had to take her to the airport. On the way, all she did was whine that she had to fly commercial and how her dad should have never sold. The plain truth was that he could not afford the upkeep, just like with the yacht he had sold, and he was taking a bath on it, the stupid Canadian. Back to the little brat. All she did was bitch and moan the whole way to the airport, and she was glued to her cell phone. What a waste of oxygen.

When we got to the airport, I pulled into the lane to unload at departures. I stopped at her airline's entrance, and she just stayed in the car. I looked at her and said, "Here you go," but she just sat there. Then I realized that she was waiting for me to get out and open her door for her. I wasn't about to do that for some pimple-faced little brat.

So, she waited for about a minute. Meanwhile, folks were beeping their horns, and I was getting looks from the cop directing traffic. Finally, she got out with this look on her face, and I was just about ready to let her have it, like, "Who the fuck do you think you are, you little twit?" Instead, I grabbed her bag, put it on the curb, and said, "Are you ok?"

She said, "I am fine now."

"Cool. Have a nice flight." Then I was gone. She expected me to carry her little bag to the check-in counter. It was a carry-on, and I was double-parked. That was the first and last time I had to do that.

By the time I got home, she had already had called her mom and told her what a dick I was and how I did not open the door and carry her bag to check-in. Myrna, the king bitch, started laying into me, saying, "You will do whatever I ask and whatever they demand."

I looked at her and said, "I don't think so."

I should have walked out that day. Rob came in and settled her down and said, "Alan, don't worry about it. We are all good. I will take care of this. Don't leave."

I said, "Ok, but I am not going to keep putting up with this disrespect."

Whatever he said to Myrna, she settled down, and that was it. I did not pick Krystal up. She had a little birthday party, maybe ten people. I think her dad paid them to show up, as I know she had no friends. Of the ten, half were family, and one was some guy she was fucking. I hope the poor guy did not marry her. That's a jail term for sure, like doing hard time. The food was easy. She wanted some healthy salads, tacos, dips, easy stuff. They had a bartender, so I did not have to deal with that, and there were two servers, and I was to leave all the leftovers there.

So those were my only two dealings with the youngest one, Krystal. If I never see her again, it will be too soon. On to the next one, Kari. They just keep getting worse. She sold real estate, or so she said—I am sure the only houses she sold were her dad's or mom's friends. She was supposed to be a beauty queen when she was younger, but she had no tits and a frog's ass. I only had one event with her, and that was enough. You will like this.

She really thought she was smart. She might have been book smart, but she didn't have a lick of common sense. To hear her talk, she was the top salesperson in Dallas. Take away her dad's deals, and she did not sell shit. What a joke. I guess she had some big listing—one of her parents' friends, you can bet on that—and she was showing it a second time to the same family. It was on a Sunday, and she called her mom and wanted me to cater a brunch for the family: champagne, fruit, the whole deal. She also wanted me to stay and serve.

I said, "It's late notice for a full brunch. Why not just do fruit, muffins, yogurt, and the champagne?"

We all agreed that would be ok. I prepared everything, drove to the open house, and set up a table. She wanted everything to be crystal. I mean, if she were closing the deal, I get it, but just for a showing? That's a little overkill and might make the buyer a little uptight, like they have to buy.

They took a quick look again, and it was not the house they wanted. You could tell by the wife's expression. Kari was already drinking a glass of bubbly, and she said to the family, "Let's have a toast to your new house. Have something to eat and drink, and let's make an offer and get a deposit." You could tell she had no experience with people and no skills, just her dad's name to go on.

The husband said, "It's not what we're looking for. We just wanted to do one more walk-through to make sure. Thanks, but we have to go look at one more house."

She was at a loss for words. She kind of stuttered and said, "I can show you anything you want to see in Dallas, and I can be your agent if you want to buy something else."

The husband said, "Thanks, but we are working with an agent."

She almost lost it. "Who is your agent?"

"We'd rather not say."

She got all bent out of shape and said, "Fine. I have other buyers to work with if you are not serious about buying," really insulting this couple.

He was cool and had class. Like lots of nice folks, he just said, "Thank you. We will be on our way."

She looked at them and said, "After all that I did, the brunch and coming over here on a Sunday, you're not buying?"

He looked at her and said, "Hell, no, and I would never buy from you or recommend you. I have never seen a more unprofessional salesperson in my life." Then they just walked away. They never touched the food or the champagne.

I could not contain my laughter. It was the funniest thing I had ever seen. What a dumb bitch. I never will forget that. While I was cleaning up, I said, "That went well."

She said, "They were not serious buyers anyway. I am sure they could not afford the house in the first place." That's it. Blame everyone except yourself. What a loser.

That was my only dealing with girl number two. Troy, her husband, I liked. He was a nice guy. I don't know why he married her, except for money. He was cool, worked for Sebastian Professional, which makes hair products, as a regional director. He made good money but not big time, but you don't need it when your father-in-law buys you half of the top floor of the W. in Dallas and pays your wife's credit card bills. I could get used to that, but it comes with a price: your manhood. I could never sell my soul. It's like being a puppy on a leash.

Last story. They were having lunch one day, just the four of them, at the house. They were having the usual conversation, talking trash about their friends and how they were better than everyone else, that kind of shit. It was the same shit every dinner, how they did this and how they did that, and it was always the best, and they had the best, and whatever they did was the best. What a bunch of losers and assholes.

Troy said something along the lines of how great it was to have a trophy wife and how it makes a man work harder to keep her. Rob jumped in and said, "Yes, you are right. We both married trophy wives, and that makes us better men." How shallow is that? I mean, you have to brag that you have a trophy wife? I lived in LA, and these two hags were no trophies. Like the other sisters, Kari had no tits or ass and was just a bitch. It'd be like military sex with her. I can hear her now, giving orders: "Stop. Start. Too hard. Too soft. Left. Right. Stop." And then, "Have you come yet, or are you done?" Myrna, I can't even think about sex with her. That's got to be rough. She was a worn-out old hag. Poor Rob. That's it for that sister. Oh, Troy, I feel for you, brother. I don't know how you can put up with that shit. Is it worth it? I am sure he is still having military sex, if he is getting laid at all.

I have to say, if it weren't for that airhead Kari, I would not have been back in Dallas. She wanted to brag that their new chef used to work for Rod Stewart. That's one of the reasons I got hired. I am sure she made up some bullshit story about how they stole me from Rod Stewart, but that's history.

Last but not least was the king bitch. Kim. She was nasty, just like her mom, and so full of herself, and they thought they were really hot. Man, what a train wreck, the whole family. Like the rest, I did weekly dinners for her and her asshole husband, Justin. Troy, at least, was an ok guy, but Justin was a complete dick, living on his old man's name. He married up, but I am sure Kim wanted to brag that she'd married into Hollywood status. The two really deserve each other because they're both assholes.

Justin's dad was the old actor Stewart Whitman, so she could say she was in the Hollywood scene.

The first good story about Kim was she was supposed to be a lifestyle guru and author of a best seller. In reality, it was all a scam. The old man paid for everything, and the books that were supposed to be sold? Let me tell you about them. You will fucking die. One of her books was supposed to have sold out, but I was putting some stuff in the third-story storage attic when I looked in one corner and saw it was full of wooden pallets. They were covered with tarps, so I pulled a few off, and beneath were stacks of her books. The old man had bought them all and hid them there. Anything to make his daughter look like she was somebody. She was also supposed to be one of the youngest females ever to make it in business, but the truth is that her dad just invented a company and said she started it and made her the president. The only thing she could run was her mouth, just like mom.

I did one party at her house, nobody famous, just a few friends she was trying to impress. All she did was complain about how the table was not set right and I could have done a better job with the presentation. I just laughed to myself. I knew my days were numbered. That was the last time I ever went to their house, and I only saw her one more Sunday dinner.

After I left, I heard they did *Top Chef* in Dallas and she and Kari were involved and somehow screwed up, which doesn't surprise me. Anyway, they got off track and screwed the whole thing up. Someone asked them a question, and they blew it off and then started bragging about who had the biggest wedding and how much it cost and so on. The *LA Times* had it right: money can't buy you taste. Martha Stewart of the Southwest, my ass. Then she compared herself to Gwyneth Paltrow. I can't believe she could think that.

Last thing about Justin. He is supposed to be this entrepreneur. I never saw the guy work. I saw him at the office one time, looking at a building to buy and trying to get Rob to give him the money. Why not? He gave the little prick a new Porsche when he bought his Aston Martin.

At one of the last Sunday dinner parties I did for the family, Rob asked about Rod Stewart and who else I worked for in LA, and I said David

Foster and Linda Thompson. When I said I got to meet Michael Bublé and what a nice guy he was and how he had that old, Hollywood look of class, I thought Kim would have a heart attack. "He is such a loser, and he is not even that good looking," she said. "He has nothing on Justin."

I go, "Yeah, you're right, only a few gold records and a couple of Grammy's. What a loser."

She almost shit. I got the look of death from her, and she said, "I went out with him and broke it off."

I did not want to throw any more gas on the fire, so I just shut up and smiled. I am sure it was the other way around. No guy in their right mind would put up with her shit and all the family baggage. Michael, I am sure, said, "Fuck this." He probably hit it a few times and the sex sucked, so he gave her the boot. He doesn't need the money; he has his own. Justin needed the money because he didn't have shit. Makes sense, don't you think?

That's all the shit I have on Kim. I did cross her path at the ranch the last week I worked there. The ranch is White Oak, 450 acres just north of Dallas. I have to say it was a nice spread. Rob bought it and let Kim do events there to make her look good. I was out there for some event to help the caterers. The whole event was a shitshow, so unorganized. I could not believe it. She had no clue about the restaurant business or catering an event, but she thought she was doing a great job. I would have fired her on the spot if she had been working for me in a hotel or event. What a circus. I am sure the guests were not happy with the cold food. It looked like shit and did not taste much better, and we ran out of wine. I can go on, but I will stop there.

There was one more thing about Justin. I almost reported them to the insurance board for this. Right before I came, they had some roof damage from a storm. He got the roofers to give him a kickback. They said that the roof leaked on a rug and damaged it, and they piled all kinds of extras on to pad the insurance bill to get the cash—twenty-five thousand is what the housekeepers told me. There are not even Americans, for Pete's sake. They are from Canada. What cheap fucks those people are from up there. Stay home, just like your friends, the French.

I guess that covers that. Now for a few stories about Rob and Myrna up. Where to start with these misfits? Rob was not a bad guy. He was just a cheap fuck and Canadian—that's bad enough. Plus, he thought he was some lady killer, but he was not that great looking. He hated to pay his bills, as he thought everyone was screwing him. That's one thing I have learned over all these years: the guys who think like that are the ones that are screwing everyone because they're crooks. It's true.

I took the Aston Martin to the shop. I had to drop it off and pick it up the next morning. It needed full servicing, which cost around $1500. It's a two-hundred-thousand-dollar car, and they're not cheap to service. Myrna gave me shit and said I should have asked before they scheduled the service. I was about to walk out that day. Rob called back the dealership and said he would not pay the bill unless they took some charges off. They knocked off a few hundred bucks, but he was still unhappy. I heard the GM say, "I am sorry, but you'd better find somewhere else to get your car serviced, as it seems, Mr. Schlegel, you are not happy with us. Have a nice day."

I will never forget what Myrna said: "Do they know who we are? We will never buy from them again." And they probably will not sell to you. What a joke.

The same thing happened at Park Place Motors, which I had dealt with in the past with the Woods. I took the Bently in. It was an older one, but it was clean. They only drove it once in a while. The brakes were shot, the tires were gone, and it ran like shit. It would cost around five grand to get it running well again. Tires and brakes are not cheap on Bentleys. Rob told me not to fix it, saying that they wear lying about the repairs. I said, "Fine. I will bring it back to the house, but I don't feel good about driving you or any family members in that car."

He said, "W won't drive it, then. We will just sell it."

The next day, he had one of his watches in the shop. I had to go pick it up at de Boulle. It was a Patek Philippe, and the repair cost around a grand. He did not bat an eyelash. I think this was because it was something people saw and he could wear it and show it off. I still wonder about that. Did I say that he was weird? For that matter, the whole gang was out to lunch, not in touch with reality. You won't buy tires or brakes for your car, but you'll get your watch fixed. Go figure. I could not get people to do work at the house unless they had a credit card on file or were paid cash that day. I have never seen such cheap, no-good fucks.

One of the only good things that came out of this job was that I got to hang out in Dallas for six months, bang a few hot chicks, and play some great golf courses. I also made a good friend, Mike Kiselak. He owned one of the roofing companies that made one of the bids, and he called me to do a follow-up and stopped by to measure. He did not get the job, as he was supposed to go through Justin, who wanted a kickback. Mike would not do that. That's when I knew I liked that guy. He was honest and had principles. We hit it off. We were both golfers, and he was a really nice guy—and spot-on about Justin. He told me about the kickback and how he thought Justin was just a little candy-ass. I said, "Yeah, I know first-hand about the little prick."

I did not know it at the time, but he played in the NFL. We met at Pappasito's, a great Mexican place I knew from the Houston Airport. We had some margaritas and dinner, and we hit it off right away. He is one of the only players, if not the only one, to have two championship rings in different leagues: one in Canada with Flutie and one in Dallas with Aikman. That's pretty cool. He was a center and no small guy. He kept himself in good shape as well.

We played golf quite a few times. He got me on the Cowboys course and a few other nice courses as well. I did a dinner party for him once. He's got a great family, a hot wife and two daughters, and he had his wife's mom and dad over. It was a birthday celebration, and I did it for free. He took me out golfing, so it was a fair trade. I made a rack of lamb. It was a great dinner and better conversation. We still keep in touch today.

Back to Rob and Myrna. Their wine cellar was the same. They would show off bottles of wine but drink cheap white wine with lots of ice. Myrna drank Cupcake. It is shit, but she loved it. I mean, eight dollars a bottle? Give me a break. They had all this nice shit and never used it. They just had it to show off. For Rob's fiftieth birthday, before I came on board, she bought him a self-portrait. It must have been eight foot by six, huge. It was up in the attic with all the books from the loser daughter. Who gives their husband something like that? First, where are you going to hang the damn thing? Like I said, Myrna was not the sharpest tool in the shed. I drove them to parties a few times, and she always got a little drunk and acted like a bitch. You could tell she was drunk, as she would start getting undressed in the car on the way home. Then, when we got home, she was ready to pass out, with her shoes in the car, dress by the door, and panties and bra in the hallway. Just a mess. I don't know why Rob put up with that shit. No class. That is something money can't buy.

They were having a large fundraiser party for Congressman Sam Johnson. This was my last big event. It was to be catered, and I was to supervise the whole show: two hundred guests, black tie. The grounds were looking a little run down. They liked to present this image that they were elites, but really they were just a couple of cheap Canadians. Rob told me to get a hold of a tree guy to clean and trim all the trees. He had been there before, and he knew the property. Rob gave me his number and said, "Make sure to get a bid before he starts the job." This was about a week before the event. Nothing like waiting until the last minute. I am sure he hated to spend the money.

I called the guy, whose name was Ron, and he said he could stop by tomorrow, and he gave me a price. He said, "It's been a year since the last time I was there, and I will only come by and give a quote if I get paid the day the work is done, cash or credit card, no checks. The last time, the check was no good, and Rob tried to beat me up on the bill." He also wanted a five-hundred-dollar deposit the day he started. I guess he knew the cheap fucks pretty well. I just loved it. I felt the same way about these assholes.

I passed the info on to Rob. He was not happy. I said, "What do you want me to tell him?"

He thought for a few moments and said, "Pay him."

It turned out that the last time, Rob said he'd been overcharged and stopped payment on the check. That did not surprise me one bit. That was why no one in Dallas liked these fucks.

I got Ron back on the phone. He said, "I can stop by tomorrow and look at the job, and I'll give you a price."

Ron was a big guy, and I want no piece of him. We talked the next day, and Rob walked around with us and told him what he wanted. Ron said, "Fine. I can do it all in the next three days, and it will be thirty-five hundred."

You'd have thought Rob was going to have a heart attack. He said, "That's a lot of money."

Ron said, "Get someone else. It's a lot of work, and I am giving you a fair price."

He started to leave, and Rob said, "Ok, I will give you half of the cash today and the rest when you finish," and the two shook hands.

Ron and I chatted for a few minutes, and he asked me how long I'd been working for them.

"A few months," I said.

"I bet you a hundred bucks you won't last six months," he said. He was right on. He told me the same stuff I had heard from other folks: they didn't pay their bills and were not liked in town.

He came by the next day to start with his crew. The place was in bad shape and needed some love. I am sure that if they were not having this fundraiser, they would not have had the trees trimmed and the place cleaned up. They only did it to impress people.

Finally, Ron was close to finishing the job, and he told me he needed final payment in cash or by credit card by five the next day. I told Rob, and he said he would have cash at the house for me. However, the next day, he headed to the office without leaving me any money. Myrna did the same. When Ron showed up, I called Rob's cell, and he said, "Tell Ron we will mail him a check." I was standing next to Ron, and he said, "Tell him, 'Hell, no.' I want a credit card or cash, or I am going to put all the tree branches and hedges I trimmed off in the middle of the driveway."

I handed him the cell, and he told Rob the same thing. Rob almost shit.

Ron gave me the phone back and said, "Michael from the office is on his way with cash." We laughed, and he said, "I will never be back again. If I had not had an open week, I wouldn't have done the work this time."

I got us some cold beers, and we bullshitted for an hour. Then Michael pulled up from the office with the cash. We chatted for a few minutes, and

Michael apologized for the mix-up. Ron said, "Tell that fuck not to call me again." Then we shook hands, and he drove off. I would hate to have that guy pissed at me. He's no pussy, that's for sure.

The grounds looked great, and the party was this weekend. When Rob and Myrna came home that night, they were not happy with Ron or me. Myrna said to me, "Why do we have to pay him today?"

I looked at her and said, "That was the deal we made with him."

"I don't know why we have to pay him cash."

I looked her dead in the eyes and said, "Ron told me that last time he was here, it took forever to get paid. You argued about the bill and did not want to pay him, and he still got shortchanged in the end. That's why he wanted to be paid in cash. Furthermore, he told me to tell you don't ever call him again."

Rob said, "We won't. He is not the only tree guy in town."

It turned out there was only a handful, and they all talked. I am sure Ron told the rest of the guys, "Don't work for this guy unless you don't mind getting paid." I liked that guy. I am the same way. Fuck these rich pricks. They never want to pay. They think they don't have to because they're special--yeah, special assholes. They were not happy with his work, but I tell you, the place looked great.

The weekend came, and it was game day, the big party. The caterers set up tables outside, and when people pulled in, two hostesses greeted guests and poured champagne while valets parked the cars. They even had a red carpet going to the main house, and they acted like it was the Oscars. But there were no VIPs, only the congressman Sam Johnson. The rest were military personnel, friends of the family, or friends of the congressman. The party went well. The caterers were first class. There were lots of finger foods and a few bars around the patios, full service. These guys did it right.

The caterer was a female chef, Kim, and we became close friends. She had a little cooking school and a nice catering company. She got paid the same way: cash or credit card, half now, half on the day of the event. No one trusted these guys.

The party was going well when Myrna called me aside and said, "Why are these people touching everything? And they are drinking too much."

I said, "It's a fundraiser, and I cannot tell them not to have more than one drink."

"Ok. Then close down one bar. That way, the guests will have to wait to get a drink, and that will slow them down, and maybe they will start leaving early."

I was shocked. That was the first time I'd ever been told that. I told Kim, and she just laughed and said, "That's par for course."

Five minutes later, Myrna said to slow the hors d'oeuvres to save a few more dollars and get the guests out of there. I have never in my career seen such a shitshow.

After it was all over and the caterers had left, Myrna and Rob were having a drink in the living room. They were still complaining about the guests drinking and eating too much. Myrna made a comment I will never forget, about how the guests were not up to her standards but they should get a lot of press and their names in the paper and ride that until the next year. Do you believe that? Like I said, all they cared about was making themselves look like they were the pillars of Dallas when all they cared about was getting their names in the paper or on TV. The good thing about Dallas is that the people with the real money and class know this and just laugh at them. I am sure of that.

That was my last event with them. I knew I would be quitting in a few days. It was getting close to yacht season in Lauderdale, and I had just sold the *Sea Rooster* and had a hundred extra grand in the bank, so to the hell with these misfits. I hated to leave Dallas, though. The city has the hottest chicks, and they are all so nice. I had quite a few, from the hostess at Rosewood Mansion in Turtle Creek to the owner of the dry cleaners and the bartender at Houston's, just to name a few. I had a hell of a run in Dallas. I have not been back since, but I am due for a trip. I miss those girls, the tight jeans and drinking beer out of a bottle. Oh, and I can't forget the cowboy hats. Love that look, along with a tight ass.

Highland Park is one of the best places to girl-watch in Dallas, and the university area and downtown as well. Too many hot chicks and just really nice folks there, and it did not hurt to be driving around town in an Aston Martin, Bently, and a new Suburban or be a private chef. It never hurts when you drop that line. They always ask, "Would you come cook for me?" And I always answer, "Of course." That was my MO and a great way to get in those wet panties. Love that.

I have never felt so good about quitting a job as I did the day I told the old hag to stick it up her tight ass. The only bad thing was that I lost a good agent. Bitch called him and said I had called her names and insulted her. She also complained that I had quit days before they were supposed to go to Canada for the summer and I had ruined their summer plans, like I really gave a shit.

Here's where it's all started. I told Rob I needed to drive the Bentley, which was just sitting in the garage. "The heat is not good for it. Either you use it once a week or I will take it out. That's what it needs. They are very temperamental."

"Ok."

"I will drive it to the golf course on my days off, get it detailed, and put like ten or fifteen miles on it once every other week."

"Yeah, do that."

"Cool. I have done this over my whole career, from the Weintraubs' old T-Bird to Rod Stewart's Rolls and Ferrari. It makes sense with these kinds of cars. Can I see the garage?"

So, sometime later, Mike and I were playing golf at the Cowboys Club on my day off. I had the Bentley, as it hadn't been driven in two weeks. We were playing with a few ex-Cowboys players, and we had a great day, including a few beers and lunch.

Afterward, I took Mike home and was back at the house by five. I parked the Bentley in the side garage and headed to my guest house. My things, by the way, were all packed up. Inside, I cracked open a cold one and was starting to relax when the housekeeper called me and said, "Myrna wants to see you in her office now."

I pounded down my beer and walked down to her office. She was in one of her bitchy moods. I said, "Yes, Myrna? You wanted to see me?"

She said, "What are you doing driving the Bentley?" By the way, this was an old Bentley.

I said, "I took it to the Cowboys Club to play golf and then had it detailed. I told Rob that it needed to be driven. That's why the tires were all dry-rotted and the oil was thick. That car needs to be driven once a week. It does not like sitting in a hot garage. It's bad for the belts, hoses, tires, and oil. You never get it serviced, so at least drive it. Rob said it was ok to drive it every week, so what's the problem?"

She went on a rage. "Rob never told you this! I run the house, and you report to me. That car is fine. I have owned Bentleys in the past, and it doesn't hurt to have them sit inside a garage."

"I don't know who told you that. Just ask anyone at the dealer."

"They're all liars. They just want your money and lie about the service on these cars."

"Ok, I am sorry. I won't argue with you. What do you want from me?"

"We never gave you permission to drive the car, especially on your day off."

"Ma'am, I live here. I never really have a day off. I'm always doing something, putting gas in the car, whatever, so what's the issue?"

She went on a tear. "I don't want you to ever drive our cars again. I'm not happy with you. You will only drive when we ask you to."

I said, "Ok, do you want to ask Rob about driving the Bentley?"

"I don't care what Rob says. I am the boss here, and what I say goes, and if you want to go to Canada with us, you had better straighten up. Do I make myself clear?"

"Yes, ma'am." I bit my tongue. I wanted to go to the Canada lake house for a month just to check it out. I thought it might be cool.

I started to walk away, and out of the clear blue, she said, "Don't walk away from me. I am not done with you yet." She had this look on her face like a mean drunk.

Then everything went through my mind. I was all packed up and could be gone in ten minutes. I could leave now or stay for one last month and then quit when I returned from Canada.

Then she said, "Get back here. I am not through with you. Do I make myself clear?"

That was it. I'd had it. I said, "Yes, crystal fucking clear. I have had enough of your shit about the cars and everything else. You can take the cars and the trip to Canada and stick them up your tight fucking ass. I have had enough of your bitching and whining. Why don't you stay in Canada? Don't come back to America. We don't need or want your kind here."

Myrna was at a loss for words, as I am sure no one had spoken to her like that before. Then I told her, "Piss off. Who the fuck do you think you are to talk to me like that? I have worked for first ladies, and they have more class in their shit than you have in your whole family. I don't need your shit or this job."

I did not let her get a word in.

Then Rob walked in, as he heard me barking at her. In a high voice, he asked, "What's the problem?"

Myrna started in about the Bentley and me driving it. "Yeah," he said, "I told Alan it was ok to drive it to the Cowboys Club and get it detailed while he was out."

She was at a loss for words and started to apologize, but that was not her style. Rob said, "Alan, don't leave. Let's work this out."

I said, "No, it's too late. I have had enough of Myrna's shit."

That was it. I went to my guest house, packed up, and drove off. I never heard from the Schlegels again. I am sure they have not changed. They better hope the well doesn't dry up, as this boat will sink for sure.

Last note: Kirby, grow up and be a man someday and not some little bitch.

Richard Riordan, Former Mayor of Los Angeles

Carroll Shelby

SHEER FASHION
LEAR'S
Wheels & Deals
A Woman's Guide
to Buying a Car
Lunch with Anna Quindlen
Outing Alcoholics
Inside a Family Intervention
Melanie Griffith Straight Up
Joan Baez
On the Road Again
Stripped-Down Shopping • The Nation's
Toughest Consumer Advocate • New Reasons
to Take Vitamins • Challenging a Spouse's Will
I loved your cooking!
love,
Melanie Griffith
APRIL 1993 $3.00

Chapter 22

DAVID GOULDEN
THE PRINCE

IT WAS NOT THE FIRST time I was out of a job, and it was my decision.

I was glad it was over. It was a shit job, and life's too short to work for assholes. I have said this many times over the years. That's one thing. If you are a good chef, you will always have a job if you want to work.

I'd been back home in Lauderdale for just a few days when I got a call from Captain Luke. I'd done a one-month gig with him a few years back on a ninety-six-footer, *Forever Young*. Luke was kind of a prick, but I did not know much about him. I'd seen him around West Palm and Lauderdale a few times. I knew the guys at the marinas did not like him, but hell, how bad could he be? No worse than some asshole owner. Man, was I in for a surprise.

He asked me what I had been up to. I told him about the Dallas gig and how I'd just gotten back into town and was looking to get back on a boat again. He was at LMC, and he asked me to stop by after lunch. He said he might have a five- or six-month gig for me. I said, "Sure, see you this afternoon."

I stopped by the yard, and he was doing some work on the boat, a brand-new ninety-three-foot Ferretti tri-deck with a huge beam. It was a good-looking boat—a pig in the open sea but a great coastal cruiser. Luke gave me a tour of the boat and laid out the summer plans.

He said, "You will have your own room and bath. It's five thousand a month, a bonus at the end of the summer, plus a car and my expenses."

I said, "Cool. When are we leaving?"

"A few weeks. We need a sea trial, and I have two crewmen lined up for the trip to Newport. They get off there. I have to hire a mate, but I have a kid lined up. We will take it to Hyannis, and that will be the home base for summer trips to Nantucket, Martha's Vineyard, Boston, New York, and Maine. No charters, just the owner and guests."

"I am in."

"I need a copy of your driver's license, the normal stuff."

"Make sure he will pay my corporation. That's a make-or-break deal."

"I will check, but I am sure that's cool."

"Who is the owner?"

He told me it was the CFO of a big company in Boston, no kids, just the wife and a small dachshund. He said, "Can you start next week? The boat is brand new and needs some pots and pans. Set the galley up. I will have a credit card for you in a few days."

"Cool," I said. "Let's go get a beer and some lunch."

We headed down to Tarpon Bend, had some lunch and a few beers, and talked about the trip. Then we shook hands, and I said, "I will see you Monday."

Luke had never been to New England. I'd been a few times, but it'd been a few years. I said, "You will like it up there, out of the Florida heat for the summer."

Just like that, I was back in the saddle again, on a new Ferretti and on my way to New England for the summer. One more new adventure. Man, what a hell of a ride for the summer.

When I got home, it was happy hour, so I called the Colonel, whom I had not seen since I'd gotten back. I said, "Hey, it's Chef Al, back in town. You up for a cold one?"

He said, "Yeah, meet me at the condo in twenty."

"I'm on my way." By the way, the condo is the junior penthouse at Las Olas Grand, not too shabby.

I got buzzed up, and we caught up over a rum and a beer. Then he said, "Let's hit the Quarterdeck. It's happy hour."

"Cool. I will drive."

"You got the Alfa?"

"Of course."

"I'm driving it."

"Cool. Let's hit it."

At the bar, the Colonel got the first round. He told me about his new hot little piece of ass, or should I say, the flavor of the month. I told him about the Dallas gig. I said, "The whole family were assholes," and left it at that.

"What's next?" He asked.

"I just got a summer gig on a new Ferretti heading to New England for the summer, leaving in two weeks, and I start prep next week."

"Congrats. Let's have some rum," he said, and then he bought one more round.

We had a few drinks, and he said, "Why don't you join me and my new toy for dinner at Timpano."

"Great." It was one of my favorite places in Las Olas.

"My treat. Congrats on the new gig. You get drinks, and I will get dinner."

"You're on. See you at eight."

I headed home, got cleaned up, made myself a martini, and said, "Man, life is great. Home a few days and already back to work and out of Florida for the summer."

I met the Colonel at Las Olas Grand, and we had a drink and walked over to Timpano. He had a new hot piece of ass, a little Filipino. Over dinner, we caught up, and I told him about the shit job in Dallas and my new gig. While the Colonel's new girl was in the bathroom, he told me about his new kid in the DR, the child of some whore he'd knocked up. What a piece of work the Colonel is, but it's not my business to judge friends. We enjoyed dinner, and I said, "I will see you in the fall. I've got a busy week. I have to get the boat ready to leave. Thanks for dinner. Take care, and we'll spend some time together when I get back. Maybe a trip to the DR is in order."

Monday arrived, and I headed to the boat to meet Luke. I have a punch list, and I got right on it. Luke said, "We have a sea trial tomorrow, and let's try to get out of here Friday evening."

I said, "I will be done in a few days."

"I want you to go pick up the new deckhand. He has no car and needs a ride to the boat."

"Cool."

"I've got one more captain and his son coming. They just confirmed, so we are all good to go."

Captain Greg and his son were going with us to Newport, so there were five of us total, counting me. The sea trial worked out, and we were all good. We took on fuel the next day. I got all the provisions and set up the galley as best I could on short notice. Captain Greg and his son showed up by cab. They seemed very professional, clean-cut and squared away. The new deckhand seemed a little dodgy. He needed a haircut and was tatted up. To me, he looked like shit. I would not have hired this kid. He'd been washing boats at Ferretti and could not tie a knot. What was Luke thinking? More on that later.

We all sat down for a crew meeting to get the game plan about leaving and checking the weather. It can get nasty around the Carolinas in the spring. At the time, I did not know that Luke had never been on a trip like this, just around South Florida. He did not have much experience, which was why he'd hired Greg. Captain Greg had done this trip a dozen times and knew the route. I could tell this was going to be one big fuck story.

Everyone stowed their gear, and we were all set to leave on Friday. I had all my shit done. The car was back at the condo, and I was good for the summer. Greg and his son were good as well. Instead of leaving first thing Saturday morning, as Luke was running behind, we missed the bridge timing, and the weather was not great. Around seven or eight, Luke said, "Let's just take off."

Greg said, "We should wait till morning."

Luke just ignored him and said, "Let's pull lines." We did, and then he backed up and damn near ran aground. What was he thinking, leaving at that time of night with bad weather coming in? That was Luke for you, real fucking cowboy. I learned this after the fact. He didn't care about the safety or well-being of the crew. I found out later he was a Boynton Beach cop and got let go. You know you've got issues when you can't make it as a small-town cop. I think the same thing happened to him in the Coast Guard. To me, that is not like being in the military, but to hear Luke talk, the Coast Guard was tough. Who are you trying to bullshit? So, now you have a little background on Luke.

We got downriver in the dark and met Greg's son at the outlet. We had a hard time in the rough water and the dark, but we got the tender tied up and headed out of the inlet and on our way north. We were in for a rough ride and quite a few tough nights with no sleep. What I learned about Luke early on is that it's his way or the highway, and he is always right. We got our ass kicked on this trip. We could have pulled into Savannah and hung out for a few days, but oh, no, Mr. Know-It-All said we would go around it. So, we headed out around Cape Hatteras, and we just got killed for two days. Luke and the whole crew got sick. We were rolling and rocking, and the tender was getting beaten up. Shit was flying around inside the boat. These Ferrettis were not made for weather like that. It was a real pig in rough water, and it was a tri-deck on top of that. I was the only one who did not get sick, but I did not sleep for two days. I thought we might roll over. It was that rough.

Luke said, "Maybe it will turn," but it was too late. We were right in the middle of it and just had to go through it. He was the worst captain I ever worked for. Besides being a prick, he did not care about the crew's safety or well-being. I would have loved to have had the owners on board. They would have fired his ass for sure for not stopping in Savannah and waiting a few days. This was the worst trip I have ever been on, and it's an easy one if you plan it right and not just go straight into the storm.

I stowed everything in sight. We lost a few pieces of glassware, and everything in the pantry was on the floor. When we got to Cape May, we discovered that the anchor on the tender had come loose and torn up the front. This was a brand-new Intrepid. The kid never put the lock on it. What a fuck-up.

Luke did not have one word to say when we docked to take on fuel. Greg and his son were still not feeling great, but they seemed a little better. We were all tired. No one had gotten a good night's sleep since we'd left Lauderdale. The whole crew went right to bed after we took on fuel. I got the interior put back together and fixed some pasta for dinner. When everyone woke up, they would have a nice, hot meal. They all slept the whole day. I just got my shit done and took a little nap, and I was good to go.

The next stop was Newport, 41 North Marine, and then it was on to the cape for the rest of the summer. I still remember the anchor. That was big. Any owner or captain would have let the guy go. That's just the bottom line; it was bad. But Luke liked being in control, and this kid just kissed his ass, so he held it over the kid's head the whole summer until he quit.

I went ashore for a bowl of chowder and a beer after dinner, and Luke said to me, "Where are you going?" I told him, and he said, "Next time, ask me."

I looked at him and said, "Really?" And just rolled my eyes and walked off the boat. Who was this fuck, my dad or some shit?

We were only in Cape May for one day and night, and then we were off to New York. Our last stop was Newport, where the boss would be getting on with a couple of guests for four days. We were not leaving the dock, just hanging out on the boat. It was his first time on the brand-new boat, and I had not met them yet, and I was looking forward to it.

Greg and I had a long talk while Luke was at the marina office, paying the bill. I looked at him and said, "That was one shitshow we just went through."

He said, "Yes, I would have pulled into Savannah and waited a few days. This boat is shit in rough seas."

"I know. What was Luke thinking?"

"He was not thinking."

We agreed and just laughed. We should never have taken that bad weather on. The rest of the trip should be much easier, all downhill. Greg and his son were still getting off in Newport, and Luke, the kid, and I would go on to the cape for the rest of the summer.

We rolled into Newport without any more issues and were still there a few days early. We got the boat all squared away, and I got all the provisions for the first visit of the boss and his guests. Greg and I traded emails and said our goodbyes. Luke told him and his son to have lunch on the boat and rent a car to get home and just send him the receipt, and he would reimburse them. This was a bad idea, but I'll get back to that later.

The boss, his wife, and their guests just wanted to stay in Newport and play tourist. I don't blame them. Newport is a cool little town with some great restaurants. It's still one of my favorite towns in New England.

The weekend finally arrived, and they showed up on the boat. I was told that David liked Belvedere martinis and his wife drank Rombauer chardonnay, so I had their drinks in hand when they arrived. It turned out that the guy was a prince, and his guests, friends of the wife, were a nice couple. I guess the wives were high school friends.

The next morning, David, his wife, and I had a little sit-down. They wanted to know more about me, and I needed some guidelines. Luke was not worth a shit on matters like this. They told me the liked an all-protein diet, very few carbs. They loved fish, nice salads, good grains, and lots of veggies. I said, "Great. That's what I like as well."

They told me that they loved Belvedere vodka, and I said, "Me, too."

David said, "Let's have a drink together and make a toast to our new chef."

Luke hated that the boss liked me from the start. I asked if there was a budget, and David looked at me and said, "We want the freshest seafood and only the best produce. We don't care what it costs." Then he asked about the Fords, if I missed working in California for the celebs, and what it was like to work for Rod Stewart. He had met Jerry Weintraub as well and was very impressed with him. Everyone is; he is a man's man.

So, I gave him the five-minute spiel about cooking for the Fords and the Bushes, playing golf with Don Johnson, and how I used to go out with

Sharon Stone's sister. I left some meat on the bone; I did not want to give the house away on the first trip.

For the next four days, I really spoiled them and their guests, turn-down service, cocktail hour, nice apps. It was a great first trip, and they were very happy. Every morning, I prepared fresh fruit and frittatas with avocados and tomatoes. For dinner, I made fish, and for lunch, I made some great salads with all my nice dressings and sauces. They enjoyed every meal. Before I knew it, the trip was over, and we were all saying goodbye. David said, "We will see you next weekend on the cape." We were going to Martha's Vineyard.

He seemed like a great guy. His wife was kind of a pain, but they all are when they marry a rich guy and don't work, just lie on their backs. David wasn't much of a stud, tall, with a beanpole build and bad teeth, like most Brits, but he had shitloads of money. I think his salary was twenty-three million. Even if you're not a ladies' man, when you make that kind of dough and drive a Ferrari and have a yacht, chicks don't care what you look like. I am sure she stalked him down at some fundraisers and then got her claws into him. She was not bad looking, a little thick, but she had nice tits, and I am sure she gave him the best blowjob he ever had. She thought she was all that, and for a nerd, he did ok. Like I said, he's a nice guy to keep Luke on all these years. Luke is still there today. I saw him last spring in Palm Beach, and he was still the same asshole.

The first trip was in the bag, and David had the whole summer planned out, every weekend until September, when we would head back to Palm Beach. I'll say one thing: David knew how to live. He had been making big money for a long time. I heard he ran Wang Laboratories for a while and some other big companies. He was a smart guy and good with numbers. He and the wife drove Ferraris, and he had a bad-ass townhome on Marlborough in Boston's Old Town. He had a pretty good life. Shit, the crew had access to two Porsche Caymans. Not a bad setup.

In this business, it's so hard to find a nice boss who pays well and wants only the best for himself and the crew. What a gig. Any captain would have been in heaven, but Luke would still complain. That guy will never be happy. Some guys are just pricks and stay that way. It's too bad. I kind of feel bad for the shithead.

We rolled out of 41 North in Newport on the way to Hyannis. The marina there would be our home dock for the summer. David had a nice house there, too. From there, we would go to Martha's Vineyard, Nantucket, Boston, Newport, and New York. It was a solid home base, and there was a great bar at the marina, Trader Ed's.

We rolled in and just happened to be the biggest boat in the marina, but that's not saying much. It's a small marine. But we were right behind Trader Ed's, a great spot. When we pulled in, all the chicks at the bar could see us. We got all the lines secured and the boat washed down, and I was off to the bar.

I bellied up to the bar and ordered a Stella. It didn't take long for me to run into the owner, John. I loved this guy from the minute I met him. He was one crazy fucker and loved pussy more than me, if that's possible. We had some great times that summer, and all his friends were first class and crazy, too. Luke came in one time with me, and he hated that I knew everyone and had made all these new friends, but like I said, Luke was an asshole and had no friends. We had lunch that one time, and that was it.

The week passed by quickly, and soon it was Friday, and the boss and his wife arrived. We would be going to Martha's Vineyard for three days. We would not tow the tender, which would make the trip a lot easier. The wind started to kick up a little in the afternoon, so before we left, Luke told the mate to secure all the top deck cushions. This kid was living proof of why tigers eat their young. The boss and wife wanted to hang out on the top deck, but because of the wind, they had drinks in the main saloon.

We cast off, and I returned to the saloon to make drinks and snacks for the boss and his wife. Luke and kid were in the wheelhouse, and we headed off. I was making the second round of my special pineapple-infused martinis when I looked out the back deck sliders and saw our cushions floating in the water. David saw the look on my face and said, "Chef, you ok?"

I said, "Yeah, I am fine, but I don't think our cushions are so good."

"What do you mean?"

"Come have a look."

The cushions floated by, and now the wind had really kicked up. He said, "Oh, shit."

I ran up to the wheelhouse to tell Captain Asshole that the cushions had blown off. He gave me this look like it was my fault, that I should have checked them. I said, "No way in hell. You told the kid to secure them, and he said he did. You should have checked them yourself, not me. I am in the galley, taking care of the boss."

He started to get huffy, but David walked in, and he shut the fuck up. David asked, "Can we try to pick them up?"

They weren't even in sight anymore, and we couldn't just do a U-turn; there were other boats in our pattern. They decided to just let them go. David said, "Just order new ones," and that was it. I would have fired both of them, but not David. He did not like to make waves. I think the new cushions cost around five grand. Me, I would have been pissed.

We got to Martha's Vineyard that afternoon. David said, "We are going out for dinner tonight, Chef. Take the night off. Tomorrow we are having two guests for dinner. Can you prepare some fresh fish?"

I said, "Sure."

"Great. Enjoy the night off, and we will see you tomorrow for breakfast."

I fixed the crew dinner. Luke was still pissed off, but he was in that mood all the time. I mean, the kid had screwed up, but Luke beat him up pretty badly. In a way, it wasn't the kid's fault. He was a boat washer at the yard, and Luke never trained him. When you pay peanuts, you get monkeys. This kid had no business on this boat.

After dinner, I got ready to go out for dinner. I returned to the galley to clean up before I took off, and Luke looked at me and said, "Where are you going, all dressed up?"

I said, "Out for dinner."

The balls this guy had. He told me, "Don't be late and don't drink."

I looked at him and said, "Really? You think I am a kid?"

Then I just walked away and went into town. Poor bastard needed a life.

I headed to Larsen's Fish Market with a bottle of wine in hand, from the boat, of course—you don't think I would buy one, do you? Larsen's is a cool spot. I ate outside and shared my wine with a young couple from Boston. It was a nice dinner. I just hung out, drank some wine, and ate some fresh fish. They do a good job. I call it an early night, as I had guests for lunch the next day and had to prepare breakfast, too. It was just nice to get off the boat and not have to deal with Luke.

I got up early and ran a few miles. For breakfast, I made one of my specialties: frittatas with herbs, sliced tomatoes, and avocados, and I made the crew breakfast burritos. The wife came down with Fred, the little dachshund. He had to go do his morning business. I've never liked small dogs, but Fred grew on me and was a cool little guy with a big personality. David came down next, and his wife returned shortly with Fed. I served them on the rear deck, and they enjoyed their breakfast.

I returned to clear the table, and they asked where I had gone for dinner the night before. I said, "Larsen's, for a piece of fish," and they said they liked the food there as well. Then they asked what I had planned for lunch. I said, "A nice garden salad, fresh halibut grilled with lemon and capers, couscous and assorted baby veggies, and fruit torte for dessert." They were not dessert people, but we were having guests today, so they wanted something light and clean.

David said, "That sounds great. The Kerrys will be pulling up next to us at around noon. They're old friends. Don't worry about feeding the security guards. They won't come on board."

I had no idea who this guy was. Then David said, "It's John Kerry, the secretary of state. He has a sailboat that he keeps at the cape in the summertime." It turned out that David's wife was a flaming liberal. She said she knew Michelle Obama and they were friends, but the Obama's never came to the boat the whole summer. I found out later on that she met Michelle at a fundraiser along with hundreds of other guests. She was so full of shit. You could tell she and David did not match. Something did not add up.

The Kerrys showed up on time, along with their Secret Service agents. They closed the dock down for a few hours. They had wine and small talk before lunch, and David introduced me and told them I used to work for the Fords. They asked about my background and what I thought of LA and the stars I'd worked for. I told them a few stories, and then I said, "I have to serve lunch."

They all sat down, and I poured some more wine and served lunch. They really enjoyed the fish and were very thoughtful and nice. They talked about the Obama's and EMI and what their plans were. David was at ease; they seemed like old friends. After lunch, David called me aside and said, "We would like to talk in private. Would you take Fred for a walk?"

I said, "Of course," and Fred and I left the boat for an hour.

The plan was to head back to Hyannis after lunch. I returned after taking Fred for a spin. He was a cool little dog. I hate to say it, but I miss that little guy. They were finishing their meeting. I would have loved to have been a fly on the wall and heard what was going on. I am sure it was some hush-hush shit.

They said thanks for lunch and that they really enjoyed the food and hoped to see me again. Then, before we knew it, we were heading back to Hyannis. The first trip was in the bag, and I really liked the boss. David was first class all the way, but his wife, I could take her or leave her. All these rich guys' wives are mostly pains in the asses. They have nothing to do but complain and bust balls. She was no different. I just hate it when these bitches come out of the ghetto—in her case, South Boston—and act all educated when they're really just cheap whores who got lucky. That's life. If I had a pussy, I would be rich as well.

After we docked in Hyannis, the boss took off. He must have told me, "Thanks for a great weekend," five times. We had a crew meeting, and Luke really laid into the kid about the cushions, but he said the boss was really happy and the first trip had gone well. We had two weeks off until the next trip. We got the boat cleaned up, I cooked us a nice dinner, and it was off to meet the gang at Trader Ed's. I said hi to everyone, had a few beers, and then went back to the boat to go to bed early, as tomorrow was a golf day. The cape has some nice courses, and the price is not too bad. We went back to Martha's Vineyard once more that summer, no guests, and just hung out for the weekend. Nothing too crazy, so we won't get into that.

The weeks flew by, as it does when you are having a good time, and the next trip was now here. I had made up a fresh batch of pineapple vodka and had lots of fresh seafood. The boss had told me he was bringing a couple with them, so I was prepared. I had been to Nantucket before, but it'd been years. I did remember that I liked it more than the Vineyards—it's not as stuffy.

The guests arrived about the same time David and his wife rolled up. I got everyone a drink, and they made themselves comfortable on the top deck. Then we tossed the lines off and were underway. This time, there were no issues with the cushions. It turned out that the guests were friends of the Obama's. The husband had just recently been appointed the ambassador to Portugal, and they were on board to celebrate.

We tied up at the marina, and shortly after, David came to see me in the galley. He said, "Alan, we are dining out tonight. We have reservations at Cru Oyster Bar but would like breakfast every day, a few lunches, and two dinners."

I said, "Fine. I can do that."

"We love your fish dishes, like you did last time, clean and fresh."

"Of course. My pleasure."

They all got changed, and I cracked open a nice bottle of wine and offered some cheese and crackers for a little starter, and then they were off to dinner. I fed Luke and the kid, got myself cleaned up, and headed into town. I went to the Club Car, a nice bar and great restaurant, and sat at the bar. To my surprise, the bartender was one of my old ski bum pals from Stowe, Aron, one crazy fuck and a great skier. He bought me a beer and said, "What the fuck are you doing here? I heard you were in California, working for all the stars."

I said, "I was for years, but now I am based out of Florida and took a summer job on a yacht doing New England for the summer."

We caught up, and I ordered some oysters with a martini and then filled up with some fresh scallops. It was a nice dinner. We exchanged emails, and I said, "Keep in touch. I will stop back in before we leave Tuesday."

I returned to *North Star*—that was the boat's name—and the guests were not back yet, so I prepped for breakfast and turned in for the night. Luke was in bed already. He never left the boat. He hated to spend a dime. I think he took us for beers one time the whole summer. Turned out he was broke. He told me he was upside down on his house, owed a lot on his credit cards, and had four cars. What the fuck? On his salary, with two kids, no wonder he was broke. He was not the sharpest tool in the shed, not even close.

The next morning was a breeze. I fed the crew and made a nice breakfast for the boss and his guests. They asked where I had gone, and I said, "I went to the Club Car for a drink and a bite."

They said, "That's one of our favorite spots."

"Yeah, it's a great spot. Do you know Aron, the bartender?"

"Yes, we've known him for years."

I told them that we wear ski bums back in Stowe, Vermont, back in the day, and they thought that was cool. I said, "Yeah, I did the ski bum thing for five seasons." We all had a good laugh.

The boss said, "We are going out for lunch today, but we'll have dinner in.

I said, "How does grilled fish with roasted veggies and a mixed green salad sound?"

"Sounds great."

"Ok. I am on it."

After feeding the crew lunch, I headed to the market to get the day's fresh catch. One more nice and easy day. I might not have said these, but I am the stew as well. That means I do heads and beds and turn-down service. It's not that bad: run a vacuum, do a load of laundry, mop the floor, no big deal.

Dinner rolled around, and they were dining on the top deck, where there was a nice view of the marina. I served some cocktails and light apps, and they were all in a great mood. I would be to if I'd just been named the new ambassador to Portugal. I served dinner with a nice Rombauer chardonnay; it went well with the grilled tuna, black and blue, with roasted red pepper salsa. They were in heaven. David loved my cooking, and the guests said they wanted to know if they could take me home—or better yet, if I could come to Portugal.

I said, "I can be had, but I am not cheap." Even David laughed at that.

Then they asked me to tell them who I liked best over the years, who I did not like, and what the Fords were like. I guess David had told them

I had worked for them. I said Betty was great, like a grandma. She and Barbara and George H. W. were hard to beat, really nice people who treated me well. I told them a few dinner stories about Weintraub and Prince Bandar and the Bushes, and I let it go at that. I wanted to leave some meat on the bone for the next dinner. I had them in tears.

I cleaned up and said goodnight, and David said, "Please, Chef, join us for a nightcap."

I thanked him and poured myself two fingers of Knob Creek. David liked a little bourbon at night. We had a nice conversation, and then I turned in. I said, "I have to be up early for breakfast. Thanks for the drink."

"It was my pleasure. We loved hearing your stories. You have had an amazing life."

"Yes, it's been a hell of a run, and I've still got a few more miles left in the tank. See you in the morning."

That night was a real feather in my cap. I made the boss look great—Luke, too, but he did not see it that way. It was all about him, his kids, and baseball. He spent half of every day on his cell, talking about baseball with parents and coaches. He was obsessed.

The next day was pretty much the same. I made breakfast, lunch, and dinner, and they turned out great. Lunch was pretty special. I did my crab-cakes with my island Jamaican-me-crazy sauce on a bed of mixed greens and with a fruit parfait for desert. It's a hit every time. Even Luke liked it.

I got cleaned up and headed to the Club Car for a drink and a bite to eat. Aron was at the bar, and it was packed. I managed to get a corner stool, and when he brought me a beer, I told him we were leaving tomorrow after lunch but would be back in a few weeks. We were having a good laugh about the old days in Stowe when, from out of the blue, Liz Chris, aka Mr. Pickwick Pub's ex-wife, rolled in. She was hot. I'd always wanted to jump her, but I'd quit doing married women a few years before. In her case, though, I would have made an exception.

Before I got the gig at the Stoweflake, I worked for her and her husband as a cook and handyman. They had just bought a little bed and breakfast on the mountain in Stowe and made it a really nice place. Liz and I became good friends. I really liked her, as did everyone in town. Chris was kind of a prick, a stuffy Brit. Liz had a rockin' little body and nice tits.

When she saw me, she was all smiles. "Chef Al, it's been twenty years or so, and you still look the same."

I said, "You look great as well," and gave her my chair and bought her a glass of wine. "It's great to see you."

"You as well. I heard you were in LA, working for all the stars."

"Yes, but I moved to Florida a few years back, and I have a little flat in the south of Spain as well."

"It seems like life has been good to you."

"Yeah, I've been lucky."

We swapped old stories, and she told me why she'd left Chris. He'd been cheating on her and had a little coke problem, and she'd finally had enough. That was five years ago. I told her I was sorry to hear that, and she said, "No, it was for the best. He cheated on me in the past, too, and I'd had enough of the lies."

"Good for you, then," I said, and we had a toast to old and new good times.

She asked how long I would be on the island, and I told her we would be leaving tomorrow after lunch but would be back a few more times throughout the summer. She was impressed that I worked on a yacht. She told me she had been working and living at the Jared Coffin House, a small B and B, real upscale.

We had a few shots, and out of the blue, she said, "Why don't you come back to my place and have a nightcap, and we can catch up more?"

I said, "I would like that." I settled up with Aron, and we were out of there. We got to her place, and she poured us a glass of wine, and we talked about the old days in Stowe. Then she said, "I always thought there was something about you that I liked," and before I knew it, she was on top of me and we were both undressed. She mounted me, and she was sopping wet. I guess she had not had sex in a while, and we went at it every way you can. She still had that nice ass and great tits. Afterward, I said, "I had no idea it would be that great."

She said, "Me, either. Let's do it again when you come back."

"Yeah, you can count on that."

We kissed once more, and I said, "I have to get back. It's getting late, but I will call soon. Take care. It was great, and I look forward to seeing you again."

"You promise?"

"Yes, of course." She knew my reputation from Stowe.

When I got back to the boat, everyone had turned in, so I kept quiet and called it a night myself.

The next morning, after breakfast, David told Luke and me there would be a change in plans. He had to be back that night, and they would have lunch on the way back to Hyannis. Luke said, "Fine. We will toss lines and get underway within the hour."

We pulled the lines up and headed back. I got to work on lunch and started to plan the rest of the week. I served lunch on the top deck: my Southwest Cole slaw with grilled swordfish, mango-pineapple salsa, charred Brussels sprouts, and lemon sorbet with my homemade chocolate bark. Everyone agreed it was the best lunch of the trip. David said, "It just keeps on getting better."

The next thing we knew, we were tying up at the marina, within eyesight of Trader Ed's. I could taste the cold beer already. We got all the guests off, and David thanked me one last time.

"My pleasure, as always," I said. "See you next week in Boston." That was our next stop. David said he would call me. He wanted me to make dinner at the house one night when we got to Boston. I said, "Sure. Just let me know." One more trip was in the bag, and all the guests were happy.

The whole gang was out on the patio at Trader Ed's, just raging as always. We washed the boat down, and I put the interior back together, fed the two knuckleheads, and was off for the night. The guys already had shots and beer lined up. The kid was eighty-sixed for the rest of the season; he'd gotten drunk and started a fight. The gang said they were going to have dinner at Embargo and asked if I was in. I said, "Hell, yes. Let's go." I had tomorrow off, and all I planned to do was play golf.

I was banging one of the staff, Patty, so I took her with us. She was fucking crazy but great in the sack and young to boot, a big bonus. We had a great dinner and drinks and then danced the night away. At the end of the night, I took Patty back to the boat for some sport fucking. It was a great time, and I will never forget the gang at Trader Ed's. I need to get back there one day.

This was halfway through the summer. I played golf, got rested for the trip, and said farewell to the gang for a few weeks. I took Patty out to the Black Cat for dinner and gave her one more fucking for good measure before I left. She was crazy, but all these bitches are.

The days off were over, and we were ready to head to Boston. We would leave the tender and cars behind, as we wouldn't need them in Boston. I could walk to the store. We cast off and left early in the morning to be in Boston by dusk. We would dock at Rowes Wharf for a few weeks. This is a great spot to be, walking distance to everything, with Faneuil Market, all kinds of restaurants and shops, Old Town, North End, the Italian part of town—I mean, you're right in the middle of it all. Well, Luke never left the boat once. He did not want to spend a dime. Boston is a cool city. I would not want to live there, but it's a great place to visit.

The plan was to have a small party on the boat for a few close friends and some folks from EMI, all the executives. I was doing dinner at the house one night. Then we would head north to Wentworth by the Sea for a few days, drop the boss off, head back in Boston, and return to Hyannis.

The boss and his wife came on the boat for dinner on Friday, just the two of them. I did a nice lobster dinner, and afterward, the boss told me to get Luke and the kid. He wanted to talk to all of us. I thought we were getting the ax or he was selling the boat.

Turned out he was inviting us all to a Red Sox game at the EMI box at Fenway Park. He said, "You can rent a car for the night or just take a cab, and the boat will pay for it." What a great guy. That was nice of him.

At the stadium, we parked in the VIP lot and walked up to the box, where there was all kinds of food and an open bar. It was a great evening— scratch one off the bucket list. On top of that, Clemens stopped by to say hi to the boss, and we all got to meet him. David was very thoughtful and had some class. Over the summer, he did a few nice things for the crew and me. It was a great game, and the Sox won, so everyone was in a good mood. I think that was the highlight of the whole summer trip. Yeah, that was hard to beat.

The next morning, I got up for my morning run. On the dock, I saw four cop cars, a crime scene unit, and an ambulance. I knew something was up. Right across the way from us, the Red Sox owner's yacht had red tape all over the place. That's never a good sign.

I asked the people standing around what was going on, but no one knew anything. So, I got my run and workout in, and when I returned to the marina a few hours later, the ambulance was gone, but a few cop cars were still around, the crime scene unit van was still there, and the yacht was still roped off.

I saw Luke and the kid on the dock, so I went over to them, and Luke said, "The chef killed himself last night. Drug OD or something like that is what he heard from the dock boys." Fucking crazy chefs—no wonder we have a name.

I was not going to let it ruin my day off. I had lunch at Faneuil and some nice wine and just walked around, playing tourist. I had a few things I wanted to see on my own, like the Museum of Modern Art and the Freedom Trail. Just walking around the waterfront is lots of fun. It's hard to beat the Alley and the Sea Grille at the wharf, a great spot and tons of hot ass to look at as well. I did everything on my to-do list and had some great lunches and dinners as well. I would put Boston on my list of places to come and see again; there's just lots of cool stuff to see and do. It's hard to believe that Luke and the kid never left the boat. I was having a great time and did not spend a fortune.

Finally, it was time to return to work. It would be a busy week. The boss called me and said, "Let's do curry on Wednesday. There will be four of us, and dinner will be at seven. Do a few apps."

"I can do that."

"I'll see you around four to get things set up."

"Great. See you then."

They had a great townhome on Marlborough, an old brownstone, really bad-ass. I liked that place. The wife just wanted some fruit and cheese for a starter, tossed salad, and curry chicken. The guests were friends of hers.

Friday night was the big party, and we had it catered. I just supervised. We did not have the refrigeration space. I hired two servers and a bartender, and we had thirty guests. All the top dogs from EMC were there, some of David's close friends, and a few of the wife's girlfriends. They were not on David's list, gold diggers and low class. What do you expect from South Boston? You can dress them up, but you can't take them out.

I picked up one of the wait staff and took her out to dinner. She was a hot little unit. The raw bar was great, and there were lots of good apps. David was happy. I did do the cheese tray and some fruit platters, easy stuff. I also got to hang out with the CEO, Joe Tucci, a great guy. He was friends with President Ford; that's how we hit it off. David had told him I used to work for them.

Unlike David, Joe was a conservative, and you could tell he was a real man's man, a sharp-looking guy, too. I am sure he had some hot ass in his day. He looked to be in great shape. David did not know the word "workout," but he was still a nice guy. Joe just had this persona about him. We hit it off, and he was a golfer, too. David invited me to have a drink with them. I thought that was cool. I had a great time talking to these two. I mean, come on, the CEO and CFO of EMC? That was a cool night, and it made my whole summer. Joe was very polite to me and took me to play golf on the cape a few weeks later. I won't forget that. Thanks, Joe, for the golf and the friendship. You're a winner in my book and a really cool guy. I never saw him again after that. EMC was sold to Dell the following year.

.The party went later than expected, so David called Luke and me aside and said, "We won't leave for Wentworth until Sunday, and take tomorrow off."

Luke hated shit like that. He would work the crew seven days a week if he could, but only because he had no life and was just miserable, the asshole. It was cool with me, though. I took the waitress out and fucked the shit out of her. I also had one more nice dinner at the North End and spent one more night in Boston. We would be heading south for the rest of the summer. All I had to do was put up with Luke's shit for two more months, but that would be a tough task.

Sunday came, and the boss and wife arrived early at the boat. David was really in a great mood; maybe he'd just gotten a blowjob from the old lady. She had those South Boston dick-sucking lips. Before we knew it, we were underway, heading north to Wentworth by the Sea. It's a small marina on the coast of New Hampshire and a great little resort. We would spend three days there, head back to Boston for one day, and then return to Hyannis.

The boss and his wife went ashore for dinner one night, and I got to go into Portsmouth. It's an old whaling town, pretty cool, with a great little marina, waterfront village, and downtown. Put it on your list of fun spots. I got the chance to play the golf course there as well. David made me a tee time. It's a great course with some holes right on the water. Three days went by, and we were back on our way to B-town.

We arrived around sunset, and the boss said, "We will see you in Newport in a few weeks." They were going to Vail. I guess they had a condo there. I was to take care of Fred, the dachshund. I was cool with that. He was a good wingman. We had two weeks until the next trip. Boss told Luke to give us all a couple of days off because they would be on the boat in Newport for ten days with a few guests and would have a big party, too.

When we got back to Haynes, we sorted the boat out and took a few days off. The kid got pulled over the next day. He had warrants in New York and New Jersey, and Luke had to call the boss to bail him out. It turned out the kid had no driver's license and two DUI's on his record. Luke had never bothered to run a check. Plain and simple, it was Luke's fault. If I were the boss, I would have fired both the fucks. But not David. He kept them both. Like I said, he was a prince and loyal guy, but to me, that's just business. If that kid got in a wreck, they could sue David for everything he had, and Luke would be looking for a new job. Any other owner would have cleaned house. The kid had issues with Luke as well, but Luke was not a drunk, just an asshole. It's hard to get kicked out of

Trader Ed's, and the kid was not allowed in for the rest of the season. That's bad. What a loser.

It turned out that David took care of all the kid's fines with a loan, but he was still not allowed to drive. I heard Luke fired him when they got back to Palm Beach. That is one of the things about the yachting industry: you get a lot of lowlifes who cannot get a job elsewhere, including drunk and asshole captains, and the stews are not much better. These kids have ruined this industry, just like the restaurant business. On top of that, they don't want to work. I will just stop there. Don't get me going on these worthless pieces of shit.

A few days later, we blew a power box again. The Italian boats always have power issues. A Viking had been next two us for a few days, but we had not seen any crew yet. They must have taken a few days off, as the dock boys were keeping an eye on it for them. Luke, being the dick he is, unplugged their power cord and plugged into their box. Bad idea and way out of line. You just don't do shit like that. This was a sport fisher, and it turned out that the captain was pretty big and looked like he could handle himself.

I was on the dock, having a glass of wine, when he came back to the boat and saw his power cord unplugged. He looked at me and said, "What the fuck? Who unplugged it?"

I said, "Luke, the captain on the boat."

He walked over, unplugged our cord, and plugged his back in. I threw Luke right under the bus. He had it coming. I guess Luke was taking a nap. Alarms started going off, and he was on the dock in two minutes and was greeted by this big and tough-looking sport captain. Sport guys hate yachties cause they're a bunch of pussies.

Luke started to say something, and the guy said, "What the fuck do you think you're doing, unplugging my power?"

Luke said, "It was just for a minute until I got the power box fixed."

"Don't ever touch my shit again, or we are going to have a problem. Run your generator."

I thought he was going to take Luke out. He was pissed, and Luke was at a loss for words. He said he was sorry, and that was it. I was hoping this guy would pound the shit out of him. Luke was way overdue for an ass-kicking, but he backed right down. He knew he was in the wrong.

Luke started the generator, and that was it. The sport captain and I went and had a beer at Trader Ed's and shot the shit. I told him all about Luke and what a prick he was. "I was hoping you'd kick his ass."

"Yeah, me, too. I was that close. He had better not touch my shit again, or he will get a beating."

After a few more beers, we headed back to the boats. Luke was in the bridge and saw us walking back together. When I got inside, he asked, "Is that guy going to be there long?

I said, "I think for the rest of the season."

"Great."

"The guy was really pissed and told me to tell you not to touch his shit again." I had to throw a little fuel on the fire.

The crew took the week off. Luke was going to Florida to see his wife and family, and the kid was also taking off. I said I would stay behind, watch the boat, and take care of Fred. I did not mind. I could play golf and have the boat to myself for a week. Plus, I could bang the crazy bitch at Trader Ed's. I took Fred out with me a few nights. He was a great wingman. They had little custom jackets made for me, and I have to say they were cool. I had a great week. Played golf a few times, went to P-town and took a day trip to the Vineyard. Fred was good company.

Luke and the kid returned, and we got ready to head back to Newport for about two weeks. After that, we only had one more leg of the trip left: back to New York to hit the Block Island Sound and the city one last time and then south to Palm Beach. Then I was done unless they fired Luke or he quit. It was getting tougher every day.

We had a change of plans on the last day. We needed a car down there to provision with or if the guests needed it for any reason, so after we cast off, I was going to drive the Porsche SUV down. Cool by me. I could stop along the coast, have a nice lunch, and take in the scenery along the way, and it would be less time I had to spend with the crew. The plan was to have guests for half of the trip, with lots of dinners and lunches out, a few harbor cruises, and a big cocktail party. This part of the country is so nice in the summer, with lots of young people out and about, great weather, and great seafood. The beaches are not too great, but there's a lot to see and do.

This would be the last stop in Newport this year. I really like it there, and 41 North is the bomb. It's just like Boston. Walk out of the marina, and you are right downtown. Two weeks is enough. You can see it all in a few days, but it's a great place to spend the summer.

I drove down the coast, had a nice lunch on the way, and met up with the boat that evening. I was having a beer downtown when I ran into Captain Greg and his son. They were doing a delivery. We had a beer, and he asked where Luke was. I said, "The prick is bringing the boat down. I drove down, as we needed a car here. We will be here for two weeks."

He laughed and told me how Luke would not pay his lunch bill the last day he was in Newport. He said it was too high and asked if Greg had put drinks on the tab. Then he only paid half, even though the bill was less than fifty dollars for two guys.

I said, "I know. I am ready to quit every day." Then I asked, "Greg, can I use you for a reference?" I did not trust Luke to give me a good one.

He said, "Sure, no big deal." We said goodbye, and then I went back to wait for the boat to get in.

We had one couple for a few days, friends of the boss's wife, followed by a few days off. Then it was time for the big party on the boat. We did the raw bar again. That week, we were having Martina Hingis and Stan Smith for a few nights. Martina was going to be inducted into the Tennis Hall of Fame, in Newport. It turned out that David was on the board and was a big supporter of the hall of fame. I am sure he gave lots of money. That was what the party was for. There were about thirty guests, most of them Newport snobs. Joe Tucci was coming as well. I liked that guy. We always had a drink together and talked golf. He thought Luke was a prick, too, but that was true of anyone who knew him. I had hired a bartender and two girls from the club to be servers. The girls were two French interns and hot. I ended up throwing a few shots into one of them. She was cool. I love that French accent, so sexy, and man, do they like to fuck.

Fred was still with me, as they were just getting back from Vail. They called me on the cell and asked me to put Fred on the phone. I thought, *You've got to be shitting me*, but he heard their voices and started to bark and kind of smiled. I almost shit myself. I got back on, and we were all laughing. They said, "We miss the little guy."

I said, "I know. He is a cool little guy, and I like him, too."

David said, "Are we all good?"

"Yes," I said, "but Luke is still getting on my nerves. I would have quit months ago if I were working for different owners. I like you guys and don't want to ruin your summer, but I am sure I will not do this next summer unless you have a different captain and crew. The kid is a liability, and Luke is just not a nice guy, and he busts my balls all the time. I've wanted to quit a few times already."

"Thank you," he said, "and hang in there. I will have a talk with Luke."

"Please mention the food bills. He says I am spending too much and questions everything I buy. You told me you only want the best. I buy only organic produce and the freshest fish I can get. He doesn't get this."

"When this next trip is over, I will have a word with him. Hang in there. We are very happy with you, and don't change anything. Whatever you are buying, keep it up. We don't care about the budget. We want all fresh and organic, like we asked you in the beginning."

"Thanks. See you soon. And Fred is in good hands."

We both laughed and said goodbye.

They showed up in a few days with the first guests, a really nice couple and low maintenance. I did some really nice seafood dinners and great breakfasts as well. They went out a few nights and treated us very nicely.

The big party on the boat would be the highlight of the season, with VIP guests, and of course, Martina Hingis and Stan stayed on the boat as well.

The day finally arrived, and we had all been busting our asses. I went out and got a fresh haircut as well. I found a great little salon on a side street, and she took walk-ins. She gave me a great haircut. She was this hot little Asian mess, mid to late thirties. We made some small talk, and I asked her if there was a golf course around. She said there was and asked if she could join me.

I said, "You're a golfer?"

"Yeah."

"Cool. Make a tee time for next week, and we will play. I will pick you up here."

"I would like that."

"Great. It is done. Thanks for the haircut, and I will call you Sunday to confirm. See you Monday."

What a great day. I got all my shit looking good and a golf date for next week with a hot little hairdresser. Man, I love Newport.

The guests arrived, including Stan, Martina, and her mother. Stan Smith, what a tennis legend and a really nice guy as well. He still looked great, though he was no spring chicken. Martina and her mom were both nice as well. She was a big girl, very athletic looking, and very humble. This was her big day. She would be inducted into the Tennis Hall of Fame, and then a party would be thrown in her honor on a big yacht. That's a great day in anyone's book.

After the ceremony, they all returned to the boat, and we went for a harbor cruise. Then the party started, with lots of champagne, finger foods, shrimp, sushi, crab, caviar. You name it, we had it. I held nothing back. This was one hell of a raw bar, and the guests were impressed. David was in a great mood, and Stan and Martina told me thanks many times as well. David said, "Not bad, Chef. What you got next?" And laughed. I think I spent around five grand on the bar and champagne. That's one of the things I liked about David: he only wanted the best and never asked what it cost. He did not care. I am the same way; I just have a smaller budget.

The next morning, the guests had one more great breakfast of eggs and crab Benedict with asparagus and roasted potatoes, always a smash. I even fed Luke, but he never said thanks. The guests had a great brunch, and we then carried their bags off and said goodbye. After they were gone, David said they were going out for dinner, and he told us to take the night off. He also told Luke to take us to dinner, adding, "Yes, Chef Al can have wine with his dinner. Don't worry about the cost."

Luke hated that; he thought he was the only one entitled to that perk. I said, "Luke, let's go to the raw bar. It's a great spot. He agreed, which

I could not believe. Dinner was great, and he was not in one of his bad moods, so we had a nice evening.

The next day, the boss surprised us all. He invited all to the tennis club for the finals of the doubles championship, box seats, just like the baseball game, only really private. It was the same setup: free food and booze, and we got to meet all the players. Martina and Stan were there, too. It was a special day that showed David's class. That's why I call him the prince. We spent the whole day there, and he said we could come back any day next week and get a free tour. "Just say you're my guests, have lunch at the club, and spend the day here. There is a lot to see." I took him up on it, but Luke and the kid were not into tennis.

Then David said, "Let's plan a crew party before I head back to Boston next week." Luke's wife and kids were in town.

I said, "Great. I will do all the cooking."

Then he said, "Alan, bring the hairdresser you are playing golf with."

I picked Sue up, and we had a great day playing golf and lunch at the club. Then I dropped her off at her place. She invited me in for a beer, and the next thing you know, we were doing the wild thing. She was great in the sack. Her body was made for it, hard and tight, like my dick. We had a great time, and she said she would love to come on the boat for the party. Chicks never say no to a date on a yacht—at least, I was never told no. I made sliders, my famous mac and cheese, salsa, guac, chips, grilled dogs, and crab and artichoke dip. It was a nice spread, and everyone had a great time, even Luke. I think that was a first, but of course, his wife and kids were there, so he had to behave. The boss was in a great mood and was still on a high about the party I'd pulled off. I always make the boss look good. That's my job, and even today, I still love what I do, and I just keep getting better. I am always changing it up and still cook healthy and clean, but with a few new twists.

Sue loved my food as well, and I had an even better evening with her once we got back to her place. We went half the night, and she was a marathon girl. I came three times, but that's counting in the morning when I rolled her over one last time. We were leaving the next day, and I probably would not see her again, and she knew that, but it never came up. She just said she had a great time and to call her if I was back in town or send her an email and invite her to Florida sometime. She owned the shop, so she could take off whenever she wanted and would love to come down and play some golf.

"Cool," I said. I had a great time as well."

I returned to the boat to serve breakfast to the boss and crew and get ready, as we had lots of work to do before we left. David was having coffee on the top deck, and he saw me walking up the dock. He smiled and said, "Good morning."

I said, "Yes, it is a great morning."

I love morning sex. Getting laid first thing in the morning is the best. It just starts the day off on a great note. If a chick doesn't want to fuck in the morning, I get rid of her right away, end of story.

I fixed breakfast for the whole boat. David said, "No lunch today. We are driving back to Boston and trying to beat traffic. Can we please have Fred back?"

I laughed and said, "Yes, but just for a few days." The dog and I were now best pals.

"I will see you next weekend," he said. "Let's go to the Vineyards one last time for the summer before the boat heads back to Florida."

After Luke and the kid left on the boat back to Hyannis, I took one last walk on the Million Mile Trail and had lunch one last time at the Landing. Sue joined me, and we had a nice lunch and said goodbye I was hoping to fuck her one last time, but she said she was sorry and booked solid all afternoon, but she really wished she could. She loved to fuck as much as I did.

I got a text from David saying he'd had a talk with Luke, and he told me to let him know if I had any more problems with him. That was cool. He wanted all of us to get along and did not want to hire a new crew, but I still knew I would not be back next season unless Luke were gone.

I took the long way back to Hyannis. They were still not at the dock when I got back, so I headed over to Trader Ed's to see the gang and have a few beers. They rolled up a few hours later, and I headed to the dock to help with the lines and get them tied up.

Not even five minutes after the boat was tied up, Luke said he was pissed at me. "Who do you think you are, going behind my back and talking to the boss? You have no right to do that, and we have to have a talk tomorrow and see if you are going to stay on the boat the rest of the season."

I said, "Fine. I don't care if I leave today. I have had enough of your shit."

He backed right down. He knew the boss was coming this weekend and we were going to the Vineyard one last time, so he really didn't want me to walk off. I would have, too, if not for the boss being the guy he was. He did not deserve to have this trip ruined. Luke said, "Fine. I want to go to the store with you and then to the cleaners to see what you are dropping off and what food you are buying."

I said, "Sure, do whatever you want." This was a first. He had nothing better to do and just liked to fuck with the crew. That's why the guy had no friends.

The next morning, as I was stripping the sheets to take them to the cleaners, he asked me what I was doing. I'd been doing this all season. I said, "They're going to the cleaners to get cleaned and pressed."

He said, "Just wash them."

"These sheets are not cheap. I don't know what you have in your house, but these sheets won't get clean in the small washer on the boat, and the wife likes them pressed. Do you have any other questions?"

"I always just wash them and just put them back on."

"Yeah, that's the difference between Motel 6 and the Ritz, and again, it's what the wife wants. Call her and ask her. Just leave the cooking and the inside of the boat to me."

He snarled and said, "Ok, but I still want to go to the store and see what you are picking up at the cleaners."

"Fine. We are leaving in a few."

The first stop was the dry cleaners. I picked some sheets up and a few of my chef coats. He almost shit. "What are you doing, getting your personal things cleaned?"

I said, "These are my work coats, and furthermore, it's part of my deal with David. He pays for them. What is your problem?"

This was Luke's first big job, and he had never had a full-time chef and crew or been on a real yacht before, so he did not have a clue. I said, "Call David, and if you still want to keep fucking with me, fine. I quit. Go find some other chef to kiss your ass. I've forgotten more than you know about yachting." I thought we would go at it, but he calmed down and maybe thought about what David told him about me: don't rock the boat, asshole.

We headed to the market, and what a fuck story that was. This guy had no clue about food or anything involving style or first-class service. He questioned everything I bought. I picked up some Vermont maple syrup, organic. It was around twenty dollars. He told me to buy Log Cabin, which he used at home. I looked at him and said, "This is not your home, and you are not the chef."

The next stop was the fish market, and it was the same shit: "Why don't you buy this?" And "Man, that tuna costs a lot." This went on all morning until we got back to the boat.

I told him, "That's it. I quit, and I am calling David and telling him what an asshole you are." He went crazy. He had a rage issue, and on top of that, he was a control freak.

I called David and said, "I am quitting. Sorry. I just cannot deal with Luke one more day." I told David the dry-cleaning story and about the two markets and the fish prices. I said, "What is up with this guy? He has issues and has to be in control of everything."

Now, David was a nice guy, but he had no spine, and he could not admit that he'd hired the wrong guy. Some of these guys are like that. They don't want to admit they made a mistake. Any other owner would have fired all of us, even me. Luke hired me, so fire the whole lot and start fresh. But not David. I knew he would not fire Luke unless he did something really crazy, and while Luke was stupid, he was not that stupid.

David said," I will call Luke and then call you back in a few." Here was the CFO of a big company; he didn't need this shit. I would have fired the whole crew, starting with Luke. I guess he called Luke and said, "Leave me alone until this trip is over this weekend. Then we will all sit down and talk." Luke was in tears. He wanted me gone that day, but he had no choice. He did not like that I was talking to the boss.

David called me the next morning and asked me to please stay and do the weekend trip. He was bringing guests, and it was only three days. I say, "Ok, but only for you. Luke has to go, or I am done after this next weekend. I cannot work with this guy anymore."

David and his guests arrived, and I did my best to keep them all happy. This was going to be a short trip of just three days. I was glad to see the Vineyard one more time. It's a great place in the summer months. David, the wife, and I had a short meeting. They were sad to see me go, but they understood. They knew Luke was a prick, but they didn't want to rock the boat.

He told me he would buy my airfare to Palm Beach and pay me until the end of the month. That was nice, first class. When you quit a boat job, you are required to take care of your own travel expenses. I guess David told Luke this, and Luke said to me, "You're lucky he is paying for that. I would have told him no."

I said, "Yeah, but your not so good. Bye and good riddance."

The next few days flew by, David, his wife, and their guests had a great time. David and I had a few chats, and I told him he was one of the best guys I'd ever worked with and I would miss him and was truly sorry it hadn't worked out. He agreed, and we had a martini together.

We went back to the boat, and Luke had to book my flight on the boat credit card, so he asked me what day I wanted to leave. I said, "A week from today."

He said, "You cannot stay on the boat."

"I know. I am staying in the guest room above Trader Ed's and then going to Vermont to see some old friends. I need a little vacation."

He did not like the idea. He would have to see me around the marina for a few more days. Fuck him, Loser Luke, the worst captain I ever worked with.

I had a great time doing the cape, and when I flew home, I was happy that I would never have to deal with Luke again.

Wayne Newton

Linda and David Foster

Emilia Crow

chapter 23

BOBBY AND JO JO JULIEN

JO JO CIRCUS

I WAS STILL IN THE cape, just hanging out with the guys at Trader Ed's. It drove Luke crazy to see me hanging out at the dock with all the guys and a bunch of hot chicks. I still had a week until my flight. I was only a half a day's drive from Stowe, and I had not been back in twenty years, so I thought: road trip. I called Haabs to see if he was in town and told him I was on my way and would see him for dinner that night.

He almost shit. "I heard you got shot by some jealous husband."

I said, "No, but I came close a few times." We laughed, and I said, "See you tonight."

That's a great drive once you get out of the city and head north. Finally, I rolled into the Sunset Grill. To my surprise, Haabs had gotten ahold of some of the old gang, and they were waiting for me: Pat, the Snake, Persiaco; Wilbur, the old bartender from the Stoweflake; Tommy from the Rusty Nail; and Ernie and Loreta from the Stoweflake.

Man, what a great time we had. Haabs cooked a great steak dinner for all of us, and we laughed all night. What great friends. They are some really special folks. I hung out for a few days and met all of Haabs's kids, three girls, all raised, and I guess some great soccer and lacrosse players.

I went over to the Stoweflake and saw Chuck, Stew, Marion, the whole gang. Chuck bought me a drink, and it was great to see all of them. I had some great times in this town and will never forget all the special friends I have there. Then I saw Chris at Pickwick's Pub, though I did not tell him I fucked his old lady that summer. We had a few drinks and talked about the old days. The years I spent as a ski bum were some of the best of my life. Love all of you guys, and I promise to get back, hopefully, for a book signing in Burlington someday, and it won't be twenty years until the next time I return. All the best to you guys, and yes, Haabs, to you, too.

I returned to the cape a day before my flight and said goodbye to the gang at Trader Ed's. They had a little send-off for me, and the next day, I was on a bus to the airport, bound for Lauderdale. When I got home, the place was just as I'd left it. It just needed a good cleaning. I chilled for a few days before calling the Colonel. Lauderdale is an easy town to get off track. People get drunk and party like they're on vacation every day. That's not my deal.

I met up with the Colonel a few days later. We had dinner and some drinks and caught up. I told him about my summer in the cape and going up to Stowe. He told me he had been well and bought a place in the DR, Punta Cana, right on the water, a nice little villa. He said, "You have to come down sometime."

"Great. I will."

"What's the next move for you, Chef?"

I told him I would take a few weeks off and get back on a yacht. I was going to try one more boat job. It's not easy. Most captains are assholes, and the crew members are young and fucked up. Plus, I was getting too old to put up with their crying and entitlement.

We had a few more drinks and called it a night. He picked up the tab. That was a first. The Colonel is cool, but he's a cheap millionaire. Fuck, I guess that's why these guys have money: they don't spend it, and they fuck everybody they can.

A week passed, and I was starting to plan my next move. Then I got a call from Darren, my realtor friend in Boynton Beach, a good old boy from North Carolina. I'd bought a rental from him. He asked me what I had been up to and if I was looking for work. I said I was, and he told me about his neighbor, a captain, who was looking for a chef. The boat would be spending the winter in the Bahamas, a 110-foot Westport, all-guy crew, no charters, only the family on board. He asked if I was interested, and I said I was. He said, "The captain will call you in a few days and wants to meet you."

A few days passed, and I got the call from the captain. We talked a bit, and he said, "Can you come up to Palm Beach tomorrow and meet me and the crew?"

"Sure," I said.

"The boat is at the Sailfish Marina. Do you know the spot?"

"Yes."

"Does noon work?"

"Sure. See you tomorrow."

"The boat is called *Jo Jo Circus*."

I said, "What the hell kind of name is that?"

He laughed said, "I will fill you in tomorrow."

"Ok. See you at noon."

I called Darren back and told him thanks and that I was meeting the captain tomorrow. He said, "Good luck. The job is yours if you want it. I got a call from the captain, and he said he liked what he heard on the phone. He went to my website and saw your CV and references and was impressed. He's already sent a copy of your CV to the owners."

If I got along with the crew, I would go meet the owners. I pulled into the Sailfish. It was a nice little marina with a restaurant and tiki bar, a cool little spot. I had been there before. I arrived on time, and the captain, Paul, was waiting for me. He introduced me to the crew, and then we sat in the galley and got down to business. Paul turned out to be one of the better captains I worked for. He was not a bad guy, a little weird, but we all are in our own way.

We had a long talk. He said, "The boat is leaving in a month and will be gone five months. I have to go meet the wife, but I am sure she will give me the go-ahead. She has already checked you out. She just wants to see if you can get along with them and the kids, three boys. She likes that you cook healthy and clean."

Next he told me about the trip. "We are doing all the Bahamas. The family will come once a month for five to six days, and then we will move the boat to the next island. Bobby has his own plane, which they will be flying in and out on, a nice Hawker. We'll start in Harbor Island and work our way south. The trip will finish in Nassau, and we will be there for a week with the whole family. Jo Jo will have her sister come one trip, and Bobby, who owns Culture Homes, is going to have eight of his top dogs on for a fishing trip."

I told him that I had been to quite a few of the islands, so it would be cool to go see some new places. We did not talk about food too much. He asked how I was with the lines and cleaning the interior, and I said I was cool with all that. Then he asked the crew to come back. Bo, the first mate, was a really nice guy from Jupiter, and Jared was from Daytona, a young kid, like nineteen. He couldn't even drink yet, but he was a real hard worker and a gentleman.

We talked about the trip. Bo ran the 57 Hatteras GT, the fishing boat, and Jared and I would handle the Westport. "Cool!" I said. "It's pretty nice when you've got a 110-foot Westport and your fishing boat is a Hatteras GT. That's bad-ass." We chatted for a while, just bullshitting, and then they headed back outside to finish up for the day. Paul told me to call Jo Jo tonight. She wanted to see me at the house tomorrow in Del Rey. After I finished up, I needed to meet him back at the boat to talk about the starting date and get some uniforms, that sort of stuff. He said, "I will tell you more about the trip then, but it will be a great five months, and you will see all of the Bahamas." I was down for that.

I called Jo Jo when I got back home, and she said, "Come by the house tomorrow around eleven," and gave me the address and gate code. I did some research on them that evening. It turned out that he was one of the richest guys in Canada and owned Culture Homes, and Jo Jo was some hot-shit doctor, a pulmonologist, whatever the fuck that is. They had three boys and were Canadian. That wasn't a good thing. I remembered the Schlegels in Dallas: cheap assholes, the whole lot. What the hell. It was a six-month gig, I would be in the Bahamas most of the time, and they would only be on the boat once a month. How bad could it be? I would find out later just how bad.

I went to the house and buzzed her at the gate just to let her know I was coming in. I have to give them credit—they had one hell of a nice place, right on the ocean, beautiful grounds, Mediterranean style, with killer landscaping. It was worth maybe twenty million or so. Not bad. The housekeepers let me in, and Jo Jo was in the kitchen, having a cup of coffee. She asked me to join her, and I said, "Of course. Thank you, ma'am."

We got right into the food, and she had a million questions. I just sat and listened until she quit running her mouth. She loved to hear herself talk. Finally, she shut up, thank God. I just smiled and said, "I can do all that. I cook very cleanly and simply, all organic when I can. I am very clean and organized and can do dinner parties at the house as well." I told her some of the dishes that most people liked.

We chatted a little more, and she asked me if I could start tomorrow night at the house. I said, "Yes, that would be fine."

She said, "Why don't you take Monday and Tuesday off, go to the boat on Wednesday and Thursday, and work at the house the rest of the week. I will pay you six thousand dollars a month and a bonus at the end of the trip. How does that sound?"

"Very fair, and I would like to come on board. Everything sounds fine."

"Great. I will see you tomorrow. See Paul, and he will get you a credit card. We would love fish tomorrow night with some of your grilled veggies and a nice salad."

"Good day, ma'am. It was a pleasure, and I will see you tomorrow."

That was it. I was hired on the spot again. On to the next adventure. I had no idea at the time how nasty she could be or how cheap they were, and their boys were just fucking heathens.

The next day, I called Paul and said, "She hired me, and we are all good to go. I was supposed to get a credit card from you."

He said, "Come by the boat after lunch. We will talk, and I will give you a credit card."

I rolled onto the boat that afternoon, and the crew was in the galley, having a beer. I joined in, and Paul told the guys, "Chef Al is on board. Let's have a beer and a toast."

I said, "I am happy to be on board and look forward to a fun season. I will only be on the boat for a few days, as Jo Jo wants me to cook at the house a few nights till we leave for the Bahamas."

They were all cool with that. Paul had had a feeling that she would do this. We bullshitted for a little while, had one more beer, and called it a night. This was a cool crew, and I knew we would have a good time on the trip.

Now, back to the family. Let's get them out of the way first.

There were three kids, all boys, around the ages of six, eight, and ten. These kids were just plain rotten, like apples on a tree. It was not their fault. Jo Jo was never around, and Bobby was never home, so they did whatever they wanted. Let's start with the youngest, Charlie. He was six, but he was still wearing pull-ups and pissing the bed. The next oldest was even worse off. He, too, was still pissing the bed at eight. On top of that, he still slept with a stuffed lamb doll and carried it everywhere, and he still sucked his thumb. The oldest was just like his dad, Mr. Know-It-All and a big pussy. What a shitty lot of kids.

Really, it wasn't their fault. When the parents don't care what the kids do and are not around to discipline them and you've got some nanny from some third-world country raising the shitheads, what do you expect? The housekeepers and nannies hated Jo Jo with a passion, but they were getting paid well and not legal, so they had to put up with her and the kids no matter how bad it got. I felt bad for the girls. They were nice, and we got along great. I just felt so bad for them. They would tell me stories that you would not believe. I will just share one with you, and you can imagine the others.

I guess the middle one was about five or six, and he broke his arm doing something stupid, as you would expect. It was a day before they were supposed to leave for Vail, and all Jo Jo did was complain about how he had ruined their ski trip. She made him stay home with the nanny while the rest of them went skiing. She only cared about herself, and from what the nanny told me, she hated the boys and did not want kids, but Bobby did, and he had all the money. She was worried about messing her body up. To me, it was nothing to speak of; she had no tits or ass.

Poor Bobby. The only sex he got was military. If you don't know what military sex is, I will clue you in. It's when some chick who thinks she is hot and that it's all about her tells you how to fuck: "Stop. Too fast. Now too slow. Hurry up. Now to the left. I meant to the right. Now faster. Stop. You get on top. Now I will stay on top." You get the picture.

One night at dinner, I was serving steak and mashed potatoes, four-ounce portions. He asked me for seconds, and I said, "Fine."

Jo Jo looked at him and said he'd had plenty and should have some more salad. This bitch was like a cow. She'd just graze all day on greens, no protein, starches, or carbs. Skinny as shit and white as a ghost. If she went outside in the sun, it was like she was dressed for the tundra: long-sleeved shirt, leggings, socks up to her ass, hat.

One night, Bobby was late for dinner. The poor guy was truly busting his ass. I served the old lady and the three fucking shitheads, and then I told Jo Jo I would make Bobby a plate and put it in the warmer. She said, "Just make the plate and leave it on the counter. For making me wait, he gets a cold dinner."

I just about shit. If she were my wife, I would have bitch-slapped her and then told her to pack her fucking bags and get the fuck out of my house. Bobby, you are a nice guy but one big pussy. Grow some balls. That pretty much sums up the family. I only met two members of her family. The gay brother, a real pain in the balls, lived in Del Rey, and the sister was just like Jo Jo. They were cheap fucks, too.

I only did one dinner party at the house. No one of interest was invited, but the dinner was pretty damn funny, and the bar story, too. She wanted to serve a watermelon salad, petit filet potatoes, asparagus, and, for dessert, fresh fruit and sorbet. They had no wine to speak of and nothing to offer the guests in the way of a drink.

The guests arrived, and Jo Jo did not have a clue. She was some sort of doctor, a pulmonologist, I think. She did not seem too sharp to me. She had no common sense at all, that's for sure.

The guests arrived, and all we had was some cheap red and white wine. Jo Jo asked the husband of one of her friends, "Would you like a drink?"

He said, "Yes, what do you have?"

"Oh, we have everything. What would you like?"

"Jack on the rocks."

You'd have thought he was speaking German. She had no clue what that was. She came to me in the kitchen and asked, "Alan, what is Jack, and do we have some?"

I looked, but there was nothing in the cupboard except some Coors Light. I told her no, and she got all huffy and went back to the guy and said, "No, we are out. What else would you like?"

"Any type of bourbon would be fine."

At this point, Bobby walked in and took over the bartending. The guests had now all arrived, and they were by the bar. Bobby tried to get them drinks, but all they had was rum, gin, some old cherry brandy, a few mixers, and that was it. So, it was rum and Cokes all around.

Bobby was at a loss for words. He said that they didn't drink and didn't keep alcohol in the house—yeah, because he was too fucking cheap. I could tell he was embarrassed, as well he should be. Don't offer guest drinks when you don't have shit. On top of that, don't serve cheap wine when you have shitloads of cash. I could tell the guests were not impressed. All the guys got their rum and Cokes and seemed happy, but the women never finished their glasses of wine. I don't blame them. It was shit.

Dinner was a joke. She wanted four-ounce filets, four spears of asparagus, and kid-size portions of pomme frites and watermelon salad. Dessert was just fresh fruit with sorbet, and I made some sabayon sauce to kick it up a notch. He did not have two bottles of the same red wine to serve, and what he had was pretty lame. It was the worst dinner party I ever did. I was so embarrassed. The guys went away hungry, and there was no after-dinner drink, which just shows that you can have all the money in the world but still have no class and be a terrible host, and Jo Jo was the worst I've ever seen. You can dress them up but you cannot take them out.

This was the first and last dinner party at the house, thank God. They had no clue how to pull off a dinner party. The next day, Jo Jo came to me with her tail between her legs and asked if I could set up a bar for them and pick out some wines for the house, three or four cases, and after-dinner liqueurs. I said, "Sure. It's going to be about a grand."

She almost shit. She said, "Are you sure?"

I rattled off a few prices, and she said, "Ok, just don't tell Bobby."

Man, these were some cheap fucks, some of the worst I ever worked for.

This was my last week at the house. We were getting ready to take the boast to the Bahamas and start the summer trip, and I had to start provisioning for the crew and guests. That was going to take me a few days, as we would be gone quite a few months. It would be nice to get out of the house. We took on fuel and waited on a weather window to take off. Our first stop was Harbor Island.

Finally, we were ready to cast off and start the trip. We headed out at dusk to get us in by the next morning so we would have light when we arrived. We would need a pilot to lead us in, as it's pretty shallow and tricky, but the locals have it down.

Like I said before, there were no celebrities on this trip, only a few more good stories about how fucked up the Juliens were and how Bobby stiffed one of the marinas we were at. We docked at Harbor Island the next day and had a week until the first visit. The first day, we washed the boat down, and then I went to get some local fish and fresh conch for the crew and get the lay of the land. I had been there several times and was familiar with the two markets, the bakery, and where to buy fresh conch.

We picked up a golf cart and were dialed in. I got some beer for the crew, and we had some fresh conch and snapper for dinner. The guys were in heaven. They'd never had a chef on the boat before. Bobby was too cheap to hire one.

Harbor Island is small, but it has two nice marinas and a few restaurants. They're overpriced and not great. It's the Bahamas; they can't cook worth a shit. Fried fish and conch, and that's it. But there are a few nice hotels, like the Pink Sands, and a few nice bars to have some rum. But after a few days, it gets old, and the diving is not great—there are lots of sharks.

The family came the next week—nothing exciting. The kids trashed the boat and tore up the jet skis. They were just little rotten bastards. Thank God they went out one night, and I got a break. I needed some Jack to calm my nerves. We were so busy with the family and the kids that, before we knew it, it was time for them to leave, and the first trip was in the bag. Paul and the mate took the family on the tender over to Staniel Cay to fly out on Bobby's private plan.

That night, I grilled up some local lobsters and made conch ceviche and mashed garlic potatoes served with lots of cold beer. It was a nice dinner, and we were all glad that they were gone. It's sad to work for someone when you hate it when they come and are glad when they leave. We had three weeks to move the boat to the next stop, so we took on some fuel and took a week off.

We had a lot of laughs at dinner that night. One thing about an all-guy crew is that there is no drama on the boat, no bimbo having her period who doesn't want to work or is in a shit mood. Guys are always cool, and we had a good crew. I miss those guys and will never forget Bo, Paul, and Jared. Red, the stew, was cool, too, even if Jared did give her a mercy fucking because I could not do it, I turned her down—all those tats she had were, let's just say, a little out there.

We were getting close to the halfway point, and now we would make a trip to Long Island. It's far to the south, and they had just built a new marina. There is also an airport to fly into and a few restaurants and resorts. Jo Jo's sister came on this trip. Two peas in a pod, both with no tits and bitchy on top of that. They headed to the beach wearing long-sleeved shirts, big-ass hats, big shorts, and long stockings, afraid of getting a little sun. They were both white as ghosts. What a trip. I only met her once, and I feel sorry for her husband—oh, that's right, she was divorced. Smart guy. Kicked her dumb ass to the curb. Bobby should grow some balls and kick Jo Jo's ass down the road, too, but he is a big pussy, afraid of losing a few million. That would be getting off cheap. What a nag.

It's a hike down to Long Island, but it was worth the trip, and they wanted to see the Blue Hole and hang out there for a week. The next and last stop would be Atlantis Paradise Island. That's a cool spot. We pulled into Long Beach, which had a brand-new clubhouse. There were a few too many sharks in the basin, big bull sharks, so I did not go diving that trip. Instead, I got the boat cleaned up and stocked, planned the menu, and then went to see the Blue Hole and the rest of the island. Oh, and I drank some beer, too.

The Bahamas are nice, but in the summer, they're just like South Florida: hot and hotter. I won't forget the Rowdy brothers. These guys looked like they could play rugby and were three hundred pounds each. The day we rolled into their bar, they were cooking a pig. We were the only yacht in the marina, and when you're on a 110-foot yacht, people take notice. The moment we walked in with crew shirts on, we were treated like family by the brothers. We could not buy a drink, and once they found out I was the chef, I had to cook dinner for them one night. The pig was great, and with the free beer and rum, man, did we get hammered. It was our new hangout for the next few weeks. What great hosts. If you're on the island, it's a must.

The only bad part was, earlier that day, I'd picked up some young island girl at the beach and banged her in a little hut. I'd told her I would come by and pick her up later and take her to dinner, but really, all I wanted was to get a piece of ass. It'd been a while, and she was young and had a great body, just a little too dark for my liking. So, I walked her back to her house after I did my job and said, "See you in a few hours," but that was all bullshit. The crew and I had had plans to go out. To make a long story short, as you can imagine, I blew her off. Well, she showed up at the restaurant and got right in my shit. Thank God for the brothers and that we were now friends. They told her to leave and not come back.

When she was gone, the crew and the brothers all started giving me shit: "What happened?" And "What did you promise her?" and "What the hell happened?" I 'fessed up and told everyone I had banged her in a hut down on the beach and had told her I would take her to dinner tonight. They all just started laughing and giving me shit. "You crazy white boy.

Now we really like you. We like the way you roll. More beer and one more round of rum for our new friends and one fucking crazy chef. You guys are welcome here anytime."

The next morning was rough, and the captain gave us all the day off. We needed it. We'd all had far too much rum. The captain was not in good shape, either. That was the highlight of that trip. We hung out at the bar every night until the family came.

I never saw the chick again. Jo Jo and the band of heathens showed up a few days later, and Bobby took the tender for a few days and went fishing, but he didn't catch shit. They spent one day at the Blue Hole and one day at a small resort with the kids, and I cooked for most of the trip. Nothing really exciting, just the same shit, with the kids tearing the boat up and just being shitheads. I won't forget how the youngest one, Charlie, took maple syrup and rubbed it on the galley sofa.

Captain Paul said, "What are you doing?"

Charlie said, "I make a mess, and you clean it up."

What a little piece of shit.

The next thing you know, they were off the boat, and we were on our way back to Nassau. Before leaving, we spent one more night with the Rowdy brothers. It was a great night, and they gave us one hell of a send-off. Love those guys. All they could talk about was the shrimp scampi I made for them. Man, that sauce was the best I ever had. That made the whole trip special. We all said our goodbyes and cast off like sailors.

Then we were off to the next port. Next stop, Atlantis.

When we got there, we would have a few weeks to get the boat cleaned and for me to get provisions and take some time off to enjoy the island. I just love Atlantis. The trip from Long Island was nice, and we arrived at what has to be one of the coolest marinas in the world—all megayachts from around the world. It was pretty bad-ass.

There was nothing exciting about this trip. It was just the family. They went to the aquarium and the beach every day and had dinner out a few nights. Like I said, nothing exciting, but I did pick up some little hottie off the yacht *Wheels Up*, a little Eastern European. We had a nice roll in the sack. That was the best part of the trip. We went fishing, did a few day trips on the tender, had some fun, and went to the casino. You know, just hanging out on a yacht in the Bahamas is not a bad life. We took the kids to Pig Island to feed the pigs—too bad the pigs did not eat the little turds. It would have done the world a lot of good. That was kind of it for the last family trip, nothing too exciting.

When the trip was over, we would head back to Harbor Island. A stew we had hired flew in to join us. Bobby wanted a female to serve drinks, wait on his guests, and clean and make the beds. Jo Jo was not crazy about this. I was surprised that she let him hire her. She was so jealous and insecure of herself. No wonder. Grow some tits and don't be such a bitch.

The last day arrived, and we could not wait to get rid of these worthless owners, mainly the kids and Jo Jo. Bobby was ok sometimes, but he was still a big pussy and a spoiled little rich prick who never had to work. Plus, he was one cheap fuck and never tipped. He only paid what he thought was fair when he got a bill for something. Bo sold the tender when we got back, full price, like $250,000, and Bobby never gave him a dime. That was cheap. Shame on you, Bobby Julien. You are one cheap fuck. Go back to Canada. French Canadians are the worst.

We had some time off, and it was well deserved. We had ten days until Bobby and his crew showed up, plenty of time to get back to Harbor Island and get the boat ready, plus now I had Red to help with the inside, so that was kind of nice.

We went fishing a few times and did some diving while waiting for the guys to show up. This would be an all-guys trip, with Bobby and around eight of his top guys. Most of these guys ended up being pretty nice, and for once, Bobby was not half bad—I am sure because Jo Jo was not around to tell him what to do. When they arrived, we had the boat ready. It was the first time I'd seen Bobby relaxed and having more than one beer. They were going to be there five days and would fish every day.

They ended up catching lots of mahi-mahi. I made great fish tacos a few times, with mango salsa and my favorite cracked conch. The guys loved it. I did a nice filet one night, with mashed potatoes and all the sides. It was the first time that Bobby was allowed to have seconds and more than a little four-ounce piece of meat. This was the best trip of the summer. All the guests were really nice; even Bobby's top dog, Bill Johnson, an American and a really cool guy. Plus, I had help. Red was not much to look at. She had nice tits and an ok body, but she was a great stew with a good sense of humor. That's why Jo Jo had picked her; she did not want someone better looking than her on the boat, but you really did not have to look too hard to find someone like that.

I won't forget the day I had the final say on Red's interview. We were talking about food, and I was laying down the rules, and I said, "You have nothing to worry about with Jo Jo. She hired you because you're not hot." Paul almost burst out laughing. I said it again: "You're not too hot, so you will be fine. That's why she hired you."

Paul told the rest of the gang, and they all thought it was cool. "Chef, you are too crazy." It was our in-joke for the rest of the trip. We would be having a beer or just hanging out, and someone would say, "Hey, Chef, don't worry. You know, you're not too hot looking."

She was a good worker. I have to say that I still can't believe Jared banged her with all those tats over her back. Jared said that when he got her from behind, all he could see was ink, but he just closed his eyes, took one for the team, and pounded away at her ass. The guys all liked her. She served drinks and had a great sense of humor.

The guys had a great time. We took them on a few day trips, and I made some great dinners. Bobby was really happy, and the guys gave us a tip, the first of the whole trip. Bobby still did not throw us a bone, but the rest of the guests did. They knew the boss was one cheap fuck.

Afterward, Bobby added one last trip with the family. One of his friends had bought a place on Baker's Bay Island, a high-end resort island with a private golf course. He was thinking of buying a lot and building on it, and he wanted the family to see it first-hand. The island had a brand-new marina as well. The trip would only be five days. I had heard about the golf course, so I was keen to go. The rest of the crew was tired and wanted to get home. Red was cool, as she would get paid for a few more weeks.

I made one hell of a send-off dinner for the guys the last night before they left, my version of a Spanish paella with all the local seafood and the fish the guys had caught. It was a big hit; even Bobby was impressed. The guys got a little buzzed that night and were all hitting on Red, even Bill, the CEO.

They were all leaving early the next morning on two separate planes. I made my famous breakfast burritos for the road for the guys. They were all hungover but said thanks and that they'd had a great time. Then they were on the tender and on their way to Staniel Cay.

Bobby told Paul, "Go ahead and let Red go. We don't need her now that the guy trip is over."

Paul said, "We hired her for the last part of the trip. We can't just let her go without paying her for the next month. That's just not right."

Bobby said that was fine, but he let Paul know that he was unhappy about keeping her. I was impressed. Paul had stood his ground, and of course, he was right. I ask you, is that not one cheap fuck and an asshole on top of that? I would have loved to put my foot up his and that bitch Jo Jo's asses. He was worried about paying a few grand more for a stew after she'd busted her ass. I have never met a cheaper prick or more dishonest person.

The trip had been a home run. Paul was happy, too, but he didn't tell me I'd done a good job until the trip was over. That's just how captains are; they think they're the best and no one else matters. I have only met a few captains who had their shit together. Most were drunks and losers who had not saved a dime or owed the IRS shitloads.

We would wait for the family to return two weeks later, and then we would head to Baker's Bay. After a short trip there, they would fly back to Florida, and we would work our way back. The end was in sight, and I was glad. I was heading back to Spain for a few months to check on my place and enjoy some time off.

Baker's Bay is a pretty bad-ass island, and the golf course is great. It's got a nice marina, a big, colonial-style house, but it's still the Bahamas, flat and with hurricanes. The locals don't like tourists, and it isn't cheap. The water is beautiful, but the diving is not great, and it all looks the same. I'd rather stay in South Florida, with happy hour, great deals, and tons of hot pussy.

We docked at Baker's Bay, and Bobby told Paul, "Don't give them a credit card. I am going to get free docking for three days, as my friend lives here and I'm thinking of buying a lot and building on it, but you have to take a tour and sign a letter of intent." Bobby was trying to get something for free. I hate these cheap pricks.

It turned out that George Strait was having a sport fishing tournament there that week and he had a house on the island. I was up at the bar with the crew, having dinner and a beer, while Jo Jo and the family ate dinner on the patio. George Strait walked in with his fishing buddies, and everyone was trying to get a piece of him. He walked by us, and I said, "Hey, George. It's been a long time. Remember me, Chef Al?"

He was so cool. "Yeah, Jerry Weintraub's chef. I thought you would still be in LA, working for fancy celebrities."

"No, I moved to South Florida a few years ago. You look great. How have you been?"

He said, "We'll keep in touch," and he gave me his number. Then he said, "I have not had food as good as yours since I left the guest house in Malibu. Take care. I have to run. It was good to see you."

We shook hands, and I introduced him to Paul and the crew. They were just in awe, and Jo Jo could not believe it. She hated not being the center of attention.

All the guys and Bobby were like, "Chef, that's George Strait."

I said, "Yeah, I know him. I was on the set of *Pure Country* when they were filming it. He stayed at the guest house for a week or so in Malibu, and we played golf and hung out."

After that, the crew never doubted anything I said. Jo Jo was just like, "So what? Who is he, anyway?" Like, "If I don't know him, he is a nobody." What a cunt. I know it sounds bad, but I just hated that bitch. She was so nasty to everyone.

Bobby told Paul, "Chef Al is the real deal. He did work for all those guys."

Paul said, "Yeah, I told you so. Look at his website and CV. He's for real."

We finished our beers and dinner, and then George swung by on his way out and said, "Take care. See you around. It was good to see you."

We hung out for a couple of days. It's a great resort. Bobby was not even a golfer. He just wanted to see the island, stop by to see his friend, and try to get a free trip on the boat and not pay for dock rent. When we left, the dock-master came out and said to Paul, "You haven't paid us."

Bobby walked out and said, "The office is taking care of it at no charge, as I am going to buy a lot." It was just a flat-out lie.

Later, Paul got emails from the marina. I am sure they did not want him back. That was just not right. Who the fuck does Bobby think he is? He is not even American. Just go home and stay up there with the rest of the Canadian assholes.

That was the last trip. We headed back, dropped them off at Staniel Cay, turned around, and headed to South Florida. The trip had come to an end. There was only a little more drama as I tried to get my final paycheck. I knew I was not going to get a bonus or tip. I was just hoping to get my last month's pay. The only thing good was that I saved twenty grand more to throw in the pot, and we did have some good times, the crew and me, not the Julien's. Plus, I got to see damn near all the Bahamas.

We got back, and there were still a few weeks left until the end of the month. Paul asked if I would stay around two more weeks to feed the crew while we were in the yard, getting some work done. I said, "No problem, but I am not going back to the house."

He laughed and said, "Cool. Just get the galley cleaned and take the extra wine back to the house."

"Sure, I can do that."

We were not back one day, and Bobby told Paul that he was selling the boat and he needed to let the mate go on the first. I felt bad for the kid. He got no bonus and no severance. Bobby was such an asshole. Who does that to people? Jared busted his ass, taking care of those fucking little brats.

We were pulling out of the yard at Rybovich when Andy, one of the big dogs and my friend, came to the boat and said, "Paul, you got a credit card to pay the bill?"

Paul said, "I have to review it. I will get back to you in a couple of days."

I'd never heard such shit. Andy was fit to be tied. Turned out that Paul was acting on orders from Bobby. He said he would not pay for this and that and knocked off about five thousand from the bill. I would have put a lien on the cocksucker's boat. Andy just agreed, but I am sure Paul and Bobby will never be allowed back in that yard again and the word was put out that Bobby Julien doesn't pay his bills. I just wished I had told him face to face what a cheap prick he is. On top of that, the asshole fucked the guys at the marina. He'd already sold the boat, but he had a year's lease with them, and they'd given him a cut rate based on that. I heard him tell the marina manager, "Sue me. I will tie you up in court forever."

I didn't think I would get my last month's check, either. Paul said, "Don't worry. He will pay you."

I said, "Yeah, fucking right."

The next day, he said, "Jo Jo wants your address to mail the check to."

I said, "No can do. I leave for Spain next week, and I will pick up my check at Bobby's office."

"No way."

"Bullshit. I am not waiting for a check in the mail that I might never get from these assholes."

"Relax, Chef. I will take care of it."

"Ok, I will wait till tomorrow. Then I am going to his office to get it in person."

The next day at noon, there was still no word. My contract was over, and it was past the first of the month. Paul was off today, so I called Jo Jo. I was cool—I did not get nasty yet. I said, "Jo Jo, I am heading to Spain on Monday, and I need my check today. I can pick it up at Bobby's office."

She said, "He is busy, but I will see if he can get it today."

This was Friday. I said, "I have to have the check today."

"Ok, I will call Bobby and ask him to get it ready, and I will call you back in a few minutes."

An hour later, I had not heard back from her. I called her again and got no answer. A little while later, I called a second time, and I left a nice message saying I was going to Bobby's office to wait for my check. They'd had a whole week to take care of this.

Then Paul called. "What are you doing, calling Jo Jo three times and leaving demanding messages?"

I said, "They were not demanding. I just told her I needed my check today. It's Friday, and I am leaving for Spain on Monday.

Paul said, "Go to the office and see Rita, Bobby's assistant. She will have your check. And don't ever call Jo Jo again, as she is unhappy with you. I am a little upset as well."

"Upset? Fuck you. They stiffed the guys at the marina, and the Rybovitch Boatyard fired Jared the day we got back. These guys have a pattern of not paying people, and you tell me to relax and that you are upset? To hell with you. One fine captain you are. You should be looking out for your crew. I busted my ass for the last six months, no bonus, no tip, no shit. Fuck them and you, too. If you want to be a prick, that's on you, Paul."

He shouted, "I cannot give you a reference with that kind of attitude about the owners!"

"Fine. I don't need one from you or these pricks. On top of that, I will tell everyone in my circle and at other marinas that if they ever get a boat again, be very careful of them, as they don't pay their bills. And as for you, Paul, you don't take care of your crew. Furthermore, you are a prick. Goodbye and good riddance." I never saw Paul again.

I headed to the office, but Bobby would not show his face. I would have loved to give him some shit, but he was hiding in his office. I got my check from Rita. She said, "Bobby seemed upset about writing this check."

"Yeah," I said, "he hates to pay his bills." She laughed. I am sure she knew what kind of people they were. I headed straight to his bank to cash it.

What drama, trying to get paid. I knew I was going to get stiffed by these fucks. So, I cleaned out the wine cellar on the boat—only a few cases, maybe three or four, but some nice reds. I took lots of liquor, though—that was a nice bonus—all the dry goods and lots of seafood. I made a good haul. Last was the whole set of brand-new, stainless-steel, all-clad cookware. It was supposed to go back in the garage at the house. No way, I said.

On Sunday, Jo Jo called and asked where I'd put the wine and liquor.

I said, "I put the wine in the cooler and the liquor back in the bar." She had no idea what they had.

"Oh, ok, and what about the dry goods?"

I said, "Not much left. I left the rest in the fridge on the boat, and there was no seafood left in the freezer."

"Oh, I thought there would be a lot left over."

"No, that's it."

Jo Jo barked back, "Are you sure you put the wine and all the food back at the house?"

"Yes, ask the housekeepers. They saw me bringing in the waters and the sodas."

She had no clue about the cookware. It had come with the boat when they'd bought it. She started to give me a little shit about something else on the credit card receipt, a gas charge from Thursday. I said, "Yeah, I filled my SUV up. I am still using it for work."

She said, "You were not supposed to use it once we got back."

"Is there anything else you want to know about?" I said. "I don't have time for your petty shit."

She barked back again, "No one talks to me like that."

I said, "Jo Jo, I have to go. Why don't you just go fuck yourself. Goodbye," and hung up.

Two minutes later, Paul called, but I did not take it. He called five times, back to back, leaving me messages: "You have to call me. Jo Jo is very upset," and on and on. I finally called him back an hour later. I had a smile in my voice. "Paul, what's up?"

He said, "You should not have talked to Jo Jo like that. We will never hire you again or give you a reference."

I cut him off, saying, "Hey, listen. I don't need this shit. I will not listen to it from you, Jo Jo, or anyone. No one talks to me like that, not ever, so save your shit for some other poor-ass crew member, not me. I don't give one shit about a reference. Now, if you don't have anything nice to say to me, good day and have a nice life. I have to go pack for Spain, as I am spending the summer at my penthouse in Marbella. Now, do you have anything else to say before I hang up on you?"

Paul was at a loss for words. Finally, he said, "Never contact Jo Jo again, or you will be sorry."

I just hung up on him. He called back a few more times and never left a message. I never called him back, and I never saw any of them again. Jo Jo sent one hate email to me, saying she could not find the wine or some shit and was going to send me a bill. I just laughed and sent a reply to her and Paul that said: "Listen to me, you two fucks. Don't ever call or email me again. I don't care if you cannot find the wine or not. If I hear from you, I will consider it harassment and forward the email and texts to my attorney. Get a life, Jo Jo. I don't want to ever hear from you and Bobby ever again. You are nasty, cheap fucks. Go back to Canada. And Paul, don't ever contact me again."

That was it never heard back from them again. I loved that moment. I'll never forget it. Who in the hell do they think they are? They had money, but they never earned it. Bobby inherited everything.

Let's close that chapter. You guys can just go fuck yourselves.

To Alan
Arnold Schwarzenegger

Chapter 24
THE ROACHES
BLUE CREST CAPITAL

AFTER TAKING THE SUMMER OFF and just kicking back in the south of Spain, I thought I should get back to the States and check on things, maybe do a little chef work. The last job had nearly killed me. I knew I was done with yachts, and I was thinking about calling it quits in a year or so. I just need a little more cash in the bank.

When I got back to Lauderdale, nothing had changed. I called the Colonel, and we hooked up for a few drinks and dinner. We talked about my trip to Spain, and he had a new flavor of the month. He showed me a few nude pics. I mean, how many guys show you nude pics of the chicks they are banging? That's how he rolls. Finally, we said goodnight, as I had a phone interview in the morning. I'd called one of my old agents, Adrian. She ran the East Coast and was from New York.

Turned out she had a part-time job, where I would be on call for a few weekends a month and make three hundred a day. The family, a young couple, had just bought a place in Palm Beach. He was a hedge fund guy, and they wanted someone to help get the house set up, the bar, wine cellar, kitchen, that sort of thing. The first gig was five days, and three couples were coming down—no kids this time. The interview was about the first trip. If they liked me, I would be on call for weekends and holidays when they came down with guests. It sounded like a pretty cool gig. They had just bought a thirty-two-foot Hinckley, so I would be in charge of hiring a captain and getting the boat ready when they came down. The wife was supposed to call me. Jen was her name.

She called right on the button and seemed very nice on the phone. It turned out she interviewed three chiefs that morning. I was the last, and we hit it off pretty well. She'd spoken to Adrian before calling me. She said, "Adrian says everyone who has hired you on yachts and for their vacations love you and that you're very flexible and have many talents. We want to hire you for a month to help us get the new house in order and cook for us. We have a few trips lined up with guests."

I said, "Sure. I would like very much to come on board."

"Great. John and I will be down in a few days for a short trip to meet you and give you the keys to the house and a credit card."

We chatted about food, drinks, and what she liked. There was nothing crazy, no weird diets, so everything was cool. Just like always, I was back at it again. My salary was twelve hundred a week to start. I was happy with that.

I had a few days until they got into town, so I did a drive-by of the new house. It was a nice pad. They called me the next week and said, "We will meet you at the house."

The first night, we got all the small things out of the way: keys to the car, credit, card food, all that sort of stuff. I liked John from the start. He was a self-made hedge fund guy. Jen was nice, too, but I could tell from the start that she had a mean side. It wouldn't be the first time I'd worked for a bitch, but she was on her good behavior. They asked if I could drive them to dinner that night as they wanted to have a few drinks and did not want to drive. West Palm Beach cops are no joke. I said, "Sure." John was a small partner in a restaurant on the island, and he ate there on the house. It happens to be one of my favorites: Buccan. If you're on the island, it's a must.

I dropped them off, and John told me, "Go have dinner on us, and we will text you in a few hours to pick us up." Damn, I liked this guy already.

I headed over to Renato's for some pasta and a glass of wine. It's one of my other favorite places. I love to eat at the bar and people-watch. I had a few hours to kill, so one glass of wine was not going to kill me.

I picked them up a few hours later, and they said that I could stay in the guest room, as they wanted to talk more in the morning and plan dinner for the next two nights. I said, "Sure," and we said goodnight. I was in for a long day of shopping the next day, so I went right to bed.

The next morning, we got a game plan together for the next month and went over the list of things for me to do and dinner for the next few nights. I picked up some fresh mahi-mahi and made fish tacos with all the sides the first night, plus my kick-ass margaritas. They were very happy and buzzed and asked me to join them in a toast to the new house and the three of us coming together.

I spent the night in the guest room again, and the next morning, while John played golf, Jen and I went over what she wanted to get done in the next few weeks. It was pretty much the standard stuff for a new home: stock the bar, wine cellar, and kitchen and get napkins, placemats, beach towels. You get the idea. She gave me free rein. She liked a few kinds of cheese, jalapeño tequila, and a couple of white wines, but the rest she left up to me, though with some price guidelines.

It was a nice few days. John was not cheap. He paid me in cash for the first week and gave me a tip of a few hundred dollars. He said, "Always buy the best fish and best ingredients. Don't skimp. We are not on a budget."

"Yes, sir."

"Always call me John, and my wife is Jen."

I drove them to the airport, and we shook hands. Jen gave me a hug and said, "Welcome to the family."

I said, "Thanks. See you next weekend."

This was a pretty sweet gig while it lasted. If not for the eight screaming kids and one nasty wife, I would have stayed around for some time. I was happy as a pig in shit. John was a prince.

The month had three trips with guests. The first was with three couples for three nights and four days. The second was with Jen's mother, her four sisters, and her daughter. That one was five days. The last trip was just them, the oldest daughter, and the three boys.

Most of the time, I made breakfast. Then the women would go shopping on Worth Avenue, spending all their old man's hard-earned money, and they would eat out for lunch. The guys would play golf and go out for dinner one or two nights. These were all young couples, maybe late thirties to early forties, so they liked to party and drink.

For the most part, they were nice, except for one couple. Turned out that they were two of the family's better friends in Greenwich and I would see them again. The guy, Gudmundur Kjernstead—try saying that three times fast—was from Iceland, some rich kid. I guess his dad owned half the country or some shit. The son owned the Trans Atlantic shipping company. The guy was just an asshole, and his wife was no better. I mean, with a nickname like "Gummy," come on. The rest of the guests were cool. One was with Blackstone, I think. He was cool, and his wife was nice as well.

I drove them to dinner one night. They all went out dancing and drinking. I did a barbeque one lunch and an Italian dinner one night: Caesar salad, melon prosciutto, a nice pasta with a veal ragu with porta-bellas, and chocolate bark and lemon sorbet. It was a really nice dinner.

They drank a nice Antinori Super Tuscan I'd picked out, and they loved it. They had a good time and thanked me all the way to the airport. Just like after the last trip, John paid me in cash and gave me a few hundred bucks as a tip. I liked this gig. It was not bad work: four or five days on and then five days off and still get paid. How long could this last? It was kind of like too good to be true. I only had a few trips left. Then I would be on call, but I knew that when I took the job.

I had a full week until the next trip. I had to restock the bar again, plan a menu for the next trip, buy food, and do a few small things around the house.

The next trip was just the family, but not all eight kids. Oh, yeah, did I tell you? They had eight kids. She was knocked up every year they were married. Who wants eight fucking kids? On this trip, only the oldest daughter and the three older boys came along. The rest of the gang stayed at the house in Greenwich with the nannies. I was getting off easy. The week went smoothly. The oldest daughter was very nice. The boys were rotten little shits, but I only had them a few days, so I was cool. John and Jen liked me and said they wanted to talk to me on Sunday in private before they left.

After dinner on Sunday, they put a movie on for the boys, and we met in the dining room. John said, "Let's have a drink."

I said, "Sure. Goose on the rocks with a lemon."

I went to get it, and John said, "No, I got this." I was thinking: *This is a hell of a way to get fired.*

John came back with three drinks and said, "Let's have a toast to Chef for coming into our lives."

I said, "The pleasure is all mine." I own that line; I've been saying that for years.

I looked at John after I had a nice sip of the Goose and said, "What's up?"

Jen said, "Alan, we really like you and want to know if you would come back to Greenwich and work for us full time. We have a guest house for you and a car, and you will work at both houses and travel with us sometimes. We will give you the same money, but now we will pay for all your expenses, travel, and food. Nothing comes out of your pocket."

I looked at them and said. "I feel good about you guys, but I don't know if I can handle eight kids."

Jen said, "Don't worry. We have two nannies. Let's try it for a month, and if you don't like it, you can just stay in Palm Beach and cook for us there and take care of the house and the boat. But we really want you to come up and at least try it."

I pounded down my drink, looked at John, and said, "Ok."

He got up with this big grin and said, "Great. Let's have one more."

"Sure."

Jen said, "Great. Welcome aboard. This will be fun."

Somehow I knew I'd just gotten rat-fucked in the ass. Oh, what the hell. I'd give it a shot. I'd always wanted to live in Greenwich. John returned with a fresh round of drinks, and we bullshitted for a while. They told me I would love it up there.

I finished my drink and said, "I have to turn in. We leave for the airport early tomorrow."

John said, "You're right. Let's all turn in."

Jen said, "Alan, we will talk after breakfast about the next trip in two weeks."

It was her birthday, and her mother was coming with her four sisters and one of the daughters, who lived in Lauderdale. It was going to be a five-day, all-girls trip. I was up for this. After this trip, I had a week off, and then I would head up to Greenwich.

The next morning, I fed the kids, and they all got packed. Then Jen and I talked for a few minutes about her birthday. I needed to get the bar stocked to make sure I had lots of caviar and champagne for the women. She said they would be going out most dinners but would want breakfast and a few lunches and dinners. She also wanted me to drive them around so they could drink and have a good time. I said, "Sounds good. I will take care of everything."

With that said, we loaded up and were on our way to the airport. John, as always, put a few bucks in my pocket. After they left, I had a week off to get ready. I headed back to the house, cracked open a cold one, grabbed a chair by the pool, and got some rays. The housekeeper was coming tomorrow, so I was done for the day.

Jen and I talked a few times over the next week, and she added a few things to the list. She was already starting to be bossy and a pain in the ass. She wanted me to put together a welcome bag for all the guests with little cards in them, along with chocolates, copies of *Palm Beach* magazine, lip gloss, sunscreen, water bottles, and beach towels. These were beach-size bags. I made it happen. It makes her happy, and I felt this was a one-time thing. I sure as hell wouldn't be there next year.

I had not even gotten to Greenwich yet, but I could tell this would be a short gig. I really wanted to live in Greenwich, even if just for a few months. Then I got the trip details, and she told me to make a pitcher of margaritas and bring it and glasses to the airport. I was like, what the fuck? I am a bartender and driver as well. I made it happen.

A few days passed, and it was show-time. I picked them up at the airport with margaritas in hand. They were in heaven, so I felt a little better. When we got back to the house, I had all the bags lined up, a nice cheese tray ready, the champagne chilled and canapés of caviar. Jen was impressed and seemed very happy. The girls all made it to their rooms, and the daughter who lived in Lauderdale arrived, so the whole gang was there and ready to party for five days.

Jen's mom looked like an old hag and was not nice, bossy and mean. The sisters were all cool, and the one daughter as well. I hit it off with all of them. They all told the older sister to chill; they knew she was a bitch. This two-time loser had spent all her money from both divorces and was now trying to find a third guy to take his money, but she better go look in the morgue for a guy. She was way past her prime and had a big, fat ass as well.

I made lunch, a nice chicken Caesar with some nice Châteauneuf-du-Pape. The girls all came down from their suites. A few should have worn a cover-up, but the middle one, divorced, did not look too bad, with a nice ass and big tits. As for Jen, what can I say? She'd had eight kids, but she was still skinny—but you know that ass was a mile wide and ripped apart. She still thought she was hot. I guess if your old man's got money, you get that shit fixed. On top of that, she just had a bad attitude, like she was better than everyone. I just kept my mouth shut. It'd only been a month, but I was ready to tell her to piss off.

The older sister took her top off, and a few of the others, including Jen, followed. They should have left them on. Jen had no tits at all. Debra, the one I had my eye on, left her top on. Her daughter was there, and so was I.

I served lunch, and they were all happy. Jen handed me a schedule for the week: dinner, reservations, lunch, shopping. She was very organized, I will say that. They were going to the grill that night, and for her birthday, they were going to the Breakers for dinner, drinks, and dancing. I would drop them off and pick them up. Jen said, "Tomorrow we'll take an Uber home because it will be late, and we are going shopping the next day, so you can rest up."

The deal for me was that when they were in Palm Beach, I would stay in the guest room, and on my days off, I would go home and stay at my place. That was cool; I did not mind that. I liked going for my morning run on the island. It had some great scenery, and there were some hot chicks out in the morning, riding their bikes, walking, or running.

The first day was a breeze, and the next day they all just lay by the pool, getting ready for the big night. I did a shrimp salad with angel hair pasta on a bed of arugula and cilantro and lime vinaigrette. They were in heaven. Home run again. They had brought gifts and would give them to Jen at dinner.

It was getting close to dinnertime, and I had a few appetizers ready for them and more chilled champagne. They stumbled down one at a time. Debra comes down first. She was the next-to-youngest one and the hottest, maybe late forties but with a nice body. She worked out—you could tell—and had a great attitude, which is key. I poured her a glass of the bubbly, and we chatted. She asked if I was married, and I said no. She said, "That's nice. Have you ever been?"

I said, "No, I just never got around to it." She laughed at that.

The others wandered down, and they were all hitting on me. The rest were all married, except for the old hag. They were just having fun, saying, "I want to take you home," and, "Don't tell my husband if I come down to your room tonight," and they were all showing cleavage. Debra was, too. I liked that. She was wearing a nice miniskirt, and I knew I would fuck her. They all had some bubbly, made a few toasts to Jen, and exchanged hugs and kisses. Then I whisked them off to the Breakers. I am sure they got plenty drunk and crazy.

I was in bed at ten and was out cold. I thought I was dreaming when I felt a warm body next to mine, and I rolled over to a nice set of tits in my face and my cock getting stroked. I opened my eyes, and it was Debra with nothing on but a smile. The next thing I knew, we were deep in it, and man was she into it. I don't think she'd had any dick in a while. She must have come three times, and man, what great head she gave, and she enjoyed it. We went at it for a good hour or so. I was wiped, nothing left. We kissed and said good night. She asked me, "Can we do it again tomorrow night?"

I said, "That would be nice. I will be waiting for you." We kissed one more time, and she went upstairs. The next day, we acted like nothing had happened, and the sisters were none the wiser.

They were all going to Worth Avenue for a good part of the day. Jen said, "We will have lunch over there, so just drop us off, and we will call you later to pick us up."

After breakfast, I cleaned up and dressed sharply, as I would not be cooking today, only driving. They all enjoyed their breakfast: classic French toast with all the sides, fresh fruit yogurt with granola, and Bloody Marys. Man, could these broads drink. At night, they would have margaritas and champagne. They were having a great time, and I was fucking Debra every night like clockwork. Once they all passed out, she would come down to the guest room and let herself in. The second night was better than the first. She was not as buzzed, and we really got into it hot and heavy. Man, that was some good ass for an older broad.

We only had two nights left, and we got them both in. Jen called me around five and said, "We don't want to have dinner at the house. Instead, we're going to have happy hour off the island and just get some apps and drinks. Do you know a good place?"

I said, "Yes, Lynora's on Clematis. They have a great happy hour and good food, and it's a cool spot."

"Great. Pick us up in thirty minutes. We will go straight there, and you can just hang out with us or go eat somewhere else on us."

"Roger that. See you in thirty."

I rolled up to pick them up, and it looked like they had bought the stores out. I am glad they were not my girlfriends, and I feel sorry for the poor bastards who got those bills. I took them to Lynora's, dropped them off, and parked. Then I walked back, and they had already gotten drinks. They offered me one, and I said, "No, I have to drive you ladies. I have to be on my best behavior." They all just smiled at me with that teasing look.

They told the bartender, who knew me, "Chef Al is the best chef, driver, and bartender. We are all sisters, and we are going to fight over him. The winner can take him home." They went on and on. I was blushing. They were all hugging me and saying, "I get him the first week," and so on. It was really great. They had a good time. I just hung out and had a pizza with them and let them have a good time. They celebrated for a couple of hours, and then we went back to the house. They all went right to bed, and I did, too.

On the last day, they wanted to take the boat out, so I had Andy lined up as captain, and I prepared all kinds of cold cuts, chips and dip, a cheese tray, some cold beers, and a nice rosé. They spent about half the day on the boat, swimming in the ocean and just having a great time.

Jen said, "Don't worry about cooking tonight. It's the last night, and we have reservations at Buccan. Would you like to join us?"

I said, "Yes, my pleasure."

We got back to the house early, and they all wanted to take a little nap before dinner. I thought they would get crazy on their last night, but they were all pretty tame. They enjoyed their food and some nice wine. I had one glass. They thanked me and said that I had made the trip special. That was nice. I drive us home. The flight the next morning was not until eleven, so there was no rush in the morning to get to the airport.

Debra came down later. This time we talked instead of just fucking. If you ask me, talking is overrated. We traded contact info, and I invited her to come down some time. I never heard from her again, but I never called, either.

The next morning, I made eggs Benny with lump crab and my famous roast potatoes, asparagus tips, and hollandaise sauce to die for, along with champagne mimosas. I think all their panties were wet. I am sure Debra was from last night. It was a great send-off, and Jen was super happy.

We packed up and headed to the airport. On the way, they all said thanks again, and Jen said, "We have something for you from all of us." She passed me an envelope and said, "You can open it now if you like. It's from all of us." It was a thank-you card with a nice note from all of them and a fistful of hundreds. I said, "Thank you very much," and Jen said, "See you in Greenwich in a week or so. I will call you and book you a flight." They all gave me a big hug, especially Debra. I think Jen knew I banged her, but she never said a word about it.

This was the first time in my career that I had waited on an all-women group for a week. It was kind of cool, and it did not hurt to get a little ass on the side. That was just a bonus.

I headed back to the house, fixed myself a killer eggs Benny, poured myself a glass of champagne, and raised the glass to myself. "Well done, Chef." I did my job and took care of a woman in need.

I got an email from Jen a few days later laying out the summer plans, with dates and trips and my flight back to Greenwich the following week. I was like, what the hell. Let's give it a shot. They had three trips planned down to Palm Beach and one family trip that I did not need to go on, to John's folks' place in Iowa.

I got to Greenwich the following week and was picked up by Jen's father. That did not sit well with me. When a boss cannot pick you up, it shows that they really don't care about you. In this case, John was just too busy with eight kids, so I cut him some slack, and he'd been a nice guy so far. The father seemed ok, but I'd just met him, so I didn't know for sure what kind of guy he was. We made some small talk on the way, about the house, kids, that sort of stuff. It turned out that John had her dad on the payroll as kind of a house manager, and the mother, too. I guess they'd hit hard times, so Jen had asked John to create jobs for them. What a crock of shit. I later heard that Jen gave money to her mom, too. I would have gotten rid of the whole rotten lot. With eight kids, John was fucked every way to sundown. She would take him to the cleaners but good. He would never see the light of day again. The old man turned out to be one cheap fuck. He never tipped and did not spend any of his own money. The mom lived in California, so I did not see her much. That was nice. I'd had enough of her on the last trip in Palm Beach.

I knew this was going to be just a summer job. I'd save a few bucks, see Greenwich, maybe go into the city one more time, and check out all the small coastal towns. I had a house car, a new Lexus SUV, and a Nissan shuttle van, like what you'd see at an airport. I mean, shit, with eight kids, you have to haul them in a bus. I hated parking that damn thing. I ended up lasting the summer, three months.

We got to the house, a large, old Victorian estate just a mile from downtown, next to some parks. It was a really nice place, great for running in the morning. John met me outside and helped carry my bags. He said he was sorry, but it was Sunday, and he was stuck with the kids. "I get it," I said. "That's cool."

He said, "Get unpacked, come down, and I will drive you into town and show you around. Then we'll come back and have a drink, and you can start fresh tomorrow."

John, you are a first-class guy. We headed into Greenwich. It's a small town, with only two major streets. He showed me the Whole Foods, seafood market, local butcher, wine store, and a few of their favorite restaurants and said he was glad to have me here, that they really needed the help. Then he showed me his friend Gummy's office. It was right downtown. John went into the city every day for work. He was up at four thirty and left at six every day. It was a tough schedule, but that's why he makes the big bucks, I guess. These hedge fund guys are just killing it. I mean, John was in his early forties and had an estate in Greenwich and a place on the island, and he belonged to a few private clubs on top of that. All these guys are like that. It's a status thing. I will never have that issue. One thing about John is that he is self-made and not a prick. Jen is a different story.

I will never forget that first day. I'd just had my coffee—no run today, as Jen wanted me to get the kids breakfast before they went to school. When I got to the kitchen, it was already a madhouse. The three older boys were fighting, and the little ones were screaming and crying. Jen was nowhere to be found, and John had already left. It was just one nanny and me. What a clusterfuck. I told the kids, "Quiet down or no breakfast." It worked for about five minutes. I made a dozen egg sandwiches and put together a bowl of fruit and served it family-style on the table—or should I say park bench. It was the biggest kitchen table I'd ever seen, seated like fourteen. The kids missed the bus. Jen finally came down and restored some sort of order, and it looked like I would be driving the kids to school after everyone was fed.

Jen gave me the school's address, and I got the kids all loaded up and was on my way. The oldest one, a girl, told me how to get there, as the GPS took you out of the way. I got them there in one piece and then returned to the house. It was still crazy there, with the three little ones and one newborn. I was like, what the fuck am I doing here? The nanny fed the little ones and put them down for a nap, and for the first time, it was quiet.

I cleaned up the breakfast mess, and just as I sat down at the table to enjoy a cup of coffee, all hell broke loose again. The three young ones were just going crazy. The nanny was not doing shit. She was Filipino and worthless. I never liked her, and she had no business taking care of the kids. I mean, what kind of parents have two nannies when the wife doesn't even work? You wonder why these kids are all fucked up these days.

Jen came down again—I guess she went back to bed after yoga. She saw I was pissed and ready to go off on the nanny. Things calmed down, and the nanny took the little ones back to the nursery. Jen looked at me and said, "If you want to go back to Palm Beach, no problem. We understand. We will just use you when we are down there."

I said, "No, I am just not used to all the kids. Give me a few weeks, and let's see if I can make it work. I don't want to leave like that. Let's try. I want to see if I can help you guys and get a handle on the kids."

"Great. I will call John and tell him you are fine, and let's do a shot of Goose. I know you could use one." John always had some in the freezer.

We did a few shots, and Jen said, "Since you are not driving the kids until the evening, if you ever need a shot, feel free to help yourself, or just buy a bottle for the guest house."

I will never forget that day. I made it a habit of never drinking on the job. I mean, after dinner, I may have a glass of wine, but that's it. I have stuck to that all these years. It's just a good work ethic. But with eight kids, three young ones, two nannies, and one deadbeat grandpa to put up with, it became part of my daily routine.

That night, when John got home, he called me into his office. I thought I was getting fired. It was just the opposite. He said, "First, thanks for staying. Now let's have a drink."

We had a few shots of the Goose, and then he said, "Take the night off. We'll take the kids out." He opened a small safe behind his desk, grabbed two hundred-dollar bills, and said, "Go out and have a nice dinner on us." I told you this guy was a prince.

I walked into Greenwich, about a mile or so, and found this little Mediterranean café, and that was the name: Mediterranean Café. I rolled up to the bar and grabbed a seat. The place was busy and had a wood-burning pizza oven. The manager walked over and asked if he could help me. I asked if I could eat at the bar, and he said, "Of course. My name is Peter, and I am the general manager. First time here?"

I told him it was, and he said, "If you need anything, just let me know. I will bring a menu over. Would you like a glass of wine or a drink?"

"A glass of red would be nice."

"My pleasure. The pizza is great if you just want a light dinner."

He brought me a nice red, and we made small talk. I ordered a Margherita pie, and it was excellent. For good pizza, you have to have a wood-burning oven. He asked what I did, and it turned out that he knew the Roaches and Jen had told him about me. We hit it off and became friends on the spot. He was a first-class guy, knew the business, and was a great host.

I enjoyed my pizza without saying a word. A waiter filled my glass, smiled, said, "You're welcome," and walked away. Nice touch. Peter returned after I had finished eating and asked how the pie was. I said, "Excellent." We chatted about food for a few minutes, and then he asked f I would like some dessert. I said, "No thanks, but I would love a double espresso and a limoncello if you have it."

Peter laughed and said, "Of course we have it. We make it on site."

"Great. Let's try it."

He returned a few minutes later with two nice glasses and my espresso and said, "A toast to new friends."

I said, "Back at you," and we smiled.

It was one of the best limoncellos I have ever had, light, crisp, better than my own. I had to get their recipe. Peter was from Hungary; the Eastern Europeans have a great work ethic. I was getting ready to say something, but he cut me off and said, "It's my pleasure." We became good friends and still keep in touch.

I got my check, and Peter took care of all my drinks. He said, "It's your first time here. Please come back and join us anytime."

"Many thanks, and I will be back."

This is my spot for the rest of the summer. I'd only been in town a few days, and I already had a new hangout and new friend. Peter and I got to be close. I came in three or four times a week. If I got a break during the day, I would stop in for an espresso.

Every day at the house was the same. On some days, there was more drama than others, but the kids were always fighting or just tearing shit up. Jen never disciplined the kids, and John was working, so he had no clue how bad the boys were. They never made it to school on time. If it hadn't been a private school, they would never have made it.

I have to say there were some good restaurants in the area. I hit quite a few of them, and they were all very nice. I decided to go all in one evening and went to Mario Batali's place. I cannot remember the name, but it was one of his flagship restaurants. It had a great atmosphere but was crazy expensive, and the food did not wow me. It was nice but not worth the money. The Mediterranean Café in Greenwich would give them a run for their money.

John was always giving me a hundred here and there to go have dinner. Plus, he took me golfing a few times at Round Hill Country Club, nice track, old money. This brings me to one of the best stories of the summer.

John asked if I would like to play golf one Saturday with a few guys and if I could be his partner. "We are playing Round Hill at ten."

It turned out that we were playing against Mark Teixeira, the Yankee first baseman, AKA Mark Tex, or just Tex. I had already met his wife, Leigh. She was friends with Jen. They did yoga together, and she was training for a marathon. She seemed really nice. She told me they met in college, so she was no gold digger. It was a great day. Tex was a really nice guy. We had a great round and drank some beers, and it turned out that he and John were pretty good friends.

The one thing that kind of pissed me off was that he was not playing because he had a shoulder issue, yet he could play golf after getting a 180-million-dollar contract. That did not sit well with me. These guys are just spoiled. They're even worse nowadays. I don't watch any of them anymore; they're way too overpaid for just playing a game.

We had lunch at the club. John was in a great mood—maybe Jen had given him a little morning ass. Tex invited us to Jeter's last home game. John said, "Yeah, I will take the whole family." I was like, great, all the fucking kids. This will be a fun day. But what the hell. Life is no rose garden.

John and I played badly, and we lost, but it was still a great day. The game was next weekend, so it was already planned: load up the van with Leigh and her kids and the Roach gang. John was not going. He had to catch up on some work. I was going to drive into the city with the two wives and all the rugrats. Yeah, I know. What the hell was I thinking? But we had a clubhouse pass, and I was going to get into the locker room to meet the players. That was pretty cool, even if you hate the Yankees. That's a bucket list item for sure.

I think it was a Sunday game. I just remember that getting all the kids ready was a pain in the ass, but for once, we were on time. It's nice when you have two moms, and Leigh's kids were pretty well behaved, unlike the Roach gang.

A few hours later, we were at the stadium. It was pretty cool. Leigh showed a pass to the cop directing traffic, and we pulled right into the underground parking lot for the players and staff. Then she took us right into the clubhouse. There was an area where all the wives and guests took their kids. They had a playroom, food, games, and nannies to supervise the kids. No beer here, but if there was anything else you wanted, you just had to ask. Leigh and Jen got the kids all settled, and then Tex showed up and asked if I was ready for the tour. I guess Leigh had called him and said I was there. We shook hands and talked about golf, and then he asked if I was ready to meet some of the players.

I said, "Sure! Is it cool?"

"Yeah, you're family," he said. That was pretty cool.

I got the grand tour. I had never seen a locker room like this; it was just over the top. There was nothing that they did not have, including a juice bar. Man, these players don't want for anything. I won't go there. I still think these guys are way overpaid for playing a game, but that's just my opinion. I really only wanted to meet Jeter. I think that guy is a real stud. He's never been in trouble, keeps his mouth shut, and never gets involved in politics. He is a real first-class guy and a hell of a player, Hall of Famer for sure and one hell of a nice guy.

I got to talk to him for a few minutes. I told him I was a big fan, and Tex told him I was a chef for one of his friends in Greenwich. We talked about food for a few minutes and then shook hands. I said, "Thanks for the time," and then we were on our way for the rest of the tour.

I met a few more players and told Tex, "Thanks for the tour and the intro to Jeter."

He said, "Cool. We have to tee it up again."

"Yeah, I would like that."

We never got to play again, as I quit the job a few months later. I saw him twice more at the house, once for a dinner party and once for a pool cookout with all the kids. All in all, he was an ok guy. One thing we had in common is that we did not like Gummy, the fuck who owned TransAlantic Shipping, a real asshole, so I knew he was not a bad guy. Gummy was just a big dick.

Back to the game. I set with all the wives in great seats. Every group had its own private concierge. Ours came by every ten minutes to check on us. Later, she brought me a dog with all the extras. I also got a signed ball. Even A-Rod signed it. I met him as well. No big deal; I never liked him. He is a cheater.

We watched the whole game, as leaving would not be an issue. We were in the employee parking lot, so it would be easy to get out. They just stop traffic and let players and guests outs. It was a fun day. Even the kids had fun, and for once, they were somewhat well behaved. When the game was over, we returned to the daycare center. The kids were hungry, and they had pizza, so we hung out there for a while.

The whole day was one to put down on my bucket list. Even with the kids, I still had a great time. I wish John had come, but he had some work to do. He was not lazy. He was a hardworking son of a bitch with eight kids and a wife who spent money like wildfire. He better keep on bringing in the dough.

We finished eating and took a pizza for the road, along with sodas. I said goodbye to the staff and thanked them for everything. They'd really looked after me. I felt like a VIP. This was a first and a last. I have not been to a game since then.

We got the gang together and went back to the van. We got in, and when I looked behind us, there was Jeter in a bad-ass Benz with a hot-as-balls blond bitch. Well, he is Derek Jeter. He waved to me, and I gave him a thumbs up. Class act all the way. I wish more athletes would take a page out of his playbook. I never saw Jeter again. Tex, I saw a few more times. He came over for a few dinner parties at the pool, along with that prick Gummy. That was the highlight of the whole summer, except for banging one of Jen's friends. She was married to an older guy, sugar daddy, rich hedge fund asshole. I guess he was not taking care of business.

We got home that evening all safe and sound, and as I was getting ready to turn in, John called me into his office. "Chef, want a cold one?"

"Sure. I have tomorrow off."

Jen was upstairs, going to bed. John asked, "How was it?"

I said, "I had a great time," and I thanked him profusely and told him the whole story.

"Cool. Glad you had fun."

We had a toast, bullshitted for a few minutes, and then said good night. As I left, he said, "Have a good day off." I really liked this guy, even if he did eventually throw me under the bus.

The following week, he took me into the city, showed me around BlueCrest Capital, and took me to lunch. New York is overrated, overpriced, and full of nasty New Yorkers. I think it's a shithole. You can have it. I never want to go back there again.

John and I had a good day, hanging out together. I think he knew my days were numbered. He was just trying to keep me for as long as he could. I am sure he knew Jen was a pain in the ass and what I had to put up with every day. I mean, the guy had been married to her for ten years.

I did one catered lunch for Jen at her friend's house. He was one of the partners of the Blackstone Group, and he owned a hundred-year-old brick estate. I have to say it was bad-ass. When I got there, as I tried to set up, the host was just busting my balls, telling me where to put stuff. This lasted about five minutes, and then I told Jen I had to get back to the house and just walked out. She said, "Ok. Thank you." That was hard for her.

We did a few more trips to Palm Beach together, nothing exciting. I always went a few days early to get the house ready, and I would get a few days off to relax. Not all of the kids came at the same time. Most of the time, it was just adults. Jack was the oldest of the boys and just a little shit-ass. These kids had private tutors, and they were still flunking.

One day, the tutor came to work with Jack, but Jack would not come out of his room. He was playing video games. The tutor went to his room and told him to come down. He would not. I went up there and told him to come out; he went downstairs for five minutes. I heard this little piece of shit yell to the tutor, "Fuck off! I am leaving," and then he went back to his room.

I called John at work and told him the whole story. He said, "Thanks for letting me know. I will deal with Jack when I get home."

Jen got home, and I told her what happened and that I'd called John because this was a pretty big deal. She called Jack in and asked him if he'd said that, and he said he did not, just flat-out lied. Of course, she took his word and blamed the tutor.

When John got home, he was pissed, and he should have been. Jen said, "It was just a misunderstanding," and let Jack lie his way out of it. She told John it was the tutor who blew up. Later, when Jen was upstairs, Jack pulled me aside, and we had a drink, and he said, "Tell me the truth."

I said, "Jack was lying, and Jen covered for his ass. The tutor was very respectful and did not raise his voice to Jack at all. Jack needs some discipline, but that's not my job. That's the truth. I was right there and heard it all."

That night, I knew my days were numbered. I'd had enough of these rotten kids. I was just trying to bank one more paycheck, but this would prove to be a hard task. I did a few more trips to Palm Beach. I got good tip money, and there were no kids most of the time, so it was pretty easy, just cooking, driving, and bartending. The last trip was just girls: Jen, her mom, and a few of the Stepford wives from Greenwich, just like the book and the movie. I don't think they cared for me too much, but I couldn't give a rat's ass. I drove them to dinner, took them out on the boat, cooked for them, made drinks, and took them shopping. I wish I could say that I banged one of them, but no luck, and honestly, I did not want to.

We were coming back from shopping one afternoon, and one of the women said, "Man, we have to buy a place on the island." I was thinking: *You don't have any money. I don't think so. It's your old man's money. You don't have a clue. Oh, we can do this and that. Are you for real? You can't even balance a checkbook.*

The next day, Jen had me drive them to buy a few houses that were for sale. One was the old Kennedy place. They were looking at homes between ten and twenty million. One house we went to was right down from Jen and John's place, and one friend was really interested in it. I think her old man was with Blackstone, a big hedge fund guy. I will never forget that conversation. They talked like I was not even in the car; it was like I did not exist.

The house was around twenty million. She did not even know if they could afford it or finance it, no clue at all, so she said, "I don't think my husband is ready to make a move yet and spend that much on a house."

Jen looked at her and said, "If you really want it, put your foot down and tell him you want this house in Palm Beach. If he says he is not ready yet, dig in your heels. No sex. Bust his balls and don't give him anything. Let the house go uncleaned the kids run wild. If he wants something, just say you are busy. Believe me. After a week, he will be kissing your ass and buying the house for you. Take that to the bank."

I was like, what cunts these Greenwich Stepford wives are, and I am sure that pussy is not great. Like I said, I will never forget that day. I took all the guests to the airport the next day, except Jen's mom. I had never seen a bunch of arrogant bitches in my life, and I was glad that I would never have to do it again. Jen's mom was no better. She was an old hag. I took them over to downtown West Palm to do some shopping and have lunch, and then we finally headed back home, as they had an early flight the next morning.

As we were driving back, we passed some condos downtown. Jen's mother told me to drive back around one of the buildings again. She wanted to take a look at it, so I turned around and gave her the tour. I just kept my mouth shut. From out of nowhere, the old bag says, "Honey, what are these going for? I need a two-two."

Jen said, "Around 250."

The old hag said, "You have to talk to John and get him to buy me a condo. That way, I can be closer to the grandkids."

I almost lost it. The balls on this old bitch. She was on her last legs, broke, and wanted John to support her and buy her a condo? You had to be shitting me. What was this bitch on, and using the grandkids as an excuse. What a fucking joke. What's sad is that Jen talked to John and they bought her a place, just like Jen's deadbeat old man, Lou. I feel bad for John. Putting up with Jen is one thing, but now he has to support her mom and dad. I would kick their whole family to the curb. What a bunch of users, just taking advantage of John. Poor guy, he will not see the end of this for years. Jen spends money like wildfire, just out of control, with eight kids to boot. That is no rose garden.

One good thing I could say about Jen is that she paid me well and gave me time off. Deep down, she knew the kids were a train wreck and putting up with them every day was no easy task, so I got a week off after every trip before I went back to Greenwich. That was one of the job's best perks, next to the golf. When they left, I had a week to get the place back in order, take some time off, and get the boat ready for the next trip. It was a thirty-two-foot Hinkley, a nice little boat.

I would call Eddie and Andrew and say, "Hey, guys, we've got the boat to ourselves. Let's line some girls up and go for a ride. That meant a whole day of drinking and fucking on the boat. Eddie would get the girls, and we'd all meet at the Sunfish marina and party all day. We would head down to Two Georges in Boynton, have lunch, and then got back to Peanut Island, maybe cruise over to Frigate's for happy hour. A few times, we went down to Del Rey. I will never forget the times we had. Great fun. Too bad John and Jen had eight kids and that Jen was such a bitch. This could have been a pretty good gig. Like they say, nothing lasts forever. At the end of the week, I'd get the house back in order and the boat all squared away and then head back to Greenwich. I had to book my own flight, and Jen's dad picked me up most of the time.

One good thing was eating at the Mediterranean Café and hanging out with Peter. I could smell the food clear down to West Palm. Then I would wake back up to eight screaming kids, fighting and just out of control.

I lasted a month longer than I thought I would. Then the shit hit the fan. That fucking Jack, what a little shit. I wish I were his dad. I would beat his ass. I bet you he would shape up in a few weeks. If he didn't, I would just keep kicking his ass every day.

One morning, Jen came down late, like she did every day. The nannies were nowhere to be found. By the time they finally showed up, it was a fucking madhouse. The kids missed the bus again, just like every day, so I had to drive them. I was pissed, and I said something to Jen like, "This is not working out. You have to get these kids under control, or I am out of here."

She said, "We will talk this afternoon. I'm late for yoga."

I just fucking laughed. You have to be kidding me. What's more important than raising your kids? It was always all about Jen.

I got the kids to school and did my afternoon shopping. Then Jen and I met in the afternoon. I still can't believe what came out of her mouth. She told me I was not a team player and if I wanted a job and to be a part of their family, I needed to get a few things straight. I held my tongue as she rambled on about the kids, how they needed this and that and how she was so busy. I almost laughed in her face, the lazy bitch. Then she said, "I am running a business here, and if you want to be a part of it, you need to do more."

I just was in awe. *You are talking about your family like it's a business? Have you lost your fucking mind, lady?* I said, "I will let you know tomorrow if I am staying or going home."

She said, "Fine. Do whatever you want. Just let me know tomorrow," and then she stormed off.

I thought: *Man, what a bitch. She needs a big boot up her ass.* She was not really even a trophy wife, even though she thought she was. She was not all that: butch haircut, no tits, personality a three out of ten. I just kept thinking: *That poor bastard John got more than he bargained for; that's for damn sure.*

One day, I was inside, cooking dinner while the boys played outside. There had been some issues with the kids next door, a little girl and her brother, both about the same age as Jack. The boys did not like them and were mean to them. They brother and sister would come over and ask if the boys could play with them, and the boys would say, "No. Just go home." The parents had talked about it, but that had not helped.

That afternoon, the brother and sister came to the door, crying. They said that one of the boys flashed the little girl and then they called the brother some nasty names. I did not see it, but I believed them. I walked them to their house. Their parents were not home, but the nanny was. She asked what had happened, and I filled her in. I said, "That's all I know. I did not see it happen, so I cannot say for sure."

That night, the parents came over. They were a little upset, and I don't blame them. They had a long talk with John and Jen. I was not there for the whole conversation, just the beginning when they asked me to come into the library and tell them what I had seen.

I said, "I didn't see it happen. I was in the kitchen, cooking dinner, when I heard a knock at the door. I went to answer it and saw your son and daughter in tears. I asked what was wrong, and they said the boys would not play with them and one of them flashed her and called her brother nasty names and told them to go home and don't come back. That's all I know. I walked your kids home and told the nanny, and then I came back home."

They all said, "Thanks, Chef. That will be all," so I left and went to my guest house.

It turned out that the little girl could not say for sure which one of the boys flashed her, as she was crying and not sure if it was Jack or not. I am sure Jen stood up for the boys, saying the little girl was lying and her boys would never do a thing like that. Bullshit.

John came down to the guest house after the other parents had left and filled me in. He said they'd all agreed that the kids should not play together and their kids should not come over until things got worked out.

He asked me what I thought, and I told him, "The boys are not nice to them, and they've got no one else to play with. That's why they come over. I would not put it past the boys to do this. John, that's my take, and if you want to fire me, I understand, but that is the truth."

He said, "Thanks for being honest."

"They need some discipline and some rules to follow." That was as far as I went. "Don't tell Jen that. She will just say I don't like the boys and it's none of my business, and it's not, but you asked, and John, I really like you. That's why I am telling you the truth."

He looked me in the eyes, and I could tell he was concerned. He said, "Thanks. Let's have a drink. I know you've got some Goose in this guest house."

We had a few, shook hands, and called it a night. I know, deep down, he was embarrassed. If you ask me, it was Jen's fault. She never disciplined the kids. They lied and cheated and did whatever they wanted, and she protected them and covered up stuff so John did not find out, like the one pissing the bed though is eight years old. That is a load of crap. I am sure these kids will grow up to be even bigger assholes and think they are better than everyone else.

I knew this was the last straw. John had no choice but to tell Jen what I thought. He was going to throw me under the bus. If he didn't, he wouldn't get any ass or head for the rest of the summer. What a raw deal. You call that marriage? It's like being in jail.

I poured myself one more and thought for a few minutes. It was time to get the hell out of here. I got on the Internet and booked a flight back to Palm Beach. If she gave me one bit of shit, I was going to tell her to shove the job up her fat ass. I would have my ticket in hand, give her the credit card back, and walk away. I packed just to be on the safe side. Then I killed my drink and passed out on the couch, and that was all she wrote.

The next morning, it was like nothing had happened. The kids were raising hell like always, Jen was sleeping in, the nanny was nowhere to be seen, and I was pulling my hair out—it was a clusterfuck, as we say in the Marines. The kids missed the bus—a given—so I had to drive them to school. When I got back to the house, I had the kitchen all to myself, a rare thing, and I quietly enjoyed a cup of coffee. The little ones were upstairs with the one nanny, so I was cool for a while. I knew Jen would be down soon and this would not end well, and frankly, I did not give a shit. I was done with this family.

I was right. Jen came down a few minutes later and started in on me. I let her talk for a few minutes. I'd had enough of her shit and was not going to take it one more day. Finally, said in a loud, commanding voice, "Enough. I have had it with the boys' lies and all of your shit. I will not lie for your spoiled kids. They all need a good ass-whipping. I have no doubt that Jack was guilty of flashing the young girl next door, as he is a little prick, and deep down, you know it as well, and it's your own damn fault. I told John this last night, and no, I don't want to be a part of this family. Who in their right mind would? Here is the credit card and all the house receipts for the last month. I booked a flight last night back to Palm Beach. I have had enough of your shit. I am packed and will be leaving soon, and as far as I am concerned, we are done here."

I thought she was going to start crying. Then she started to backpedal. "Wait. We can work this out. We don't want you to leave. We need you. I will change."

I almost laughed in her face. I said, "No, I am done. I will see myself out. I will grab my bags and wait for the Uber driver in town. I am going to have lunch and then fly out this evening. I am sorry it had to end this way."

"Let's try this one more time."

"No, I am sorry. I have had too much of this shit. Nothing will change my mind. And oh, here are the keys to the house in Palm Beach as well."

I went to my guesthouse, grabbed my bags, and called a cab to take me to the Mediterranean Café to say goodbye to Peter and have one last lunch in Greenwich.

The moment I sat down and ordered a glass of wine, John called and asked, "Where are you at?"

I said, "At the Mediterranean Café."

"Don't leave. I will be there in an hour or so."

"Cool. I will be here."

Peter came over with my glass of wine. He saw my bags and said, "What's up? You quit?"

"Yeah," I said. "I had enough of the wife's shit and those eight kids."

We had talked about the family before, and he knew I would be leaving them soon. They would come into the restaurant and just raise holy hell. I mean, they would just tear the place up, yell, complain, and make a mess.

I told him, "I got a late flight to Palm Beach. I am going to have a long lunch and a few drinks and then take an Uber to the airport. John will be here in an hour. He asked me to stay and wait for him. I told him I would."

Peter said, "In that case, maybe we should have some shots."

"Yeah, just let me get some food inside me first."

"Your money is no good today. It's on the house. The last supper."

I just laughed at the man. I loved that guy. Peter, you are the best, my old and good friend.

I had a great lunch: wood-fired salmon, couscous, and some nice grilled veggies. I could do no better, and the price was right. I just love getting comped. I was just finishing up and getting ready for my espresso and after-dinner drink when John walked in. He knew Peter, but they were not close friends. Peter walked over and greeted him, but he didn't say a word about me leaving. My bags were in plain sight, but he said nothing. Peter has class.

John said, "Hi, Peter. Let's have two Grey Goose martinis." He didn't even ask me. I said, "Sure, John. Nice to see you."

"What time is your flight, Chef?"

"Seven thirty. I'm taking an Uber."

"Bullshit. If I cannot talk you into staying, let me take you to the airport."

"I would like that. I love you, John. You're one of the best guys I've ever worked for, but I have to move on."

"I understand, but can I at least try?"

I laughed, and we had a toast. Then he said, "I am sorry about throwing you under the bus. I had no choice. You know Jen. If I left her, it would kill me. I am stuck. I did not want eight kids. It was all her. She wanted them, and now I am fucked. So, please stay. I talked to Jen. She wants to put this behind us and start fresh. We want you to help with the kids."

"John, if I were younger, I would, but I am set in my ways, and Jen just got to me, and I cannot go back."

"Come on, Chef, one last time."

I just smiled and said, "I truly am sorry, but I can't."

"Well, shit. Let's have one more drink, and I will take you to the airport."

"Yes, I would like that."

Peter walked over and said, "Hey, you guys left me out. Let me in on this toast, too. Chef Al, we will miss your smiling face around here. All the best, and you are welcome here anytime. Keep in touch."

I will never forget that evening. John and I talked all the way to the airport, and he told me, "Keep in touch when you are in Palm Beach. We will go tee it up sometime." We did keep in touch for a few years. I saw them out in Palm Beach, but we never got to play golf. I am sure Jen put the squash on that deal. But that's cool.

At the airport, we said our goodbyes and shook hands. John said, "Here are a few bucks to get you home."

"Thanks. John. All the best to you. Take care."

What a first-class guy. I miss him to this day. John, you're a prince.

I had a nice flight home. I felt good about what I'd said to Jen, and I was glad the job was over. I was looking forward to getting back to Palm Beach and taking some time off.

Sean Young, Sally Kirkland, Lee Grant

PAUL SAUNDERS
AKA MR. PANTIES

A FEW DAYS PASSED, AND I was just chilling in Palm Beach when the phone rang. It was Gayle Parsons. I'd been the chef on a yacht in the Bahamas, *Dealership*, a six-month gig, and Gayle and her husband, Lyn, had been guests for a week. They were good friends of the owners, Vern and Marie Kraus. Vern was a big car guy, owned lots of dealerships, thus the yacht's name.

Gayle explained that they lived in Palm Beach Gardens and wanted me to do a dinner party for them. I said I could, and then she told me that she'd invited a couple that was looking for a full-time chef and she had told them all about me. She said they were a really nice couple, the guy had tons of money, and they wanted to offer me a job.

I said, "Cool. Give me the dates, and we are on."

Dinner went off without a flaw. I did my signature grilled salmon with tzatziki, roasted potatoes, asparagus, and grilled red peppers, always a hit. The guest who wanted to hire me, Paul Saunders, went out of his way to tell me about the house they were building. I did not like the guy from the start. I could tell he was an egomaniac. I know the type. Vicky, the wife, just praised every word Paul said. I should have known better.

After dinner, Lyn invited me out for drinks. Vern and Marie gave me a big hug and said they'd had a great time when I was the chef on the yacht for those six months. Vern said, "If we had not sold the boat, you would still be on it."

I said, "I know. I feel the same way about you guys as well, and all your friends are great." I had a great time on *Dealership*. I miss that boat. We all raised a glass to *Dealership*, and then we talked about Harbor Island and what a great trip we'd had.

I cleared the glasses and was cleaning up in the kitchen when Paul came in and asked if I could come to their house next week and meet them and talk about working for them. I said, "Sure, I can do that." Then I headed back out to the patio to join the other guests. Vern talked about Harbor Island again and my conch ceviche and pineapple martinis, and we had a few more drinks. It was a really nice evening. Gayle and Lyn and Vern and Marie are the best. I wish Vern had never sold the boat. That was a great gig. Vern was one of the best, if not the best, guy I ever worked for, and Marie, what a great lady.

I went to see Vicky and Paul the next week. They were living at the Ritz Residences on Singer Island while their new house was being built. The house would be done the next summer. It's some monster on Manalapan, right on the beach, thirty thousand square feet or some crazy shit like that. I had a cup of coffee with Vicky. Paul was about twenty minutes late. I should have walked out right then and said, "Fuck this prick." I was looking for one last gig to get me by and save a few more dollars. This would be no easy task.

Vicky and I chatted about Gayle and Lyn—they were from RVA as well—and she asked how I liked working for Vern and Marie. I said, "I love them. If he had not sold the boat, I would still be working for them."

When Paul finally showed up, he got right to the point. I think he had something else going on, so he kept it short. They wanted to hire me for December, and if all parties got along, they would hire me full time at the first of the year. It was the middle of October, so this was still two months away. I told Vicky, "Since I don't know you, I need a two-thousand-dollar deposit, and my fee is a thousand a week plus expenses. If I block out the month, I want to make sure I get something in case you folks cancel on me." Vicky looked at Paul, and they agreed. I said, "Fine. I will block the whole month out."

Paul asked if I was a skier, and I said I was. He said, "We need you to go to Vail for a week as well."

I said, "Sure, I can do that."

He got up, saying he had to take a call, and then we shook hands and said goodbye. Vicky and I talked for a few minutes about food and their holiday plans. I said, "I can do all that, and we will keep in touch. If you need something, just call me."

"Great. Let me get you a check."

We said goodbye, and then I was off to have lunch at my favorite lunch spot in Palm Beach, the Avocado Grill. I love to girl-watch there as much as I like the grilled octopus. Vicky seemed very nice but a little weird. I felt good. I had four grand for December booked and a nice tip as well, so I would take a few months off, chill, and just do a few private parties. I always land on my feet.

Where to start with the Saunders? This was my last gig for now. They turned out to be some of the weirdest fucks I've ever worked for. I mean, this guy wore panties and a woman's training bra. Tell me that's is not weird. I did a few private parties over the next month and one short yacht job to the Bahamas for some friends of Vern and Marie's. Then it was show-time.

December was right around the corner, and Vicky and I talked every day. I will say one thing: she and Paul were good with dates the first month. After that, every time there was a change of dates, guests, you name it, they could not get their shit together. This just drove me nuts, and Paul never apologized. That would be beneath him, as he thinks the world revolves around him and fuck everyone else. If not for that coronavirus shit, I would have left, but there were no jobs out there.

The first week, I cooked for just Paul and Vicky and got the house ready for Christmas. The next week, we flew to Vail in Paul's Challenger aircraft. They owned the penthouse at the Willows, a really nice place. The kids would arrive in a few days. He sent the plane for them.

We spent a week there before returning to Palm Beach. It was an easy week. I made breakfast and a few dinners, cleaned up a little in the morning, and that was it. Paul has two sons, Brock and Hutch, both married and with kids. Both wives are total bitches. They didn't work, but to hear them talk, you'd have thought they wear royalty. They remind me of the Schlegels in Dallas, only not as bad, but still nasty. I just acted like I really liked them and had a smile every day just to put on a show.

I liked being back in Vail. I got together with some old friends. Old Pepi was still alive and kicking, and skiing as well. What a cool old guy. All I can say is that he is a legend, end of story.

I quickly realized that I'd made a mistake by taking the full-time job. I still kick myself in the ass when I look back. Paul did not even offer to buy me a ski pass. It's like $180 a day to ski Vail. What a rip-off. I will never ski there again; it's just stupid money. In all my past jobs, my boss always took care of a ski pass for me. That's when I knew he was one cheap prick. I have to 'fess up. He did buy me lunch at the Game Creek Lodge one day, but I found out later that he had to spend a minimum every season and he hadn't spent a dime, so it wasn't like he was doing me a favor. He let me know he was treating. Big Daddy, as he called himself, always let you know he was the best and was buying.

Still, I got some ski time in. I also took my old girlfriend to Jackson's Steakhouse. That's one nice piece of ass. We had a nice dinner, too. Only one of the sons made this trip, Hutch, or Paul Jr., the youngest. He wasn't a bad guy, but like every rich, spoiled kid, he had no idea what it's like to work for anything. His wife, Taylor, was nothing special, but she thought she was.

The skiing was great. There was lots of snow, so everyone was happy. Vicky was not much of a skier, but she had the best equipment. She just tried to make Paul happy. It was all about him every day. Every meal, he came first. She could not make a decision without talking to him. That is so weak and no way to live life. Poor bitch. I just kept my mouth shut.

It was a short trip, and then we were on the plane back to Palm Beach.

Brock, the older son, would join the rest of the family once we got back. Paul was going to send the plan to RVA to pick him up, and they would spend the rest of the holidays and New Year's in Palm Beach. They would go out for a few nights and have breakfast every day and a few lunches, but it was not a bad schedule.

Brock's wife, Sara Alexander Squire—I mean, come on; what bitch needs three names?—Was right up there with the Schlegels from Dallas in thinking her shit didn't stink. After two kids, that ass was getting wide. Poor Brock had to put up with her shit. I don't believe some of these guys. They have all the money, but they still put up with these bitches' shit. I would send them packing, just write them a check and be done with them. Many don't work; they just stay home and spend their husbands' money. What guy in their right mind would put up with that shit? I just watch it from the sidelines. What do I know? I am just the hired staff, a poor chef.

The rest of the holidays went off pretty easily. I did a Mexican buffet one night, turkey chili with all the sides, and fish tacos. On Christmas Day, I made a roast and turkey, and for New Year's day, I made prime rib. The whole family was happy with my cooking, and I guess they liked my personality, because they wanted to hire me full time. I put on a pretty good front. I did not like this family at all, but I did like the money, so I just put on my smiley face every day.

It turned out that I would only have two put up with the kids and grandkids a few times a year in Palm Beach. They wanted me to spend the summer in Richmond, Virginia, where the office was and the rest of the family lived. They didn't entertain much, as he has no friends, mostly just the kids and family members, his brother and sister and Vicky's sister. I can count the guests on two hands.

The job did not sound bad, aside from working for an ego freak and a slightly weird wife. Plus, it's nice to get out of South Florida for the summer, and RVA sounded pretty good. I just wanted to kill a few more years and then get the hell out of there and back to Spain, so I decided to take a chance with this couple. How bad could it be? I did not know how weird these two were.

It turned out that this guy made his money in hedge funds and then branched out into doing venture capital, golf courses—you name it, he is into it, just a greedy fuck. What else, I am not sure, but I do know this guy is no angel. He got one of the largest fines in Wall Street history for trying to manipulate some companies' prices and, I think, front-running. Let's just say you don't get that kind of money without doing some shady shit and fucking everyone along the way. I heard him on the phone more than once doing front-running. Robbie would say, "Are you sure you want to do this?" And Paul always answered, "Just do it." One time, Paul gave Hutch, the younger son, twenty million to start his own fund, I think just to do trading on the Grey market for Paul.

I think the guy is a crook. I have many stories about him, but let's cover the front-running first, and you tell me. I am sure you will agree. You don't get that kind of money without fucking some guys in the ass along the way. He might even have been fucked in the ass himself, but I think he likes that. Maybe that's why he wears the panties.

There is a company called Siga. Paul was on the phone with Robbie Stamper, and he could not get a large order filled for Siga.

His son Hutch was buying as well at a lower price. He was trying to get the price higher, so he got an order filled—I mean, a big order. Rob said, "You know this is front running. I ran it by our attorney, and she said you should not make the trade. They can trace you to Hutch via emails and phone calls. This is not good."

Paul said, "I don't agree. Fill the order. I don't care."

"Are you sure?"

"Just do the order."

Guys like him never learn. It's greed. He got the largest fine ever on Wall Street, and he still doesn't care. It was a couple of million. I say take all their profits back and then fine them. Rich people only get hurt when you take their money. Then they learn. Paul's case was just pure greed. That was only one case. I am sure this prick has been doing this for years. That's why he opened a hedge fund for his kid in a different location. If you ask me, it's just not fair. Throw these fucks in jail and take some of their money. Then they will learn.

He tried to get Trump to step in and help with some patents they had pending. What a low life. That was one of many cases I overheard as he talked on the phone to Robbie and Hutch. On top of that, he would brag about what he was doing. So now you know what kind of guy this is.

I made it through the holidays, and I was thinking: *Do I want a full-time gig again for some rich asshole?* Then I thought: *What the fuck. I can always quit. Take the money.* When we got back from Vail, nothing exciting happened in Palm Beach. It was just family stuff, pretty easy, except for fucking the Brazilian nanny. She was a little thick, but she had a pretty face and big tits. Big girls need some fucking, too. It was a little rough, but she was young, and that shit was wet as soon as I got down to it. That is always a good sign. Plus, the thicker ones appreciate it a little more because they don't always get it.

We did Christmas family dinner with all the grandkids, and I served the meal family-style: roast turkey, mashed potatoes, green beans, tossed salad, and all the sides. Paul gave me a nice tip.

So, I started the new year off with a new family and not a bad gig. Over the next two years, I got two more trips to Vail and was able to ski at a private ski mountain, Yellowstone Club. Paul had just bought a lot there and joined the club and was thinking of building there. I mean, how many houses does one family need? Greed and ego. House in RVA, the new place in Manalapan, the Singer Island Ritz, Vail. New York, Yellowstone Club, St. Croix and now the Greenbrier in West Virginia. That's just way too much damn money. Nobody needs that many homes.

I would be traveling to all the houses, but I never went to New York, which was a good thing. I cannot stand the city. It's just a shithole, not to mention all the nasty New Yorkers. You can have that place. Most of the job was in RVA and Florida. I liked RVA. It's a nice place with lots of young people, not like Palm Beach, land of the gray-hairs.

The first few months just flew by. The house in Manalapan would not be ready until the summer. I hung out at the Ritz. Paul had a sweet downstairs that opened right onto the sand. I would take my break down there in the afternoon, have a coffee, and look at the girls on the beach. I miss that.

Before I get into some of the stories, let me tell you a little about Paul. The first month I worked for him, I tidied up the bedroom and picked up dirty clothes from the floor, mostly women's panties, Victoria's Secret thongs, lace. You know the type. I am sure you've bought some for your wife or girlfriend over the years. I know I have. I thought: *That old broad Vicky is still wearing some sexy shit. That's cool. I mean, I would not want to see her in them, but that's cool.*

So, I picked up a pile of these panties and put them in Vicky's clothes basket. I mean, that's what anyone would do. That is, if you're normal. The next day, Vicky was doing her laundry, and I was in the kitchen. Paul came in for his breakfast and shake, and the first thing he said was, "I like that you are cleaning up our dirty clothes and fixing the bed in the morning. That's all great, and we like that, but whatever is on my side of the closet is mine. Especially the panties. They're mine."

I said, "Cool. Got it."

He looked at me, and I just smiled and said, "Ok."

Then he said, "The reason that I wear them is that they are so comfortable."

"Sure."

I mean, give me a break. Who believes that shit? A string up your ass, and what about your nuts in a ball bag? Come on. I still laugh about that morning. That was only the first. There was more later. Wait until you hear about the training bra.

He dressed for shit in skintight clothes, but he thought he looked good in them. Yeah, if you're Brad Pitt. Paul is like six three or four and 156 pounds, skin and bones, no ass. He thinks he is a stud and that women think he is sexy, but people just laugh at him. And poor Vicky would not say a word, even when he walked around in a ball bag in front of his kids, mother, and guests. The front desk at the Ritz told him that he was not to wear one inside unless he had a cover-up on. He made a big stink, but that was the rule. And on top of that, the gray hair on his chest looked like a weed patch. What a joke. I could not believe that Vicky put up with his shit, but she had nowhere to go.

The guy never tipped, and he complained about everything. He took whatever he could get for free: candy, bottled water, fruit from the front desk, you name it. If it was free, he'd take more than his fair share and more. He would have dozens of opened waters on his desk and on the counter in the kitchen. Instead of one apple, he would take all he could carry. He was just a cheap fuck. He was the same way with to-go stuff or buffets at the golf clubs. If only he knew that everyone was laughing at him.

I told all my friends and the gang in RVA about the panties, and they all thought that was par for him and just laughed. The joke with my golf buddies was that when we teed up and cracked the first beer, I'd say, "Ok, guys. Which one of you fucks is wearing panties?" Then someone would always say, "I've got my ball bag on. What about you, Chef?" And we'd all laugh. This is where the name Mr. Panties came from.

Paul was very inconsiderate as well and cared about nobody else's time but his. He was always late and made his guests and everyone else wait for him. As for his kids, they had no choice but to do what Big Daddy wanted or goodbye trust fund. What a joke. I would tell him to stick that money up his ass, but they had no balls.

One good thing was that I met some really nice friends. They worked at the Ritz, and I still keep in touch with them today: Rafael, the desk manager, and Dirk, the GM, really great guys. They were good to me.

We did one more ski trip the first year to Vail. It was just me, Paul, Hutch, and his wife and their new baby. Vicky did not make the trip. I thought: *Yeah, this could work for the next two years.* I'd have to put with some shit and be around some weird rich guy, but I'd save some money and get a few free ski trips. I still needed to work some, so I'd just hang in there.

Skiing was great that year. Paul took me to Game Creek again, but I had to buy my own ski pass. The trip lasted a week. Willow Creek had a terrible breakfast buffet, so I made breakfast every day. I also made lunch on the slopes and a few dinners. This was the last trip with the family to Vail. Paul had just bought a lot in Yellowstone Club in Montana and was going to sell the place in Vail. I guess they were just done with it. I was, too. I loved that place and the town. I mean, there are a lot of rich assholes, but it's a great mountain to ski. I miss it, but it costs too much money to ski and go out, so I will not return.

Back in Palm Beach, everything was soon back to normal. Vicky said she missed my cooking and was glad I was back. I quickly got back into my routine. Most of the time, I cooked for just Paul and Vicky and maybe for a dinner party every few weeks. There were a few bright spots about the job. It just sucked being around super-cheap people who complained about everything and thought they knew it all. That got old fast.

The next few months were pretty easy. The kids did not come down, and there were no house-guests. Paul and Vicky would be going back to RVA on the first of June, and I would drive up and spend the summer there. I thought that would be cool. I could drive over to Ohio, see my favorite cousin, Lisa, and stop by and see my mom. Plus, on the way, I could hit the Bourbon Trail. That was on my summer bucket list.

I didn't meet any interesting people the first year. A few of the folks living in the building were nice, just nobody of any great importance. Before spring came, we had two dinner parties. Either the guests knew Paul or he wanted to know them. They all wanted something or just to brag. Most people cannot stand the prick. I mean, if you're a guy, would you hang out with a weird fuck who wears panties and brags about himself all the time? Hell, no. So, you get the picture.

Here are a few dinner party stories from the Ritz. You might know these two couples, but if you are an investor, stay clear unless you want to take it up the ass. Paul has done well in the market and investments, but his clients and investors have taken it in the ass big time. Plus, he won't pay his bills.

More on that later. Let's cover these two dinner parties. I was embarrassed even to pour the wine; that's how cheap this fuck is. He had invited the neighbors and Zygi Wilf, the owner of the Minnesota Vikings and some pro soccer teams. He is on the *Forbes* list, a big-time real estate developer. I'm not sure how Paul met him—probably playing golf. This guy was out of Paul's league. He came over with his wife and two of his kids. They seemed like a really nice family. The kids were in college and very polite, and his wife was nice as well. As for Zygi, that is a different story. Don't get me wrong. He wasn't a bad guy, but like all billionaires, it was all about him. He had to be the center of attention, and only what he was saying was important. It was the only time I ever saw Paul at a loss for words. He couldn't get one word in, and it was killing him that he was not the center of attention for once. I am sure he wanted to brag about the new house he was building, but Zygi was in command, and the other guests wanted to know what it was like to own a pro team. Zigi talked about the corporate Gulf-stream, while Paul had an old, rundown Challenger on it's last legs. It broke down every month, and I didn't fly on it after the first few trips.

I never even got a chance to tell them what was for dinner, as they were deep in conversation about football. I served my signature red snapper with the mango salsa, wild rice, and roasted veggies, with a fruit tart for dessert. Thank God Al from downstairs brought some nice wine. He knew Paul served shit for wine, and I am sure he did not want to have a nice dinner and drink some shit wine that Paul said was great. Al knew the drill. He had been over a few times. We chatted and laughed about it. Everyone knew how cheap Paul was. The smart ones didn't come back, or they brought some good wine to drink.

Zygi had been in trouble in New Jersey after deceiving investors. You could tell the minute he started talking he was dirty. That was something he and Paul had in common, along with their big egos and little dicks.

I finished cleaning up, and Al came into the kitchen and said, "Thanks. That was a great meal." He was the only one with some class. He was not impressed with Zygi, and that made two of us. Paul was the kind of guy who just wanted to brag that the owner of the Vikings had come over for dinner, like some kid. Zygi never came back—nobody did—but to hear Paul talk, they were best buddies.

The next day, all Paul could talk about was this guy. He asked what I thought of Zygi, and I really talked him up, saying he was on the *Forbes* list and what a nice guy, everything Paul wanted to hear. I've learned over the years while working for these rich pricks that someone always has a bigger dick around the corner. Really, how much does one man need? Six, eight homes? Come on. It's all ego.

The other dinner party was with Paul's friend Jeffrey Citron, a Jew from New Jersey. He had been over a few times. Like the rest of the gang, he knew it all, and everything he had was the best. It's funny, but I am sure all these guys talk behind each other's backs. Like I said, none of these guys have any true friends. It's sad. It's all about dollars and what they have. So weak. I heard Paul say more than once that he only liked making money.

Citron lived large, with a big yacht, houses all over the place, a Gulf-stream, all the toys. I was surprised that he didn't have a trophy wife. His wife was no prize and was getting a little fat. I would have told her to drop some pounds, and if she didn't, I would have given her the boot. On top of that, she was young. I think they were both in their late forties, young to have that kind of money. He'd made it when he was young. He'd started and sold the phone company Vonage for hundreds of millions. Then he'd started high-frequency trading, sold that for even more money, started an e-trade company, and sold that. I mean, the guy just kept killing it.

I don't know who was worse, Paul or him. He had been by a handful of times, and they acted like friends, but they couldn't stand each other because they were alike. Even their wives were fucking messes. Dinner was not much to talk about. They just talked about their yachts and summer in the Med. Then Paul would brag about the house he was building at the Yellowstone Club or the house in Manalapan that would be done next year.

I couldn't tell the guests what was on the menu because they were all trying to get a word in edgewise. I just put dinner down and waited. Then I told them what was for dinner. None of these folks were foodies. The Citrons had a wine cellar from hell. He just bought whatever was the best that year and bragged about it when he came over. What an asshole. I do not miss that prick.

The next few months just flew by, and finally, I headed up to RVA. It was a nice road trip. I spent the night in Charleston and half a day in Savannah, and of course, I put it on the house credit card. It was like a free road trip. Sometimes the perks are not so bad.

I got to RVA two days later, checked in with the boss, unpacked in the guesthouse, and made plans for the summer. It's really a nice spot out in the country. Manakin Sabot was about thirty minutes away. RVA is divided into about four or five parts: downtown, Short Pump, the stadium, and the fan district. I really enjoyed my time there and met some really nice friends. I lived out in the country, but in a few minutes, I could be downtown or in Short Pump, having a nice lunch at West Coast Provisions, my favorite spot, Tazza, which has great pork tacos and a nice grilled salmon, and of course, Red Salt.

This was my first summer with the Saunders in RVA. I would be back for one more summer, but that would be a short one because of COVID. That first summer, it was the same drill as Palm Beach. I did only one dinner party. I don't count the kids; that's family. Like I said, Paul and Vicky had no friends. Vicky could have had some, but no one wanted to hang out with Paul. He was rude and weird. He would have guests over and just take off or show up late. He did that with the kids and guests alike. He would just get up and leave, or he'd bring out blueprints of the house he was building and talk about how much he was spending on the place. I got the "tool" thing from Jack and Deb's son, who was home from Clemson. He came up with that when I first met him. He asked, "How is working for the tool?" And I just laughed. He hit the nail on the head. Paul is a real tool, and that's putting it lightly. From then on, I've described Paul as a real tool; that fits him well.

That summer, I went back to Ohio to see my mom and Lisa, my favorite cousin, in Columbus, and on the way, I stopped at the Greenbrier for a round of golf. It was way overpriced, but it was on my bucket list. It's old and rundown and living on it's past reputation. I would not go there again. Paul was building a house there, only five million or so, after he'd just moved into the new house in Manalapan. This guy has way too much money.

On my way to Ohio, I made one more stop: the Bourbon Trail. That was on my list as well. The first stop was Woodford Distillery. Then I went to Four Roses, followed by a few more. This is a pretty spot in Kentucky, with all these horse farms and big, big money. Across from the Woodford was the farm owned by some Wall Street fuck whose horse had won the Derby a few years back. What a bad-ass place. Several of the farms were just over the top. This was a really cool trip, and I highly recommend it.

But once you've seen one distillery, you have seen them all. Some have some history, but they're all pretty much the same, so after hitting a few, I called it a day and headed off to Columbus to see Mom. That was a cool trip. After seeing her, I had to get back to RVA. Paul and Vicky would be home in a few days, and I was supposed to be house-sitting while they were in the Med for two weeks. I got back, everything was fine. I still had a few days to rest and get the house in order before they returned. I met up with the neighbors, a great crew: Jack and Deb, and Chester and Vicky.

Here's a little bit about Dr. Chester Sharp. Besides being a great guy, Chester changes kids' lives. He is one of the top orthopedic surgeons in the country, but you would never know it by talking to him. He's very humble and just a great human being, and his wife, Vicky, is a star. She's a little high maintenance, but that's ok. She was a cheerleader at Virginia Tech and all through high school, so you know the type. Ball-buster and not cheap, but I liked her. Every time we went out, some family or kid would come by and thank him for fixing something. Chester would stop whatever he was doing, look at the person's hand or foot, and ask them if they were ok. On top of that, he makes trips to third-world countries and trains doctors and does surgery on these kids for free. He is also one of the top sponsors for the Special Olympics. That is a full plate, and you never hear him brag about it. He is just giving back, unlike Paul, who, if he does something, wants everyone to know, and if there is nothing in it for him, forget about it; he will pass. It's always about Big Daddy, Mr. Panties.

Doc, my hat's off to you. You're one hell of a great man. All the best to you and Vicky. I hope to see the whole RVA gang in Spain. You know I love you guys. You are the best. The world needs more guys like you, and that's no bullshit. Keep up the great work.

Before Paul and Vicky got back, we all had a nice night out at Hermitage. That's the golf course that all these folks belong to. Chester and Jack would never let me buy. We would hang out, smoke a cigar, enjoy a great dinner, have some good conversation, and drink a little brown stuff, aka bourbon. We did that quite a few times that summer, and I did one nice dinner party at Jack's place with the whole gang, Italian buffet. Big hit. I miss those guys.

I had some good times with Jack and the gang, and I met a few golf buddies while playing Hunting Hawk. Tim and I were playing Hunting Hawk with this tall kid, Matt—I say "kid," but he was in his thirties. He could hit the ball a country mile. It turned out that Matt and Tim knew a few of the same folks, so it was a nice round. He was a nice, smart young man, and we hit it off. Plus, he had one of my dream jobs. He worked for Cigar International, doing marketing, sales, and events. What a great gig.

We finished the round, and I bought the beers. Matt had a nice sample box in his car, and he gave it to me. What a great day. I said, "Let's get together next week and play again." I love Tim, but he is a hack. This kid had game, probably an eight handicap. It's nice to play with a good golfer. It makes me play better. With Tim, I just can't get into the grove. Plus, he smokes way too much pot for me. Matt and I played the following week at the Hawk again. It was close for both of us. I told him I was a private chef for Paul Saunders. Matt said he thought he'd heard of him and James River Capital. He asked his dad if he knew him, and you won't believe what his dad said. Oh, by the way, Matt's dad is a pretty big-time attorney in RVA, and one of his clients is the Pruitt family. They own all the land around the Short Pump area and the mall. He said, "Yeah, I know the cheap prick. Tell the chef to tell Paul to pay me the thirty grand he owes the firm for the last three years. We did some work for him, and he never paid us. He has that rep around town."

I just laughed. That sounded like him. I am sure it's true. Why would his dad make that up? I just thought: *What the hell. This is my last job. One more year to get my Social Security check. I just hope I can hang in there.*

Paul and Vicky returned, and I had to go back to the grind. It was not so bad when it was just them, but add in the kids, nanny, and grandkids, and it was a clusterfuck. Thank God they only came a few times a year. Paul was tough enough by himself. I had to bring him lunch every day, as he was too cheap to go out for lunch. His assistant, Robin, did everything for him. I still can't believe the shit she did for him and the shit she had to put up with. I am surprised she has not sued him or that some other employees have not sued. I know one flight attendant made a complaint against him and asked not to fly with him again. She was with the Delta Wheels Up private charter service.

The first week they were back, I knew this was my last gig. I brought Paul his breakfast in his office, and the guy was standing in the middle of the room in nothing but a pair of women's panties, a bright red Victoria's Secret G-string, just like modeling the shit. I looked at him and said, "I'm really sorry. Here is your breakfast."

As I was leaving, he said, "Chef, wait a minute. I just like the way they feel. That's why I wear them."

I looked at him and said, "Sure. Whatever makes you feel good." Then I just smiled and walked out.

I'd known that he wore panties for a while. When I first started, I put them on Vicky's side, and he told me that they were his and not to touch them. I knew he was weird then. This was about the time he started wearing a Nike training bra as well. He said it helped support his shoulders. What a crock of shit. He is just one weird dude.

Not much happened during the winter in Palm Beach. Only a few people came over, and none are worth talking about. I did meet a few interesting guys at Trump International in Palm Beach. Paul belonged to the club. I dropped him off to play there, and I was supposed to pick him up and take him to the airport to fly back to RVA on business. Before he teed off, he gave me a tour, and then we headed to his locker. All the lockers had the members' names on them, as all private courses do, but next to his was Rudy Giuliani's.

As we headed out, who should walk around the corner, but the man himself. He said hi to Paul, and Paul introduced me. We shook hands and chatted for a few minutes. I said, "I've always respected you and thought you did a great job in New York. We need more men like you in office."

We had a nice chat, and he joined me for breakfast while Paul played golf. I asked him if I could get a photo of us together, but the Don does not like photos being taken in the club. I was cool with that. He was a first-class guy. We need more guys like him in charge of things. Then this country could get more done. I was very impressed that he took the time to have breakfast with me. I will never forget that morning. We finished breakfast and said our goodbyes, and I thanked him for taking the time for me. That was way cool.

A few weeks later, I met the man himself, Donald, in the grill room. I was with Paul. We did the fist bump, and I told him I was a fan of his and voted for him. We spoke for a few minutes, and it was pretty cool, but I could tell he was an egomaniac, just like Paul. They think they're special; all these rich pricks are the same. But it was cool to meet the Donald. Yeah, he is one interesting dude.

We did one more ski trip that winter, to Yellowstone Club. If you don't know Yellowstone Club, it's a private ski and golf course community in Montana. It's where the billionaires go to get away from the million-aires. If you ask me, it's just a bunch of Wall Street crooks and A-list celeb-rities from LA. The mountain sucks, and the Warren Miller Lodge is just ok, nothing great. But it's ultra-private. If you're really rich and like being around other assholes, you will like it there. Paul paid about seventy grand for a ski locker, no shit, and it was about six feet wide and high and two or three feet deep. That's just fucking crazy for a ski locker, and he bought two.

Brock and his family showed up a few days later, and I was back working my ass off, making breakfast and dinner and running to the store every day for shit. Everyone had to have something different, and it was all just a pain in the ass. The only good thing was that I did get a little ski time in, and Paul bought lunch a few times on the mountain.

There was a restaurant at the top, kind of high-end. The second time we had lunch there, he told us all that if we ate the hot buffet, we had to pay for ourselves. We were only allowed to eat the salad and soup buffet. The hot side was fish, meat, and veggies, a proper ski lunch. It was an extra sixteen dollars, and the other was around fourteen dollars. He said it was a rip-off and, if we wanted it, we had to pay for it ourselves. I told you this was one cheap prick. So, I never had lunch with him again. Fuck you. Invite me to lunch and tell me what I can and can't order. That's like two-year-old shit.

I never took him up on lunch or golf again. I did not want the drama or the bullshit. I just skied on my own and ate in town when I was off, because, on the mountain, you cannot pay for anything; you just sign for it.

A few days passed, and it was time to head back. It was a ten-day trip. On the last night before we were to leave, the nanny was getting something for the baby in the kitchen. It was about two in the morning. As she came up the steps, there was Paul, in the middle of the living room, with his panties on, kind of dancing by the fireplace. When he saw her, he just turned around and kept dancing. She got the baby's food and hauled ass back downstairs.

The next morning, she told Brock's wife, Alexandra, what had happened. She was worried that Paul might tell them to fire her because of what she had seen. So now the cat was out of the bag. They all knew grandpa had issues. I was in the kitchen when all of this was going down, and I caught the tail end of the conversation. This was before Paul came down. Vicky said to the nanny, "I am sorry you had to see Paul like that. He just likes to be in touch with his feminine side."

I almost burst out laughing. What a crock of shit. He is just one weird fuck. He is not in touch with anything. I have to give Vicky credit. She stood by her man, or whatever the hell he thinks he is. But like I said, she has no life without him. She has let herself go, so no guy is going to pick that shit up. Plus, she has a gut now. She's no catch for sure, and she is a little weird, so they are kind of made for each other.

Weird and weirder. The kids already knew Big Daddy was a panty-wearing fruit, and I think the wives did, too, but they were all part of the trust fund, and they knew they would never have to work the rest of their lives as long as they went along with whatever Big Daddy wanted. If you ask me, that is no way to raise a family, and it's sure as hell no way to live, waiting for the old man to die. He will live forever. He is too mean and cheap to die early.

That was the highlight of the Yellowstone trip. It was my last time there, and I have no desire to ever go back; it's just not that great.

We were all up early, and I made breakfast. Then the SUV was loaded, and like always, Paul was late, either on the phone or doing whatever he wanted. We were all waiting when Vicky came out and said to Brock and me, "Paul is having a vertigo attack, and he cannot get up. Can you help him get to his feet and carry his bags?"

We headed into the bedroom, and he was fully dressed but could not get out of bed. He asked us to pick him up, and we carried him out to the SUV. Then I came back and got his bags. No sooner had we driven a few miles than he was back to normal. Vicky was holding his hand like he was a little baby. "Oh, honey, are you all right? Should I call the doctor? Do you want anything? What can I get you?"

"Yeah, shut the fuck up and give me a blowjob." That's what I would have said. I think it was all for show to get attention from the rest of the family. Oh, poor Paul. What a shitshow.

We were an hour late, but it was his plane. They were not happy, but what were they going to do? We dropped the kids off in RVA, got some fuel, and headed back to Palm Beach. We skied Vail one more time that year but never returned to Yellowstone. That was the one trip I will never forget. I would spend one more summer in RVA, but it would be a short one because the Corona-virus was just starting to get out of hand and Paul is a hypochondriac. So, we were stuck in RVA, and I was living in hell.

The kids came over every weekend for dinner. Paul wouldn't leave the house. I felt like a slave at their beck and call. I knew this was not going to last long. The guy was driving me crazy every day: "Are you ok?" "Did you go somewhere?" "What did you do on your off day?" All I can tell you is that it was a boring summer, no dinner guests, just the kids.

I did have some fun playing golf with my RVA gang. That was the best part. I have one more golf story. If you are a golfer, you will understand and think: *Wow, what a prick. Who does he think he is?* I could not believe this myself. It was a first for me, and I even felt embarrassed, and Vicky did for sure, but she was used to the shit he pulled. It was a Sunday afternoon. Paul had promised all summer to take me to play Kinloch. He was one of the founding members, and when you go to the club with him, he is sure to tell you. Then he'll tell you that it's the best course in the country and show you that his name is on the board. Everything he does, owns, or has anything to do with, you can bet it's the best—at least, according to him. That shit just gets old. We headed to the course in separate cars. Vicky was going to join as well.

I got the grand tour. It's a really nice club but not the best in the country. I will take Sherwood any day of the week. That's a bad-ass club. We hit some balls, and they were running a little behind, and Paul was already pissed off. "What do you mean, backed up?" He told the starter.

"I am sorry, Mr. Saunders. We just had a few foursomes go off. It might be a little slow."

Paul barked back, "I hope not."

We teed off, and he was already in a rush. You have to walk this course and have a caddy, and Paul was moving at a forced march. I had played with him a few times already, and I kept saying I would never play with him again, but I wanted to play this course. After all, it's supposed to be the best in the country.

The front nine went well. We waited a few times, and Paul hit into the group ahead of us a few times. He was just rude, complaining, "These guys are playing too slow." What he needed was a good bitch-slapping, but he might have liked that. We got to the turn, and now it was backed up on this par five. He got on his cell, called the head pro, and started giving him shit: "Why did you play these foursomes back to back? You know I had a tee time, and you put me behind them." I mean, he was being a real dick.

Before we teed off, the head pro rolled up, and Paul said he wanted to play through the groups ahead of us. The pro said, "There are three foursomes."

Paul said, "I don't care. They're playing slowly. And I am playing through."

The pro said, "I will be back. I will meet you on the next tee."

I could tell Vicky was embarrassed, but it was her own fault. She could always leave the prick. She liked the money too much, and sadly, I think she worshiped Paul.

We got to the next tee box, and the pro was there. He walked over to Paul and said, "You're good to play through."

Paul hit way short on the par-three. I was sure the guys on the green were laughing and thinking, who is this asshole? I topped my shot, as I just wanted to get off the course, and Vicky just picked up. As we walked up to the green, I had my head down in embarrassment. Paul said, "Thanks, guys." He chipped on two puts, and we walked away. The look on these guys' faces said it all. I felt bad to be playing with these assholes.

I thought that was it. Then we got to the next par four, and there was the pro again. We were playing through this other foursome. I said, "Paul, I will pick up."

He said, "No, come on."

I just walked on, and Vicky did, too. These guys were like, what the fuck? We paid good money, too. Who is this fuck? We did that for two more holes. I have never been so embarrassed on a golf course in my life.

That was the last time I played golf with Paul, and I will never play with that prick again. He was just plain rude. I used to feel sorry for Vicky, but it's her own fault. She can leave the asshole any time. I did not get to play the whole course. That sucked, but what the hell. Vicky said on eighteen, "I will take you out here again, just us two." It never happened. I am sure Paul would not pay for the round unless he was playing with us; he'd be afraid he might miss out on something. The only good thing was he took me to the pro shop and bought me a shirt and hat. That was the least he could have done, and for the next year, he brought it up: "I took you to Kinloch and bought you a shirt and hat." Yes, he is that cheap, and if he bought you lunch last year, you will hear about it for months to come.

I am sad to say I took him up on the invitation to go to a Final Four game. This was the year UVA won the national championship. I think they were playing Western Kentucky, and I got a last-minute invite, as someone did not show up. It was Paul Jr., his wife, Vicky, Paul, and me. We got there just in time. Paul is always late, and he makes people wait for him. That's just how he is. I got the tour, and we went to the private dining room. Food and beer were all comped before the game. It was pretty nice, but these colleges are making too much money. As we ate, Paul told me how great this was, how much he'd had to donate, how it's the best school, and just more and more bullshit.

We made it to the seats, and yes, they were right on the floor. I would have enjoyed it more if I hadn't been forced to hear every five minutes how much he'd spent to get the seats. He just wanted me to stroke his ego.

Finally, thank God, the game started. This was a first, but I didn't need to be told ten times how this was the best and how lucky I was. I had been asked to go to games in the past. It was always last minute, and I was last on the guest list. I would see Chester, and he would ask if I had gone. He was one spot above me, but he never wanted to go. He said it was not worth the bullshit. Now I knew what he meant. This was my last game. I have to say it was cool on the floor, but having to do all that ass-kissing made it not worth it.

By now, I was counting my paychecks so I could quit the job and get away from this cheap prick, and I am getting close. Just a few more, and then I would be on my way back to Spain. I was tired of these rich assholes. I'd had a great run, but now I was getting close to hanging my spurs up. It'd been a wild ride, and this was my last gig.

Here is a funny story. Vicky, Paul, and I were in the kitchen, talking before dinner, and somehow Paul Jr. came up in the conversation. I mentioned the Julien boys and said how spoiled they were and that the eight-year-old was still wearing pull-ups. Then Vicky said, "Paul Jr. wet the bed until he was ten."

I said, "What? You have to be kidding me."

Then Vicky, who is always right—at least, she thinks she is—said, "Oh, that's normal."

I looked at both of them and laughed. I said, "I don't know where you folks come from, but pissing the bed at that age is not normal, and neither is wearing pull-ups."

Paul said, "I don't agree."

"Really?"

He went on to say that he wet the bed until he was fourteen. He even went in his pants. What grown man would tell anyone that? I would be so embarrassed. That just put the icing on the cake. I don't know who raises their kids like that, but that is fucked up. Finally, I got up and walked away to serve dinner. What a shitshow.

All these guys are just weird, and the wives are even worse sometimes. They have too much time on their hands and nothing to do. If you want to talk about lazy, Vicky wouldn't even walk down the driveway to get the mail. She seemed to think it was beneath her. If I were off for a few days, she would let it sit there, or she would ask the housekeeper, Marie, to get it. That's just lazy, and she needs the exercise. Get out and walk. It just drives me crazy.

One weekend, she got a package on Saturday, and I was off. The delivery man left it by the gate, as it was closed and the family had stepped out to play golf. I came in on Monday, and before I could start my routine, Vicky paged me to come to her office. I was like, oh, shit. What does this bitch want now?

Vicky said, "There is a package down at the gate. Would you go get it?"

I said, "Sure. When did it come in?"

"Saturday."

"Why didn't you go get it? It rained yesterday."

"I was too busy, and I was waiting for you."

I looked at her and just shook my head. Vicky said, "What's wrong?"

I said, "What are you going to do when I am gone?"

She said, "Oh, Chef, you won't leave us."

"Oh, yeah? Don't hold your breath," I said and walked away.

I think she still wipes the two boys' asses because they can't do it themselves. When the kids were there on Thanksgiving for the first time at the new house, Vicky bought not one but three kinds of pillows for these spoiled fucks. The dinner conversation was all about if the pillows were all right and the mattresses were ok. Hutch said they were fine. Brock said that one was too hard and the other was too soft. You've got to be shitting me. These ungrateful pieces of shit, staying in a thirty-five-million-dollar house, all rooms with an ocean view, never had to open their wallet, yet they still complained about the pillows. Brock told Vicky the name of a company that made pillows he liked. Then she said, "Give me the info, and I will order some." What a joke. Hey, Mom, can you wash my dick for me as well?" That was the whole dinner conversation. I think she spent around fifty grand on mattresses and pillows. Just too much money for one family.

Paul told me I don't know how many times, "You can never have too much money," and, "My hobby is making money." He bragged all the time about how much he had, but he wouldn't spend it or, for God's sake, tip anyone. The kids are all the same. All they talk about is money.

Paul only cares about himself and has an ego you cannot believe. He knows everything, and he has the best of everything, and he will tell you that. He dresses for shit, all this skintight stuff, and half his clothes are thirty years old. He won't get rid of anything. I was on my way to RVA the first summer, and I forgot my traveling golf club bag. He had five sitting in the spare garage. Three were like new, and two were pieces of shit. I asked him if I could have one of the old ones, and he told me, "No, I might need it."

I almost laughed in his face. I said, "Are you serious?"

He said, "Yes, I might need it."

I would have been embarrassed to use it. I just needed it for the trip back, and then I'd throw it in the trash. That's how bad it was. What an asshole. I told Jack and Chester the story, and they just laughed, and Jack said, "I have an old bag you can have." The next day, I threw it in Paul's face, saying what a nice guy Jack was for giving me his spare traveling bag. He did not say shit. Fuck him.

He asked me to drive him a few times, but after the last trip to the airport, I never drove him again, and I told Vicky, "Don't ask me. I am not doing it." All he does is complain, and he is a rude driver. He's lucky someone hasn't pulled him over and kicked his ass. He thinks, because he is special and has a Porsche Panamera, he owns the road. He cuts people off and drives right up your ass, just like those nasty New Yorkers on 95 in South Florida. He has no respect for other people.

That's Paul Saunders, a complaining little whore. When he gets hurt, he has to tell the whole world. I won't forget how, during one of the last few weeks before I quit, I had a dinner party for six guests, including Louis Capona and Peanut, whom I'd met before and lived down the street, a super-cool couple, and RJ and his wife. He is a big-time investor. Dinner was on the patio. Paul was wearing these skintight, see-through white pants. They looked like something Vicky should be wearing. You could see his G-string through them. *He had on a skintight shirt, too, like out of Saturday Night Fever.*

He didn't even have the wine chilled, and he offered no one a drink. Thank God for Vicky, or the guests would not have had a drink or wine for dinner. Lewis had a glass of Pouilly-Fuissé, and it was warm. Lewis said to Paul, "You need to chill the whites."

Paul said, "No, you serve them at room temperature." He didn't have a clue.

Lewis looked at me, and I just smiled. Paul did not want me to handle the wine. He didn't want me to open up anything good. Everything he had was cheap except the stuff guests brought him. On top of that, he thinks he knows wine. It's a joke. I finally got the salads out, and Paul was still working on the wine. It should have already been chilled and on the table. It made me look bad. So, now Paul had to rush to get the wine out and pour it, which he had no business doing. He poured each guest four ounces so they wouldn't drink the whole bottle.

On the way out to the patio, he tripped on the step and fell right on his side and elbow. He saved the wine—I have to give him credit for that. He got blood on his white pants. I think he was a little tipsy. He doesn't usually drink, and he'd had a taste of vodka. That might have done him in. How embarrassing—falling on your ass in your own home while doing something you had no business doing in the first place. I just laughed inside.

For two weeks, all he did was cry about his elbow. The same thing happened when he had a little skin cancer on his calf and they had to cut it off. You'd have thought the prick was dying. That was all I heard for weeks: "Oh, I might be dying. I've got cancer on my calf." It was like six stitches. What a pussy. I still laugh about that. And Vicky just held his hand and wiped his ass. "Oh, yes, honey, I am here for you. Whatever you need."

That kind of sums up Paul: cheap, selfish, demanding, and Mr. Know-It-All. As for Vicky, she was just a little weird. Ask anyone at the Ritz, and they will tell you that they're both weird, rude, and cheap, the worst couple in the building. I don't know Vicky's whole story, but to marry Paul, she can't be all together. I mean, how many wives would put up with their old man wearing women's panties and just being a selfish prick? On top of that, the guy had to read a book on how to make love to a woman. That's pretty sad.

Vicky is a piece of work, too. She would ask me to clean her purse if there was a spot as big as fly shit on it. The same with the carpet or furniture, yet her car was a fucking train wreck. She'd ask me to load and unload her golf clubs. One time, she asked me to go to the post office. It was around Christmas, and she thought the envelopes were too big to mail and wanted to make sure there was no extra postage. I just told her they were fine. I didn't even go to the post office. I knew they were ok. She might have had a Ph.D., but she still couldn't spell her own name. She had no common sense, just like Paul and the kids, yet they think they know it all.

She's just let herself go. In a way, I cannot blame her. Paul is not fucking her, and who would anyway? She's an old broad with a gut and no tits. I mean, she could have some work done, and she damn well needs it. But why? Paul; doesn't care. She has lost all her self-esteem, and she needs to hire someone to show her how to dress. She dresses like shit. Paul is not much better. Maybe these two tools were meant for each other.

Vicky once told me not to touch her wine. It was cheap, so I cooked with it sometimes. Come on, cupcake. She said, "Don't use it. I want to keep track of how much I am drinking." Give me a break. I think she was worried I was drinking that cheap shit. She might have two glasses a night with lots of ice. I saw her drop food on the floor and, like some homeless person, pick it up and eat it. It might be just one chip or a piece of lettuce from the salad. She also ate with her fingers. Paul was the same way— no-class nouveau riche. Can't take them out of the gutter. On top of that, she had a gas problem, always farting. The best thing is that she thinks she is still hot. Not in a million years would I jump on that shit. I told her the story about Paul telling me not to talk to the staff during working hours, and she just said, "Paul is right. Keep it to a 'hi' and 'good morning.'" Who do these fucks think they are?

When the kids and grandkids came down, I would be given a list from hell for these spoiled shits: three kids of milk, cashew, almond, and fat-free; three kinds of yogurt; special snacks. They would even have Amazon deliver stuff. Oh, I also had to have the two wives' special rosé. I mean, it was unbelievable, the shit they did for these kids. No wonder they can't wipe their own ass. They never have to. If they all crashed in his plane, I couldn't give two shits. The world would be a better place without these assholes.

What's sad is that Paul's brother and sister are normal. They don't have his money, but Rick is a big-time attorney, and his sister, Kirk, is one of the top dogs for Mary Kay. She went to school with the two sisters from RVA. She has to know her big brother is a tool. It's the money. But the sisters back in RVA said that he was out there when he was young and never grew up. I mean, shit, the guy was pissing the bed till he was fourteen. I heard none of the girls wanted to go out with him. He was just weird, so that tells you something about Vicky. No one wanted her, either.

On top of that, they both have bad taste. Their furnishings needed to be torched. The stuff was fifty-five years old and just ugly. The guest house was falling apart, and the linens were old. Everything was old, cheap, and ready for the dumpster. His golf shoes were thirty years old. I tried to throw them away, and he got them out of the trash and told me not to touch his stuff. They were in the spare garage in a junk pile, same place as the golf bag I asked for. I could go on and on. Vicky would keep half a sandwich for weeks in the fridge. I would toss it, and she'd say, "Why did you get rid of it? I was going to eat that today." Two weeks old? Are you fucking for real?

I think you've got the whole picture. It's just too bad. Vicky has no life and is married to a weird, panty-wearing tool. It's only going to get worse. He is coming out of the closet. I would bet on that.

The kids were birds of a feather. Both got jobs out of college thanks to daddy, first as interns and then going to work for him. Dad gave Paul Jr. twenty million to start his fund and hired his wife. Give me a break. Who can fuck that up? Taylor was a jock and ate with her mouth open and her elbows on the table. To hear Vicky talk, she was Wall Street elite.

Brock still works for daddy. To hear him talk, he runs the show. Same deal with Hutch: he had a job briefly before returning home to work for his dad, where he can do what he wants, take off when he wants, and make millions. Not a bad life. Just wait for the old man to croak and get your trust fund. Some people think that's great. It's no way to raise kids. You need to teach them a work ethic and the value of money.

I would love to see the boys start out like I did and see where they would be today. They could not make it on their own. I would bet the ranch. So much for the boys. It's the same with all these wealthy families. It just makes me sick to hear them talk and brag about what they have.

What really makes me mad is that Paul and his piece-of-shit partner, Keven Brandt, got the biggest fine ever from the SCC for an individual. Paul was fined almost four hundred thousand dollars for market timing and was suspended for sixty days, a slap on the wrist if you ask me. The good thing is that it's still on his record. Google it if you don't believe me. I don't think it was fair. I will never forget the stock deal where he lost around a hundred million dollars. He cried for a week and never left the house. I just laughed. If you really want to hurt the ultra-rich, hit them where it counts, their wallets. Without their money, their no one. He had to give more cash to Paul Jr., as he took it in the shorts as well.

I remember how, when the market was tanking during the COVID shutdown, I had to hear Paul cry every day, "I am losing millions." Then he would say, "I will be broke. Now I just hope I don't get COVID and die. What a big pussy. I would love to see this guy end up broke. It'd teach him and his ungrateful kids to go out and get a real job. They would be lost. And Vicky? Shit, she would be in even worse shape. It will never happen, but I would love to see it.

I guess that just about covers the Saunders and James River Capital. This is kind of a cool follow-up. One day, after lunch, I got a call from the front gate saying there was a delivery for Paul Saunders. I walked outside, and an armored truck was waiting there, along with three armed guards. I went up to Paul's office and told him. He was on the phone, so he came down a few minutes later. I asked him, "Paul, what the hell is going on?" He had not given me a heads up about this.

"Oh," he said. "I forgot to tell you. I'm having some gold coins delivered."

These guys unloaded ten million in gold coins, American Eagle. They unloaded boxes for half and hour. You'd think that with ten million, he would have thrown the chef a bone. Fuck, what is one coin when you've got that many? Plus, he bragged that he had more in Richmond, thirty million in coins. Man, I bet the IRS would like to know that. But again, like I said, all that money cannot buy you friends and happiness. I am sure he doesn't care.

I have to tell you how my last gig ended. I knew it was coming to an end when I did not get shit for my birthday, no card, no money, nothing, but I got the last say. You will like this story. All the kids and grandkids were coming down for spring break, along with two nannies. That would be ten guests for ten days plus two more couples for a few days. They wanted me to take care of everyone myself: make lunch and dinner every night with no help, cook, serve, clean up, everything. That is a hell of a lot to ask of any one person. Vicky said, "We will get the housekeeper and the gardener to help." He was a former alcoholic and still had the shakes, and they were both smokers and worthless.

So, I came up with a plan. I thought about this a lot. They just took me for granted, and I'd had enough of their shit. I thought this would be the perfect time to get COVID. I called Vicky the day the gang was coming and told her I'd gotten COVID and would not be in all next week. I had nothing prepared, so they would have to feed themselves, and Vicky could not cook for shit. Neither could the other wives; they were just worthless. I am sure it ruined the kids' stay, as they'd thought they would have Chef Al waiting on them, cooking for them, and cleaning up after them.

Months down the road, before I moved to Spain, I got a call from the old nanny. She and her sister had quit. She asked how I was doing after having COVID. I told her the truth. "I could not put up with their bullshit one more day, so I faked the COVID. I knew that would ruin their holiday and I would get some kind of payback and put a smile on my face." She agreed, and we laughed. I said, "They deserve it. They're just not nice people." We chatted for a while, and I said, "I am moving to Spain in a few weeks. Keep in touch." Then we said our goodbyes.

After the kids left, I called and said, "I am not coming back. I have had enough." I dropped the keys off and called it a day.

Over the last few years, I had met some great friends in RVA, Jack, Chester, and the two sisters, some old friends in Vail, the gang at the Singer Island Ritz, Raphael and the gang, what a great crew, and Louis Capona from Manalapan. Oh, and I cannot forget his girlfriend, Peanut. They're both great.

Louis, I hope to see you in Lake Como down the road, one of my favorite spots. I always told you that you are a prince. I will cook for you anytime. We will invite Paul over and ask what kind of panties he is wearing tonight. I thought you would get a laugh out of that. Take care, and see you down the road. Love you guys.

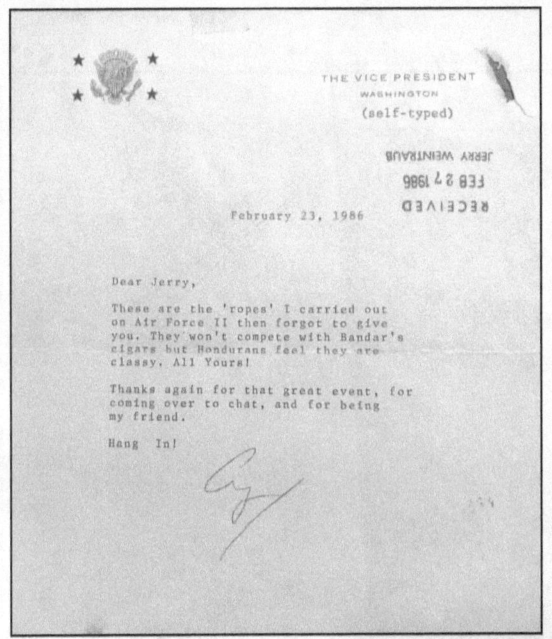

THE VICE PRESIDENT
WASHINGTON
(self-typed)

RECEIVED FEB 27 1986 JERRY WEINTRAUB

February 23, 1986

Dear Jerry,

These are the 'ropes' I carried out on Air Force II then forgot to give you. They won't compete with Bandar's cigars but Hondurans feel they are classy. All Yours!

Thanks again for that great event, for coming over to chat, and for being my friend.

Hang In!

chapter 26

YACHT CHARTERS, FREELANCE CAPTAINS, AND PILOTS

THESE LAST FEW STORIES ARE about yacht charters, freelance gigs, captains, and pilots. Most of these gigs were a week at a time, usually trips to the Bahamas or around South Florida. There are a few names I am sure you will know, and just like you see in the press, they are assholes. I am here to tell you first-hand.

However, let's start with one of the nicest couples I have ever worked for.

Vern and Marie Kraus

Yacht *Dealership*

I got this gig from my old pal Andy at Rybovich. We were at his house one Sunday, having a few beers with the guys, when one of his captain buddies showed up, Jim Cartwright. I had met him but never worked for him. He asked me if I wanted to do a six-week gig in the Bahamas. "Great owners," he said, but they all say that. We would stay at Harbor Island the whole trip. The boat only moved from Jupiter to Harbor Island.

I said, "Yeah, I am in ."

Jim said, "You just have to meet the owners next weekend at their house in Jupiter. They keep the boat at Admiral's Cove, and they live there as well."

We had a few beers and bullshitted, and then I headed home. These guys were a bunch of potheads, and once they got stoned and started talking shit, it was time to hit the road.

Next Saturday rolled around, and I was on my way to meet the owners at the marina. It was around ten am. I walked down the dock to *Dealership*, a real nice ninety-two-foot Princess, pretty new as well. When I got to the boat, Jim was there, and he looked like shit, hungover and smoking a cigarette on the back deck. This guy was a chain smoker, had a drinking problem, and was a pothead. I don't know how these guys get jobs. We chatted for a few minutes, and he said, "Vern is on the phone. Give him a few minutes."

Finally, Vern's wife, Marie, waved us in from the back deck. I introduced myself to them, and we shook hands. Jim took off to wash down the outside, and Marie asked if I would like some coffee. I said, "Yes, that would be nice."

We all had a cup together, and Vern and Marie both jumped in. "Chef, we love your website. We just wanted to meet you face to face and see if we all got along." I liked that.

We chatted for about fifteen minutes or so. I told them I had been in the Marines. They liked that. They told me about their kids and their guests for the upcoming trips. She had written down dishes from my site, and she wanted to have a few of these for dinner. I said, "Sure." They told me they would take care of buying the wine for the trip. I would handle all food and other beverages. I said I could do that.

Vern said, "Alan, what do you need to make for the trip?"

I said, "My rate is a thousand a week."

"Sounds fair to me."

Marie agreed. "Sounds fair to me as well."

We talked for a few more minutes about Harbor Island. I said, "I've been there several times, and it's a great spot, with lots of cool day trips from there."

Vern said, "We will be flying into Staniel Cay."

I said, "I know it well. There's a nice little restaurant there."

We shook hands, and they said they liked my personality and I would be a great fit for all the guests and them, too. Vern said, "Jim will get you a credit card, and we will see you in Harbor Island in a few weeks. We have to go back to Atlanta Monday. If you need anything, call Marie."

We exchanged numbers, and I said, "Thanks. I look forward to the trip," and that was it. I hung around to talk to Jim and get a game plan together, dates, guests, all that. He said, "Marie will get you all that. Let's go get lunch at the Dive Bar."

I said, "Sure, let's hit it."

I did not know Jim very well before this trip, and he seemed ok except for the drinking and smoking two packs a day. It was none of my business if he wanted to kill himself. Jim is ten years younger than me, but he looked ten years older, with a bad back and messed-up teeth. He owed the IRS shitloads of money, which I found out later. It's sad to see guys just waste their lives away. Jim was not a bad guy; he just happened to have issues. Life is what it is.

We had a nice lunch at the Dive Bar, another of my favorite places in Jupiter. They've got a great happy hour, and it's a great place to girl-watch. I told him I would start shopping next week and get the menu ready for the month and I would be by the boat Monday to start taking inventory and see what I needed.

"Great," he said. "See you then."

I had a good feeling about Vern and Marie, and my gut was right. Throughout this book, I have been saying how these rich assholes are nasty. Well, Vern and Marie were a nice change. After twenty years, I had finally found a great couple to work for. Their friends are all super nice, and their kids were not spoiled little pricks.

First, they are all from the South, where they teach manners and respect. That's a good thing. Vern made his money in the car business, as you would expect with a yacht named *Dealership*. In Atlanta, he is the man, Krauss Auto Group, but you would never know it by talking to him. Ford, Benz, McLaren, he has them all. I never made it up there, and he ended up selling the boat after the last trip with me.

Back in Jupiter, we were set to head to Harbor Island. I had all the provisions done, and the boat was stocked up and ready to sail. We would be towing a thirty-two-foot Boston Whaler for the trip.

Jim brought one of his old mates on the trip. The guy turned out to be just like Jim, a drinker, a smoker, and on his last legs. A few days later, we got to Harbor Island. If you have never been there, put it on your list, and stay at the Pink Sands Hotel. It's a special place; my old friend runs it. I took Vern, Marie, and some of their guests there, and they loved it. The food is great, and the sand is pink.

We were staying at the Romora Bay Marina. It's a really nice spot, with a pool and a bar on the water, and the food is pretty good, too. For the next six weeks, this was our new home, not a bad way to spend some time. We had a week until the first set of guests arrived—six trips, all with different guests.

Vern told me that I should let him know if anybody gave me a hard time or acted up. I thought that was pretty cool. The toughest part of the job was getting smokes and buying beer for Cartwright. I have seen slobs, but he was one of the worst. His hygiene was terrible, too, and his room was a pigsty. I don't know how he got the job. I mean, the guy was a good Capitan, but they're a dime a dozen in South Florida and not all drunks. He started being a prick a few days after getting to the island. He even asked me to clean his room. I said no way, and he was not real happy. Once the guests arrived, I only saw him in the morning and at dinner. I was busy cooking all day and cleaning the inside of the boat, so Jim had no time to give me shit

On the first trip, Vern and his guests loved my food, my pineapple martinis, and the way I waited on them. Vern called me aside on the third day and said, "Thanks. You are doing a great job. I had no idea of the level of service you give, Alan, and we love your cooking."

I said, "Thanks. It's my pleasure." That was very nice of him. Marie told me the same thing.

I could tell Jim was a little bent out of shape because the guest could not stop talking about last night's dinner, the fish tacos we'd had at lunch, or the kick-ass margaritas. I pulled out all the stops on the first trip and never took my foot off the gas. They never had the same meal twice. Marie told that Vern had not enjoyed himself like that in years. They did day trips over to Staniel, went fishing on the small boat a few days, and went to Compass Cey to see the sharks and Guana Island. They did something every day.

The second trip was with Vern's partner and his family; all the trips were six days. Dan and his gang from Atlanta were great, and they gave me one of my biggest tips a week of work: a thousand dollars. That was pretty special. They came into the galley the last morning after breakfast and handed me an envelope with a card in it that they had all signed. It was pretty cool.

I did some of my best dishes: Spanish paella, grilled fish tacos, pasta, flat iron steaks with chimichurri. I did a great job with the wine pairing, too. They all said the best part of the trip was Chef Al. That was great. It was my first yacht charter where all guests were super nice and very kind. It's nice when the guests enjoy good food and see the love I put into it. All the guests were Vern's close friends, except for Dan, his partner. You could tell they all thought the world of Vern, and now I know why; he's one hell of a gentleman. Vern, you are the best.

The trips would end early Monday morning, so on Sunday, I'd make eggs Benny with all the sides, my famous roast potatoes, grilled asparagus grilled, hollandaise sauce to die for, fresh fruit with Chantilly cream—it's like having sex, I have been told—Bloody Marys, and fresh mimosas. It's hard to beat that for a send-off brunch. I put a lot of love into the brunches.

After the second trip, I felt Vern, Marie, and I had a bond, and we are still friends today. Toward the end of the second trip, Vern asked if I could cook at their house once in a while and come back on the boat for a trip in the future. I said, "Sure. It would be my pleasure."

The last trip was just Vern, Marie, and one couple, Gayle and Lyn Parson, whom I became good friends with. They lived in Palm Beach

Gardens. Gayle was an interior decorator, and Lyn owned shitloads of apartments in Richmond, Virginia. I really spoiled them with some great dinners and lunches, including Vern's favorite, shrimp scampi. They all had a good time, and Vern was very thankful. Marie was, too, and she said, "We look forward to having you over at the house to cook." We all said our goodbyes the next day, and they were off. That was a quick six weeks, but what a great time, and I met some really nice guests.

When I got back home, I already had a message from Gayle and Lyn about doing a dinner party at their house. It was kind of a repeat of the last trip. Vern and Marie came over as well. They had a friend from RVA looking for a chef and someone to help take care of the big house they were building, and Gayle had told them about me, and they wanted to hire me. It turned out that Vern was selling the boat and his plans had changed, and he did not need me full time, so I was out of that gig.

That was a great gig except for the drunk captain. He got the ax, too. He needed to get fired. The moment we left Harbor Island, he and the halfwit Brit he'd hired as a mate were already drinking beer like it was their boat, and I mean pounding them down and talking about the old days. This guy was in his late sixties and overweight, to put it nicely. I mean, the guy could not see his dick, and he huffed and puffed just going up the steps. He had no business being on a yacht in his shape and health. Thank God we got to Jupiter safe and alive. That was the last time I ever did a trip with those fucking monkeys.

I told Vern about it when he asked what I thought about Cartwright. I never lie. Ask me something, and if you don't want to know the truth, don't ask, because you won't like what I tell you.

Gayle and Lyn's friend who wanted to hire me turned out to be none other than Mr. Panties. Lyn and Gayle, I wont hold that against you. It's my fault; I took the job.

I made a nice dinner that night: grilled salmon with tzatziki, grilled veggies, farro, and my lamb patties for an appetizer and hummus and roasted red pepper salsa flat-breads. All the guests enjoyed everything, and the lamb and flat-breads were a hit. Dinner went smoothly, as always. Gayle helped serve. After dinner, I was asked to join them for a drink, and we talked about Harbor Island and how they all had a great time. Paul did not get a word in, as we all just talked about the trip.

As soon as I started to clean up, this tool was in my face, asking questions, bragging about this house he was building and how he wanted me on board. I said, "Give it a rest. Have your wife call me, and we will talk about it. I will need a deposit if we decide to go further." I left it at that.

This was the last dinner party I did for Gayle and Lyn. I was busy, and COVID arrived. When I think of you guys, it always puts a smile on my face. Love you two. All the best. You know you have a room at the new guest house in Spain. Keep in touch.

Jordan Zimmerman
Zimmerman Advertising, Boca Raton, Florida
Florida Panthers

Now here's a real prick for you. I got a call from an old agent, Adrien De Winter. She was with PCI and ran the New York show, and she'd gotten my name from a friend in Dallas. I should have known better. Most of the time, these agents have shitty jobs that nobody will take. She told me, "It's a two-week gig and a grand a week cash. The guy's full-time chef is on vacation, and it's just breakfast and dinner five days a week."

I thought: *What the hell. It's still two grand, and the chef will be there the first day to give me the rundown. How bad could it be?* I never knew someone could be such an asshole. I did not know that Zimmerman had a crazy diet, or I would have never taken the job, not even for a week. He is vegan, but he's also a steroid head, so the guy is eating healthy but putting drugs into his body. It makes no sense. I mean, this guy's face and eyes were red, and talk about rage. Man, what a walking time bomb.

Anyway, this prick owned one of the country's largest PR firms and part of the Florida Panthers hockey team. He had a big house in Boca and a few hot cars, and he was working on his second wife. They were on the outs during my two weeks. She moved out the second week I was there. I don't blame her. What a dick. She was not bad; I am sure she was just there for the money, as this guy was not much on looks, and I am sure he could not get it up with all the juice he was doing. They had a nasty little daughter together, maybe around five. What a little twit, spoiled rotten. I would have taken her ass to the woodshed and beaten her ass.

Every morning, the guy had to have a special protein shake, and I had to pack his lunch for work. He left the house every day at six on the dot. The shake was from hell: these seeds, those seeds, homemade almond butter, almond milk, just crazy shit, and he changed it every few days. He had to have two: one at the house and one for the road. Lunch was just stupid: three or four main courses, grains, and veggies.

On top of that, he was just fucking picky. I barely made it through the first week. I was like, shit, what did I get myself into? I did not meet anyone famous or powerful, just his son. He only came over for dinner once, and I will never forget it. The dinner was for the father, son, and one of his big clients from Toyota. I think he had the national account for them, and this was some guy high up in the company. It looked like they were losing the contract, and he was pissed. I guess his kid fucked something up, but the way he laid into him in front of me, this guy, and the staff was totally uncalled for. I mean, he called him stupid and every name in the book. I did not like the kid, but no one deserves to be talked to like that in front of other people. Just no class.

The other story is about a date he had at the house on a Sunday. He asked me to come in and just do lunch for them. The week before, the wife had moved out. I am sure he used a matchmaker for rich pricks. She was just looking for a meal ticket. She was good looking—I have to say that—and she brought her son with her. He was about six or seven, and I guess she'd brought him so he could meet Zimmerman's daughter.

I arrived at the house around eleven to start lunch, and she showed up a few minutes later, but there was no sign of Zimmerman. I fixed her a glass of wine and got something to eat for her son, and they hung out by the pool. Lunch was supposed to be at noon, but there was still no sign of the dickhead.

I told her, "I am sorry. I don't know where he is."

She called him a few times, but he did not pick up. Finally, he showed up around one thirty and said he was not hungry. He told the date, "Have lunch by the pool, and I will join you in a few minutes." That seemed weird, but what the hell.

I brought her a nice chicken Caesar; that's what she wanted. He had a big desk by the window that looked out over the pool and the Intercoastal, and I could see he was on the phone. She could see him, too. I came out, poured her one more glass of wine, and said, "I feel terrible about the lunch."

She said, "That's ok. I don't think there will be a second date if this is what I am up for."

I thought: *Good for her. This guy is a real prick and deserves no one.*

He finally came out when she was just about ready to leave. They chatted for a few minutes, and I cleaned up. Then she got up and said she had to get her son home and it was time for her to be on her way. I will say that he at least walked her outside. I finished up and took off. I wanted no part of this shit.

The second week was more of the same shit. Every day was like pulling teeth. He would complain about the drink every day, too much this, too much that, nothing was right. On my second-to-last day, he was running late or some shit, and his shake was not quite done. It only took two minutes to blend, and he started giving me shit, saying that I was the worst chef and couldn't even get a shake made on time.

I looked at him and said, "Listen. I don't know who the fuck you think you are, but no one talked to me like that. You can get your own damn shake and shove it up your tight ass." Then I headed for the door. I'd had enough of this asshole's shit. He said, "Oh, wait a minute. I need my lunch and shake."

I said, "Ok. It will be five minutes." I mean, who doesn't have five minutes? You are the boss.

I fixed the shake and gave him his lunch, and he said, "Chef, can you put my case in the car?" I just walked away, and that was it.

What an asshole, just like Barry Diller. Who do these fucks think they are, treating people like that? I didn't come back for the last day. He called the agent and complained, saying he would not pay for an incompetent chef. Surprisingly, while I didn't get a tip, I did get paid. He wanted to mail the check, but I said, "No, I will pick it up at the office."

You will like this. I went to the office, and it looked like it had been designed by the villain from the James Bond movie *Tomorrow Never Dies*. When you walked in, there was a long hallway with nothing but pictures of him and twenty or thirty TVs playing a video of him talking at a conference. Then, at the front desk, there was more of the same. I thought Trump was bad at his golf course, but this blew that away. I mean, what an ego, and this guy was one ugly dude.

He would say, "Sleep is for the sick and the old. I will get plenty of sleep when I die." He also said he only slept for two or three hours a day. That's why this guy was all fucked up, plus the roids he takes. Oh, and as you would guess, he had no personality.

I picked up my check, and his assistant said, "They last two weeks on average." That should tell you something about this guy. I got my check and never saw or heard from him again. The agent called me and said that she wouldn't be able to place me again, that Zimmerman claimed I had talked back to him and was not professional. What a joke. I told her to lose my number and not call me again for the shit jobs working for assholes.

That wrapped that up. I would love to see him on the street and give him a good tune-up. He is way past due for an ass-kicking. Hey, Jordan, wherever you are, the Hampton's or Boca, you can kiss my ass, you prick. Go do some more juice.

Ron Bruno
Bruno Supermarkets, Bruno Events, Birmingham, Alabama
Yacht *Forever Young*

This was a nice little gig. It was also the first time I worked with that loser Luke, captain of *North Star*. I met him at a Neptune networking event for yachties in Lauderdale, and we had a beer together. He seemed like an ok guy. A few months later, I got a call from the prick from out of the blue, and he asked if I would be interested in a two-week gig.

"The job pays a grand a week and a tip. We'll leave West Palm, towing a small tender, and the first stop is Ocean Reef. The owners will board, and we'll stay there a week. Then we'll head to Miami and dock right in front of the Fontainebleau for the second week. The owners will get off there, and we'll bring the boat back to West Palm. There will be no guests, just the owner, his wife, and their son. There will be a big party, which you will need to have catered, forty people. I want you to manage the event, but hire a company, because he wants a full-blown buffet."

I said, "Cool. I can do that."

"Lastly, we need to hire a female stew. Do you know someone?"

"Yeah, I can line one up."

He gave me the dates, and then he said, "The owner might want a sample dinner in West Palm on the boat in the next few weeks."

"Sure, but he has to pay me for the day."

"I will tell him."

"I don't work for charity."

It turned out that the owner was some hotshot from Alabama and would be hosting the football team and Nick Saban on the boat. The national championship game was being played in Miami, with Alabama and Notre Dame vying for the title. He was some big booster, and his son went there as well. The son's best friend was the kicker, and the dad was friends with Saban.

I thought: *These will be cool.* Plus, I had never been to the Ocean Reef Club. It turned out that once was enough. Once you have been there, you don't want to go back. There are tons of rich assholes there. You can have that place. The Fontainebleau was cool. That was the best part of the trip.

I got a call from Luke the next week. He said, "The owner would like you to cook for him and his son this Friday. He likes fish. Just pick it up, and he will reimburse you. Be at the boat at six. I won't be there. They will be expecting you, and they are pretty casual."

I said, "Cool. I can do that."

I thought I would go with one of my staple dinners: grilled salmon with a mustard dill sauce, jasmine rice, grilled asparagus, and my signature house salad mixed, greens with a lemon-mint vinaigrette. And they wanted vanilla ice cream and some fresh berries. Pretty simple, and it's always a hit.

The same was true this time around. The owner, Ron, and Greg, the son, were impressed. We had a glass of wine after dinner and talked about the trip. I told them I would take care of the caterers for the party before the game. I would oversee them and help serve, and I would take care of all the food for the rest of the trip, breakfast, lunch, and dinner. We shook hands, and then Ron said, "I like your style, and we look forward to the trip. Dinner was great, and I am sure you will work out." I said it was my pleasure, and we called it a night.

I had two things to take care of: hire a caterer in Miami for the party and line up a stew, a pretty easy list. I also had to plan a menu and buy some food, but that was pretty easy stuff, and we would be close to markets in Ocean Reef and Miami, so no big deal. I just had to put up with Loser Luke. He was not too bad on this trip, and it was only two weeks. He did not show his true colors until I got on *North Star* down the road, but we've already gone through that. No use beating a dead horse or kicking a man when he is down, though, in Luke's case, I might make an exception.

The next morning, Luke called me and said that Mr. Bruno approved of me and everything was a go. "Come by the boat this afternoon, and we will talk about getting a stew. We have plenty of time to line one up."

I said, "Cool. See you after lunch."

"Oh, and by the way, can you drive a tender?"

"Sure."

"Good. We will take it out this afternoon so you can get used to it."

That afternoon, we went for a boat ride, and then I worked on my menu and started on my shopping list. We would be taking off in a week.

I lined up a cater up the next day, just lots of finger foods, a cheese tray, veggies, and hors d'oeuvres. I would make a big batch of gumbo for the main course, self-serve with small plates. We interviewed stews the next day. Luke did not like any of the ones I lined up, so I said, "Cool. You hire one. I don't want to get involved. We had a few good ones, and you passed on them, so you are on your own." It was the first of many disagreements. He was a micro manager and had to be in charge and have the last say.

He ended up calling a crew agency and paying for it when he could have hired one through DayWork123 for free or one of the ones I'd brought by. They were all very capable of doing the job. I mean, there would only be four guests for two weeks, and they'd eat a lot of meals off the boat.

We were finally just about ready to head down to the Ocean Reef Club in a few days. Luke hired a stew from Crewfinders, and she seemed nice. She was a little young and did not have a lot of experience, but I could tell she would do fine. From what I had been told by the son and dad, the Brunos were pretty casual. They seemed ok and not very demanding. They were from the South—always nice folks, well, most of the time.

I was right. They turned out to be very nice folks. Ron was a little on the cheap side, but besides that, he was a nice guy. Greg, the son, and his wife, Lee, were also super nice.

We headed out early in the morning, which would put us at Ocean Reef around sundown. I drove the tender until we got out of the Intercostal. Then we tied her up to tow and headed off. The Brunos were flying into Miami and driving down to the club. They would be there the next day, so I had a day to prepare. It was a nice ride down, and there were no issues. I fixed lunch for the crew.

I have been in some tight marinas, but Ocean Reef is no joke. It was getting dark, and I could tell Luke was a little concerned. We got in ok with some help from the dock-master. Thank God he was there. Once we were tied up, I cooked the staff a nice dinner, and we talked about the next few weeks and got a game plan together. Then we called it an early night. We would be there for about five days. Talk about a boring place to stay for more than a few days. Unless you are a guest, the place sucks. It is in a swamp, and there are lots of bugs. I felt like I was in Costa Rican rain forest, just getting chewed on by the fuckers.

I guess they have a pretty good golf course. It's private, like the whole place. Unless the owners give you a pass, you are only allowed into the staff area. There is a little bar and cafeteria. Talk about low rent; it just plain sucks. I went there twice. I had to get off the boat, and there was nowhere else to go. On top of everything else, it's no short walk from the marina. Five days, no big deal. I just thought about being at the Fontain-bleau lobby bar next week, and that put a smile on my face.

The Brunos showed up the next day, and I had lunch ready for them. Ron and his son played golf one day. They took the tender out fishing. Other than that, it was a pretty chill few days. Lee was super nice. This job was the only time in my career that the wife apologized for the husband in advance. I will never forget that day. It was like the first day Ron and Greg were out playing golf. Lee was by herself on the boat, so I fixed her a nice lunch, and we chatted for a few minutes. She was a first-class lady. I could tell that right away, and just a nice person.

She looked at me and said, "Alan, I can see you've been around. I just want to let you know ahead of time that Ron is cheap, and he will drive you nuts over the smallest of details. He still gets on my nerves, and it's been twenty years. Sometimes I just have to get up and leave the room, so be forewarned and don't take it personally. That's just how he is." I thought that was pretty cool.

The stay was nothing special, no guests, just a boring week. The stew went out one night and was late getting up on deck the next morning. She was a little hungover but not too bad. I mean, there is no excuse; she should have been home early or not have drunk so much, but she was young, and this place was pretty boring. Luke, being the prick he is, had her in tears and was ready to kick her off the boat. He yelled at her, saying she could not leave the boat for the rest of the trip. He was way out of line. I told her to file a complaint with the crew agency when she got back. He deserved it. She was young and needed the experience, so she kept quiet. What a shame. I told her, "Don't worry about it. You can use me as a reference, and I will help you get a job. It will be ok, and Luke will calm down. He is just a hothead and full of hate." That made her feel better.

The rest of the stay in Ocean Reef went well. I made some great meals, Luke calmed down after a few days, and things returned to normal.

Finally, the week was up, and we were on our way to the big show. The owners were going to the game, but I would be watching it at the Fontainebleau. We would all meet at the hotel, and we would be docked right across the street from it. I will never forget that or the tip: nothing. Like I said, he was a cheap guy. We would be there for five days.

Lee wanted to do some shopping, and we had the big catered party the day before the game, with the team and Saban coming over to the boat. They would leave the next day, and then we would head back to Palm Beach and be home that night.

We left early in the morning and were docked and all tied up by dinnertime. They went out for dinner that night, so I just had to feed the crew, and then I went to a bar for a cold one and did some girl-watching. It was a far cry from the boring Ocean Reef Club.

I made a few nice meals over the next few days, but they went out for lunch a lot, so I was not getting killed except for having to put up with Luke. He was not a happy guy, but life must go on.

Everything was going great with the trip. The owners were happy, and the big party was tomorrow evening. I had been in contact with the caterers, and everything on their end was good. I had planned to help serve and oversee the party, and I made a big batch of seafood paella. The stew would help serve and bus as well, and the caterers were sending two waiters.

The party went off with great ease. Ron and Lee were very happy. Luke did not even care. He just stood watch with a frown on his face like always. I got to meet Saban, shook his hand, and met a few of the players. You would have thought it was Saban's yacht, as he walked around like he owned the place. I guess, in Alabama, he is a god. He sure as hell acted like it. It reminds me of the joke: What do God and Nick Saban have in common? Saban thinks he is God. I am sure everyone knows he is a prick, so I won't beat him up too badly.

The players seemed to have a great time, and I met some of Greg's friends, really nice kids. Afterward, we cleaned up, I tipped the crew out of petty cash, and that was a wrap.

Ron came in and told me thanks and great job. That was nice. Luke added nothing and just went to his cabin and called it a night. The next day was the big game, so I made a big breakfast, and then they were off.

I watched the game at the lobby bar at Fontainebleau and lost a hundred bucks. Notre Dame got killed. It was not even a game. I still had fun. Bruno was not bad, and his wife and son were great. The one exception was when he beat up on the stew for not cleaning out the toilet bowl brush trays and leaving a little water in them. I mean, shit, who goes around looking inside them? Only a prick who has nothing else to do but find something to bitch about.

I should have known better when Lee apologized the first few days. I got a kick out of that.

On the day they left, he came into the kitchen and was going through the cupboards and the freezer, looking around like a madman. I asked him if I could help him find something. He looked at me and said, "I just wanted to see how much waste there was, and I was looking for that bottle of pinot. It was almost a full bottle, and it was very expensive."

"I am sorry, but there was only one glass left, and I drank it."

"Don't argue with me. It was full."

I just walked away, thinking: *You cheap prick, worried about one glass of wine, and it was not that great, like a twenty-dollar bottle, if that.* I just laughed. That was the last time I would ever see that cheap fuck. I knew then there would be no tip.

We took care of all the bags, and they left after breakfast. Lee and Greg said thanks, but Ron did not say shit. I guess he was still pissed about one glass of so-so wine. Give me a break. On top of that, he told Luke the same story, and Luke reads me the riot act. I thanked God that he was on his way back home and, after one more day, I would have not to put up with Luke's shit.

We got back to West Palm without a hitch. The stew said goodbye, Luke and I got the boat all tied up =, and I was packed up and gone in five minutes. Not a bad trip. I made a few dollars and got to see the Ocean Reef Club and hang out in Miami.

I never heard from the Brunos again. That's a good thing. I saw Luke again on *North Star*. We all know how that ended up. What a complete asshole. Loser Luke.

JR and Loren Ridinger
Market America, Miami
Yacht *Utopia*

This was one crazy yacht. I did a few charters to help my friend Mark out. He was the captain, an old Texas boy and friend of Cole's. That's how I met him. He was one of the few nice captains I worked for. Just like Cole, he didn't have a big ego. Anyway, the owners, I only met a few times. They wanted to see if I would fit in with their celebrities, friends, and clients. I felt like I was back in LA with these assholes. I'd thought Mr. Panties was bad, but this guy took the prize, and his wife was just as bad. If not for Mark, I would have never taken the gig. He needed a chef in a bad way. The last guy had walked off, never a good sign.

These folks were so full of themselves. They had a few businesses, but the main one, Market America, was the real cash cow. It was kind of spin-off from Amway. JR had worked for them in the day and started his own gig. All I know is that the pair of them are real pieces of shit. I thought I could handle a few charters. The second charter was canceled; they just stayed on the boat and partied in Miami, so not a bad deal, and Mark was happy. The next trip was supposed to be to Cancun, and it was also canceled. We just went for a few day trips out and around Miami with the guests. They stayed on board during the day and then went out a few nights in Miami. I still got paid, and it worked out well. Mark was off the hook, and I also made a few bucks.

They kept the boat right behind their house in Miami. It was like a revolving door with crew and staff at the house, which should tell you something about this pair. I got calls for a year or so to come back as a house manager, chef, and even purser on the yacht. They couldn't keep track of who had quit or been fired. The owners and their guests were nasty; you can have that freak show.

I only have two stories about the guests; that was enough for me. The first guest was none other than J. Lo, or should I say "J.Hoe." That woman has sucked a mile of cock to get where she is. Talk about one nasty, self-absorbed bitch. There you have it on a silver platter. Just ask Mark Anthony.

A-Rod had enough of her shit, too. She's only been married, what, three times? She says she is still just the girl from the neighborhood. Right, that is such bullshit.

She showed up with the young dancer she was dating for a few months or so. They and their whole entourage were a bunch of assholes, rude, just ordered the staff around. They wanted to be waited on hand and foot and provided food around the clock. They had one of the deckhands drive them into Miami until the wee hours of the night and just busted this kid's balls, and they left no tip on top of that. I don't know where J. Lo's kids were, but you'd have thought she was a teenager from the way she partied and carried on with this dancer. No mother with any class would behave like that and treat people the way she does.

They were supposed to stay for a week, but thank God it was only a few days because we canceled the trip to Cancun. I would have walked off if I'd had to put up with their shit for a week, and Mark would have thrown them overboard. It's crazy how fame makes these people think they're just better than everyone else. They are all so shallow and weak, and the same goes for the people who follow them and live on every word they say like it's gospel. Most of them are dumber than a bag of rocks, and J. Lo is no different. They trashed the boat and ordered all of us around like we should bow down and feel grateful that we were in their presence and got to wait on them.

I will never forget how she acted like she was the first lady. Like they say, you can take a tramp out of the gutter, but you can't take the gutter out of the tramp. Same story, old news. Everyone knows she is a pain in the ass and hard to work with, but no one wants to speak up. Someone needs to grow a set of balls. I know I do. If I were a director, I would tell her to shut the fuck up and get off my set. She is not that hot, and that big ass, you can have it. Actually, she is not Oscar material, average at best. I would not even cast her. There are far more talented people out there, and to put up with her shit? Not no, but hell no. They stayed drunk and partied like there was no tomorrow. That was the last time I would see J. Lo, thank God.

The next trip was not any better: the Williams sisters. Talk about ghetto; that's putting it lightly. Their trip was short, as something came up. We just took them out a few times for a cruise around Miami, the same deal we did with J. Lo.

I now know why Serena is the most disliked female athlete in the world, and her sister is not too far behind. They call others racist when they are the ones, pots calling the kettle black. I tell you one thing. Serena takes a man-size shit. She is no small girl. Large panties around that big ass. In my worst nightmare, I could not imagine waking up next to that shit. She is scary.

They had about five in their group, a few gay guys and some other women. They were all rude and very demanding. They trashed the boat and complained about everything; you just could not make them happy. We had to drive them all over Miami while they were drunk off their asses until the wee hours of the morning. Then they wanted to be dropped off one night at some club and said they would find their own way back to the boat. On their way back, they got lost and could not find it. One of the deckhands had to get out of bed and go get them. This was around four in the morning. It was just rude and showed their lack of respect for the staff. Thank God their stay was short. They did like my chicken wings; that was the only saving grace.

I don't get it. They have everything in the world and still have to act like assholes, treat people badly, and pull that race card shit. Go back to Compton and cry your sob story to someone who gives a shit. They stiffed the staff as well.

Celebrities and sports stars, I don't know where they get off on acting like they are something special. I did a charter with Mariah Carey and one with De Niro on a different yacht out of Jupiter sometime back, and it was the same: trashing everything, being demanding, and leaving no tip. I could have and should have kicked the shit out of De Niro. That guy is a real piece of shit. He needs a good ass-kicking, and Mariah needs a good bitch-slapping.

Getting the Williams sisters and their gang to the airport was an ordeal. They were running late, and we had to rush to get them there on time. Thank God I will never have to cook or wait on nasty people like that ever again. It just leaves a bad taste in my mouth.

I hope you have enjoyed my stories. I've tried my best to call it like I see it. I met some great folks over the years and some real-first class assholes. Folks in my line of work know I am telling the truth about some of these rich pricks, but you have to keep your mouth shut because you are still working. I am at the end of the road, so I am letting it all hang out, and I've called it as I see it.

Richmond VA, Friends

Chapter 27

LONG, WILD RIDE BUT NOT DONE YET

IT'S BEEN A LONG AND crazy ride, from West Jefferson, Ohio, to Beverly Hills, New York, Palm Beach, and everywhere in between. Sports stars, CEOs, presidents, and first ladies, I have cooked for them all. I have met some really great people and some real assholes along the way. I've gotten more than my fair share of hot ass, banged hot actresses and a few old ones as well, a *Penthouse* model, I don't know how many guys' wives—I lost track a long time ago—daughters, nannies, and housekeepers. What the hell; someone has to do it. From trashing Albert Gurstan's Ferrari to stealing Rod Stewart's Versace shirts, I've pulled some shit over the years. On top of that, I never got caught.

It's hard to believe I did all this. Sometimes I have to pinch myself. I look back over the years and say, "Man, I have been one lucky guy." I have lived at some really great places and on some great yachts as well. Most people dream of shit like this. It sounds great, but it comes with a price. It's not your home, it's not your yacht, and you are an employee at their beck and call. It's not all that great when you have to eat shit all day and put up with nasty wives, spoiled kids, asshole bosses, or all of the above—then you are in real deep shit. I know. I have seen it all.

There is not much I have not seen, and I know what I am talking about when I say it's no walk in the park. I am sure there are some great bosses out there with shitloads of money. I just never had the right fit. Chefs don't leave great jobs like.

On a side note, it's nice to know karma exists after all. My old captain Luke, the prick, got the fucking he deserved. Just before I took off for Spain, I was in Nora's, having dinner at the bar, a pizza and a Stella, my beer of choice. I'd just left Mr. Panties' house, so I had my chef's coat on. Some young guy asked to sit next to me, and I said, "Of course."

He saw "Chef Al" on my coat—I have them custom made, but of course, you know that—and he asked if I was the chef there, as he was new in town. I replied, "No, I am a private chef. I work on yachts and at estates."

Then he asked if I'd ever worked with Captain Luke on *North Star*, a yacht owned by the Goulds. I said, "Why do you ask?"

He said, "Because everyone says you are the only one to stand up to Luke and tell him to fuck off. David and the wife still talk about you and will never forget you. They said you always had great stories and the dog loved you."

I said, "That's me," and I bought him a beer.

He was just starting a job as the wife's personal assistant and steward on the boat. She never hires women. I liked that, no drama. It turned out that the boat was heading back north to Boston and the cape for the summer. I said, "Congrats on the job," and told him a few things about the family and to stay clear of Luke at all costs. Everyone knew he was a dick and control freak and just a real asshole on top of that. I said, "I cannot believe David has not fired him."

He said, "I'll get the next beer, and what I have to tell you will make your day."

It turned out that they had just fired Luke for stealing and were going to file charges unless he gave the money back. I guess it'd been going on for a year or so. He had been buying boat parts and selling them to other owners, doing work on the side while saying it was for *North Star*, and billing for work that never got done and then keeping the money. Well, they caught him and fired him on the spot, and of course, Luke did not confess. He said it wasn't true, that it was all a misunderstanding and he could explain, but David, a CFO and no dummy, would have no part of it and said, "Get off the boat now and don't come back."

What really made my day was the next bit of info. The kid told me that David had already hired a new captain, and a few days later, Luke was working on the boat next door for some other owner he was screwing, and he tried to fight the new captain. The new guy called David and the marina security. This is Palm Harbor, pretty high-end. David knew the owners of the yacht next door, and he called them and said, "Luke did not quit. I fired him." He explained why and told them they should do the same and not allow Luke on the property. Then marina security walked Luke off the property.

I had never heard such good news. I mean, if you knew Luke, you would feel the same way. The guy is just a dick with a capital D. So, as it turns out, every dog has its day, and Luke got the fucking he has deserved for all those years of stealing, badly treating his crew and others, and just being a piece of shit. When I think about that, a smile comes to my face.

I am a lucky guy. I have traveled the world, drunk the best wine and liquor, dined at some of the best restaurants in the world, and lived for most of my life on someone else's dime. That's how I got ahead, not counting never marrying, which saved me a fortune. Women are like hurricanes: they all come in warm, wild, and wet, and when they leave you, they take the house and everything in it and leave you high and dry. Like one of my old bosses used to say, "Yeah, my last wife made me a millionaire, but going in, I had fifty million." True to the bone. I know. I have seen it first-hand.

Looking back, the best parts were skiing Vail and Yellowstone Club and eating and drinking whatever I wanted. I'd just go into the cellar or bar and grab whatever I needed. Knob Creek, Maker's Mark, whatever I felt like, I just helped myself. That's what Chef Al does. I look at it as my job: quality control. I have to make sure the wine and booze are good. It's a tough job, but someone has to do it.

With all that said, let's put this book to rest, and I will get on with my next chapter, and I tell you, it won't be boring. I hope you enjoyed my stories. Tell your friends to buy a copy, and let's get this on the *New York Times* Best Seller List. Thanks, and as Haabs would say, get on with your bad self.

That's a wrap.

Chef Mike and Chris, Newport Beach

ACKNOWLEDGMENTS

I HOPE YOU ENJOYED THE book. I have had one hell of a ride. I've seen some pretty weird shit over the years and worked for some really nice people—and my fair share of assholes, too. I have met many interesting people, sports stars, CEOs, presidents and first ladies, and A-list celebrities. I have lived in some of the best addresses in the US, flown in private jets, driven just about every car you can imagine, and lived on yachts all over the world. I have had some great times and plenty of stories to tell over a nice glass of bourbon with the guys. I've also had more than my fair share of pussy.

I would like to thank my mentor, Mike Gayner, in Newport Beach, California. Thanks, Mike, for everything you have taught me. I would not be where I am today without your help and guidance. You are the father I wished I had, and you treated me like a son, and I will never forget your kindness. You made me a better man. Mike, I love you, and from the bottom of my heart, you're the best thing that ever happened to me, and I will never forget our friendship. Chris, I love you as well. You are the best. Beaver, I will never forget you guys.

The Vero Beach gang, oh, man, how I love you guys. Doc, Don, Will, what great times we have had. I thank you guys for putting up with my shit and never getting tired of hearing my stories and about all the ass I've gotten over the years. I guess it helps when I cook for you guys and bring out the brown stuff. That's a fair trade. I will never forget our bond, guys, and I look forward to all of us having dinner at the new guest house in Spain and getting into the brown stuff. We will smoke some cigars and talk some shit.

Special thanks to Glen Edelstein of Hudson Valley Book design for putting up with my s#%t, and designing the perfect book cover and interior.

Thanks to Michael D. Wandzilak for the book title and all his support.

My favorite cousin, Lisa, and her husband, Roger, from Ohio, thanks for believing in me and the great friendship. You both are super people, and I am proud to say you're my cousin and friends.

Lastly, I cannot forget Colonel Jeff Smith, Fort Lauderdale, one of the best guys I've ever cooked for. I am honored to have known you and say you are my friend. Thanks for everything. Jeff, you have been good to me. Just open that wallet a little more often. All the best to you and Ella.

I also cannot forget Bryan Dopp, my friend for over thirty years, just a damn good guy. I will never forget the times we had. Lots of pussy, crazy times in Mexico, the desert in California, Vegas, it's been a long ride. Take care. All the best.

Most of all, I cannot forget my social media guru, web host, and editor, Mike Wandzilak, a great friend who really believed in me. Thanks for all your hard work, and I could not have done this without you. I will never forget you, your wife, or your son. I look forward to our next dinner. Love you and the whole family.

I know I am leaving out lots of folks. I am blessed to have so many great friends from around the world, and I thank you all. If you know me, you know you have not heard the last of me. I have some big plans and one hell of a bucket list. So, tell all your friends to buy the book, and you are all welcome to my humble little house in the south of Spain. And follow me on Facebook and chefal.net for my travel blogs.

This is not the final chapter. I still have a lot of living left and a new bucket list. So, stay tuned for the next wild ride. I promise you it won't be boring. Love all of you.

Like I've been saying for years, every day is a Superbowl. Go out and get it.

ABOUT THE AUTHOR

CHEF ALAN MICHALS is an accomplished, professional culinary chef and private estate manager with an extensive background that encompasses working in private homes and estates, as well as five star restaurants and on-board mega yachts. As a highly respected expert in his field for more than 25 years, he is a formally European-trained Chef who possesses the latest and most modern techniques in food preparation and the culinary arts. Chef Al has comprehensive experience delivering exceptional and unique private chef services for celebrity, entertainment and high-profile clientele.

www.ingramcontent.com/pod-product-compliance
Lightning Source LLC
Chambersburg PA
CBHW032018140726

47988CB00017BA/13